Britain's Betrayc

CW00584596

The Story of The Anglo Indian Community

Frank Anthony

An Anglo Indian Heritage Book

6 656 976 000

Warning and Disclaimer

Britain's Betrayal In India

The Story of The Anglo Indian Community

Frank Anthony

Simon Wallenberg Press

Frank Anthony

Frank Anthony (Born 1908-Died 1993) was a prominent leader of the Anglo-Indian Community in India.

Frank Anthony was born in Jabalpur, in 1908. In 1942, he was elected the President-in-chief of the Community of the All India Anglo-Indian Association.

In October 1946, Mr. Anthony was selected as one of India's principal delegates to represent the country in the first delegation from independent India to the United Nations.

In 1948 and again in 1957, he was one of India's representatives to the Commonwealth Parliamentary Conference. Anthony's greatest contribution was in the field of Anglo-Indian Education.

In 1947, he was elected Chairman of the Inter-State Board of Anglo-Indian Education. He was also the Founder-Chairman of the All India Anglo-Indian Educational Trust which, today, owns and controls five schools.

The Anglo Indian Heritage

*Frank Anthony's The Story of the Anglo Indian Community
is the first book in the Anglo Indian Heritage series.*

The Others are:

These Are The Anglo-Indians by Reginald Maher

*Hostages to India: The Life story of The Anglo Indian Race by
Herbert Alick Stark*

Cimmerii? Or Eurasians and Their Future by Cedric Dover

*The books are called the Anglo Indian Heritage books as they
chronicle the rich and colourful history of the Anglo Indian
Community. This small community has had outstanding
achievements at every level of society for hundreds of years
but that record of achievement has been hidden, passed over
or co-opted as British and Indian History. These Books are
an attempt to fairly represent the history of the community
by works by Anglo Indians themselves.*

CONTENTS

DEDICATION

This book is dedicated to my small but gallant Community which I have had the privilege to lead for the past 26 years in a tumultuous period of Indian history.

New Delhi,
31st December, 1968.

INTRODUCTION

ONE of the six politically recognised minorities of India, the Anglo-Indians face the future in a politically tumultuous, reborn India, set in a resurgent Asia, with hope not unmixed with anxiety.

This is perhaps the first attempt to chronicle, fairly comprehensively, the story of the Anglo-Indian Community. Several books have been written on the Community. Herbert Stark's 'Hostages to India' and 'Call of the Blood' were perhaps the best written and the best known. Unfortunately, they are out of print. They also suffered from the defect that they only dealt with certain limited phases and periods of Anglo-Indian life, and failed to bring the account down even to fairly recent times.

This book is something more than a historical record. I have, therefore, deliberately described it as a story. Important aspects of the Community's life, its social and psychological pattern, the considerable educational and cultural contributions it has made to India, the beauty and capacity of its women, the incomparable Anglo-Indian nurses, the indelible impress the Community has left on the military annals of British Indian history and the saga of continuing service to Independent India inscribed by Anglo-Indians in blood and in valour are some of the topics dealt with. The book is not intended to be an unvarying paean of glorification. The split psychology of the Community, its alleged social exclusiveness, and, not seldom, overweening Community arrogance towards its fellow-Indians are only some of the inhibitions that have been underlined. The Community also had a certain resentment complex towards the British. This characteristic it displayed in common with the other Indian communities: it was perhaps an inevitable reaction between a subject people and a ruling community.

I have sought to be as objective as possible in my treatment of a living subject. Inevitably, for one who has had the privilege of being the Community's accredited leader and who has represented it, virtually single-handed, in the central political field since 1942, complete detachment has perhaps not always been attainable. Above all, I have sought to avoid any deliberate bitterness. The fact that the past 26 years have represented perhaps the most critical period in the history of the Community, during which I have had to battle not only for the political but the economic and cultural existence of the Community, often against bitter and even seemingly hopeless odds, must undoubtedly colour some of my views and writings.

Notable History

Brought into existence deliberately by the British, used throughout British Indian history to serve and often to save British Imperial interests, treated for the most part in a churlish manner, this comparatively microscopic Community, which has forged a not negligible, and, in many respects, a notable history, was cynically betrayed by Britain before its withdrawal from India.

The Anglo-Indian Community has been perhaps one of the most misrepresented people in the former British Empire. Since Independence and the exodus of many thousands of Anglo-Indians to Britain and the Dominions, there is, today, perhaps some slight awareness abroad of who and what this Community represents. But the Anglo-Indians overseas, whatever their number, cannot give even a partially correct impression of the achievements and actual position of the Community in India.

The average Briton or American who has not visited India, if at all aware of the existence of the Community, usually has a completely false, if not fantastic, idea as to our origin, way of life and general position in India.

In fact, many members of other Indian communities have only a vague, often misinformed even warped idea of the background of the Community, its social life and traditions and proud contribution to India.

The origin and growth of the Community have been along quite formal and legitimate lines. The Community's attachment to its Christian religion has been deep and abiding. The sense of filial duty and affection has been specially marked. The sense of sacrifice of parents for the welfare and education of the children has run like a golden thread through the Community's life. The Community has been at least for the last 100 years rigorously endogamous, that is, it has married within its own limits, with the exception of those Britons who settled in India and who usually married Anglo-Indian women. In the result, over a period of 300 years the Community has emerged as a homogeneous racial-cum-linguistic-cum-cultural entity.

Peripatetic writers in search of lurid detail and cheap sensationalism usually hit upon the lowest specimens in the Community. Very often, the specimen was a low-caste member of some other community, masquerading as an Anglo-Indian and seeking social and economic betterment. From such specimens unscrupulous writers, in their desire to rake in the shekels and oblivious to all canons of journalistic decency, have often generalised in sweeping libellous terms against hundreds of thousands of members of an essentially fine Community. Even writers, in fact Anglo-Indian but masquerading as British, have purported to draw on the Community for producing penny-shovelling exercises in near-pornography.

The achievements of the Community were not chronicled or publicised. On the other hand, there was always a marked official inclination to deny us the credit of our exploits. For instance, hundreds of Anglo-Indians won awards for gallantry in World Wars I and II. Some of them won the V.C., others the D.S.O. and a large number the M.C. and the M.M. Either no publicity was given to them or the awards were published under the caption 'India-born Officer'. The names, being European, the reading public usually inferred that it was a Briton who had won the award. I have been able to salvage the names of at least 9 members of the Community who have won the Victoria Cross. In the words of a well-known British writer, Professor John Coatman, "Every page of British Indian history bears testimony to their (Anglo-Indian) devotion and valour." The Anglo-Indians have forged their achievements in the face of a chilling round of the most bitter social and economic disabilities. At certain periods in our history, our treatment by the British was not only deliberately discriminatory but advisedly repressive and even unnaturally cruel.

This story helps to affirm the dictum of Lord Olivier, a well-known British scientist, that persons of mixed blood are potentially among the most competent vehicles of humanity. It exposes the pretentious nonsense spoken and written about the superiority of the so-called pure races. The Anglo-Indians have added a not negligible page to the history of mongrels, the most energetic forging the history of the moment. I am reminded of the words of the Rt. Hon. H.A.L. Fisher that, "Purity of race does not exist. Europe is a continent of energetic mongrels." In a sense, both Olivier and Fisher were scientifically wrong. Cedric Dover, an internationally famous Anglo-Indian author and biologist, was more right when he said, "There are no half-castes because there are no full-castes."

American ascendancy has been the immediate result of the ebullient energy born from the multi-racial crossings that represent the American ethnic melting pot. I have little doubt that the British will show a fresh phase of resurgent vigour as a result of the present Anglo-Indian 'invasion' of the British Isles. In India the most virile races are admittedly in the North. They symbolise the accumulated vigour drawn from a succession of invaders of diverse races.

Days Of Prosperity

I have sought, in this book, to cover the main periods in the life of the Community. The first period may roughly be said to cover the time between the founding of the British settlement at St. George, Madras, in 1639, and 1791. Those were days of prosperity and great influence for the Community. There was no discrimination between Briton and Anglo-Indian. The Anglo-Indian sons of British fathers were taken freely into the covenanted ranks of the British services and reached the highest positions of trust and responsibility. Ninety per cent of Britons, including the most highly placed, married Anglo-Indian women. The main contribution during this period was to the military history of India. This was only to be expected, as the Anglo-Indian Community was drawn predominantly from professional soldier fathers or unashamed military adventurers who lent their swords to the highest, usually Princely, bidders.

Indelible Military Impress

The second stage covers the period from 1791 till what is generally known as the Mutiny of 1857. This was a period of calculated and increasing repression, political, economic, and social by the British. Misguided fear because of the growing strength and influence of the Anglo-Indian Community led to a succession of measures aimed to drive the Community out of the armed forces, to forbid it from going overseas for further studies and to debar it from entering the officer ranks of either the military or civil services. On the one hand, this long period of cruel repression led to terrible unemployment and the economic debasement of a large section of the Community : on the other hand, this period also produced some of the brightest facets of Anglo-Indian history. Proscribed by the Fatherland, prevented from joining the forces in which their British fathers served and often commanded, the sons, with soldiering in their blood, offered their swords, forged in the military traditions of their fathers, to the leading Indian Princes. This was a period which produced a galaxy of Anglo-Indian soldiers who have left an indelible impress on the annals of Indian military history. This was the period of Gardner who founded Gardner's Horse, Lt. Col. James Skinner, the founder of Skinner's Horse, and Col. Henry Forster who founded the Shekhawatie Brigade later known as the 13th Rajputs. All three regiments are proud units of the Indian Army today. This was also the period when the most powerful Indian Princes eagerly sought after and employed Anglo-Indian officers to lead, train and discipline their armies. Perhaps the most powerful military forces of this period, popularly known as 'The Great Anarchy', were those of Madhoji Scindia, the leading Maharatta Chieftain. A very large proportion of the officers in Scindia's victorious armies were Anglo-Indians, some of them holding the very highest positions of command. At this period, the Nizam of Hyderabad's armies also had a large percentage of Anglo-Indian officers. Other leading Indian Princes freely employed Anglo-Indians. Thus at the early age of 25 General Bensley was the Commander-in-Chief of the Maharaja of Alwar's forces. General Jean Baptiste Filose was, for many years, the supreme Commander of Gwalior's armies.

This period of bitter economic discrimination was brightened by the increasing efforts at self-help in the Community. This was the age of John Ricketts and Henry Derozio. In a sub-chapter, some worthy names in the Community have been salvaged by me, although I do not pretend to have touched even the fringe of the galaxy of members of the Community who deserve a place in the scroll.

The part played by the Community during what is known as the Mutiny was decisive. It may be a subject for controversy but no more than the part played by the Sikhs or the Gurkhas who also largely fought alongside the British. At least the Anglo-Indians were motivated by ties of blood. But controversy aside, the role of Anglo-Indian soldiers such as General Sir John Bennett Hearsay who was in Command in Bengal, General Van Cortland who pacified the Punjab and the crucial services of Anglo-Indians in key civilian positions such as Forjett, the Anglo-Indian Commissioner of Police in Bombay who forestalled the Mutiny in that Province, and the supreme fighting qualities of certain predominantly Anglo-Indian units such as the Madras Fusiliers who fought at the relief of Lucknow and the capture of Kanpur and Pearson's Battery from Agra are facts of history. Even the cynically arrogant Curzon was constrained to say (in referring to the services, during the Mutiny, of George Brendish, the Anglo-Indian boy telegraphist) while unveiling the obelisk which stands in the Delhi Telegraph compound, "The Electric telegraph saved India." Those words are inscribed on this obelisk. ✓

Post-Mutiny Period

The post-mutiny period may be said to cover the years from 1858 to 1919. Some attempt at amends by the British for their past ingratitude to the Community was sought to be made, but it was made in a halting, niggardly manner. The Community's services were welcomed but welcomed only in a subordinate capacity. Here, again, self-interest perhaps was at least an equally important motive with the British Administration. Without the selfless services of the Anglo-Indians the Railways, the Posts & Telegraphs, the Customs, the Police, the Marine services could never have been built. In a hundred years, India was covered with a network of railways and a telegraph system to which comparatively little has been added since. And during those 100 years the outstanding part in building these key services was played by the Anglo-Indians. Penetrating inhospitable jungle terrain which was riddled with every form of danger and deadly disease, Anglo-Indian men, separated from their families and homes for many years, built what are today India's greatest national assets. An Anglo-Indian railwayman was lucky if he saw his wife and family at intervals of five years. That was a normal concomitant of their near-heroic service.

The Gidneyan Era

The period from 1919 to 1942 may appropriately be described as the Gidneyan era. In 1919 there emerged on the Anglo-Indian scene Col.—later Sir Henry—Gidney, an Ophthalmic Surgeon of international repute, gifted with a phenomenal memory, a connoisseur art-collector, a 'bon vivant' with a connoisseur's eye for beautiful women and a big game hunter with a record bag of tigers. Although often maligned, Gidney gave more than 20 years of dedicated, fighting public service to his small Community. In place of disunity in the Community's ranks he forged unity. Living his motto, 'The Impossible is Possible', Gidney wrested for his Community a place of recognition and increasing respect in the sub-continent of India.

During the critical days of political unrest in India the Community played its own, perhaps misunderstood, part. In the Volunteer Corps, later known as the Indian Defence Force and, yet later, as the Auxiliary Force, the Community constituted the overwhelming element. This was India's second line of defence. During World War I when India was denuded of British troops, it was the Indian Defence Force, consisting almost entirely of Anglo-Indians, which maintained the security and stability of India.

The services of the Community in the fighting forces during World Wars I and II represent almost a saga of which any much larger community anywhere in the world could be justly proud.

Independence And After

The period 1942 to 1950 marked a grim, unceasing struggle, the burden of which fell on me, to find a place of recognition for the Community in an Independent and, basically, a politically hostile India. It underlined the final and supreme act of cynical betrayal by the British Cabinet Mission and the departing British Administration.

On the eve of their departure from India, British politicians entrusted with the transfer of power were so impervious not only to natural emotions but to an elementary sense of conscience as callously, and it would appear deliberately, to spurn and betray the Community. On the eve of Independence, when the existence of the Community was trembling in the balance, even the modest demand for a single seat in India's Constituent Assembly was rejected. Fortunately for the Community, although betrayed by the British, either from motives of unnatural indifference or of unworthy political expediency, it was given to me, by God's grace and the generosity of the Indian leaders, to find for the Community a place in the Constituent Assembly and through the Constituent Assembly not only a recognised but a special position in the Constitution of Republican India. Perhaps it is correct to say that this small Community of about 300,000 souls has achieved a unique position in the annals of Asian history. Thus while the Anglo-Burmans have disappeared from the political scene in Burma, the Burghers from Ceylon, the Anglo-Indians, proportionately much smaller in numbers in a sea of over 500 million people, have been able to find a specially recognised place in the Indian polity. It would be correct to say that the Anglo-Indians are the only minority of European descent to survive in Asia as a recognised entity.

The post-Independence period was marked by an almost miraculous recognition given to the Community in the New India which was denied to other much larger minorities. It was marked also by uncertainty among a large section of the Community as to their future in India. It was marked by the exodus of an appreciable number of Anglo-Indians. On the other hand, it was also marked by the outstanding contributions of Anglo-Indians to the New India. The decisive part played by the Anglo-Indians in the critical Kashmir campaign was but one example. More than 50% of the fighter pilots of the Indian Air Force were Anglo-Indians: they helped retrieve by their persistent gallantry and often reckless heroism what seemed to be an utterly hopeless position and to drive the invaders back literally from the gates of Srinagar. A large proportion of the officers leading our land forces in the Kashmir and Hyderabad campaigns were members of the Community. The late Capt. Eric James Tucker symbolised the spirit of service to Independent India. His was the only citation for gallantry to be read at the Republic Day Parade in Delhi, at which the Duke of Edinburgh was present, in January, 1959. The citation was a heart-jerking account of sheer reckless heroism in the face of certain death when he was leading a company of troops against Naga hostiles.

At a special investiture held in 1965, the President of India decorated 63 heroes with awards for gallantry made in the field during the Indo-Pakistan conflict: 7 of the 63 were Anglo-Indians. By any standards that was a proud record for a microscopic community.

The Anglo-Indian Community is essentially urban. Its immediate history during the past 125 years, when it was canalised into Government service, tended inevitably to give it not only a Government service complex but made it look away from trade and industry where it had once played a notable part. With the lapsing of the special constitutional guarantees, in 1960, affording quotas in certain Central Services, the Community has more and more entered trade, business and the professions to its increasing advantage.

The Community is cent-per-cent literate. Although largely practical by aptitude, a relatively high percentage take to higher education. With the education trust created by the All-India Anglo-Indian Association, that tendency has been given a further impetus. In a sense, the opportunities for the Community have been greater since Independence than ever before. Anglo-Indians have, for the first time, achieved positions commensurate with their character and ability. Many Anglo-Indians, since Independence, have become heads of important departments. The Armed Forces are a significant example. From Generals downwards, there are several hundred Anglo-Indian officers in the Defence Services today.

Post-Independence Battles

In the chapter under the above heading, I refer to some of the legal battles that I have had to fight on behalf of the Community. Decisions were wrested from our Supreme Court, which gave a charter of educational freedom not only to the Anglo-Indians but to all the linguistic minorities.

The menace of Hindi Imperialism poses a threat not only to the linguistic minorities, but to the unity of India. Despite the unremitting hate campaign of the politically powerful Hindi chauvinist bloc, English has not disappeared. On my private resolution in Parliament emerged what has come to be known as the Nehru formula. Under that formula English will continue to be the associate official language as long as the non-Hindi speaking people so desire. That position has now been recognised statutorily. Nagaland adopted English as its official language in September, 1967. Except by the obscurantists and the revivalists, English has been recognised as the last remaining bond of educational, administrative, judicial and, indeed, emotional integration. The Supreme Court has put its imprimatur on my thesis that English is an Indian language because it is the language of a recognised Indian minority, the Anglo-Indians. The legal dictum affirmed by the Supreme Court is that English is not only an Indian language, but the dominant Indian language because it is the language of the Constitution, the language of the Supreme Court and the High Courts and the language of authoritative legislation.

A grave threat not only to the Anglo-Indians but to all the minority groups is the growth of a fanatical, resurgent Hindu revivalism. Certain groups and parties make no secret of the fact that they repudiate completely the secular ideal which was so passionately preached and practised by Jawaharlal Nehru. There is a latent powerful potential in Hindu society, especially in the Hindi States, which fosters the urge to establish a Hindu Rashtra or a theocratic State. The two-nation theory and Partition have given a tremendous fillip to the forces of revivalism in India. Continuing Pakistani intransigence and three acts of aggression have given increasing grist to the political mill of the revivalist parties. If like Pakistan India becomes a theocratic State, the lot of practically all the minorities will be unenviable. At best they will live on sufferance : even worse, they may face calculated oppression.

The Women Of The Community

No book on the Community would be complete without a reference to the women of the Community. They, in a very special way, have made a notable contribution to India. Free from caste and communal inhibitions, Anglo-Indian women have made a contribution to India's nursing services that was unique : 80% of India's nursing services, military and civilian, right up to Independence was drawn from the Anglo-Indian Community. In peace and in war they served India selflessly. They set standards which were comparable with the highest to be found in the most advanced western countries.

Few nursing communities in the world could point to the exploits of Helen Rodriguez whose almost incredible heroism during the Japanese campaign in Burma earned her the George Medal. Gloria Berry, the Anglo-Indian Air Hostess who was killed when the 'Kashmir Princess', one of our largest planes, was sabotaged, exemplified the spirit of the women of the Community. Her cold, calculated courage in the face of certain death earned her the posthumous award of the Ashoka Chakra Class I. She was the first, and, so far, the only woman in Independent India to be so decorrated for supreme gallantry.

No mention of Anglo-Indian women would be complete without a reference to their striking beauty. This has been the subject of comment by writers of different periods and diverse nationalities. Catherine Worlee who first married a British member of the Indian Civil Service, Grant, and later Talleyrand, Napoleon's Foreign Minister, as Princess Talleyrand was one of the most famous international beauties of her time. She was not an exception. Neither was the beautiful and talented Kitty Kirkpatrick, who was the original Blumine of Carlyle's 'Sartor Resartus'. Throughout the history of the Community, in spite of political, economic and also social discrimination which was practised against the men of the Community, until the opening of the Suez Canal in 1835 the most outstanding Britons in India married Anglo-Indian women. Many of the leading families in the British Peerage, today, were fortunate to receive this re-invigoration of Anglo-Indian blood. One of the premier Duchesses, today, comes from a rather humble Anglo-Indian family in Uttar Pradesh.

Sporting Prowess

Reference has also been made to the fact that the Anglo-Indians have a unique record as a sporting Community. In spite of its numerical smallness the Community, both the men and the women, bestrode the sporting world of India like a Colossus. In hockey, India's national game, its skill was outstanding. In the Indian hockey team that covered itself with glory in the 1928 World

Olympics and put India on the world map of sport, of the 11 playing members 8 were Anglo-Indians: of the 3 spares, 2 were Anglo-Indians. In boxing, for decades, Anglo-Indians knocked out all other contenders, including the best that the British Army in India could produce. The first and, so far, the only Indian to annex an individual World Championship for his Country was Wilson Jones the world amateur billiard champion in 1958 and 1964.

What Of The Future

I do not believe that the Community will be absorbed or disappear because of some allegedly inevitable historical-cum-biological processes. This has not happened to the Parsees, an equally microscopic community. Like the Parsees the Anglo-Indians have a certain inherent community sense which in the final analysis will ensure continuing cohesion and identity. History tells us that after the demission of the Portuguese from the Indian scene the Luso-Indians rapidly sank in the social and economic scale. But unlike the Luso-Indians, the Anglo-Indians have, as observed by Bishop Heber, a surly community pride which is perhaps part of their British inheritance. This proper pride, which should be distinguished from meretricious arrogance, leads to a powerful identity of community thought and action, and a stubborn resistance to submergence and the loss of racial, cultural and linguistic attributes which distinguish the Anglo-Indians.

The Community, today, through its schools is in the educational vanguard. Anglo-Indian teachers are the best qualified to purvey education through the medium of English. The demand for entry into the Anglo-Indian schools remains clamant and insatiable. The long and increasing waiting lists of applicants to Anglo-Indian schools have to be seen to be believed. Ironically, the most clamorous in the queue are the most raucous among the Hindi chauvinists.

Through the Frank Anthony Schools' Scheme the Community, today, has given the greatest hostage in its history to its future progress and well-being.

Fortunately, the Community has a highly organised All-India Association which enables it to achieve an almost unique measure of cohesion in furthering its social, economic and civic interests. With its network of branches spreading from Delhi to Quilon and from Bombay to Shillong the Association has enabled the Community to make up in powerful organisation what it lacks in numbers. I have the privilege of being the elected President-in-Chief of the Association since 1942. The Community's problems are many and the Association's tasks are diversified and difficult. The Association is the life-line of the Community.

In the words of Lord Linlithgow, one of the last Viceroys of India, "The Community has made a contribution of a real and permanent nature to India: it has produced many figures of outstanding capacity in the past and the work done by its members has been of real, lasting value." Despite the pressures and the difficulties I have a steadfast faith in the future of the Community and the continuing contribution it will make, out of all proportion to its size, to India.

CHAPTER I

WHO IS AN ANGLO-INDIAN?

EVEN the British in India had no precise appreciation of who and what an Anglo-Indian really was. Thus, British recruitment to the Armed Forces, even during World War II, exemplified this confusion. One brother, because he was somewhat dark, would be recruited into the Indian Army: the other brother, because of his comparatively light skin, would be recruited into the British Army. The dark brother would receive his commission as an Indian officer: his lighter skinned brother—a twin perhaps—would be employed as a European or King's commissioned officer.

Often this discrimination was not the result merely of confusion but stemmed from a policy initiated at the beginning of the 19th Century. Yet there was, also, real ignorance among the British officials and their wives, cut off as they were from social contact with the Anglo-Indians and other Indian communities, not only as to the factual position but, above all, as to the real range and meaning of the term 'Anglo-Indian'.

Outside India there was, and undoubtedly still is, a vague perhaps even derisive concept of the term 'Anglo-Indian'. A hyphenated designation, implying a community of mixed blood, perhaps conjures up a contemptuous vision jaundiced by some cheap novelist's description of a down-at-heel, treacherous half-breed. But in India, both in fact and in law, the position is very different from popular fallacy or even the well-meaning and patronising British officials' vague notions.

Name Changes

In its application to the Community, the term 'Anglo-Indian' is of fairly recent origin. The Community has, in fact, traversed several name changes. The earliest names were not specific Community designations. They were more a popular description. Country-born was generally in use. There was no stigma, no

derogatory sting in the term.   It was fondly used by the British
father of his Anglo-Indian son.   Indo-Briton was perhaps the first
Community designation to be employed.   After that the Community was generally known as 'Eurasian'.   At the beginning of the
19th Century, there was an organised move to substitute the term
'East Indian'.   The petition presented to the British Parliament
by John Ricketts in 1830 urged the recognition of the term 'East
Indian'.   The designation 'Eurasian', however, continued to be
more or less current from about 1823 to 1910.   Thus, the Association founded by E.W. Chambers in 1876 adopted this description
as a Community designation.   The term 'Eurasian' has been attributed to the Marquess of Hastings.   An examination of this
question, however, shows that Hastings did not, in fact, describe
the Community as such.   He was the Governor-General from
1813 to 1823 and in none of his speeches and writings did he employ
the word 'Eurasian'.   On the other hand, he did employ the term
'Indo-Briton'.

As the term 'Eurasian' began to acquire a derogatory connotation, the Community moved to be recognised by the term 'Anglo-
Indian'.   In 1897 the Secretary of State for India was petitioned
by a deputation to give official recognition to the use of the term
'Anglo-Indian'.   This was refused.   Till then, this term was used
to describe Britons working or resident in India.   Dr. Wallace,
however, founded what was rather grandiosely described as, 'The
Imperial Anglo-Indian Association'.   He is credited with the
extravagant observation, "Britishers we are and Britishers we ever
must be.   Once we relinquish this name 'Anglo-Indian' and permit
ourselves to be styled 'Eurasian' or 'Statutory natives of India',
we become estranged from our proud heritage of Britishers."   Lord
Curzon was also approached for approval of the use of the designation 'Anglo-Indian'.   The arrogant Curzon denied the request
in typically Curzonian fashion, with almost publicly expressed
sarcasm.   In 1911, however, Lord Hardinge, the then Viceroy,
sanctioned the use of the term 'Anglo-Indian' to describe the
Community in the census drawn up in that year.

Dual Status

In 1870 Parliamentary Statute referred to the Community as
'Statutory Natives of India'.   Paragraph 346 of the Montagu-

Chelmsford Report classified the Community as Anglo-Indian. The Army authorities continued to define and accept the Community as European British subjects. This dual status was underlined in a reply made by Earl Winterton, Under-Secretary of State for India, in the House of Commons in December 1925, when he said, "For purposes of employment under Government and inclusion in schemes of Indianisation, the members of the Anglo-Indian and Domiciled European Community are Statutory Natives of India; for purposes of education and internal security, their status, so far as it admits of definition, approximates to that of European British subjects." This dual status operated adversely against the Community in two ways. Although to protect its economic interests, the Community was defined as 'Statutory Natives of India', for defence and education it was classified as European. Not only Indian but British officials, when the question of the Indianisation of the services was being pursued, interpreted it to mean de-Anglo-Indianisation. Indianisation was interpreted so as to exclude or squeeze out the Anglo-Indians. The treatment of the Community as European for certain purposes, especially for defence, made the Anglo-Indians liable for service in the Indian Defence Force, India's second line of defence. This force was usually called upon to maintain order during communal riots. Inevitably, its task was difficult. In maintaining order the I.D.F. incurred the hostility of the major communities as often the suppression of communal riots meant shooting down, impartially, both Hindu and Muslim miscreants.

Definition

Because of this unsatisfactory state of affairs, the late Col. Sir Henry Gidney, my predecessor-in-office, sought and succeeded in securing the inclusion of a definition of the Community in the Government of India act of 1935, which was framed by the British Parliament. Under that definition all persons of European descent in the male line, whose parents were habitually resident in India, were and are Anglo-Indians. Generally and also in official quarters the term 'Anglo-Indian' was, after 1911, taken to signify persons who were of European descent in the male line but of mixed European and Indian blood. Thus both in official circles and in the Community itself a distinction was often sought to be drawn between Anglo-Indians and the so-called Domiciled Europeans, although economically, politically and socially the interests of both were identical. Thus, even the Association under Gidney subscribed to the designation, 'The All-India Anglo-Indian and Domiciled European Association'. A large number of its members were those who claimed to be of unmixed European descent, that is, Domiciled Europeans.

In fact, however, the definition of the term 'Anglo-Indian' as set out for the first time in the Government of India Act of 1935 made it clear, beyond a peradventure, that the term 'Anglo-Indian' included all persons of European descent in the male line whether of mixed or allegedly of unmixed blood. After that year, the term 'Domiciled European' became, legally at least, an anachronism, although it continued to be used. Even today, there is a microscopic organisation in South India which calls itself an Anglo-Indian and Domiciled European Association. The term 'Domiciled European' was obviously always a misnomer. Persons of European descent domiciled in India could be domiciled Indians but not domiciled Europeans. In spite of this clear legal position, British officials continued to maintain an often studied discrimination between the so-called Domiciled Europeans and the Anglo-Indians. While socially both Anglo-Indians and Domiciled Europeans were, in common with all Indians, ostracised from the 'burra' clubs as country-born, the so-called Domiciled Europeans were usually given preference in the matter of employment.

At most there could be one generation of Domiciled Europeans, namely, those Europeans who settled in India. Their children were Anglo-Indians. The definition of Anglo-Indian does not postulate mixture of Euro-Asian blood but merely requires European descent in the male line of parents habitually resident in India. Thus even assuming, contrary to the ethnic verities, that the original British families settled in India for two, three or more generations had no admixture of Indian blood they were and are Anglo-Indians. For instance, a person like John Masters, the fairly well-known author of the rather lurid novel, 'Bhowani Junction', who described himself as second or third generation European domiciled in India, was, in fact, Anglo-Indian. So also were a large number of actors and actresses who migrated to and achieved fame in America and Britain. One does not have to mention the names of certain well-known actors and actresses, past and present, in America and Britain who migrated from India. Their pronounced brunette complexions—not ascribable entirely to the Indian sun—were and are a permanent testimonial to their Anglo-Indian heritage.

Apart from being accorded certain special, even unique, guarantees in Independent India's Constitution, which came into effect on the 26th January, 1950, the Anglo-Indian Community was the only one to be defined. The definition is given in Article 366 (2) of the Constitution. It is, in effect, a reproduction of the definition set out in the Government of India Act of 1935. Article 366 (2) reads,

> "An 'Anglo-Indian' means a person whose father or any of whose other male progenitors in the male line is or was of European descent but who is domiciled within the territory of India and is or was born within such territory of parents habitually resident therein and not established there for temporary purposes only."

The Tar Brush

As a one-time student of Anthropology, I have always been extremely doubtful of the validity of the ethnic purity claim of the so-called Domiciled Europeans. With intermarriage between Britons and Anglo-Indian women, which represented the marital usage for about 200 years, few, if any, European families in India really escaped a touch of the Anglo-Indian tar brush. But it suited the British historian, particularly when these Anglo-Indians distinguished themselves, to appropriate the credit for the British by describing the person as European or at best as 'India-born'. Thus, when an Anglo-Indian pilot won the VC—his name being British—it was claimed that the recipient was British. But on the rare occasions when an Anglo-Indian was involved in a crime the British papers would take care to refer to him as an Anglo-Indian. Thus, in Fitchett's 'Tales of the Indian Mutiny' the gallant Anglo-Indian boy telegraphist George Brendish was described as an 'English boy'. Even after the departure of the British from India, the tendency to filch the credit of the achievements of the Anglo-Indians has not ceased. Thus, fairly recently, an appeal was sent out to locate Miss Fitzgibbon, the daughter of Andrew Fitzgibbon, V.C., to enable her to attend the Victoria Cross exhibition to be held in London from the 4th to the 11th May, 1962. Typically, a journal entitled 'This is Britain' described Fitzgibbon as the youngest 'British' VC, stating that he belonged to the Indian Medical Service. The Indian Medical Service was a superior cadre and, at the time when Fitzgibbon won his VC, a preserve which only Britons could enter. While one Indian-owned English-medium paper described Fitzgibbon correctly as an Anglo-Indian, the then British-owned 'Statesman' carried a series of accounts of Andrew Fitzgibbon, the youngest 'British' VC. In fact, Fitzgibbon, who won his VC on the 21st August, 1860, during the capture by Indian forces of the North Taku Fort in China was a member not of the superior Indian Medical Service but a young hospital apprentice of the Bengal Subordinate Medical Department. This 15-year old Anglo-Indian apprentice, while the troops were storming the fort, coolly attended to wounded sepoys and a doolie-bearer, in circumstances of the greatest danger. He was severely wounded in the process. 'The Statesman' went to the extent of mentioning that Miss Fitzgibbon was last heard of when she was living with a 'British' family called 'Pewseys'. In fact, she last lived with a family by the name of 'Pusey': Mr. Pusey was at one time a Sergeant in the Madras Police, which cadre was reserved for Anglo-Indians.

Blame The System

The Community has been blamed for the twin defects of escapism and renegadism, of the albescent even the strongly sun-stained crossing or trying to cross the colour line and denying their Community. Yet I would blame more the system than the individual. British policy, in fact the whole artificial Imperial Code, from the beginning of the 19th Century, placed a premium on renegadism. It was only by denying their Community that able Anglo-Indians were allowed to achieve positions commensurate with their character and ability. I could name scores of members of the Community, not only of the alleged Domiciled European variety but of the clearly mixed descent variety who achieved the highest positions as members of the Viceroy's Executive Council, Governors of Provinces, senior Generals; one became Surgeon-General to King

George V.. They were lost to the Community because of a policy that was at least amoral in its rigid insistence on alleged purity of race as a passport to achievement.

Herd Consciousness

On the other hand the Community has shown an intense herd consciousness. This is perhaps, to some extent, in imitative emulation of the social exclusiveness practised by the British or even to some extent an inherited quality from the caste-conscious British and Indian social patterns. Marriages were jealously confined within the walls of the Community. It was regarded as social anathema to marry even a light-skinned, most highly placed, member of another community in preference to an ebony-hued, poor Anglo-Indian. For generations there has been no inter-marriage with other Indian communities.

Colour has been one of the lesser determinants for the Community. Persons who might, because of their extremely dark complexion, provoke amused incredulity at their seemingly non-existent claim to the prefix 'Anglo' have over and over again been able to produce irreproachable evidence of European descent sometimes in the first generation. It is not uncommon for an Anglo-Indian family, within its confines, to exhaust the gamut of the colour spectrum, one daughter being completely Nordic, fairer than the average Briton, another albescent, a third lime-coloured and a fourth a beautiful, delicately framed brunette. In the Community there are also not a few whose sable hue would hold favourable comparison with the most highly polished mahogany. And yet despite this kaleidoscope of colour, they have been blended into one cultural, social and economic group by bonds which distinguish them from the other communities and identify them with one another.

In a sense, the term 'Anglo' may not be literally correct as it would denote persons only of Anglo-Saxon descent in the male line. Inevitably perhaps, because the existence of the Community is identified with the British regime in India, the bulk of the Community is of British descent: equally inevitable, perhaps, the offspring of the former European regimes—Portuguese, French and Dutch—have intermarried with the Community and have been assimilated to it socially, culturally, linguistically. I deal with these and other aspects more fully in the chapter entitled 'The Social and the Psychological Pattern'.

Endogamous—Mother-Tongue English

After the Mutiny, there was virtually no inter-marriage with the other communities of India. The Briton, who settled in India, almost invariably married an Anglo-Indian. Many of the better placed Anglo-Indians, after going abroad for studies, married British or European women. As a result of this endogamy the Community has emerged over a period of over 100 years as a distinctive racial-cum-linguistic-cum-cultural entity. This is in accordance with the genetic law that where peoples originally heterogenous are endogamous, that is, marry among themselves they develop the characteristic described by biologists as homozygosity. Apart from identity in clothes, in that the Anglo-Indian men and women all wear what is commonly known as European dress, they have certain common customs, manners and cultural affinities, with the supreme bond of English as their mother-tongue.

That English is the mother-tongue has been axiomatic and taken for granted. This was the reason why it was not put into the definition either in the Government of India Act of 1935 or in Article 366 of the Constitution. Thus with the de facto transfer of Pondicherry to India, the leader of the persons of French descent there had addressed me for permission to open a branch of the All-India Anglo-Indian Association. I replied that while culturally his community perhaps had much in common with the Anglo-Indians, the Association regretted that it could not have a branch there because a sine qua non of membership of the Community was the mother-tongue, English.

In fact, the Anglo-Indian Community is, perhaps, the only racial minority in India. In the words of Sir Campbell Rhodes, "Of the many races that comprise the people of India, the majority have come through the passes of the North-West Frontier, or, in earlier years, from overseas. The Anglo-Indian Community, which has distinct racial characteristics, is one of the few communities that can claim possession of an Indian birthright."

Inaccurate Census

The census figures concerning the Community, especially in

pre-Independence days, were notoriously inaccurate and even absurd. Even the Census Commissioner admitted that these figures were incorrect. Many Anglo-Indians, according to him, were wrongly returned as Europeans. His estimate, in 1931, was that the Community was approximately 200,000 strong. But even that estimate was patently wrong. At that time, there was no clear idea of the term 'Anglo-Indian'. Even the official conception was that any one with a light complexion was European. My estimate is that, in 1941, the number of Anglo-Indians was between 250,000 and 300,000.

The Government decided that the 1961 census would not show caste or community except in the case of the Scheduled Castes because of their special guarantees in respect of recruitment to the services. This was one of the near-hypocritical offerings at the altar of national integration. Religion would still be shown. In effect, this meant that the designations Hindu, Muslim, Sikh, Parsee, Christian would still appear in the census. The only community designation to be eliminated from the 1961 census was that of the Anglo-Indians. The All-India Anglo-Indian Association considered this position and ultimately decided not to make it an issue. One of the main reasons that prompted this decision was the recent attempts at infiltration by the 'Feringis' of Kerala, who claimed to have been of Portuguese descent but who during the whole British regime had nothing to do with the Community culturally, socially or otherwise and were classified as a backward class of Indian Christians whose mother-tongue was Malayalam. It was felt that the Community was still clearly identified by its mother-tongue, English. The 1961 Census showed 2,23,781 Indians with English as their mother-tongue. This figure would represent almost exclusively the Anglo-Indian Community except in Maharashtra where a fair number of others, I should imagine Goans, also returned English as their mother-tongue. This census exposed the fraudulent claims of the Feringis that there were tens of thousands of Anglo-Indians in Kerala. The Census showed the total number of persons with English as their mother-tongue in Kerala, men, women and children, as being not more than 7000. This would make an adult population of barely 1,500 which would be the correct assessment of the number of Anglo-Indians in Kerala. I deal with this issue more fully in the chapter entitled, 'The

Social and the Psychological Pattern'.

The largest concentration of the Community has always been in West Bengal, especially Calcutta. The Madras State comes next : Maharashtra (the former Bombay State) follows and then come Uttar Pradesh, Mysore (especially Bangalore), Andhra Pradesh, Madhya Pradesh (especially Jubbulpore), Bihar and Orissa, with Kerala at the end. The number of Anglo-Indians in Delhi would not be more than about a thousand adults or perhaps less. In the Punjab the number has fallen to a few hundred as also in Assam and Rajasthan.

CHAPTER II

ORIGIN AND GROWTH

First Betrayal

THERE is a vague and perhaps widespread belief that the Anglo-Indian Community, like some other mixed communities perhaps, was the result of a haphazard process of miscegenation between outcaste Englishmen and outcaste Indian women. There is also perhaps the cynical insinuation that the origin of the Community is largely shrouded in the blankets of incontinence. In fact, nothing is further from the truth. The Community has developed along quite formal and legitimate lines.

The history of the Community is the history of the British connection with India. The British advent into India was in quest of trade. In fact, the spread of British influence and domination was accidental and unplanned. It was the story of factories consisting of glorified huts being extended into buildings of a more permanent character, ultimately becoming centres first of military and then of civil power. As Sir John Seeley, the historian, has said, "Conquest is not the right word for what happened. The Indian Empire was virtually thrust upon the British." The East India Company had been permitted by Emperor Jehangir, in 1612, to erect a factory at Surat. This was their original Headquarters. In course of time factories were erected at several places. The factory, which was established at Madras, in 1639, rapidly grew into the largest and most important settlement of the trading centres of the East India Company. As these factories grew, not only British factors and writers but soldiers came out in increasing numbers. They began understandably to look around for women to marry. At that time the sea journey to India took at least six months. British women were virtually unobtainable. Even wives were not permitted to accompany their husbands and to face the rigours and hazards of life in India. Under these circumstances the men began to cultivate the society of the women of

Portuguese and French origin in the Madras settlement. As they were Christian, the British men preferred to marry them. These persons of Portuguese and French extract were, however, Roman Catholics. There was, inevitably, an increasing tendency for the British soldiers and writers who married these women to change their religion. At that time England was convulsed by the reformation movement and was a hotbed of anti-Catholicism. A cry of protest was raised at the Court of Directors of the East India Company which evolved a new policy. In any case the number of women of French and Portuguese extract available for marriage was soon exhausted as the number of British men coming out to these settlements steadily increased. On the 8th April, 1678, the Directors of the East India Company thus addressed the President of Madras : "The marriage of our soldiers to the native women of Fort St. George is a matter of such consequence to posterity that we shall be content to encourage it at some expense, and have been thinking for the future to appoint a Pagoda to be paid to the mother of any child, that shall hereafter be born of any such future marriage, upon the day the child is christened, if you think this small encouragement will increase the number of such marriages."

The Pagoda was then equivalent to eight or nine shillings, that is, then worth about five rupees.

A deliberate policy of avowedly encouraging intermarriages was thus initiated. As a result of this policy the Anglo-Indian Community was officially brought into existence.

Intermarriage

These marriages were by no means confined to the middle and lower classes. The British secured their wives in two main ways, either by treaties with Indian Chiefs and Ruling Princes or from among widows and family camp-followers left on the battlefield. It was customary, particularly among the Mohammedans, for the soldier's wife or slave girl to accompany him on the march. Usually the women were baptised and the marriage ceremony performed according to Christian rites. This period has been described as the 'Brahminising period' of English rule, when it was thought that these alliances with the local people would attract the sympathy and support of the Indians.

As not only the trade but the territories of the East India Company expanded, the commitments, both trading and military, grew correspondingly. The Directors of the East India Company, inspired for the first time by visions of Empire, initiated a policy of encouraging Britons in the humbler ranks to make India their home. In pursuance of this object an allowance of 5 rupees for every child was made to a soldier in the ranks. These marriages were not only officially encouraged, but were considered as entirely respectable. The offspring of these unions were usually well and often lavishly provided for. Many of them intermarried with some of the leading families in the British aristocracy who perhaps would, today, resent any imputation of any dark strain in their pedigree.

Some Famous Names

The history of marriages between distinguished European and Indian families would make romantic reading. More than that, they would either illuminate or darken, according to the point of view, the lineage of many of Britain's leading families, reaching to the highest ranks of the British peerage and in respect of whom there has perhaps never been any suspicion of even a touch of the tar brush. A brief reference may be made to some of these unions, the descendants of whom either merged in Britain or with the Anglo-Indian Community. Job Charnock, the founder of Calcutta, snatched a Hindu widow from the funeral pyre of her deceased husband and married her. One of their daughters, Mavis, married Sir Eyre Coote, one of the most brilliant and spectacular figures of Clive's times. A fact not generally known, perhaps conveniently suppressed by the British historians, was that Eyre Coote was an Anglo-Indian. Colonel William Linnaeus Gardner, ancestor of the Gardner family once in the British peerage, married the Nawab of Cambay's granddaughter, who was also an adopted daughter of the Moghul Emperor. Gardner was nephew of the first Lord Gardner and founder of the well-known Gardner's Horse, a famous regiment in Indian history. The Gardners are a numerous family well-known in the Anglo-Indian Community. Major Hyder Young Hearsey married another sister and granddaughter of the Nawab of Cambay. Hearsey founded the famous Anglo-Indian family of Hearseys including General Sir John Bennett Hearsey of Mutiny fame. In fact, these unions represented almost a marital usage of the times. Colonel Kennedy married a Rajput Princess. Their daughter was the first wife of General Sir Abraham Roberts, father of the famous Field Marshal Earl Roberts, at one time Commander-in-Chief in India. The son by this first marriage, and half brother to Lord Roberts, was in one of the Burma Services. Colonel Kirkpatrick, the British resident in Hyderabad, married an Indian lady and their exceptionally beautiful daughter Kitty was portrayed by Thomas Carlyle in his 'Sartor Resartus' as the original Blumine. The House of the Earl of Duffus has descendants in the Community who take pride in the family name of Sutherland. General Sir Hugh Wheeler of Kanpur fame had an Indian wife.

Such an account might include a reference to Emperor Ashoka and Thomas Becket. In his book on the Community entitled 'Our Reproach in India' H.P.K. Skipton writes, "If ancient legend speaks truly Emperor Ashoka and our own Thomas Becket were of mixed European and Asiatic race and both were remarkable and forceful men."

Walter Reinhardt, described by some writers as an unsavoury, even infamous character was, nevertheless, rather typical of the age. Through many vicissitudes but generally through ruthless fighting he achieved a position of eminence as a free-lance soldier. He and his brigades were in considerable demand by Princes of the day. Ultimately, he was taken into the service of the Emperor and put in charge of the Fort at Agra. He was known as General Sombre (or Sombru). Reinhardt died in 1778 leaving his estates and his principality of Sardhana to his favourite slave girl and second wife who achieved fame as Begum Sombru or Sumru. Much has been written about this remarkable woman who later married a French adventurer, Col. Le Vassoult, who committed suicide to avoid capture by his enemies. Reinhardt's son, Aloysius, by his first wife who was a Muslim lady, married the daughter of General Lafevre: the daughter of this marriage married George Dyce, an Anglo-Indian from the Upper Military Orphanage of Calcutta, who was then serving as Commandant of the Begum's forces. Of their children one daughter married Baron Peter Solaroli. The son, David Ochterlony, who was adopted by Begum Sumru took the additional name of Sombre. David Ochterlony Dyce Sombre inherited more than half a milllion pounds from the

Begum in 1836 and became the most celebrated personage of the English season of 1838. In 1840 he married the Hon'ble Mary Anne Jervis, daughter of the second Viscount St. Vincent: he also won a seat in Parliament as Member for Sudbury. A more detailed account of this controversial, maligned figure will be given when describing his contributions as a poet and writer.

Elihu Yale was President at Madras from 1687 to 1692. He was said to be a wise and progressive Governor and was known for his generosity both public and private. Yale purchased for the Company a place called Tevenapatam to the south of Madras which was duly fortified and was destined to play an important part in later history. The fort at Tevenapatam, now called Cuddalore, was named St. David after Elihu Yale's little son David who, unfortunately, died in his infancy. Yale remained in India for seven years after resigning office and having amassed an enormous fortune he left India for England in 1699. Shortly afterwards, he was made Governor of the British Colony of New York. His name is remembered in America, the land of his birth, through the University of Yale which he generously endowed. His tombstone inscription runs as follows,

> "Elihu Yale was buried 22nd July, 1721.
> Born in America, in Europe bred,
> In Africa travelled, in Asia wed,
> Where long he lived and thrived—in London dead.
> Much good, some ill, he did, so hope's all even,
> And that his soul through mercie's gone to heaven."

It has been said that Elihu Yale's wife was an Anglo-Indian.

Thomas Pitt was the second son of the Rev. John Pitt, Rector of Blandfort, Dorset. He was born in 1653. While still young he came out to India but not in the Company's service. He lived as a free-trader at Balasore in Orissa. He returned to England when still comparatively young and settled in Dorset. He was elected as a member of Parliament. Later on, he came to terms with the Company and in 1698 he was appointed Governor of Fort St. George, for a period of five years. His tenure was extended so that he was Governor for the unusual term of 11 years. His Governorship was regarded as the golden age of Madras in respect

of trade and the increase in its wealth.   Pitt did a great deal to improve Madras and also to strengthen its fortifications.   He was also
a big diamond dealer.   On one occasion he purchased an enormous
diamond for £ 20,000 which he eventually sold to the Regent of
France for £ 135,000.   In 1680 he married Jane Innes at Calcutta.
She is believed to have been an Anglo-Indian.   They had three
sons and two daughters.   His eldest son Robert was the father of
William Pitt, the first Earl of Chatham and one of England's
greatest statesmen.   On his return to England he purchased large
properties and was repeatedly elected a Member from his own
constituency.

These examples could be multiplied many fold. A separate
book written about these unions would be of some historical but
perhaps of greater romantic interest.

Intermarriage With British

With the growth of the Anglo-Indian Community the practice of
intermarriage with women of other Indian communities fell not only
into disuse, but even into disrepute. More and more Britons began to
seek their brides from among the Anglo-Indian women. The British
women found it impossible or were not even permitted to come
out to India in appreciable numbers. The regulations of the East
India Company at first prohibited the British women from sharing the lives, the hazards and the privations of their fathers,
brothers or husbands in the India of those days. As time went
by, every new arrival, from Governor and Member of the Council
downwards, found a wife for himself from among the daughters
of Anglo-Indian homes. Thus, there were towards the end of
the 17th and the beginning of the 18th Centuries what were known
as the Upper Orphanage and the Lower Orphanage. The Upper
Orphanage Schools were aided by British Military officers. Many
of these orphans were first or second generation Anglo-Indians,
that is, their mothers were either Anglo-Indian, Hindu or Muslim,
married to British officers. There was also the Lower Orphanage
Schools for the children or wards of non-commissioned officers or
privates. To these orphanages according to their ranks went
practically all Britons to find a wife. It was the endeavour of
the promoters, "To render the girls agreeable and engaging in
their deportment so that they might make eligible marriages in

the settlement", and the marriages were usually arranged for the girls at what would now be regarded as an extremely tender age. Thus, "The promoters regretted that several of the young ladies who had reached the age of 13 years and yet had received no proposals of marriage which the Managers could approve of."

The Briton in India at that period was no different from the Briton who remained behind in his own country. The moral code in England had reached a particularly low ebb. The Anglo-Indian Community has thus descended from the same stock, moral or immoral, as the British of those days. In some ways life was easy, extravagant and even licentious. In other ways the times required rough, ruthless but also courageous living. Not only was the dress extravagant and utterly unsuited to the climate, but so also was the food consumed. The daily menu was remarkably elaborate. The wealthier merchant had several servants : he usually had between 100 and 150 servants : the less wealthy anything between 50 and 100. Even a young officer during a campaign was accompanied by 7 or 8 servants, 15 or so coolies to carry his luggage, his wine, his brandy, tea, his live poultry and his milch cows. Europeans and Anglo-Indians lived close to and were much influenced by Indian customs. Those who could afford it, ate and drank intemperately. The staple drink was 'Arak' which was later replaced by Madeira and in the 19th Century by whisky. Not only the men but even the women smoked. The chewing of betelnut was a general practice.

Vital Bulwark—Welcomed As Equals

From 1650 to 1783 India was torn by internecine tribal and clan warfare. The confusion was made worse confounded by the Portuguese, the Dutch, the French and the British fighting either among themselves or taking sides with the warring Indian Chiefs.

By about 1750 the number of Anglo-Indians exceeded the number of Britons in India. This increase was welcomed by the Company as it gave them the necessary man-power to draw upon. As the territories of the Company expanded, it became involved in warlike activities. Bound to the British by ties of blood, language, dress and habits the Anglo-Indians formed a vital bulwark of the growing power of the East India Company. In the beginning of the 18th Century Britain was largely occupied in fighting wars in the European Continent and was unable to provide European troops for campaigning in India. In the words of Herbert Stark, "The brunt of the fighting fell on the Anglo-Indians. But for them the French would have expelled the British from India." Stark proceeds, "All Anglo-Indians who were physically fit were enlisted into the Company's forces in every branch. In times of emergency they were called up or volunteered for active service, and gallantly fought under Clive at Arcot, Sriramgaon, and Trichinopoli in the Second Karnatic War; and at Wandiwash under Eyre Coote. They perished in the Black Hole of Calcutta. They were in the line of battle at Plassey. They participated in the campaigns which put an end to French aspirations in India. They were massacred with their English comrades by the soldiery of Mir Kasim at Patna (1763), fought in the battle of Buxar (1764) and were present at the capture of Allahabad. They took part in the Rohilla War (1772), the First Maratha War (1775), and in the Second Mysore War (1780)."

"By the time the Treaty of Versailles was signed in 1783, the Portuguese, the Dutch and the French ambitions in India had been crushed largely with the help of Anglo-Indian officers and soldiers."

While the East India Company was growing, its territories expanding and its wars being fought, the Anglo-Indians were welcomed and treated as equals. The covenanted and commissioned ranks of the services were open to them and also the combatant ranks of the British army. They suffered no disabilities, either social or economic. If their fathers could afford it, they were sent to England for their studies and usually entered the covenanted ranks of the civil services or came out as officers in the British Regiments in India. Those who could not afford to go to England for their studies, usually entered the Warrant Officer and other ranks of the British army. The Anglo-Indians, like their British fathers, had to subscribe to certain restrictions. Like the British, they were not allowed to acquire land for agriculture. They were not permitted to live more than 10 miles from the nearest town or settlement. By background, tradition and training, war and soldiering were their heritage.

By the beginning of the 18th Century the East/India Company regime began to acquire the trappings of colonial government.

The government was centralised in the Governor-General who was assisted by a Council of about 4 members. By this time also the Anglo-Indians had forged for themselves a position of respect in the Administration. Many of them had literally fought their way by capacity, work and character to the highest civil and military positions in the Country. They were treated by the Indian population not only with respect but even with deference. By that time they had become perhaps the most wealthy and influential Community in India. Members of the Community filled the highest posts in the civil and military departments. There was no discrimination, either social, economic or racial.

First Betrayal

Discrimination and deliberate oppression were, in the next few years, to be the return for their vital services. There had been almost constant friction between the Directors of the East India Company and the Government in India in the matter of patronage and the filling of appointments. The complex of greed, baseless fear and brazen ingratitude was to be the guiding motive of policy towards the Community in the next few years. For some time the shareholders of the East India Company had watched with growing dissatisfaction the Englishmen returning from India who had become inordinately rich, sometimes in a comparatively short space of time. A feeling began to mount that positions of responsibility and influence should now become the perquisite of the relatives and sons of shareholders in England and that appointments should no longer be made by the Government on the spot and least of all to persons born in India or with an intermingling of Indian blood. Motives of greed were fortuitously buttressed by happenings in the Spanish possession of Haiti. This was an island in the Carribean which had been discovered by Columbus and annexed by Spain. The French also gained a footing in Haiti. In time a large population of Mulattos, persons of mixed European and Negro blood, came into existence. The French supported a policy of liberalism towards the Mulattos; this was not, however, favoured by the Spaniards. In the American War of Independence which came to an end in 1785, the French had joined hands with the Americans against the British. They had sent a number of their Mulatto troops who had fought side by side with the

Americans helping them to throw off their yoke. Subsequently, the French resiled from their policy of liberalism and joined hands with the Spaniards in seeking to oppress the Mulattos, and also the Negro population. Having once tasted freedom, the Mulattos were not easily crushed. Mulattos such as Oge, Rigaud, Pinchinet and Banvais, rose in revolt and led the Mulatto and Negro troops until they had wrested their freedom and the Black Republic was established. Several Mulattos suffered unspeakable atrocities. They were broken on the rack and were hanged before freedom was achieved. This event in far-off Haiti was seized upon by the shareholders of the East India Company to reinforce their attempts to capture key posts in India for their sit-at-home offspring.

By this time the British forces in India had been considerably emasculated owing to England being constantly at war. The canard was generated that Indian soldiers led by Anglo-Indian officers might well emulate the story of Haiti and drive the British out of India. As the first step in this policy of monopolising the posts in India for themselves the Directors of the East India Company, under pressure from their shareholders, directed their first attack against the wards of the Upper Orphanage School at Calcutta. This school, which had been founded in 1782, catered for the orphans of British Military officers. Many of these orphans were first generation Anglo-Indians, that is, their mothers were either Hindu, Muslim or Anglo-Indian married to British officers. On the 14th March, 1786, an order was promulgated prohibiting practically all these wards from proceeding to England in order to complete their education after which they usually entered the covenanted civil services or became officers in British regiments in India.

There was also a Lower Orphanage for the children or wards of British non-commissioned officers and privates. There was a flame of indignation among the British Officers in India. Their sons and grandsons, reared in the sound and sight of cannon and amidst the dust and din of battle and sudden death, were now to be deprived of their traditional occupation of bearing arms. It was pointed out that this discrimination was directed against Anglo-Indians and more especially against orphans of British officers who had given their lives in the service of the Company. It was underlined that any Indian could proceed to England for further studies and that those British fathers who could afford it could and would send their Anglo-Indian sons to Britain for further studies or to settle in England and that this order was wanton and heartless. The shareholders, however, won the day. In fact, this first victory merely whetted their appetite for still further oppression and expropriation of worthwhile cadres in India. Increasing pressure was brought by the shareholders on the Directors of the East India Company until in 1791 they resolved that persons of Indian extraction were precluded from employment as officers in the Civil, Military or Marine services of the Company. This prohibition was published in the Calcutta Gazette of the 14th June, 1792. Thus a blanket embargo was placed on Anglo-Indians entering the official cadres of the civil and military services.

The appetite of the shareholders grew with feeding. Worse was to follow. Not satisfied with closing the officers cadres to the Anglo-Indians, the shareholders felt that they must go a step further if their policy was to be completely successful. The Government in India represented by the Governor-General-in-Council had fought successively losing battles and ultimately succumbed in 1795. The Governor-General-in-Council was prevailed upon or compelled to pass a resolution by which all persons unless descended from European parents on both sides were disqualified from service in the army except as fifers, drummers, bandsmen and farriers, that is as non-combatants. In the words of Herbert Stark, "Within a brief period of 10 years, lying between 1786 and 1795, by the standing orders of the Great East India Company Anglo-Indians had been reduced to the status of a proscribed and down-trodden race." This policy was immediately implemented and Anglo-Indians were discharged en masse from official positions in the civil service and the army.

Apparently conscience was not part of the make-up of the Directors of the East India Company. As soon as Anglo-Indians had served their purpose in the Maratha War of 1803 they were faced with the final blow. One Viscount Valentia had been commissioned by the East India Company to visit their possessions between the period 1802 to 1806. His visit coincided with the currents of suspicion and nervousness that had been generated against the Anglo-Indians by what had happened in far-off Haiti. In 1806 Lord Valentia with the assumed authority, which globetrotters usually arrogate to themselves, without any real knowledge or experience of the subject he was treating wrote as follows, "The most rapidly accumulating evil of Bengal is the increase of half-caste children. They are forming the first step to colonisation by creating a link of union between the English and the natives. In every country where this intermediate caste has been permitted to rise, it has ultimately tended to its ruin. Spanish-America and San Domingo are examples of this fact. Their increase in India is beyond calculation: and though possibly there may be nothing to fear from the sloth of the Hindus, and the rapidly declining consequence of Musalmans, yet it may be justly apprehended that this tribe may hereafter become too powerful for control. Although they are not permitted to hold offices under the Company, yet they act as clerks in almost every mercantile house; and many of them are annually sent to England to receive the benefit of an European education. With numbers in their favour, with a close relationship to the natives, and without an equal proportion of the pusillanimity and indolence which is natural to them, what may not in future time be dreaded from them!"

On the basis of that criminally ignorant report, an order was issued in 1808 discharging Anglo-Indians from all ranks of the British Army. The first great act of betrayal of the Community was ruthlessly implemented. Yet another major blot was thus unashamedly placed on the already shame-scarred escutcheon of the Directors of the Company. Thereafter a dense, impregnable wall of social and economic discrimination was drawn around the Anglo-Indians. Some escaped by claiming to be European. They achieved wealth and distinction. A premium was thus placed on renegadism.

CHAPTER III

FREE-LANCE SOLDIERS

Scholars and Poets

BETRAYED by the Administration, driven out of the services, Anglo-Indians nurtured in the profession of arms followed the only course open to them. They offered their services to the Indian Princes and to soldiers of fortune. The Maharatta Chieftains, the Nizam of Hyderabad, the Nawabs of Bengal and Oudh, the famous Tippu Sultan of Mysore, the Rajas of Rajputana, the Jat Chiefs of Agra, Bharatpur and Alwar, and Ranjit Singh, the Lion of the Punjab, welcomed the Anglo-Indians as officers. Madhoji Scindia, who founded the Gwalior dynasty and built up the most powerful princely army of the time, employed a large number of Anglo-Indian officers to train and lead his soldiers. Anglo-Indians also joined free-lances such as the turbulent Irishman Raja George Thomas. Others raised their own Corps of infantry and cavalry.

This was the period of Indian history which has been described as 'The Great Anarchy'. At that time India was torn with internecine strife. The power of the Mughals had crumbled and the Country was overrun by Chieftains and Warlords. Because of the military genius of Gen. Count deBoigne, Commander-in-Chief of Madhoji Scindia's armies, the power of Scindia had spread over the greater part of Hindustan from the Nerbudda to the Sutlej. Hundreds of thousands of floating soldiery transferred their allegiance according to the prospects of loot and plunder.

The territories even of the most powerful Princes such as Scindia and Holkar never had any real peace. The peasantry enjoyed neither security of person nor of property. The forces of the Maharatta Chiefs were constantly out in detachments raising armies, reducing forts or punishing refractory officers or zamindars all over Rajputana, Malwa and Bhopal. The system of plunder indulged in by the leading Princes inevitably encouraged local populations, which were predisposed to marauding, to take to plundering the Country. In fact, most of the Princes encouraged such marauding bands as affording additional means for enlarging their own sphere of military plunder. As a result, before 1814 the Country was overrun by predatory bands, known as the Pindaris, who systematically ravaged every district from the Krishna to the Marwar desert. In 1814 they were estimated to consist of about a hundred thousand horsemen of all sorts and conditions. Treacherous, indulging in every form of barbarity, these banditti laid waste the Country with fire and sword.

James Skinner

A detailed account of Anglo-Indian soldiers of this period would make thrilling reading. This was the period of Lt. Col. James Skinner. An almost fabulous figure, he raised Skinner's Horse which achieved world fame. It continues till today as one of India's finest units. The tradition has also continued of associating one of Skinner's descendants with this famous regiment. This is not the place to give any biographical sketch of Skinner. A brief reference will have to be sufficient. James Skinner was born in 1778 and was the son of a Scotsman, Ensign Hercules Skinner, who rose to the rank of Lt. Col. His mother was the daughter of a Rajput Zamindar : she had been taken prisoner at the age of 14 during the war with Raja Cheit Singh. Of the three sons, David went to sea and James and Robert distinguished themselves as soldiers. On the mother's death the boys were sent to a charity school. From there they were removed to a boarding school. James was subsequently apprenticed to a printer in Calcutta. Disgusted with the unimaginative chores of the printer's trade, he ran away with the intention of going to sea. For six days he wandered in the bazaars offering to work for anyone who would hire him. Surprised by a servant of his elder sister's household, he was taken home and duly chastised. He was then put to copy law papers in his brother-in-law's office and in return received his food. After about three months Skinner was visited by his godfather, Col. Burn, who, finding that the young lad's heart was set on soldiering, gave him a letter of introduction to General deBoigne, the Commander-in-Chief of Madhoji Scindia's armies.

Skinner soon became efficient particularly in the use of the sword

and the lance. In recognition of his valour at the battle of Chand-
kori General Perron, who had succeeded deBoigne, promoted him
to the rank of Lieutenant. At the siege of Chittor Skinner saved
Scindia's life. To express his gratitude, the Maharaja held a
special Durbar at which, after embracing Skinner, presented him
with a charger, a sword, a shield and a pair of gold bangles set
with diamonds. Skinner's valour won him further laurels. He
was promoted to be a Captain and his brother Robert, who received a Commission from Perron, was appointed to his Corps. In
an encounter with the army of the Raja of Oonereah, Madhoji
Scindia's soldiers deserted him : Skinner's Horse alone remained loyal.
In the battle Skinner was shot through the groin and left on the
field with more than a thousand of his slain soldiers. Skinner has left
a graphic account, in Persian, of the terrible sufferings of that night.

Skinner records that Jaswant Rao Holkar, one of the leading
Maharatta Chiefs, was always jealous of Scindia's power. Holkar
raised an army and attacked part of Scindia's forces which were
led by Colonel Hessing, an Anglo-Indian officer. Hessing's brigade
which had become detached from the main body of Scindia's forces
was surrounded and cut to pieces by Holkar's army after putting
up a gallant resistance for 15 days. Skinner records that in this
encounter 16 Anglo-Indian officers were killed : many of them
had been to school with him.

At this time events were moving to the culmination, in 1803, of
war between the British and the Maharattas. The Maharatta
Chieftains had enormous forces at their disposal. On behalf of
Scindia Perron himself commanded sixteen to seventeen thousand
regular infantry, fifteen to twenty thousand cavalry and the usual
complement of artillery. Had the Maharattas not been divided
by their age-long rivalries and feuds, they could have mustered a
force two hundred to three hundred thousand strong. When Lord
Wellesley declared war against the Maharattas, all Anglo-Indian
and British officers serving with any Maharatta Prince were ordered to leave. Skinner was among those officers. While being dismissed, however, from the Maharaja's service, he protested against
his dismissal. He was completely Indian in the sense that he
had been brought up among and served with Indians. He had no
ties with Britain. His father was dead and his brother had been
given a Commission by Begum Sumru. In fact, he had little con-

fidence in British faith. Finally, he was persuaded by his fellow-officers to meet Lord Lake, the Commander-in-Chief of the British forces. He was treated with extreme cordiality and offered a Command by Lord Lake and given the right to raise a troop of horse. Skinner, however, had a deep sense of loyalty. One of the terms which he insisted on was that he would not fight his old comrades-in-arms: nobody would draw sword against Madhoji Scindia, whose salt he had eaten, or Perron under whom he had served. Ultimately, Skinner became a great favourite with Lord Lake. He formed his Corps of cavalry from a body of Perron's men who had served under him. The men, in fact, insisted on serving under 'Sikander Sahib', as James Skinner was known. 'Sikander' was a corruption of Alexander, the reference being to Alexander the Great.

Skinner's first action under the British colours covered his Corps with glory. Having captured the fort of Malaghur from Madho Rao, he was congratulated by Lord Lake and placed in general command of the country between Aligarh and Delhi. During that period with only 800 men he cut up about 5000 Sikhs at Saharanpur and made prisoners of the confederate Chiefs who had assembled on the banks of the Jumna.

Because of the jealousies existing among the Maharatta Chiefs, all their schemes for unity came to naught. Scindia and Holkar, in spite of efforts to unite, failed to do so. Ranjit Singh of Lahore also backed out from supporting Scindia. Holkar, Bhonsle, who was Maharaja of Nagpur, and Scindia, although promising to work together never did so and were destroyed one by one by the British. The regular brigades received no assistance from the cavalry and were, during the battles, deserted by the officers who led them. It is interesting to reflect that had the Anglo-Indian officers, who had distinguished themselves in the service of the Maharatta Chiefs, remained to lead the otherwise courageous Maharatta soldiery, the history of British arms in India might well have been differently written. Holkar first tortured and then barbarically put to death eight of his best officers. The most eminent of these was Col. Vickers, an Anglo-Indian, who was mainly responsible for Holkar's victory over the Peshwa's army at Poona on the 25th October, 1802. Vickers with seven officers, all Anglo-Indians, were beheaded in one day.

Lord Lake met the remnants of Scindia's forces and after a bloody battle totally destroyed them.

Skinner and his men saw considerable service against Amir Khan, the most powerful of the predatory Chiefs of this period. In an encounter with his forces, Robert Skinner displayed particular gallantry. Lord Lake sent a letter in Persian to the Corps commending their services. Skinner's Horse covered itself with so much glory that when they were passing through Delhi, the Resident, Col. (afterwards General Sir) David Ochterlony, inspected them and unbuckling his sword gave it to their Corps Commander, James Skinner. On the 19th December, 1805, Holkar and Ranjit Singh sued for terms. In January, 1806, at the end of the campaign all the irregular troops were discharged. Skinner's was the only Corps of irregular cavalry that was retained and made permanent as a reward for their courageous and faithful service.

On Lord Cornwallis' death in Ghazipur, in 1805, his successor Sir George Barlow ordered, among other reductions, the disbandment of Skinner's Horse. With tears in his eyes Lord Lake, the Commander-in-Chief, communicated this news to Skinner. His men received pensions and gratuity, while James and Robert were granted Jagirs yielding Rs. 20,000/- a year. Shortly after this, however, when it was decided that British subjects will not hold land, the Jagirs were withdrawn and pensions were granted. This pleased neither of the two brothers nor their friend Lord Lake.

Not long after there was trouble with the Sikhs. Once again, the British Administration rushed for help to Skinner. He was asked to raise a Corps for the settlement of the Harriana District. On the death of his brother in 1825, Skinner's Corps was reduced in strength. Skinner's reaction was an eloquent commentary on the administration's policy at the time.

"I was, however, still at the head of 1200 horse: and in 1822 I went to Calcutta, where I was very kindly greeted by Lord Hastings. He promised that he would not lessen my command by a single man; but no sooner had he left the Country than my Corps was at once reduced to 800 men. Rapid, indeed, has been my fall. In the Maharatta service from 1796 to 1803, I had always a well-grounded hope of rising in rank and fortune; no question was ever raised as to my birth there. When I entered the British service, I believed that I had found a field in which the fruits of zeal and fidelity would be matured and reaped in perfection; and no exertions on my part were spared to forward this object. I imagined myself to be serving a people who had no prejudices against caste or colour. But I found myself mistaken. All I desired was justice. If I was not to share in all the privileges of a British subject, let me be regarded as a native and treated as such. If I was to be regarded as a British subject, did the hard labour and ready service of twenty years merit no more than a pension of 300 rupees per month; without either rank or station and after the distinct and repeated promises of the permanent maintenance of my Corps, was it fair that I should be left liable to be commanded by the youngest subaltern in the army, deprived of the hope which I had so fondly entertained of passing my old age tranquilly in that service to which my better years had been devoted? But I thank my Creator that there remains one source of satisfaction—one consolation under every disappointment; and it is this—that I have ever discharged my duty as a soldier with honour and credit; that during the space of twenty years, in which I have served with Europeans, no one can ever upbraid me with dishonouring 'the steel', or being 'faithless to my salt' : that, finally, though I have failed in gaining what I desired and deserved—that is rank—I have proved to the world that I was worthy of it."

In 1826 on the recommendation of the Government Skinner was made Commander of the Bath. The British Government was further pleased to declare, "This officer has so often been brought to our notice that his services must no longer be neglected; therefore, let the gift of rank be bestowed by the Crown." The rank of Lt. Col. was granted to both Skinner and Gardner. It would appear that Lord Combermere had to wear down the opposition of some of the British military officers who did not view favourably the conferment of this rank on Skinner.

In 1831 Skinner was directed to proceed with two Risalas of his Cavalry to Rupar where a grand meeting had been arranged between the British Governor-General and Ranjit Singh. The latter attended this Durbar superbly dressed. He wore on his left arm the famous Koh-i-Noor diamond. Lord Bentinck presented Skinner with an elegant silver vase on which there was an inscription acknowledging Skinner's outstanding services.

On the 4th December, 1841, the lion-hearted leader of the famous

'Yellow Boys' passed away. He died at Hansi after a short illness.
On the 17th January, 1842, his remains were disinterred and escorted by the regiment to the church which he had built in Delhi.
Four miles from the city the cortege was met by a vast multitude.
Sixty-three guns were then fired corresponding to his age. Full
military honours were paid to him. It was said, "No Emperor
was ever brought to Delhi in such state as Sikander Saheb."

Skinner was as modest as he was a dashing soldier. It is said
that he used to have a wooden ladle placed before him at meals to
remind him of his humble origin. He was short, sturdily built and
dark in complexion. Apart from his skill and courage as a soldier
and leader of men, Skinner was a Persian scholar and kept his diary
in that language.

The Gardners

Col. William Linnaeus Gardner was the founder not only of the
well-known Gardner's Horse, which continues today as one of
India's proud regiments but also of the rather prolific Gardner
family. William Gardner was gazetted as an Ensign in the 18th Foot
on the 7th March, 1793. He was the eldest son of Major Valentine
Gardner who was the elder brother of Alan, First Lord Gardner.
He became a free-lance soldier and had a most adventurous
career. Before 1798 he entered the service of the Maharatta
Chieftain Jaswant Rao Holkar and raised a brigade of infantry for
him. Holkar sent him on a mission to negotiate a treaty with the
independent Princes of Cambay, a State on the west coast of India.
Gardner married Princess Mehr Manzul-un-nissa when she was
13 years of age. This granddaughter of the Prince of Cambay was
eventually adopted by Akbar Shah who succeeded Shah Alam as
the Emperor at Delhi. It would appear that in 1804 Gardner was
in the service of the Raja of Jaipur. When he joined the British,
he raised a cavalry Corps known as Gardner's Horse.

Gardner served as a leader of this irregular horse unit with the
rank of Captain under Lord Lake. Later with the rank of Lt. Col.
he rendered invaluable service under Sir David Ochterlony. His
unit was first known as a Corps of irregular cavalry and afterwards
was described as Gardner's Local Horse.

Gardner was a skilled rider and swordsman. He was held in
very high esteem by both Indians and Europeans. He was des-

cribed as a gentleman and a soldier of pleasing address and uncommon ability. Gardner and his wife are said to have led an
ideally happy life. He resided at his estate at Khasgunj in Etah
District. He died there on the 20th July, 1835, at the age of 65.
His wife is said to have died of a broken heart within six months
after the death of her husband.

Col. Gardner had two sons and a daughter by his Princess wife.
Alan, the second son, who died in 1828, was married to one Bibi
Saheba Hinga. They had two daughters, Susan and Hurmuzi.
Susan married Prince Anjam Shikoh: Hurmuzi married in 1834
Stuart William Gardner, an Ensign in the 28th Native Infantry,
the son of Rear-Admiral Francis Gardner, nephew of the second
Baron Gardner and grandson of the first Baron Gardner. Their
son Alan Hyde succeeded to the title. He married in 1879 Jane,
a converted Princess of the House of Delhi who had a son in 1881.

The Gardner family lived in a princely style but ultimately their
estates were mortgaged and then lost. In 1883 Alan Hyde Gardner
claimed the title of fourth Baron. On the death of Alan Hyde a
few years before 1889, his son Alan Legg, who was Reference Clerk
in the Library of the Government Secretariat of the United Provinces, claimed to have succeeded to the title.

Hyder Hearsey

To this period also belonged Major Hyder Young Hearsey, one
of the most colourful Anglo-Indians of that time. He was the son
of a Jat lady by Capt. Henry Hearsey. By coincidence he was
given the name of Hyder, which was the name of one of England's
greatest enemies at that time, Hyder Ali of Mysore. It is believed
that his second name was 'Jung', meaning war, which was subsequently anglicised to Young. Hyder Young Hearsey was educated at Woolich. Owing to the ban against the admission of
Anglo-Indians into the Company's Army he would have been denied a Commission but for the influence of his cousin Col. Andrew
Hearsey, Commandant of the Allahabad Fort. His first appointment was as aide-de-camp to the Nawab Wazir at Benaras: he soon
effected an exchange into the Maharatta service under Madhoji
Scindia. Partly because of his knowledge of French, Hearsey
was made aide-de-camp to General Perron who was then commanding Scindia's armies. Ultimately because of Perron's partiality

to certain French officers, Hearsey and Hopkins, another Anglo-Indian, left and entered the service of Raja George Thomas. Subsequently Thomas fell out with Madhoji Scindia and a French officer by the name of Bourguin was sent with two divisions of the Maharatta army to conquer Hissar, Thomas' principality, and to reduce Hansi, the capital. In the various actions that ensued, Bourguin was repeatedly defeated by Thomas and his lieutenants Hearsey and Hopkins. Finding that he could not reduce Hansi by the normal methods of warfare, Bourguin resorted to treachery and sought to bribe Thomas' soldiers into desertion. Soon Thomas found that he had not sufficient men to man the walls of his fort. With Hearsey he withdrew into his citadel where he was besieged by Bourguin but without decision. Eventually Thomas was induced to give up the citadel named George-ghur. He was allowed to march out with all the honours of war, to retain his arms, his family and his private property : he was also paid three hundred thousand rupees.

Shortly after this Hearsey left Thomas and raising a troop of 5000 men in the Mewathi country, began to subdue the district for himself. In 1804 he received an invitation from Lord Lake to come over to him. Hearsey accordingly disbanded his men with the exception of one regiment of picked cavalry. With these he fought in the battle of Deigh. As a reward his men were formed into a cavalry regiment under his command. Hearsey was sent to quell the insurrection of Rohillas which he did successfully. Sir George Barlow, acting Governor-General, however, ill-advisedly ordered the disbandment of his Horse and even refused to pay the soldiers the pension that had been promised by the Government.

In the following year Hearsey went exploring the sources of the Jumna and the Ganges. In 1809 he found himself undertaking a more attractive task of expelling the Gurkhas from the Oudh Terai. His campaign was completely successful and he took the Gurkha Chieftain a prisoner.

Hearsey had become acquainted with the Raja of Tehri Garhwal who was living in very straitened circumstances at Bareilly. The Raja was the representative of the Chand family that had ruled over Garhwal for many centuries. He was the heir of Raja Pradhuman Shah who was driven from his dominion by the Gurkhas in 1803. Pradhuman Shah made a valiant attempt to recover his territories, but was defeated and killed near Dehra in 1804. His successor, despairing of regaining his territories and throne, offered to sell part of it to Hearsey. The transaction seemed to be extremely rash in nature because of the inclination of the British authorities to avoid war with the Gurkhas. Hearsey was, however, not only absolutely fearless but of an enterprising character. He entertained the idea of reconquering Garhwal for the Raja and himself. The sale was, therefore, concluded by a formal deed. According to this deed the Raja sold to Hearsey the Pargunnas of Doon and and Chandee. This was in 1811. Hearsey thus owned the whole territory between Kalsi and Gonda.

After the Gurkha war of 1815, the British Government reinstated the Raja in parts of his dominion, but certain parts which included the Doon and Chandee and the present district of Garhwal were retained by the British. Hearsey brought his purchase to the notice of the Government which bought the Parganna of Chandee from him for a sum which was to be payable to Hearsey and his successors in perpetuity commencing from the 1st of January, 1812. In the same deed Hearsey promised that when the Doon valley came into the possession of the Company, he would sell that property also to the Company. But for reasons best known to it, the East India Company failed to complete the purchase of the Doon and the efforts of Hearsey's descendants to get the British authorities to honour these transactions consistently failed.

In 1814 Hearsey and Dr. William Moorcraft journeyed into Chinese Tartary and were the first foreigners to set eyes on the Mansarowar and Rakastal lakes. On his return Hearsey submitted his report to the Government with an illustrated map and received a present of 6000/- rupees. In the following year Hearsey was engaged in another campaign against the Gurkhas.

The capture of Bharatpur was the last campaign in which Hearsey fought. The old warrior emerged from his retirement to volunteer his services in spite of the many wounds that he had received during his many campaigns and despite the churlish treatment meted out to him by the Company. After the fall of Bharatpur Hearsey retired to his house in Kareli where he lived in great state and happiness until his death in 1840. His wife, a Princess of Cambay, survived him for about ten years. He left two sons and a daughter who married General Sir John Bennett Hearsey of Mutiny fame.

The two sons, John and William, entered the service of the King of Oudh in 1836 as they were unable to get commissions in the Company's service because of their mixed descent. On the annexation of the Province in 1852 both brothers were given commissions with the rank of Captain and distinguished themselves during the Mutiny.

It is interesting to note the number of Anglo-Indian officers involved in the battle between the Maharatta and the Nizam's armies. One of the most powerful Princes of the time, the Nizam of Hyderabad, employed a large number of Anglo-Indian officers to train and lead his armies. On the 11th March, 1785, the Nizam's armies met the Maharatta forces at the battle of Kardla. The armies of the Maharattas and the Nizam were almost equally matched in numbers and equally well disciplined, being officered largely by Anglo-Indians and Europeans.

The battle was really indecisive. The Nizam, who was an old uncertain man, insisted on retreating when his Moghul cavalry, on which he relied unduly, broke up in confusion under heavy fire from the Maharatta rocket batteries. In the Maharatta army there were many senior Anglo-Indian officers such as Col. Hessing, Michael Filose, Derridon and many others. One of the most distinguished Anglo-Indian officers of the Maharatta armies was Col. Sutherland who married the niece of General Perron, the then Commander-in-Chief of Madhoji Scindia's armies, and the daughter of Col. Hessing. Sutherland fought gallantly for Holkar and settled at Mathura where he was buried.

In fact General Perron himself had married an Anglo-Indian girl by the name of Derridon (the original name was perhaps deRidon). He had two daughters, one of whom married a French nobleman. The Derridon family was living at Koil in 1838.

General deBoigne

General Count deBoigne was one of the most colourful and decisive figures in those stirring times. His military genius and his many qualities of head and heart made him not only the Commander-in-Chief of Madhoji Scindia's armies, but uncrowned King of Hindustan. On the 2nd February, 1794, Madhoji Scindia was perhaps the most powerful Prince in Maharatta history with the exception of Shivaji. The kingdom he left behind was the most powerful in India.

Its strength was due as much to the military genius of deBoigne as to the statecraft of Scindia. It is said that deBoigne's conduct was governed throughout by the highest of principles. In 1795 in the palace of Agra there was a solemn parting between deBoigne and his young master of the House he had served so long and faithfully. deBoigne had resigned the service of Daulat Rao Scindia, the grand-nephew of Madhoji Scindia.

deBoigne had contracted in India a marriage, according to the usages of the Country, with the daughter of a Persian Colonel. He had two children, a son named Alabux and a daughter named Banu. They accompanied their father to France and were subsequently baptised into the Christian faith, the son being named Charles Alexander and the daughter Anne. Charles married the daughter of a French nobleman. On the death of the father the estate passed to him.

deBoigne left behind in India two daughters by another marriage. In letters written to Col. Sutherland he showed his continuing concern for these daughters. His landed estate in the Etah District had been assigned to the support of the two girls.

A brief reference may be made to the extraordinary adventurer Raja George Thomas, the Irish sailor who had deserted from the Navy in 1782. Thomas served under Begum Sumru and achieved great distinction. He was placed in command of her forces which at first consisted of five battalions of infantry, some cavalry and about 40 guns and included about 300 Anglo-Indians and Europeans of various ranks. In 1788 he took part in the campaign on behalf of the deposed Emperor Shah Alam. By his skill and daring he succeeded in turning defeat into victory and saving the person of the Emperor. Thomas also served under Madhoji Scindia and then carved out a principality for himself. He was the undisputed Raja of the Harriana province with his capital at Hansi. Ultimately he was brought to bay by the troops of Scindia under the command of one Bourguin who, however, allowed him honourable terms of surrender on the 1st January, 1802. He went to Sardhana, the seat of Begum Sumru, where he spent some time. The Begum took charge of his wife and family. He had married one of Begum Sumru's maids of honour by the name of Maria. Thomas himself was a Protestant, but Maria was a Roman Catholic and so were her children.

George Thomas completely identified himself with his soldiers. He was virtually illiterate in English but a scholar of Persian. Jacob Thomas was one of the four children of George Thomas. He served as an officer for many years with Begum Sumru. On her death the Sardhana forces were disbanded and Jacob Thomas joined Ranjit Singh in March, 1838. John Thomas was the eldest son who was known more for his literary activities and for his Urdu verse.

Colonel Henry Forster—C.B.

Henry was the son of Henry Pitts Forster of the East India Company's Civil Service who came out to India in 1783 and was subsequently appointed Master of the Calcutta Mint. The father constructed, at Bhowanipore, a circular summer-house in the centre of a tank. This was known as 'Forster's Folly'.

Henry was born in 1793. Being of mixed descent he was disqualified from obtaining service under the Company. Finally, he joined what was the resort of all aspiring soldiers of the day, the Mahratta Army. In 1816 he was appointed Adjutant of the second regiment of Skinner's Horse.

The following year he saw active service under General Sir John Malcolm in the Pindari campaign and helped to run to earth Cheetoo, the lawless freebooter. He fought in the battle of Mahinpore, aided Baji Rao, the last of the Peshwas, in quelling a mutiny among his Arab mercenaries. In 1818 he was assisting Skinner's Horse to weed out the Pindari hordes from the districts of Dhar and Jubboa. In 1819 Forster was made a Lieutenant and transferred his services to Roberts' Local Horse. In 1822, however, he rejoined Skinner's Horse where he was placed second in command. Eight years later he became Adjutant of the 3rd Local Horse at Bareilly, and in 1834 he marched the regiment to Neemuch.

About this time the Government of India directed him to raise a force for the suppression of a serious revolt in the Shekawatie Country in Rajputana. This important task he carried out successfully and furnished a brigade composed of two regiments of Cavalry, two of Infantry and two batteries of Artillery commanded by himself and officered by his three sons, Henry, William and Thomas. With these levies he won—not without being wounded—

the battles of Sikur, Gudhi and Khetri and captured the fortress of Raluk from the insurgents.

During the first Punjab campaign of 1845-46 the Shekawatie Brigade was actively employed. It was present at the battle of Aliwal where Henry Forster (Senior) had a horse shot from under him. On one occasion during the campaign Forster was ordered to send a guard of four companies of the Shekawaties as escort for the Commander-in-Chief, Lord Gough. Forster selected the flank companies of each of his regiments. When Lord Gough rode down to the escort ranks and enquired where the officer in command was and what regiment he was inspecting, he was informed that the regiment was an Irregular one. Lord Gough then exclaimed if an irregular regiment is like this, what must the regular be! Forster received the Punjab medal and clasp of the campaign and made a Companion of the Bath. It is noteworthy that although Lord Gough urged the East India Company to promote Forster to the rank of Colonel for his services, the Court of Directors declined to accept the recommendation of the Commander-in-Chief. Gough, however, proved a staunch friend and in 1854 obtained for Forster a Colonelcy in the Queen's Army.

The strength of the Shekawatie Brigade was subsequently reduced to one regiment of Infantry, later known as the 13th Bengal Native Infantry which was stationed at Dinapore under the command of Col. James Michell, the grandson of Henry Forster. During the whole period of the Mutiny the loyalty of the regiment was never suspect and unlike other regiments were allowed to keep their arms. This dependability was due to the love and confidence of the men in Henry Forster and his son William who succeeded him in the command.

On the outbreak of the Mutiny Forster again was detailed to reduce the mutinous 34th N.I. and Ramghur Infantry in Singhboom, Manbhoom and Chaibassa. After having accomplished this Forster was ordered to perform a similar task at Sumbulpore. On his arrival there he was appointed Commissioner. His health being impaired as a result of a prolonged attack of fever, he proceeded to England on medical advice, returned to Calcutta, took up his residence at Ballygunge and died in 1862.

Col. Forster first married Miss Kellner who was murdered at Delhi during the Mutiny. His second wife was an Indian lady who left a legacy of Rs. 40,000, to the District Charitable Society. With one exception all his daughters were married to officers of the old Indian Army. His son Major William Forster married Miss Hearsey; both their sons were in military service, one in the Indian Army and the other in the 5th Lancers. Col. Forster's youngest son, Major-General Thomas Francis Forster married his cousin Anne, a sister of Sir George Kellner who retired in England. Their son Arthur, of the Punjab Police, married Miss Alice Skinner. A handsome marble monument in the Lower Circular Road Cemetery marked Col. Forster's grave and had the following inscription:

"In memory of
Colonel Henry Forster, C.B.
(H.M's Indian Army)
Who died at Calcutta
on the 9th October, 1862
Aged 69 years."

Poets and Scholars

IT is significant that during this period of anarchy and strife many Anglo-Indians distinguished themselves not only as soldiers but as outstanding writers of Persian and Urdu verse. Up to 1750 and indeed for about 50 years beyond that Europeans and Anglo-Indians mixed freely with one another and with members of the other communities. There was close social and cultural intercourse. Persian and Urdu were the principal languages. Because of this close intercourse a significant feature was the complete mastery by many Anglo-Indians of both Persian and Urdu. Unfortunately, much of the literary production of that time and the undoubtedly great influence that Anglo-Indians had on both Persian and Urdu literature have been forgotten. Writing of this period Mr. R.B. Saksena, a retired civil servant, said, "Englishmen in India and Anglo-Indians not only distinguished themselves as writers of Urdu and Persian verse, but were equally eminent in the domain of English verse." Continuing Saksena writes, "Their poems reveal a remarkable knowledge of oriental literature, mythology and religion, local colour and history and minute details

of Indian life and scenery.   Many of them were authors of established reputation."

The Filose Family

One of the most distinguished Anglo-Indian families of this
period, the members of which achieved distinction both as soldiers
and scholars, was the Filose family of Gwalior.   It played a notable part in the history of Central India.   The founder of the
family was one Michael Filose who arrived in Calcutta in 1770 A.D.
Ultimately he found service with deBoigne.   Filose had two sons,
Jean Baptiste and Fidele by an Indian lady.   Michael Filose ultimately commanded a Corps under Madhoji Scindia which numbered eleven battalions.   When he left for Europe, the command of
the battalions was taken over by his two sons.   Jean Baptiste was
one of the few officers of European descent who fought alongside
Madhoji Scindia against the British.   After Scindia's defeat Jean
Baptiste joined him and remained in his service for many years
as Commander-in-Chief.   Jean Baptiste was perhaps the only
military adventurer of Hindustan who survived the disaster of
1803.   Jean Baptiste had a colourful career.   Before Scindia's
defeat by the British, he used to go out on 'kingdom taking' expedi-
tions.   He was the Commander-in-Chief of the State Army which
consisted of thirty thousand regular sepoys and the famous artillery
which had remained with him since the days of deBoigne.   Jean
Baptiste served the Scindia House for 37 years and died in 1846.
He built up a reputation not only as a great soldier but as a great
scholar of Persian.

The greatest poet the family produced was Sir Florence Filose.
He was born in 1829 and died in the Gwalior State at the ripe age
of 83.   He married one Mary Anne and both of them were buried
in the Filose Chapel at Gwalior.   Florence Filose had two sons,
Col. Albert Filose and Major Clement Filose.   Sir Florence's elder
brother was Col. Sir Peter Filose who died in Gwalior on the 4th
July, 1872 : he was head of the criminal administration of Gwalior.
The youngest brother was Lt. Col. Sir Michael Filose who was
born on the 18th April, 1836, and died on the 5th February, 1925.
He served under four Maharajas.   A famous architect he designed
and constructed the famous Jai Vilas Palace.   At the Delhi Darbar of
1911 his Majesty the King conferred the K.C.I.E. on Michael Filose.

General Joseph Bensley was born on the 15th October, 1846, and died on the 1st November, 1871, at the early age of 25. He was not only the General Officer Commanding the Alwar Forces but had a reputation for several accomplishments. He was proficient in music and composed Hindi songs. His range and versatility were deemed to be remarkable, the more so because he did not have any special poetical master. Joseph Bensley married a daughter of John Puech, an Anglo-Indian, and sister of George Puech.

George Puech

George Puech is deemed to be the most prolific of Anglo-Indian poets of Urdu. Born in Koil on the 1st December, 1827, he was taught Urdu and Persian privately. According to Saksena, "George Puech occupies a very high niche in the temple of Anglo-Indian poetry and an honourable mention as a Urdu poet amongst writers of Urdu verse. He had the rare distinction of writing with ease in Persian and Urdu. He had a remarkable knowledge and considerable command over these languages and wrote well and copiously." The younger sister of Puech married James Gardner, grandson of Col. Gardner.

The Palmers

Another well-known Anglo-Indian family of this period was the Palmers. The founder was General William Palmer. His second marriage was to a Muslim lady of Delhi who is said to have died in Hyderabad in 1828 and was buried in the Palmer cemetery in Hyderabad. By this marriage he had many sons and daughters. The most famous was William or 'King' Palmer who entered the military service of the Nizam in 1799. 'King' Palmer rose to the rank of Brigadier and retired in 1810. He founded the famous banking house of the Palmers. Incidentally 'King' Palmer built up such a successful banking business that he was able to lend to the Nizam, when he needed it, one million pounds. 'King' Palmer's daughter married Col. Meadows Taylor, the famous author of the 'Confessions of a Thug'. In his memoirs Col. Meadows Taylor testifies to the scholarship of his father-in-law, who was an accomplished Persian scholar.

Dr. Benjamin Johnston

Dr. Benjamin Johnston of Hyderabad, son of Capt. Benjamin Baillie Johnston, a British officer in the Nizam's army, was not only a skilful physician but has been acclaimed as a poet of great ability. Saksena observes, "From the specimens of his verses it appears that Johnston was a poet of great ability who could compose verse in Urdu and Persian with ease and fluency. He shows mastery over language and technique. The Tazkiras testify to his scholarship." Dr. Benjamin Johnston's sister, Anne, married John Francis Anthony, a successful Anglo-Indian lawyer and my paternal grandfather.

The Gardners

No Anglo-Indian family, however, has produced so many poets of Urdu and Persian as the Gardners. The most notable was Suleiman Shikoh Gardner. He was the eldest son of James Valentine Gardner by a Muslim Princess, the adopted daughter of Prince Suleiman Shikoh, son of Emperor Shah Alam of Delhi. Gardner was born in 1831 and died at Ghaoni, the family residence, in 1902. Inheriting a large family property from his father he lived the life of an Indian nobleman. He had a wide circle of friends, the Maharaja of Alwar being one of the closest. It is said that Gardner was fond not only of poetry but of wine and women. His tastes, however, were scholarly and he was specially proficient in Persian, Arabic and Hindi. He spoke all these languages as if they were his mother-tongue and had a reputation as a born poet. In the words of Saksena, "His Hindi compositions are remarkable. He shows amazing command over the Urdu language and is an outstanding poet of merit amongst Anglo-Indian writers of verse and Urdu poets generally."

The Indian Bourbons

Another leading Anglo-Indian family that produced both soldiers and poets of distinction were the Bourbons of Bhopal. There is a strong tradition that the family descended from John Phillip Bourbon, Prince of Navarre. In 1540 John Phillip Bourbon of Navarre, a member of the younger branch of the family of Henry IV, King of France, came to India. He landed in Madras and then went off to Bengal. He ultimately arrived in Delhi where the Emperor Akbar conferred on him the title of Nawab and placed the imperial Seraglio in his care, having first taken the precaution of marrying him to his Christian wife's sister Lady Juliana. This office remained in the family till 1734 when Nadir Shah sacked Delhi.

The history of the family really begins with Salvador Bourbon. Col. Popham, the British resident of Gwalior, gave him a Jagir and a house in the State. Salvador was employed by the Begum of Bhopal and remained in her service till her death. He was recalled to the Bhopal service and made Commander-in-Chief of the forces. In that capacity he was actively engaged in defending the State against the Maharattas and the Pindari freebooters that infested the Country. In this task he was assisted by his cousin Pedro Bourbon. Ultimately Scindia and another Maharatta Chieftain Bhonsle, the Raja of Nagpur, sent their combined forces to Bhopal to avenge their previous defeat. The Bhopal army was defeated by this combind force of over 80,000. Salvador retreated with a small force of 3000 to guard the city. His heroism fired the inhabitants to endure a siege of six months and led ultimately to the raising of the siege. Madhoji Scindia now sent a force, under his famous Anglo-Indian General, Jean Baptiste Filose, with instructions to destroy the city. Salvador went to meet the invading General as he wished to secure time to enlist the intercession of the British through Col. Ochterlony who was then Resident at Delhi. The two Anglo-Indian Generals met and Salvador persuaded Filose to stay operations. In the meantime the British intervened and the city was saved.

The Pindaris were constantly attacking and harassing the southern border of the State. Salvador went out with an army against them and after ridding the frontier of these pests, he was sent to Nagpur on a mission of peace to Maharaj Bhonsle of Nagpur. During his absence his patron Minister, Wazir Mohammad Khan, died but not before he had conferred on Salvador a valuable estate for his great services. Salvador died shortly after that and was succeeded to his estate by the younger of his two sons, Balthasar.

The late Minister's son was elected the Ruler of Bhopal. He at once appointed Balthasar Bourbon as his Minister and sent him to General Adams who was operating in the vicinity against the

Pindaris in order to secure a treaty with the British. In order to achieve this Balthasar volunteered to supply a contingent of Bhopal troops. This was accepted and he served the British with distinction accompanying General Adams as far as Kotah. The treaty was executed in 1818 and Balthasar Bourbon's name appears as representing the State.

About a year after this the Ruler was accidentally shot. His young widow was left in an unprotected position and but for the skill shown by Balthasar, who was then a Minister, her position would have become impossible. He carried on the administration for 8 years so well that the then Agent conferred a fresh Jagir on him. That was in 1828.

Balthasar married, in 1821, Elizabeth, daughter of Captain Johnstone of the Bengal Army. Capt. Johnstone had married a Pathan lady of Delhi who was related to the Imperial House. Balthasar's wife was subsequently known by the title of Madam Dulhin. She adopted a son Sebastian. The family was forced to flee by Nawab Jehangir who confiscated their lands which were subsequently restored by Sikander Begum.

Balthasar Bourbon was a considerable poet of Persian and Urdu. In the words of Saksena, "There is no doubt that he is a poet of high order. He has a thorough command over the language and is well versed in the technique of poetry." Saksena continues, "His position as an Urdu poet of repute is undoubtedly high amongst Anglo-Indian poets of Urdu."

Sebastian Bourbon, who was born in 1830, married the daughter of Captain Bernard, an Anglo-Indian officer of Sardhana. Sikander Begum appointed Sebastian to command her forces against the rebellious members of her House. Because of the service of the Bourbons, Sikander Begum was able to crush all rebellious attempts in her State. Col. Kincaid in his 'Bengal Past and Present', writes, "The latter history of the family furnishes a sketch of Bhopal history for the last three quarters of a century. The fidelity of the Bourbons is not more admirable than the generous acknowledgements and rewards bestowed upon them by the Chiefs they served."

An interesting sidelight is found in the fact that in 1861 the Begum of Bhopal, Sikander Begum, made a tour of India. She was attended by a troop of Amazons which contained a number of ladies belonging to the Bourbon family.

After the death of Madam Dulhin in 1882 there was a special investigation by the political authorities into the circumstances and history of the family. There was said to have been a family history compiled in the 18th Century and carried by a priest to Goa. There is also an interesting paper by Col. Kincaid in the Asiatic Quarterly Review of January to April, 1897.

John Roberts was the son of General Sir Abraham Roberts, K.C.B., and the half brother of Lord Roberts, V.C. John Roberts married a Muslim lady and became a Mohammedan. In his will General Sir Abraham Roberts, K.C.B. of 25, Royal York Crescent, Clifton, Bristol, dated the 18th January, 1873, made bequests to his wife Isabella Roberts, his daughter Harriet Mercer Roberts, his son Lt. Col. George Roberts and his son Lt. Col. Frederick Sleigh Roberts, V.C. He also made annuities to Ann Roberts, resident of Benares, William Roberts and also to John Roberts, resident of Lucknow. The latter were his children by an Indian wife. John Roberts has left poems which show complete familiarity with Urdu. According to Saksena, however, they were not of a specially high order.

Dyce Sombre

It has already been mentioned that Begum Sumru lavished her entire wealth on David Ochterlony Dyce. He was carefully educated by her and received his education in a Delhi college. He was a scholar both of Persian and English. In a deed of gift to David Dyce, her adopted son and heir, the Begum stipulated that he should proclaim himself as one of the family by adding that name to his own. It was thus that he took the name of David Ochterlony Dyce Sombre. The Begum died on the 27th January, 1836. At the age of 30 Dyce Sombre found himself the master of a fortune amounting to half a million pounds. Two of the Begum's old friends wrote to Dyce giving him differing advice. Lord Combermere urged him to visit Europe, while James Skinner addressing him an ode in Persian strongly dissuaded him from such a step.

Dyce went to England. Although very dark in complexion, he attracted considerable attention not only because he was highly placed and had sponsors among Royalty, but also because of his considerable wealth. In 1838 he was introduced to Mary Anne Jervis, the only surviving daughter of Edward Jervis, Second

Viscount St. Vincent. He was married on the 26th September, 1840, when the bride was 20 years of age. In the following year Dyce Sombre was elected Member of Parliament from the borough of Sudbury. Apparently he had followed the then rather widespread practice of trying to buy a 'pocket' borough. He was unseated on a petition for bribery and corruption. Dyce's marriage was unhappy. He accused his wife of infidelity. According to him English society of that time was not only corrupt but had no morals. He alleged that many English noblemen had offered him their wives in exchange for cash payments. Mrs. Dyce, already heir to her husband's immense wealth, was successful in having him declared to be unbalanced and put under restraint. Dyce escaped the consequences by fleeing to Paris. He did everything possible to disprove the allegation that he was in any way unbalanced. In 1850 he presented a petition to the House of Parliament. He died in July, 1851, and in a will left all his property to the founding of a school in India for boys of mixed parentage. He made the Chairman and Deputy Chairman of the Court of Directors his executors. They fought the case up to the highest court but ultimately lost and the whole property went to Mrs. Dyce.

Mrs. Dyce Sombre remarried, on the 8th November, 1852, George Cecil, 3rd Baron Forester, who died on the 14th February, 1886. There were no children of the marriage. During her lifetime Lady Forester maintained the palace at Sardhana and founded the Forester Hospital and Dispensary at Sardhana. After her death the palace and the adjoining grounds were bought by a Catholic Mission. The palace was then used for the purpose of an Anglo-Vernacular school and as an orphanage for Christian boys.

Dyce travelled extensively in Europe and was a scholar not only of English but of Urdu and Persian. He wrote to many of his Indian friends in Persian and English. In the words of Mr. Saksena, "It is unfortunate that no specimen of Dyce Sombre's verses in Urdu or Persian are available. It is incontrovertible that he was a scholar of Persian and Urdu. It is also a fact that he was a poet and could even compose verses in English. He had a number of books and manuscripts which he took to England and kept them as his dearly prized possesssions." Saksena reproduces certain verses in English which were in manuscript and sent by Dyce to Lord Lyndhurst. A sample is given below.

1. I hate your dreary English land
   Its clime and hearth so cold;
   Its mercenary altars raised
   To Mammon and his gold.

2. I hate your dreary English land
   Its scandals, trade and mist—
   Where e'en your women's lips are chilled
   However warmly kissed.

3. Give me the sunny land of Gaul
   Its bright wines, its wild blisses;
   Give me the Paris Bacchanals
   Dishevelled Locks and Kisses:

4. Give me French hearts, as light and gay
   As their own glad champagne;
   Give me those lips that always smile
   Those arms that always strain.

5. Farewell, my Lord; when next you have
   Some spouse a 'madman' made,
   Don't let his keepers take him to
   The Burlington Arcade.

6. For me while France affords a home
   Your land, I 'll ne'er regret it:
   Shall I e'er cross the sea again
   Here's wishing you may get it.

Boulogne.   Dyce Sombre"

In the words of Saksena, "Dyce's life was sad and his end tragic, but he appeared to be more sinned against than sinning."

Hearsay's Petition

In about 1875, Captain Hearsay, son of General Sir John Bennett Hearsay, drew up a petition in verse. One verse was particularly significant, as it underlined the discriminatory treatment meted out to the Anglo-Indians. It read;

"We have treated all Indians with kindness
This Country we've made it our own,
For this reason our children get nothing
Because they have never been home."

CHAPTER IV

DIFFICULTIES AND SELF-HELP

The Age of Ricketts and Derozio

SOME WORTHY NAMES

THE next 50 years saw the Community gripped in the fierce toils of economic bitterness. The pall of discrimination imposed by the British on the fortunes of the Community was, however, illumined by a spirit of self-help and sturdy independence.

Finding the opportunities for soldiering drastically restricted or even completely destroyed, the Community branched out into trade and commerce. Above all, there was an increasing awareness of the need for educational facilities in order to equip the Community to compete. Numerous private schools were established in places like Calcutta. I deal with this aspect rather fully in the chapter entitled 'In the Educational Vanguard'.

John William Ricketts, who later presented the Anglo-Indian petition to the British Parliament, was the centre of the Community's endeavours. Son of Ensign John Ricketts of the Bengal Engineers, who fell in the siege of Seringapatam, Ricketts was born towards the close of 1791. He was brought up by some friends who took him to Calcutta and placed him in the Upper Military Orphanage of Kidderpore. He left the School before he was 16 years of age.

Ricketts was a person of literary tastes and culture. When a boy he enjoyed reading Addison and later in life frequently contributed polished articles to various journals. He published a series of religious addresses and exercises for Sabbath Schools entitled 'Feed My Lambs'. By persuasion he was a Baptist.

Like James Kyd, his great contemporary, Ricketts was a thoroughly practical man and whatever he undertook was marked by ability, energy and earnestness of purpose.

On the 26th October, 1816, he married Miss Sarah Gardner

who was, it is believed, a ward of the Kidderpore Upper Orphan
School and the daughter of a military officer. She was said to be
remarkably beautiful and survived her husband by 12 years.
Besides the children he lost in their infancy, Ricketts had five sons.
Thomas, the youngest, was killed at Cawnpore during the Mutiny.

It was the guidance and initiative of Ricketts that led to the
establishment of the Parental Academy in 1823. It was, in fact,
the first Anglo-Indian school in the sense that it was established
and administered by Anglo-Indians. I deal with the position
and ultimate fate of this School in the chapter 'In the Educational
Vanguard'.

In 1828 Ricketts set up the Commercial and Patriotic Association
with the object of training Anglo-Indians to participate in agriculture, trade and commerce. The Apprenticing Association was
also started in Calcutta with the object of meeting the premium
to be paid by Anglo-Indian lads apprenticed to engineering firms.
In 1828 a Marine School was also established on the Company
ship 'Princess Charlotte of Wales'. This was intended to train
Anglo-Indians for the Merchant Navy. At Bombay, Madras and
Hyderabad associations were formed to enable Anglo-Indians to
take up agriculture and qualify for trade and commercial pursuits.
Many of these commendable efforts were unfortunately blighted
by a series of bank crashes, throughout the Country, which destroyed the savings of the bulk of the Community.

At a meeting held in November, 1825, in Calcutta, it was decided
to present a petition to the British Parliament. Apparently there
was a long incubation period before the petition was finalised. A
Committee was formed which included John Ricketts, H. Derozio,
C.F. Byrn, Wale Byrn, William Byrn, Willoughby Dacosta, P.
Mello, G.R. Gardener, J.J.L. Hoff, H. Martindell, C. Pote and
W. Sturmer. The document passed through the hands of two
eminent barristers, Theodore Dickens and Mr. (afterwards Sir)
Thomas Turton. The advocates were paid 40 gold mohurs each
for their advice: the last-named gentleman also accepted from the
Committee a gold watch with a chain and seal valued at Rs. 600.

At a public meeting held in the Town Hall on the 20th April,
1829, Ricketts was unanimously elected Agent of the East Indians,
as the Community was then known. It was resolved that he should
convey the petition to England and that a fund should be raised

for this purpose. Subscriptions amounting to Rs. 17,000 were ultimately raised.

Ricketts arrived in London on the 27th December, 1829, and on the 29th March, 1830, the petition was placed before the House of Lords by Lord Carlisle and on the 4th May, 1830, before the House of Commons by the Hon'ble Mr. W. Wynn.

Some of the main items of the petition were as follows.

1. There was no uniform civil law applicable to members of the Community.
2. There was no law governing succession to their property.
3. There was no law which indicated whether they had the right of bequeathing property by will.
4. There was no law to declare which of their children should succeed in case of intestacy.

    Regulation VIII of 1813 of the East India Company had expressly included the East Indians as "Native subjects of the British Government" and thereby subjected them to the same disabilities as members of the other communities.

    By Regulation III of 1818 they had been deprived of the protection of the Act of Habeas Corpus.
5. In the interior areas they were subject to Mohammedan Criminal Law which often operated not only in an arbitrary but barbarous manner.
6. They were excluded from all superior and covenanted offices in the Civil and Military Services, and from all sworn offices in the Marine Service of the East India Company. This restriction was first adopted by the Company on the 9th November, 1791, prior to which there was no impediment.
7. They were not only excluded from superior offices which were open to Christian subjects, but they were also treated as ineligible for most of those subordinate appointments in the Judicial, Revenue and Police Departments and even in the Military Service which were open without reservation to Hindus and Mohammedans.
8. By the order of the Commander-in-Chief of His Majesty's Forces dated the 27th February, 1808, they were

expressly disqualified from holding Commissions in the British Army.

9. They were not permitted to be employed under the Indian Princes without the special permission of the Supreme Government. This rule was supposed to apply to Europeans and Americans, yet the restriction was applied in practice to the East Indians.

10. Any plan proposed by others or by themselves for improvement of the Community, instead of receiving the support of the Government, had consistently met not only with neglect but with positive rejection; every attempt to provide the blessings of education and improve the moral and civil status of the East Indians had invariably been discountenanced and discouraged by the Court of Directors.

Some of the main points raised by Ricketts in his evidence before the House of Lords' Committee were as follows.

The petition had been signed by 600 or 700 persons most of whom were immediately descended from European fathers and Indian mothers or from their descendants by intermarriage.

Ricketts pointed out that Anglo-Indians were not recognised as British subjects by the Supreme Court of Calcutta, if residing in the mofussil: they were subject to the jurisdiction of the mofussil courts which were regulated by Mohammedan Law. They could appeal to the Sudder Dewany Adawlat of Calcutta but had no right of appeal to the Supreme Court of Calcutta although the Dewany Adawlat had the power of enhancing the punishment without any fresh evidence being adduced. They were not permitted to act as pleaders in any of the courts.

Members of the Community could not hold a Commission in the Company's or the King's Army. They might be drummers and fifers, but, as Ricketts pointed out, he was not aware of a single instance in which a member of the Community had advanced even to the rank of Corporal.

Some members of the Community were admitted in the Civil and Military Services prior to the prohibition issued in 1808 by the Commander-in-Chief. After that members of the Community took service under the Indian States but they were required to return to the Company's territory on the outbreak of war. Thus Anglo-Indian officers with the Mahratta Army from 1801 or 1802 were ordered back to the Company's territories on pain of the most drastic penalties.

To use Ricketts' own words, "Treaties with Native States prevent Europeans from taking service; but, as in this instance, we are recognised sometimes as Europeans and at other times as natives as it suits the purposes of the Government. We are recognised as native except within the jurisdiction of the Supreme Court, and yet the officers who were employed by the Mahratta States of Scindia and Holkar were threatened to be dealt with as traitors if they did not return to the Company's territories!"

"The public and private schools for the education of the children of East Indians have never received assistance from Government in any shape whatever. We are excluded from participating in the grant for the education of the natives of India. We outnumber the Europeans very considerably and our number is increasing owing to the increased number of Europeans and of intermarriages. We are chiefly employed as clerks in the public offices of Government. During the Nepal War East Indians were employed in the Irregular Corps, but the corps was disbanded."

Referring to education, Ricketts pointed out that the Community were educated at the Orphan Military Asylums, Upper and Lower : to the Upper went the orphans of officers who married Indian women, to the Lower of British soldiers married to the women of the Country. There were also the Parental Academic Institution and the Calcutta Grammar School. But there was no opportunity for college education in Calcutta except in the Bishop's College which was confined to missionary purposes.

Ricketts mentioned that members of the Community were employed as missionaries and teachers and acquitted themselves creditably in those positions. He stated, "The influence they possess in such occupations would be very much increased by the removal of the restrictions to which they are at present subject. It is a thing for which the natives themselves cannot account that the Government should reject, as it does, their own offspring, and treat them with marked neglect and proscription.... As natives of the Country and as fixtures of the soil, the East Indians might be rendered instruments of great good to the Country. If the real interests of India be sought, they cannot be more effectively promoted than through the instrumentality of those who have been born, educated, and are destined to spend their lives there." Ricketts gave instances of highly placed Europeans married to Indians. Among those he referred to was one Harington, a member of the Governor-General's Council. He also mentioned, that, "The ladies of half blood are extensively married to Europeans." Ricketts referred to the fact that many members of the Community after having been educated in England, Scotland and Ireland were, on return to India, so frustrated by the disabilities imposed on them that they often returned to Europe to seek a living there. He gave the instance of the son of a British General. The son had obtained the degree of Doctor of Medicine, but he found the discrimination in India so intolerable that he returned to England in 1825 and practised there.

In his evidence before the House of Commons' Committee, on the 24th June, 1830, Ricketts mentioned that a large proportion of British officers in the Company's service married women of the Community. He pointed out that before 1791, the Company's service, Civil and Military, was open to the Community. Thus, stated Ricketts, the Bombay Army was commanded by General Jones, a member of the Community, during the campaigns of 1803 and 1805. The then Quarter-Master-General of the Army, Col. Stevenson, was also a member of the Community. Among members of the Community in the King's Army, Ricketts mentioned Major Deare, Captain Rutledge, Lt. Mullins and others. He referred to Drs. Lumsden, Breton and Lycke, members of the Community in the medical profession. Lycke practised in Calcutta and retired in England after having amassed a fortune. Members of the Community were also engaged as indigo planters, school masters and architects. Ricketts referred to the business houses such as Lackersteen, Vrignon, Mendes, Baretto and Brightman. He mentioned that James Kyd was the master shipbuilder of the Company in Calcutta. He referred to the fact that members of the Community had been in the Company's service in various professions and were as much respected as any European.

Ricketts also added, "There is no distinction made by natives between East Indians and Europeans: the distinction emanates from the authorities of the Country. They first originated the distinction and then used it as an argument for keeping us where we are. The prejudices against us have diminished of late. A much more liberal policy has been adopted towards the descendants of European fathers by native mothers by the Dutch, French, Spaniards and Portuguese in all their settlements. Two-thirds of the Council of Ceylon are composed of gentlemen born on the Island."

The petition to Parliament resulted in the insertion of the clause in the Charter Act of 1833 proclaiming that all persons without reference to birth or colour were eligible for the Civil and Military Services of the Government.

Ricketts' efforts were warmly appreciated by the Community and on his return he was entertained in Madras where he disembarked. When he arrived in Calcutta, there was a large meeting held at the Town Hall on the 28th March, 1831, where he was accorded a hearty welcome.

Charles Pote, the distinguished Anglo-Indian artist of the period, painted, free of charge, a portrait of Ricketts, which can still be seen in the office of the All-India Anglo-Indian Association in New Delhi.

Ricketts was buried in the old Gaya cemetery at the foot of the Ramsila Hill. His grave was marked by an imposing monument 12 feet high, resting on a base 12 feet square by 2 feet deep, surmounted by a slab of dark blue basalt. In an obituary notice which appeared in the 'Friend of India' the following tribute was paid: "To his spirit and perseverance the East Indian Community are mainly indebted for the change that has occurred in their position in general society and in the regard of the Legislature—a change little more than begun, but nevertheless striking, and advancing quietly to greater and greater importance:" and further, "Mr. Ricketts was not perhaps largely endowed with the peculiarities generally required in an agitator or a popular deputy. He had little of that warmth of temperament which attaches the multitude to a leader and not much of the suavity and address desirable in an Advocate. He gained attention from his earnest honesty of purpose and his matter-of-fact sort of argument. In other times these qualifications would not have served his purpose, but happily there was a spirit abroad which readily sympathised with the claims he had to urge."

One of the four Houses in the Frank Anthony Public Schoo., Calcutta, is named after Ricketts.

Henry Derozio—First National Bard Of Modern India

While Ricketts was the public and political spearhead of the Anglo-Indian movement of the time, the intellectual and emotional leaven was lent especially by the outstanding figure of Henry Louis Vivian Derozio.

Some commentators have put the 10th April, 1809, as the date of birth of Derozio. The more authoritative view is that he was born on the 18th April, 1809. This Anglo-Indian boy genius was cut off by a cruel fate when he was not yet 23 years of age. Despite the fact that he died so very young, Derozio left behind verse which for sheer lyrical beauty, wealth of classical allusion, poetic metaphor and vivid imagery make him, in my humble opinion, perhaps the greatest poet of English that India has so far produced. By some who have studied Derozio's works—the first flowering of his remarkable poetic genius—he has been acclaimed as the first national bard of modern India. He has also been claimed as Bengala's Bard. Unfortunately, unlike Rabindranath Tagore, there was no one to publicise the quality of Derozio's poetry or to give him his rightful place in the pantheon of the poets of English.

Derozio was a typical product of this time. He was brought up against the background of the repressive economic and social system under which the Community laboured. He represented the attempt of the ambitious Anglo-Indians to break through the chilling round of social and economic disabilities. This book is not the proper place to write anything in detail about the out-standing quality of Derozio's verse. No work on Indian history and more especially on Indian literature would be complete without a special place being accorded to Derozio. His father was partly Portuguese and partly Indian. His mother was an Englishwoman. Derozio's early education was at the Dhurumtollah Academy of David Drummond. Drummond represented one of the finest specimens that Scotland had sent out to this Country. His influence both scholastic and poetic are said to have created a lasting impression on young Derozio. Derozio was only 23 when he died. Yet at that young age he had achieved a considerable niche for himself both in the world of letters and in journalism. In the words of Cedric Dover, "He was the apostle of freedom, the prophet of a united India before India had dreamt of unity." Derozio left school at the age of 14 and yet in the intervening period he composed verse of a quality which attracted favourable attention even from the London press.

At 18 he gave up work with his uncle, who was an indigo planter at Bhagalpur, and decided to carve out for himself a literary career. His first book consisted of several verses and poems which he had contributed to various journals. It was an immediate success. The second volume was produced early in 1829 and included the Fakeer of Jungheera, a Metrical Tale, and other poems. They were given a cordial and encouraging review. The New Monthly Magazine (March, 1828) remarked, "The thoughts and topics are not unusual, but they are expressed and treated with grace, elegance and spirit. The language is elevated and poetical; and the versification is flowing, polished and serious."

At this time Derozio was working as Assistant Editor of 'The Gazette'. Immediately after the appearance of the Fakeer of Jungheera he was appointed as Lecturer in English history and literature at the Hindu College. In the words of Cedric Dover, "He was not yet 19 when he entered upon his new duties, but he exercised an influence that remains unrivalled. He shook the Hindu religion to its foundations and was the real mover of the theistic schism which exists today as the Brahmo Samaj movement of Raja Rammohan Roy, his friend and contemporary."

A contemporary describes Derozio's outstanding influence as follows, "The students in their turn loved him most tenderly and were ever ready to be guided by his counsels and imitate him in all their daily actions in life. In fact, Mr. Derozio acquired such an ascendancy over the minds of his pupils that they would not move in their private concerns without his counsel and advice. On the other hand, he fostered their taste in literature, taught the evil effects of idolatry and superstition, and so far formed their moral conceptions and feelings as to make them completely above the antiquated ideas and aspirations of the age. Such was the force of his instruction that the conduct of the students out of the college was most exemplary, and gained them the applause of the outside world, not only in a literary and scientific point of view, but what was of still greater importance, they were all considered men of truth. Indeed, the (Hindu) 'College boy' was a synonym for truth."

Early in 1831 Derozio was dismissed from the College as his dominating influence on the students created a wave of alarm among the management which was much too hide-bound by convention and tradition to allow Derozio's radicalism and questioning scientific approach to life and values to gain currency among the students. Replying to some of the criticism levelled against him, Derozio wrote, "Entrusted as I was for some time with the education of youth peculiarly circumstanced, was it for me to have made them pert and ignorant dogmatists, by permitting them to know what could be said only upon one side of grave questions? Setting aside the narrowness of mind which such a course would have evinced, it would have been injurious to the mental energies and acquirements of the young men themselves. And (whatever may be said to the contrary), I can vindicate my procedure by quoting no less orthodox authority than Lord Bacon. 'If a man', says this philosopher (and no one has a better right to pronounce an opinion upon such matters than Lord Bacon), 'will begin with certainties he shall end in doubt.' This, I need scarcely observe, is always the case with contented ignorance when it is roused too late to thought .... If the religious opinions of the students have become unhinged in consequence of the course I have pursued, the fault is not mine. To produce convictions was not within my power; and if I am to be condemned for the Atheism of some, let me receive credit for the Theism of others. Believe me, my dear Sir, I am too thoroughly imbued with a deep sense of human ignorance, and of the perpetual vicissitudes of opinion, to speak with confidence even of the most important matters. Doubt and uncertainty besiege us too closely to admit the boldness of dogmatism to enter an enquiring mind; and far be it from me to say 'this is' and 'that is not', when after the most extensive acquaintance with the researches of science, and after the most daring flight of genius, we must confess with sorrow and disappointment that humility becomes the highest wisdom, for the highest wisdom assures man of his ignorance."

Indignantly refuting the accusation of inculcating parental disrespect, he quotes instances to prove that he has 'always endeavoured to cherish the sentimental feelings of the heart, and to direct them into proper channels', though he condemns 'that feigned respect which some children evince, as being hypocritical and injurious to the moral character'. The third charge he dismisses as 'ridiculous', remarking that 'it is a satisfaction to reflect that scandal, though often noisy, is not everlasting'. And in concluding he enquires pertinently 'whether the expediency of yielding to popular clamour can be offered in justification of the measures adopted by the Managers of the College towards me?' He believed that there was a determination on their part to get rid of him, 'not to satisfy popular clamour, but their own bigotry', but feels that 'to complain of their injustice would be paying them a greater compliment than they deserve'.

Cedric Dover writes, "We get an insight of the remarkable qualities of Derozio's mind and thinking to say the least for a young man of barely 22. These are indicative of his extraordinary character and ability. Derozio now took seriously to journalism. He had a vast circle of the most influential friends which included leading figures among the Anglo-Indians, the British Community and the Hindus. He organised and edited the 'East Indian' which rapidly grew in influence. It is said of this paper that it advocated, 'the claims of every question, honest and true and liberal, with an eloquence and ability and a power of judgment of which East Indians may well be proud. At the same time he contributed to a host of other journals. Most of these contributions were poems."

Derozio's intellectual pursuits were not only deep but also diversified. To quote Cedric Dover once again, "It is known, however, that he translated the work of De Maupertuis on Moral Philosophy, that he delivered a series of lectures on philosophy before crowded audiences, and that he wrote a criticism of Kant, which Dr. Mill said was 'perfectly original and displayed powers of reasoning and observation which would not disgrace even gifted philosophers.' And his contemporaries were fond of saying that there were only two places where the most recent books issued by British publishers could be found : the shelves of the most enterprising booksellers and the library of Derozio, frequently the latter alone."

Continuing Dover writes, "But the fruits of philosophy need time and atmosphere to mature—and Derozio missed both. So we cannot add his name to the roll of philosophic accomplishment, but we can accord him a place in the gallery of the world's poets. He must be regarded as a genuine member of the Romantic Movement, and had, says Professor B.B. Roy (in an article published in the Calcutta Review some twelve years ago), 'the same free-thinking mind, the same challenge to orthodoxy, the same fundamental melancholy, the same love of mythology, and the same command over the resources of the English language.' It is an error to describe him, as certain uninformed critics do, as an imitation Romantic, though much of his verse is imitative and ornamental, for we can also find in it the pure gold of utterance."

Dover continues, "The Fakeer of Jungheera, with its vivid imagery, its dramatic touches, its gems of poetic metaphor, and the Enchantress of the Cave, with its robustness and fidelity of details, were earnests of Derozio's potential ability. But it is in his sonnets that he is at his best. Here we can enjoy with him the simple beauties of nature, and appreciate the vigour, the vision and the patriotism which permeated his life and work. 'Harp of My Country', he cries, 'let me strike the strain'—and he pours forth song. Such song as this:

> "Oh, Freedom! there is something dear
> Even in thy very name,
> That lights the altar of the soul
> With everlasting flame.
> Success attend the patriot sword,
> That is unsheathed for thee!
> And glory to the breast that bleeds,
> Bleeds nobly to be free!
> Blest be the generous hand that breaks
> The chain a tyrant gave,
> And feeling for degraded man
> Gives freedom to the slave!"

"Or this:

> "My Country! in thy day of glory past
> A beauteous halo circled round thy brow,
> And worshipped as a deity thou wast.

Where is that glory, where that reverence now?
Thy eagle pinion is chained down at last,
And grovelling in the lowly dust art thou:
Thy minstrel hath no wreath to weave for thee
Save the sad story of thy misery!
Well—let me dive into the depths of time,
And bring from out the ages that have rolled
A few small fragments of those wrecks sublime,
Which human eye may never more behold;
And let the guerdon of my labour be
My fallen Country! one kind wish from thee!"

"And if he was melancholy, it was the melancholy that impels
action. He was too vigorous, too philosophical, to be actually
depressing. He knew that

"....man's energies can make
An atmosphere around him, and so take
Good out of evil, like the yellow bee
That sucks from flowers malignant, a sweet treasure—
O tyrant fate! Thus shall I vanquish thee,
For out of suffering shall I gather pleasure."

"So the note of hope rings through much of his verse, as in these
lines:

"Your hand is on the helm—guide on, young men,
The bark that's freighted with your Country's doom,
Your glories are but budding; they shall bloom
Like fabled amaranth Elysian, when
The shore is won, even now within your ken,
And when your touch shall dissipate the gloom
That long has made your Country but a tomb,
Or worse than tomb, the priest's, the tyrant's den.
Guide on young men; your course is well begun;
Hearts that are tuned to holiest harmony
With all that e'en in thought is good, must be
Best formed for deeds like those which shall be done
By you hereafter till your guerdon's won
And that which now is hope becomes reality."

"And there is hope become reality in this enthusiastic fragment:

"Towards yon grey isle the waters flow,
Then, brothers, brothers, bravely row.
The rising gale hath filled our sail,
It bends our slender mast;
And now the word is, like a bird
We'll reach our home at last ....
And see! our isle of rock is won
Now, brothers, brothers, bravely done."

"Finally, there is this bright and poetic vision of the future in which he sees:

".... through mists of coming years
'rising spirit speaking peace to man.
The storm is passing, and the Rainbow's span
Stretched from North to South; the ebon car
of darkness rolls away; the breezes fan
The infant dawn, and morning's herald star
Comes trembling into day. O! can the sun be far?"

I have referred to the fact that when Ricketts returned from England there was a meeting in the Town Hall of Calcutta on the 28th of March of that year. At that meeting Pote, the famous Anglo-Indian artist, proposed that a second petition should be presented to the new Parliament. In seconding this proposal Derozio made a speech which is significant not only for its language, but also for his appraisal of the supercilious, if not indifferent, attitude which the average British Parliamentarian could be expected to show to the efforts of the East Indians to secure better treatment and improvement of their position. Derozio said, "What have we hitherto done?" he asked, "What have we yet obtained? Have our rights been restored, our claims conceded? No, Sir, we have but just taken the field. And now shall we rest upon our Arms? The spirit of exclusion has only been startled upon his throne. But there sits the demon still, mocking our efforts, and grinning over his triumph. Our hearts must not falter, our nerves must not slacken. Let us not trust our cause to men, who have nothing for us but empty professions .... Do you suppose that any member of the Legislature, touched by so much tenderness, will address either House of Parliament in some such way as this?—"Gentlemen, here am I, overflowing with the milk of human kindness, anxious to restore to that long-neglected and unjustly treated race, the East Indian, those rights WHICH THEY DO NOT DEMAND THEMSELVES."

"No, Sir, such will never be the language of legislators. The benevolence of statesmen seldom incommodes them to such an alarming degree. And the very facts which Mr. Ricketts' Report communicates to us, should lead us to distrust noble Lords and Honourable gentlemen. What are those facts? Lord Ashley felt for us! We thank his Lordship. He promised to present our Petition. This was generous. But, when the time came for his Lordship's hand to follow up the benevolent suggestions of his heart, that hand became suddenly paralysed. Weighty matters of State pressed upon his mind, and the Petition was left to make its own way into the House of Commons. I am apprehensive (though I only suggest the possibility) that matters of State may be as burdensome to our other sympathising friends in Parliament, that such paralytic attacks, as we see do sometimes affect Lord Ashley, may be common to others who are deeply interested in our welfare. To protect ourselves against such mischances, it would not, perhaps, be the most unwise course to petition the Legislature again."

"Gentlemen, you have nothing to fear from firm and respectful remonstrance. Your calls for justice must be as incessant as your grievances are heavy. Complain again and again. Complain till you are heard—aye, and until you are answered. The ocean leaves traces of every inroad it makes upon the shore. But it must repeat those inroads with unabated strength, and follow them up with rapidity, before it washes away the strand."

British commentators on Derozio have written mostly with typical arrogance and with the inhibitions of European smugness and self-assumed superiority. Typically, Bradley Birt has twisted the whole motive of Derozio to suit this European sense of overweening arrogance. Thus in 'Harp of My Country' Derozio has apostrophised the deadening effect on the Indian people of slavery and colonialism, obviously singing in the larger Indian context. Yet

Bradley Birt perverts this motive to suit his own imperial ballet and would confine Derozio's lament merely to the wrongs which had been done by the British to his own Community.

Speaking on the occasion of Derozio's anniversary in 1926 Professor B.B. Roy, a well-known professor of English in the Calcutta University, among other things said, "I am quite convinced that full justice has not been done to him and to refer to him as 'the Keats of Anglo-Indian Literature' is, to my way of thinking, an entirely wrong way of looking at him. English literature is one and indivisible; the bisection of it on a racial basis is unfortunate in the extreme and should not be tolerated. The best that has been written in the English language is worthy of a place even in the most exclusive histories of English literature, no matter what colour the skin of the writer may have. Towards pure artists like Derozio, there should be a more liberal attitude than has been displayed by European writers on Anglo-Indian literature."

Concluding his lecture, Professor Roy said, "From whatever point of view, therefore, we might look at Derozio, we must be struck by his greatness, his nobility, his fineness of temper and maturity of mind. Every Bengali and every Anglo-Indian should study his life and his life's work as an essential part of their education. This should be particularly so today. He was the prophet of a United India, before there was an awakening, either among Indians or among Anglo-Indians. This message of unity and concord comes with singular force in a time which is troubled by unhealthy and blundering communalism and by a deep unsettlement of political and social values."

Derozio was struck down by cholera and died on Monday, the 26th December, 1831, and not on Saturday, the 23rd December, as stated by Thomas Edwards. Owen Aratoon in his edition of "Derozio's Poems" (1872) reproduced a photograph taken from a lithographic miniature published by Stapleton. A copy of this today hangs in the office of the All-India Anglo-Indian Association, New Delhi. It shows Derozio dressed in a high-collared dress-coat which was the fashion of the day, his neck swathed in the white neck-cloth which was also the fashion of the day. The photograph shows that he had a round face and long black hair which was parted in the middle. He was slightly built and had the reputation of dressing not only carefully but foppishly. Some commentators referred to him as very dark, but others have questioned this description. Some writers have said that he suffered from much conceit: others referred to this as more a pride in the knowledge of his outstanding qualities. He was generally acclaimed as a person with a loyal, kind and affectionate temper. Some writers have deplored the fact that neither the people of Bengal nor the Anglo-Indians have thought to raise an appropriate monument to Derozio. Mr. Susobhan Sarkar writing the foreword to a recent publication edited by Mr. Subir Ray Choudhuri referred to Derozio as 'A great son of Bengal' and suggested the erection of a statue preferably in the neighbourhood of that of David Hare, the other famous benefactor in the early history of modern education in India, the rebuilding of the burial place of Derozio and the renaming after him the road near Moulali where he lived and died.

One of the four Houses of the Frank Anthony Public School in Calcutta is named after Derozio.

Some Worthy Names

Charles Pote

In this sub-chapter I have made a reference to a few worthy Anglo-Indians. Hundreds of worthy names have been lost in the mists of time. The achievements of hundreds of others have not been chronicled or have been filched for the British Community.

Charles Pote was perhaps the greatest artist that the Community has so far produced. He was a contemporary of Derozio at Drummond's Academy where he received a sound education. Leaving school he followed the advice of James Kyd and instead of entering Government service in a subordinate capacity, decided to pursue his special talents and opened an artist's studio in Dhurrumtollah street. He was fairly successful in his profession. Eventually he became the Headmaster of the Dacca Pogose School, an institution founded by Nicholas Pogose. While in Calcutta Pote took a great interest in the Parental Academy. He also took a prominent part in the movement that led to a petition of the Community to Parliament presented by Ricketts. When Ricketts returned from England, Pote made an eloquent speech. On that occasion after he resumed his seat, Derozio addressed the meeting. He began by observing that had it been his desire to attract admiration, the brilliant address of his friend, Mr. Pote, would deter him from making such an attempt.

Pote excelled as a miniature painter. Among his larger pro-ductions, however, was the portrait of Lord Metcalfe which was, at one time, in the Town Hall of Calcutta, and another portrait of David Hare in the Hare School, a painting of William Ricketts which now hangs in the office of the All-India Anglo-Indian Association, and the Altar piece at the Armenian Church of Dacca. A painting of Derozio was apparently lost or destroyed.

Two companion pictures by him entitled L'Allegro and Il Penseroso were much admired at Dacca. He died at Dacca and was followed by a crowd of pupils and admirers.

Pote was a free-thinker and was laid to rest without the rites of Christian burial. Our artist sleeps in a nameless and forgotten grave.

James Kyd

Born in 1786, James Kyd was the son of Col. Robert Kyd, Bengal Engineers, Military Secretary to the Governor. The father, Col. Kyd, wrote a celebrated research work on Botany. He was responsible for laying out the Royal Botanical Gardens. James and his brother Robert were sent as boys to England to get a training in shipbuilding. On their return in 1800 they were apprenticed to one Waddell who was at that time Master Shipbuilder to the East India Company. Seven years later the brothers pur-chased the dockyard of Kyderpore which later on passed into the hands of Government. Both this suburb and Kyd street are named after the family. It is also probable that Kyd-ganj in Allahabad and Kyd island owed their names to the same source.

James Kyd succeeded to the position of Master Shipbuilder to the East India Company. In 1814 he visited England in a vessel which he had constructed and named 'General Kyd' after his father. James Kyd was held in the greatest esteem by the Governor-General. He rendered yeoman service to members of the Community. He was the author of several pamphlets in which he advised the lads of the Community to look away from Government service and strike out for themselves independent sources of livelihood instead of treading on each other's heels in their hurry to enter the lower grades of Government service.

James Kyd was a member of the Asiatic Society. He was also a member of the Management of the Parental Academy which was founded by the Anglo-Indians in 1823. He died on the 26th October, 1836, at the age of 50. The Governor-General wished to have a public funeral in his honour but it was declined by his brother with modesty. A Bengal obituary observed, "Mr. James Kyd was universally recognised as the Head of the East Indian Class to which he belonged. Where will they ever find his equal?"

Captain John Doveton

Doveton is an illustrious name, often mentioned in the history of the campaigns in Afghanistan, Mysore and Central India. Although neglected by his relatives, John belonged to this house. One of his uncles, when making enquiries after his dead brother, found that the brother's son was a poor, friendless orphan at a charity school in Madras. He succeeded in obtaining for his nephew a commission in the army of the Nizam of Hyderabad. John's service dated from the 21st March, 1817. He rose to be the Captain Commandant of the 7th Regiment of Infantry—a rank next to that of a Brigadier. John Doveton inherited a large fortune. He resigned his commission and went to London, where he died in 1853. Doveton was of the Baptist persuasion and his political views were ultra-radical in character.

John Doveton took a great interest in the education of the Community and bequeathed £ 50,000 for that purpose. This sum was equally divided between the Parental Academy of Calcutta, the name of which was then changed to the Doveton College, and the Doveton Protestant College founded at Madras. An oil painting of Doveton hangs, today, in the office of the All-India Anglo-Indian Association, New Delhi.

Lawrence de Souza

Lawrence Augustus de Souza was a partner of the firm of Messrs. Thomas de Souza & Co. He was the nephew of the late Count Anthony de Souza. The Community has occasion to remember his name with gratitude for the trusts he left. These trusts continue to enure for the benefit of members of the Community.

The Lawrence de Souza scholarships are looked after by the Official Trustee of West Bengal in which task he is assisted by an

Advisory Committee which includes of a nominee of the All-India Anglo-Indian Association. These scholarships were originally awarded to Anglo-Indians going overseas to compete for the I.C.S. Today, the scholarships are awarded to Anglo-Indians preparing for the I.A.S. or the Central Government Service examinations: a few are also given for other courses of study.

The de Souza Homes, another Trust founded by Lawrence de Souza, are administered by the official Trustee of West Bengal: he is assisted by the nominees of the Calcutta branch of the All-India Anglo-Indian Association and the Calcutta Rangers Club.

Lawrence de Souza died in London on the 27th September, 1871. His remains were brought to India and were buried in the Church of the Sacred Heart, Calcutta, which had been erected by his grandmother, Mrs. Pascoa Barretto de Souza.

His brother, Sir Walter Eugene de Souza, was educated partly in England at Downside College, Somerset. Sir Walter was Consul for Portugal at Calcutta 1870-1878 and Consul-General from 1878 to 1884. He was member for Westminster on the London County Council. For his munificence to charities he was knighted in 1879. He was also a Count of the Roman Empire and held other foreign distinctions. Walter Eugene de Souza also founded a trust for the Community: it is a comparatively small trust and is administered by the de Souza-and-Doucett Charitable Trust.

Sir Robert Warburton

Robert Warburton was the son of Lt. Col. Robert Warburton of the Royal Artillery who married an Afghan lady, the niece of Amir Dost Mohammad. The son was educated at Mussoorie and later in England. He came out to India with a commission in the Royal Artillery and served in the 21st Punjab Infantry in the Abyssinian campaign of 1868. He was appointed to the Punjab Commission in 1870. He is famous for his work in the Khyber where he was political officer from 1879 to 1897 and became a legendary figure. Warburton raised the Khyber Rifles. He was awarded the CSI in 1890, became Brevet-Colonel in 1893 and served in the Tirah expedition from 1897-1898. He was decorated with the K.C.I.E. in 1898. His book 'Eighteen Years in the Khyber' was published in 1900. He was known as the 'Warden of the Khyber'.

Sir William Willcox

Although the Encyclopaedia Brittanica refers to Sir William Willcox as a British engineer, he was obviously a member of the Community. Born and educated in India, he qualified as an engineer from Roorkee. He designed and carried through the Aswan Dam in 1898. His most important undertaking, however, was the irrigation of 3,500,000 acres in Mesopotamia which began in 1911.

Sir George Kellner

George Kellner was one of the most respected members of the Community and played an active part in the promotion of its interests. He was educated at the Parental Academy, the school founded by the Community. After that he entered the service of the Government of India and was Inspector-General of Accounts. After that he was Financial Commissioner and a member of Council in Cyprus from 1878 to 1883. He then became the Assistant Paymaster-General in the Court of Chancery in 1884. He was decorated with the K.C.M.G. in 1879 and died on the 10th June, 1886.

Watts—Dewan of Travancore

Son of an Anglo-Indian, born and brought up in the Travancore State, Watts received his early education in the Maharaja's College. He went to England where he was called to the Bar and then returned to India. He was Dewan of Travancore for several years.

Doctor Wallace M.D.

The date of birth of James Robert Wallace is given as the 20th January, 1856. He was educated at the Lawrence Military School, Sanawar, and the Medical College, Calcutta. He went to England for further studies in 1879 where he qualified for the M.D. He returned and entered Government service but resenting the disabilities imposed on the Anglo-Indians he resigned. In 1892 he was a director of the Eurasian and Anglo-Indian Association. At that time the term 'Eurasian' was applied to the Community, and the term 'Anglo-Indian' to Europeans settled in the Country. In 1897 and again in 1902 he was deputed to represent the grievances of the Community to the Secretary of State and members of Parliament. Nothing is known of the results, if any, of his representations. In 1901 he was elected President of the Imperial Anglo-Indian Association. In another Chapter I have referred to his grandiloquent proclamation to the Anglo-Indians, "That Britishers we are and Britishers we ever must be." He, however, laboured hard for the Community. He died in 1903.

Thomas Beale

Thomas William Beale started life as a clerk in the office of the Board of Revenue of the North West Province as it was then known. He was a profound scholar and assisted Sir H.M. Elliot in his work on the Mohammedans in India. He wrote the 'Miftah-ul-Tawarikh' and an Oriental Biographical Dictionary. He died at a very ripe age in 1875 at Agra.

Charles Richard Hardless

Charles Richard Hardless died on the 19th July, 1944, at the vintage age of 78. He retired as the handwriting expert to the Government of India. If ever a man deserved the epithet of self-made it was Hardless. He started life well down at the bottom of the ladder. He rose to be the first official handwriting expert to the Government of India. He has been referred to as 'The Father of the Handwriting profession' in India.

Leaving school he joined the Telegraph Department on Rs. 50/- a month. He brought to bear on his work his innate sense of devotion to duty. He was made Superintendent of his office at an exceptionally early age. But Hardless was looking for fresh avenues. At that time he came into contact with handwriting identification work. He pursued it with characteristic energy and thoroughness. It was not long before he acquired such efficiency that he attracted official attention and his services were requisitioned by his own Department, the Posts & Telegraphs. He studied and worked till his knowledge and efficiency grew and the post of handwriting expert was created by the Central Government.

As time went on, he became more and more absorbed in his work. He soaked himself in it, ate it, drank it and dreamed of it. He wrote books and articles and evolved certain theories and principles which came to be recognised not only in India but abroad. One of his books is a standard work on the subject of handwriting. The name of Hardless is still a legend not only among handwriting experts but the legal profession throughout the Country. From 1920 to 1921 he was Honorary General Secretary of the All-India Anglo-Indian Association when Gidney was the President-in-Chief.

H.J. Mulleneux—OBE, J.P.

Harry J. Mulleneux died on the 6th November, 1958, at the age of 70. He was educated in Bangalore. After completing his apprenticeship in Bombay he joined the G.I.P. (now the Central Railway) in the bottom rung. From this humble beginning he rose to the top and retired as Chief Electrical Engineer.

Mulleneux was an inventive genius and put into use many electrical devices. One of his important contributions was the electrification of the railway up to Igatpuri and Poona. During World War II his services were enlisted by the War Office in London. He was largely responsible for the device which led to the mine-detector and the elaboration of mine-sweepers. He was decorated for his services with the OBE. A loyal worker of the All-India Anglo-Indian Association, he was elected to represent the Community in the Bombay Legislature. That was when the Community had elected seats.

Frank Clinger Scallan

Born in Calcutta in 1870, Frank Clinger Scallan was a well-known Anglo-Indian artist and writer. Scallan completed his education at the Calcutta Boys' School after which he joined the Survey of India, where he served for more than 40 years. After his retirement from service he spent much time in Europe. He travelled to England, France, Italy and Spain a number of times and was a pupil of the late Jean Paul Laurence Academie Julian in Paris. His works were exhibited in the Royal Scottish Academy, Paris Salon and also in various art exhibitions all over India. He got the highest awards for black and white in India and a silver medal in the Calcutta Fine Art Exhibition in 1924. He was elected a member of the Graphic Art London in 1920 and a member correspondente of Soc. des. Aquafertistes (Society of French Etchers) the same year.

His etchings were particularly noteworthy. The titles of some of his original Indian and Foreign etchings were, Kashtaharani Ghat, Monghyr, 1901, A Riverside Temple, Monghyr, 1903, A City Gateway, Lahore, 1917, The Ajmer Gate, Old Delhi, 1918, The Women's Bathing Steps, Udaipur, Rajputana, 1918, Proladh Ghat, Benaras, 1919, A Ballygunge Tank, Calcutta, 1919, In the Court of the Golden Mosque, Lahore, 1919, A Street in Udaipur, Rajputana, 1920, The Canal Chitpur, Calcutta, 1920, The Sweetmeat Seller, Bishnath Temple, Benaras, 1920, A Lascar's Tea Shop, Kidderpore, 1921, A Persian Wheel, Lahore, 1921, Stairway in the Bazar, Darjeeling, 1924, The Non-Cooperator, 1924, A Kashmir Beggar, Lahore Baba Mast Ram Das, 1927, The Inverted Ploughs, 1928, In the Bazar, Delhi, 1936, The Kos-Miner in the Field, Delhi, The House on the Wall, Lahore, The Cloud Messenger, Isola dei Pescatori, Lake Maggiore, 1934, Rio San Pole, Venice, 1934, Rio S. Formosa, Venice, 1934, Antilers, South of France.

Scallan's paintings and sketches included, The Swayamvara of Yasodhara, Buddha in the Forest, Camel Rider, the Taj Mahal, Brindaban Bihari Ghat, The Talau, The Temple of Jhangira and Jammu Masjid, Darjeeling, Poster 'Inverted Plough' (Kalka Farming), Mahabarat, The Tobacconist, Simla Hills 26, Pictures of the Alphabets Vendors-Malaga, Spitans Coffee House, Market Place, San Remo, Italy, All that is left of the Old Residency of Cossimbazar, 1921, San Remo (Sketch), War with Prithvi Raj, Illustrations in the Indian King Reader, Book II.

After his return from Europe, Scallan took to writing mainly of a historical nature. He was an illustrator for various important publishers and Government departments in India. He was also a poet.

Scallan lived to the age of 80. He died in November, 1950, and was survived by his widow who was still living in Calcutta.

CHAPTER V

ANGLO-INDIANS AND THE MUTINY

TO write of the valour and exploits of the Anglo-Indians during the Mutiny or the First War of Independence, as it will probably be redesignated, is a delicate if not politically dangerous task. In his book entitled 'The Call of the Blood' Stark has recorded, often in detail, accounts of the decisive, sometimes seemingly superhuman, heroism of Anglo-Indian men and women. The task is delicate, because to write unreservedly about events in India at that particular period might easily be misunderstood in an Independent India. And yet no account of the Community would be even partially complete without some narrative of the position and the heroism of the Community during that critical period. There is no intention to apportion blame. Whatever is written should not be misunderstood. It is part of the scroll of history. Anglo-Indian valour, reckless heroism, disregard of danger and death should not be interpreted as a glorification of any anti-Indian feeling, no more than to record the part played by the Sikhs would be to portray the Sikhs as being anti-Indian.

The deeds and services of the Community during that period do not represent anything of which they should be ashamed. According to their history, tradition and background they did their duty. In fact, they served beyond the call of duty. It is this aspect of courage, of devotion to duty that this period serves to throw up in bold relief. These qualities, in fact, run through the history of the Community: they have projected themselves in the service of Anglo-Indians to Independent India.

An adequate record is difficult, because of the trend to be found throughout British Indian history of lumping the exploits of the Community with those of the British. No real attempt has ever been made to distinguish between the achievements of the Anglo-Indians and the British. Certain features, however, stand out.

The British administration was caught not only unprepared but was shaken to its foundations and might well have been completely overrun. Some of those who have written of the Anglo-Indian contribution have stated, on good authority, that but for the part played by the Community British Indian history might have been differently written. This is said not in any anti-Indian spirit nor in any spirit of overweening self-adulation.

The Mutiny was characterised by excesses and atrocities on both sides. In the first fury of the Mutiny, Anglo-Indians equally with Europeans were caught up in a maelstrom of violence and sudden death. Usually no attempt was made by mutinous troops or those who joined them to distinguish between Europeans and Anglo-Indians. Whole families of Anglo-Indians were wiped out. In his book Stark gives lurid details of almost indescribable individual heroism on the part of Anglo-Indian men and women caught up in an orgy of mob violence and other excesses. It would take a considerable volume to refer in any detail to the exploits of the Community at this flaming period in India's history. Only the briefest reference to some of the outstanding exploits is possible.

Delhi And The Punjab

The first name that comes to mind is that of the Anglo-Indian youth Brendish. Brendish, who was only 18 years of age, was a telegraphist posted at Delhi. Only a few years before the electric telegraph had been introduced into India. At twilight during the period of evensong on the memorable Sunday, the 10th May, the Mutiny broke out unexpectedly and prematurely at Meerut. The message was flashed by telegraph to Delhi. It was received by the Anglo-Indian telegraphists George Brendish, Charles Todd and Pilkington. Meanwhile the storm of the mutiny had burst also over Delhi. Todd went out to repair the telegraph line between Delhi and Meerut which had been cut. He was met by rebel troops and killed. A stream of refugees from Delhi and the surrounding areas hurried past the telegraph office which Brendish and Pilkington refused to leave. Brendish kept flashing messages to wherever it was possible to send them. Unable to get into touch with Meerut, he sent the following telegram to Ambala, "We must leave office. All the bungalows are being burnt down by the sepoys of Meerut. They came in this morning. We are off. Don't call today. Mr. C. Todd is dead, we think. He went out this morning, and has not returned yet. We heard that nine Europeans were killed. Good bye." From Ambala this message was relayed to Lahore, from there to Peshawar and other military stations of Punjab. As a result sepoys throughout the Punjab were disarmed. Referring to this action on the part of Brendish Sir Herbert Edwards speaking to a London audience said, "Just look at the courage and sense of duty which made that boy, with shots and cannon all round him, manipulate that message which, I do not hesitate to say, was the means of the salvation of the Punjab." Sir Robert Montgomery, Judicial Commissioner of the Punjab, was even more emphatic when he said, "The electric telegraph saved India." These words are inscribed on the obelisk which stands in the compound of the Delhi Telegraph Office and which was unveiled by Lord Curzon in 1902. Curzon repeated Montgomery's words. Little is known of what became of Pilkington.

Brendish was not, as some historians have written, killed after sending the message. After Delhi had fallen he joined the Meerut Light Horse which was recruited from the uncovenanted services and consisted of a large number of Anglo-Indians. From there he joined the Bengal Yeomanry Cavalry, another predominantly Anglo-Indian Unit, which was disbanded in 1895. After this Brendish rejoined the Telegraph Department. The manner and the quantum of the recognition of his services are significant. They are significant for the tardy and niggardly manner in which Anglo-Indian achievement, however outstanding, was recognised or appreciated by the British administration. He was made a gift of a month's pay which was Rs. 30 or £ 2. After a proper period of forgetfulness, lasting over 40 years, the next instalment of recognition came with his retirement on full pay. In 1902 a final instalment of recognition, properly modulated, was made to Brendish in the shape of a Medal of the Victorian Order.

The major contribution of Brendish to the salvation of the Punjab from being overrun by the mutinous troops was complemented by the exploits of another Anglo-Indian, General Henry Van Cortlandt. The Punjab has been known traditionally as the 'Sword Arm' of India. The message from Brendish had enabled tens of thousands of potential mutineers to be disarmed. In spite of that there were over 30,000 sepoys who had been disbanded in the Punjab and who had joined other mutinous elements. There were only a handful of British troops in this area and they together with those units of Indian regiments that could be relied upon were too inadequate to deal with the widespread depredations. The Grand Trunk Road up to Delhi and beyond had to be kept open, isolated communities of Europeans protected, if possible, from the general carnage which had swept over several families caught up in out-of-the-way places. The administration was desperate and virtually helpless. To their rescue came an Anglo-Indian, one of the romantic and legendary figures of Anglo-Indian history. He was Henry Van Cortlandt.

Van Cortlandt's story is typical of the milieu in which the Anglo-Indian had to struggle and also typical of the cruel social and economic policies which were part of the then British code in India. Henry was the son of Lt. Col. Henry Clinton Van Cortlandt of the Company's Army. The son was educated in England and given a military training. He returned to India hoping to get a commission alongside his father in the Company's forces, but as with the majority of the Anglo-Indians the policies of prejudice proved too much. Because of his Indian blood from his mother's side, Van Cortlandt was denied admission into the Company's army. Trained to soldiering he took service with Ranjit Singh, the Lion of the Punjab. When the first Sikh War broke out Van Cortlandt took up service with the British and was appointed as a Political Officer. On the cessation of the hostilities he was re-employed by Ranjit Singh. With the outbreak of the second Sikh War Van Cortlandt was embodied in General Edwards' army. He rendered particularly distinguished service in the battle of Multan.

With the annexation of the Punjab, Van Cortlandt joined the civil service. When the Mutiny broke out he was performing his duties as a civil servant. With growing restlessness he watched the tide rising against the administration. Trained to arms, with soldiering in his blood, he volunteered to raise a cavalry unit. In time of stress, throughout British-Indian history, the administration unhesitatingly called upon the Community which was, after their loyal and selfless service was completed, as unhesitatingly discarded. Van Cortlandt's offer was accepted with alacrity.

His own reputation and the reputation of his father enabled him, within a comparatively short time, to raise the Harriana Light Horse. With this body of troops as his nucleus Van Cortlandt, who now enjoyed the rank of General, achieved a series of victories which ultimately ended in the complete pacification of the Punjab. With an auxiliary of Bikaner troops, he broke the mutineers at Hansi and went on from there to recapture Hissar. With his victories at Mungali and Jamalpore he subdued the whole of Punjab up to Rohtak which is only a few miles from Delhi. By his series of lightning and uninterrupted victories, General Van Cortlandt reclaimed the most vital and strategic districts, such as Sirsa, Hansi, Hissar and Rohtak.

In addition, his victorious forces cut off huge bodies of mutineers under Prince Muhammad Azeem and prevented them from swelling the already swollen tide of mutineers who had proceeded to Delhi to join the general fighting there. When the mutiny had been quelled, Van Cortlandt's outstanding and vital services were recognised by the award of the Companionship of the Bath. He was also made the Commissioner of Multan. Van Cortlandt retired from service in 1868 and died in London on the 15th March, 1888.

Lucknow

The Mutiny had broken out at Meerut on the 10th May, 1857. In Lucknow the fateful day was the 30th May. Sir Henry Lawrence was the Chief Commissioner and was invested with plenary powers and also given the rank of Brigadier-General.

The only force Lawrence had with him consisted of 300 British troops. To augment this totally inadequate number, he raised a corps of volunteers and constabulary. This corps was part Infantry and part Cavalry. It was recruited from among Europeans and the Anglo-Indian civil population. With these volunteers and a handful of troops Lawrence withstood and made history during the siege of Lucknow. He faced over 50,000 mutinous troops.

Running true to form the British historian has not cared to identify the names and the achievements of the Anglo-Indians. As usual, these names and achievements have been included with the British. It has been possible, however, to rescue some of these names for Anglo-Indian history. In his book, Stark has made a reference to a number of Anglo-Indians who fought with the daring and abandon of professional soldiers. Charles Crabbe was a mere lad who was specially mentioned for his bravery in facing shot and shell and performing his duty in an exposed position. In a sortie another Anglo-Indian by the name of Hyde rushed one of the enemy batteries killing three mutineers, shooting two and putting the third to the sword. Young Campagnac in spite of an injury to his leg was seen hobbling about, rifle in hand, where the fighting was the thickest. Incidentally, Campagnac's grandson, Charles Campagnac, is, today, a colonel in the Indian Army and one of its finest boxers. Other names mentioned by Stark for conspicuous gallantry were those of McGrennen and Hill. Sequeira, without hesitation, manned a post which was a veritable death-trap. When the Commanding Officer asked the name of the NCO who had had the criminal stupidity to put Sequeira in such an exposed position, he refused to disclose the name of the NCO. Among other names rescued from oblivion were those of Ramsay and Apothecary Thompson. Ramsay was a telegraph assistant who was working day and night at his post till he was killed by a bullet. In his account of the Mutiny, Rees says of Thompson, "Next to God, Dr. Thompson had been the means of saving many lives." The defence of the Residency and the siege of Lucknow are now landmarks in the annals of Indian history.

Even in a historical record of outstanding courage and unusual gallantry one particular aspect of this grim period deserves to be specially mentioned. Seldom, if ever, have schoolboys been called upon and answered the call to fight as men and soldiers! During the siege of Lucknow 14 boys of La Martiniere School, which is still one of the leading Anglo-Indian schools in the Country, were required to do duty as soldiers. The position allotted them was known as the Martiniere Post. They not only carried arms, but stood shoulder to shoulder with the professional soldiers and the civilian volunteers at every phase of defence and attack. The names of those 14 Anglo-Indian lads deserve to be inscribed on a special scroll of bravery. They were—

(1) Edward H. Hilton
(2) David Arathoon
(3) William Clark

(4) John Horny
(5) Danier Isaacson
(6) James Luffman
(7) James Lynch
(8) David Macdonald
(9) Lewis Nicholls
(10) Donald Macdonald
(11) George Roberts
(12) Joseph Sutton
(13) John Walsh
(14) Samuel Wrangle

In the words of Skipton this was. "The only public school in the British Empire with a record of active military service."

Half the meagre forces with which Lawrence withstood the siege of Lucknow from May till September, when Lucknow was relieved by troops under Sir Colin Campbell and Sir James Outram, were civilians. Apart from the scorching heat and then the pouring rain, the garrison was reduced to starvation rations: suffering and disease took their increasing toll. The deaths sometimes rose to as many as 20 in one day. And in all this tragedy there was the inspiring example of courage and endurance not only by civilians, but by boys. The women in the garrison, half of whom were Anglo-Indians, showed a stoicism and courage equalled only by their men. They cooked the meagre rations, they tended the sick, the wounded and the dying. They helped to forge a tradition for the Community, in war and in stress, which has been maintained by subsequent generations of Anglo-Indian women.

Sir James Outram in his Divisional Order of the 15th October, 1857, offered his, "Special congratulations and thanks to the European and Eurasian portion of the garrison."

R. Gubbins, Financial Commissioner for Oudh, and next in rank to Sir Henry Lawrence, in his "Account of the Mutinies in Oudh and of the Siege of the Lucknow Residency" writes, "Sufficient justice has, I think, scarcely been done to the clerks and uncovenanted service. The admirable conduct displayed by this class, which contained such men as Kavanagh and Williams",.... and again .... "All behaved well during the siege, and were often very conspicuous in repelling the fiercest attacks of the enemy. They deserved, I think, better at the hand of Government than

they received, or had at least received, when I left India."......
"The uncovenanted service, let me again say, distinguished itself
very remarkably at Lucknow. Individuals belonging to it on
several occasions volunteered and took part in sorties when the
enemy's guns were charged and spiked. And its members should
have no cause to complain that their gallantry and good conduct
have gone unrewarded." The Anglo-Indians were the uncovenanted service.

Cawnpore

The flames of the Mutiny spread to and ultimately enveloped
Cawnpore on the 6th June. The tragic fate of the Cawnpore
garrison and their acceptance of the terms offered by Nana Sahib
and the ultimate slaughter of men, women and children are not
for this book to relate. The total garrison of about a 1000 of
which ultimately there were only 2 survivors, contained about 300
Anglo-Indians. A reference to Cawnpore is, however, indicated
because of the two outstanding attempts made by Anglo-Indians
to carry messages to Allahabad in order to bring relief to
the beleaguered and desperate Cawnpore garrison. Those two
Anglo-Indians were Blenman and Shepherd. Disguised as a
cook Blenman tried to get through the enemy lines. He eluded
seven pickets, but was ultimately caught by the eighth. He saved
himself by immediately inventing the story that he was a chamar
(leather worker) and that the revolver he was carrying had been
taken by him from a European. He ultimately returned to the
beleaguered garrison. G.O. Trevelyan in his book on the Mutiny
paid a tribute to his gallantry during the terrible privation and
fighting. General Wheeler, the Commanding Officer, at last decided to accept the terms of Nana Sahib for safe passage as further
resistance was impossible. Blenman was among those who were
killed by Nana Sahib's troops at the Suttee Chowra Ghat.

W.J. Shepherd was the other Anglo-Indian who volunteered to
go through the enemy lines and seek relief for the beleaguered
garrison. He was a clerk in the Commissariat Department at
Lucknow. Barely recovered from a bullet wound, Shepherd
volunteered to try and get through to Allahabad. He was
disguised as a cook. Shepherd, however, did not go very far and
was caught by Nana Sahib's troops. He was tried and sentenced

to three years' imprisonment. He was fortunate. With the re-capture of Cawnpore by General Havelock he was found alive and released.

Bombay

While the Mutiny had been scotched in the Punjab, the flames enveloped Delhi, Cawnpore, Lucknow and leaped their way to Central India. Bombay was a focus which, if overrun, would have extended the Mutiny through Western India and the Madras State. The spirit of disaffection was no less strong in Bombay than elsewhere. The British authorities and more especially the British officers of Indian regiments were lolling in a sense of false complacency. In spite of what had already taken place in other parts of the Country, British military officers refused to believe that their own set of men could ever be disloyal. They felt that any indication of suspicion on their part would create wanton resentment and perhaps disaffection among the men, where none existed. Fortunately for the British at this time the administration of the Bombay Police was in the hands of an Anglo-Indian, Charles Forjett. Forjett had started life in a humble capacity in the Survey of India Department. By dint of hard work and merit, he climbed the rungs till he became a Superintendent of Police and uncovenanted Assistant Judge, then Deputy Commissioner of Police, Bombay, and finally Commissioner of Police and Sheriff of Bombay. In his book 'Our Real Danger in India' Forjett has traversed the critical and momentous events in which he was a central figure. While deprecating unnecessary suspicion, Forjett was convinced that the events in other parts of the Country demanded the utmost precaution and vigilance. He approached Lord Elphinstone, the Governor of Bombay, and asked for and was given a free hand to take all measures that he considered necessary. The first thing Forjett did was to collect around him a strong and reliable nucleus of mounted Anglo-Indian and European Policemen. They were a handful consisting of 50 men. He refused to disperse these men through the city and maintained them as a hard core under his immediate command. There was an incident which, if not firmly handled by Forjett, might well have precipitated the mutiny of the troops in Bombay.

A Christian soldier belonging to the 10th Regiment of Infantry had bumped into a procession carrying a Hindu deity. The drunken soldier assaulted the members of the procession and knocked over the deity. The nearby policemen took the soldier into custody. When word reached the Regiment, a number of soldiers proceeded to the police lock-up, assaulted the policemen on duty and rescued their comrade. A European policeman with 4 men went to the military lines and insisted on the policemen, who had been seized by the soldiers, being released. The sepoys surrounded the policemen who had to fight their way out, killing 2 of the soldiers and wounding others. On this the sepoys took to arms and were faced by 5 or 6 of their European officers with drawn swords. As soon as news reached Forjett, he rushed to the spot with his 50 mounted policemen. The British officers implored him to go away as they felt that his presence would only incite the troops to violence. Forjett's mounted policemen were well-armed and refused to listen to the British officers. He ordered his men to open fire on which the sepoys thought better of the whole matter and the incident ended quietly.

Forjett was now in the process of being convinced that the men were restless and had been infected with the fever of disaffection. He then arranged to keep a close watch on the sepoys. Not only did he send out hand-picked men, in disguise, to mingle with the sepoys when they visited the market, but Forjett himself in one disguise or another did the same. Being dark-skinned Forjett had no difficulty in assuming various disguises. As a result he discovered that the house of one Ganga Prasad had become the rendezvous for the secret meetings of the sepoys. He got hold of Ganga Prasad and on pain of unspeakable penalties induced the latter to agree to admit him in disguise into one of those secret meetings. From an anteroom Forjett was able to overhear the conversation which left him in no doubt that the troops in Bombay were completely disaffected and were planning an uprising. The broad facts which emerged were that an uprising had been arranged for the last day of Muharram, a Muslim festival. It had, however, been postponed owing to the draconian measures taken by Forjett and was now fixed for a day during Diwali.

Forjett knew that if he relayed his information to the British officers, they would immediately discount his information as being exaggerated or even baseless. He, therefore, arranged to take

Major Barrow, the senior British Officer, along with him to one of the meetings. Barrow was dumbfounded when he heard for himself the conversations: in spite of his original scepticism, he had to accept the evidence of his eyes and ears. As a result, the ringleaders were duly court-martialled and sentenced. The whole movement was nipped in the bud.

Illustrative of the typical British neglect of the services of members of the Community, Forjett received no official recognition for his outstanding work. Certain verbal encomia were, however, duly recorded not without a certain sense of patronage. By a resolution dated the 19th June, 1858, the Governor-in-Council recorded, "That the expectations raised by the appointment of Mr. Forjett to the executive command of the Bombay Police have been amply realised."

On the 23rd May, of the following year, the Secretary of the Judicial Department wrote, "The Right Honourable the Governor-in-Council avails himself of this opportunity of expressing his sense of the very valuable services rendered by the Deputy Commissioner of Police, Mr. Forjett, in the detection of the plot in Bombay in the autumn of 1857. His duties demanded great courage and acuteness, and great judgement, all of which qualities were conspicuously displayed by Mr. Forjett at this trying period."

Praise from an even higher source duly arrived. Sir Charless Wood, Secretary of State for India, conveyed to him, "The gracious approbation of Her Majesty the Queen of your conduct during the critical period of the Mutiny and the disturbances in India."

The Indian and European communities in Bombay presented Forjett with an address and, with the approval of the Government, gave him a purse of 3850 pounds in token of their gratitude for his "zealous energy" and the successful application of his "almost despotic powers". Forjett died in London on 27th January, 1890. He continued to be resentful of the niggardly treatment he had received from the British administration and salved his injured feelings by recording his experience in his book entitled, 'Our Real Danger in India' where his services have been chronicled.

In recognition of his services Forjett was granted an extra pension and his son, F.H. Forjett, granted a commission in the Army. Forjett's son saw service mostly with the 26th Bombay Native

Infantry, which in the 'seventies' and 'eighties' was popularly known as the 'Black Watch', since three of the senior officers were Anglo-Indians: they were the Commanding Officer John Miles, who is said to have had a dominating personality, John Heath and F.H. Forjett. The family name was said originally to have been Forget, suggesting French descent.

Calcutta

That the flames of the Mutiny did not erupt in Calcutta was due to the grizzled Anglo-Indian soldier General Sir John Bennett Hearsey, who was the military commander of the district, which included Calcutta the then Capital of India. The mounting spate of news from all directions of uprisings and the massacre of Europeans, both military and civilian, kept Calcutta on the edge of nervous expectation. Sunday, the 14th June, 1857, has been described as "panic" Sunday. The growing snowball of rumour given momentum by a certain amount of panicky, wishful thinking gave birth to the story that the disbanded sepoys were on their way from Barrackpore to slaughter the Europeans of Calcutta. Trotter tells of the almost wild stampede led by high European officials, both civil and military, to Fort William or to ships on the river. Fortunately nothing happened on "panic" Sunday. It was confirmed later, however, that there was ample basis for the alarm. The Maharaja of Gwalior was to entertain European guests to a display of fire-works on "panic" Sunday. It was arranged that the fire-works would be the signal for an uprising at Fort William, Calcutta, of the sepoys who, after killing their officers, would join the sepoys from Barrackpore. Thereafter, they would proceed to the palace of the deposed King of Oudh at Garden Reach and link up with his force of about 1,000 armed retainers. The final part of the plan was that these ex-soldiers would lead a mass of the Muslim population in Calcutta to wipe out the European population. The plan failed because of a downpour of rain which prevented the fire-works. The uprising was, therefore, postponed to the 23rd June, which was considered to be trebly propitious. It was the centenary of the Battle of Plassey; it was also the occasion of the Hindu festival of Rathjatra and of the Muslim festival of Bakr Id. The plan was forestalled by General Hearsey disarming and disbanding the sepoys at Barrackpore. The guards posted to different parts of Calcutta although not removed from their posts were disarmed. Hearsey was a tough, battle-hardened, fighting general and one of the most trusted advisers of Lord Canning, the then Viceroy. He belonged to the well-known Anglo-Indian family of Hearseys.

Volunteer Corps

In these conditions of anxiety, nervous tension and fearful expectation the Government decided to create the Bengal Yeomanry Cavalry. It was a volunteer corps. For this corps a large number of Anglo-Indians volunteered. In October, 1857, the Yeomanry Cavalry proceeded from Howrah to Raniganj by train. From there they marched via Gaya and Patna across the Ganges into Tirhut. They moved through Dharbhanga and other places towards the Nepal Terrai.

Early in 1858 they marched into the Gorakhpur district and ultimately arrived at Almora. They fought a series of actions and at Gonda, in conjunction with certain other units, routed the forces of the Rajah of Gonda. The main body of the enemy, however, was yet to be dealt with and the opposing forces met on the outskirts of Bulwaghat. Nash describes the battle as follows, "One hundred and twenty-two sabres with the Colours at their head prepared to charge. The words 'March, Trot, Gallop', in rapid succession, have scarcely passed the lips of the leader, when on dash the Yeomanry like greyhounds slipped from the leash. They sweep over the plains, they plunge into intercepting ravines half full of water that momentarily check their race into the jaws of death; they tear through the stream in the teeth of a shower of grape from the enemy's one and only 18 pounder. Still on goes the squadron, with every nerve braced, every sabre gripped : knee to knee the onward wave still roars as it were 'Now for the gun! Now for the gun!' as the scowling black monster from its gaping muzzle vomits for the last time another deadly discharge of grape into our faces : but with free rein, neck and neck, with outstretched strides the maddened and gallant horses fly like the irresistible shower of the iron hail that had just flown over their heads. Yet mutineers, with muskets levelled from the shoulder, stand like posts and draw not a trigger. A few strides more, and bayonet and sabre will cross one another. When, lo! in an instant up spring hundreds of sepoys on every side as if out of the very ground itself. They have been crouching like tigers prepared to spring from behind the village, and from behind the thin line of their front rank by which we had been decoyed. It was now too late to check the headlong rush: and, had it been attempted, in the confusion that would doubtless have followed, the destruction of the whole squadron would probably have been the result. No sooner, therefore, were these numerous assailants disclosed, than the next moment a stream of musketry, like a sheet of fire, met us with terrible effect and literally cut down a section of the squadron, and encumbered the spot where this withering volley was received with men and horses struggling in dying agony."

"But nothing could daunt the remnant of that devoted band. They plunged in among the enemy with an ardour that could not be resisted. In an area of Heaven knows how few square yards, the killed and the wounded lay crowded together as they had fallen. Some of the latter, with their garments on fire, were unable to move; others fell and died without a groan; others, weltering in their blood, or bleeding to death, dragged themselves up into a sitting posture, and, with revolver in hand, watched the doubtful fight; and others again, having escaped severe injury and having lost their horses, were standing over their helpless comrades and shooting down the scattered sepoys as they approached within revolver range of that gory spot."

"While all this was going on, the undaunted remnant—roused to almost superhuman efforts—having ridden into and over the mutineers, drew their revolvers, and an unrelenting and indiscriminate carnage ensued. And now the left squadron, noticing their comrades hard pressed, also raced into the melee; and then the clank of steel, the rattling of musketry, and the yell of the mutineers."

In the cold weather of 1858-59 the Yeomanry Cavalry were employed in operations in the Baraich District of Oudh. Here by their fighting qualities they gained the dreaded name of the 'Shaitan Paltan', that is, the Devil's Regiment. Finally they operated against the sepoys on the Nepal frontier. They had been commanded by Major Richardson of the 81st Irregulars; Captain F.C. Chapman was the Second-in-Command. The Cavalry consisted of 4 Troops, one of which was commanded by Lieutenant deHoxar, member of a well-known Anglo-Indian family from

Northern India. The corps was disbanded at Patna in 1859. Before breaking up the men were addressed by the Viceroy as follows, "I cannot allow the Officers and Men of the Bengal Yeomanry Cavalry to disperse without expressing in general orders this acknowledgement of the excellent services they have rendered. The gazette of the 23rd March, 27th April, 11th May, 6th and 13th July, 13th August, 12th and 19th October, 23rd November, 1858 and the 11th and 18th January, 1859, all testify that the Bengal Yeomanry Cavalry have borne a distinguished part in the several operations therein recounted. Long marches, exposure, fatigue, and harassing patrol and picket duties have from the first fallen to the lot of this young Corps, and they have borne the whole in true soldier-like spirit. The Governor-General-in-Council conveys his best thanks for the good service they have rendered to the State, and in disbanding the Corps, which from the 27th instant will cease to belong to the British Army, he wishes its members a hearty farewell."

In St. James' Church, Calcutta, the following tablet was to be found: "BALWAN, ALMORAH, BIKRAMJOTE, NUKUGGUR, HURRIAH, JUGDISPORE, DOOMAREAGUNJ, BURRAREA, TOOLSIPORE, A.D. 1857-1858. Erected by the Officers, Non-Commissioned Officers and Men of the Regiment of Bengal Yeomanry Cavalry, in memory of their Comrades who fell in action with the enemy, or died of their wounds or disease: CAPTAIN A. GIFFARD; LIEUTENANT S. STROVER; CORONETS L. MARTIN, A.W. MARSHALL, H.P. TROUP, C.S. GAYNOR; SERGEANTS C.H. SAVAGE, W.A. CURRAN, W.H. BENNET, W. WILLIAMS; TROOPERS, G. WESTERLY, T. TAYLOR, E.O. TURNER, H. RANDOLPH, F. MILTON, J. BROWN, R. MAY, G. RICHARDSON, G. ANDERSON, J.D. ALLINGHAM, E. FITZGERALD, J. ERROL, T. BURKE, W. GRIFFITHS, J. THOMPSON and T. HUNTER." The tablet contained the names of several Anglo-Indians.

Anglo-Indian V.Cs.

To this period belongs perhaps the first identifiable Anglo-Indian V.C. Thomas Henry Kavanagh, a clerk in the Deputy Commissioner's office at Lucknow. Kavanagh was the first and, so far, the only civilian in India ever to have been decorated with the V.C. On the military side the first Anglo-Indian to win the V.C. was Andrew Fitzgibbon. In fact Fitzgibbon was the youngest person ever to have been awarded the Victoria Cross. The next identifiable Anglo-Indian V.C. was Robert MacMillan, an orphan Anglo-Indian boy from Madras, who won this coveted distinction while serving with the Sherwood Foresters in the Ashanti War of 1873.

Belated Recognition

The Queen's proclamation of 1st November, 1858, marked the official end of the Mutiny. Much of the exploits, daring and unwavering courage of the Community during a period which broke the spirits and the minds of many men and women have not been salvaged for history. Much of this achievement has been lost under the general designation 'British'. Much of it has also been lost to historical record for want of chroniclers. What has been salvaged stands out as a shining monument to the courage and devotion to duty of the Anglo-Indian Community. The knowledge of their deeds is made all the more splendid by the fact that for the greater part of a century before the Mutiny they had been subjected to bitter economic and social disabilities and even to deliberately cruel discrimination. Yet, when the occasion arose, they formed civilian regiments and served shoulder to shoulder with the most seasoned and battle-inoculated soldiers, both British and Indian. Their dogged endurance, their capacity to march and fight in the deadly heat of an Indian summer, or during the torrential rains, at last evoked a belated recognition of their qualities. The Volunteer Corps of Patna, the Lahore Light Horse, the Uncovenanted Men of the Lucknow Volunteer Cavalry, had written in deeds of reckless heroism a valourous and stirring history. The Lucknow Volunteer Cavalry had met and repelled the repeated onslaughts of over 50,000 mutineers. The First Madras Fusiliers, Pearson's Battery, the Mounted Volunteers of Agra, the Yeomanry of Meerut, the Cavalry Regiment of Calcutta, all of which units contained a large proportion of Anglo-Indians, had made a notable contribution to the final result of this dark and uncertain period of history.

As part of the recognition of the fighting qualities exhibited by the Community, it was announced that the Government had decided to raise a regiment of Anglo-Indians, from all parts of the Country, for service in Bengal. Lord Canning was among the first and the most enthusiastic in his appreciation of the courageous services of the Community.

The Metropolitan See was occupied, at that time, by one of the greatest prelates who have ever adorned this high office. In his thanksgiving address at St. Paul's Cathedral, Bishop Cotton pleaded on the 28th July, 1860, for the setting up of a number of well-equipped schools for the Community. In his minute of October, the Viceroy pleaded in ardent terms for fairplay to the Anglo-Indians: "If cared for betimes, it will become a source of strength to British rule and of usefulness to India. The Eurasian class have a special claim upon us. The presence of a British Government has called them into being. They serve the Government in many respects more efficiently than the native can serve it, and more cheaply and more conveniently than the European can."

Lord Canning's scheme for the advancement of the Community was largely still-born because his term of office expired in 1862. Bishop Cotton also died in 1866. After Canning, there were no less than four Viceroys during the next twelve or fourteen years. It was only on the 13th August, 1881, that Lord Lytton, recalling the intentions and promise of Lord Canning, issued his minute on which the Government of India decided on the 15th October, 1881, to make European education (which included the Anglo-Indians) a Department of Public Instruction. I deal with this aspect more fully in the chapter entitled, 'In the Educational Vanguard'.

CHAPTER VI

THE GIDNEYAN ERA

Betrayal Again

L T. COL. SIR HENRY GIDNEY represented an epoch of over 20 years in the life and history of the Community. A reference to Gidney's service to the Community involves, inevitably, a reference to the position and achievements of the Anglo-Indians from 1920 to 1942.

Henry Albert John Gidney was born on the 9th June, 1873, at Igatpuri. Igatpuri is situated in the Western Ghats about 80 miles east of Bombay. A comparatively small place, Igatpuri, however, represented an important railway centre, where an appreciable number of Anglo-Indians employed on the railways lived and worked.

Gidney was brought up in the Methodist Episcopal faith. From the Methodist School in Igatpuri, Gidney was transferred to the Baldwin Boys' High School, Bangalore, a well-known Anglo-Indian School. Gidney finished his schooling at St. Peter's High School, Mazagaon, from where he matriculated at an unusually early age. Gidney was an all-round sportsman, being good at billiards, boxing and tennis. In later life, he was a keen and successful big game shikari.

Gidney was unusually ambidextrous. To this congenital quality he ascribed much of his prodigious if not phenomenal memory. Passing out from school, Gidney joined the Indian Medical Department (British Cadre) which was reserved for members of the Anglo-Indian Community. He was trained at the Calcutta Medical College, where the I.M.D. students pursued their studies along with medical students of all communities. Gidney was barely 16 years of age when he joined the Medical College in 1890. During the 4-year course in college, his academic record was spectacular. In the first year examination he stood first: in the second year examination he again stood first. While doing his medical studies, Gidney sought to improve himself academically: he took the Intermediate Arts examination from the Allahabad University. In the third year medical examination, Gidney not only retained his first place but secured 3 gold medals. He climaxed his stay in the Medical College by passing out first, beating on the way every other student including the best civil medical students from all the other Indian communities. This time he won 5 gold medals and 6 other honour certificates for every senior subject.

The Indian Medical Department (British Cadre) was a subordinate service open only to Anglo-Indians. It was attached to the British Army in India, and hence the tag—British Cadre. Gidney was fired by an irresistible ambition to enter the senior service—the Indian Medical Service. After only 2 years as an Assistant Civil Surgeon, he was able to get 6 months furlough to proceed to England, an unheard of concession in those days. Within 6 weeks of his arrival in London, Gidney appeared for his London Entrance Examination. This was also a record. Being short of money, he appeared for certain competitive inter-hospital examinations and annexed 3 out of 5 scholarships. After 6 months he decided to appear for the I.M.S. competitive examination. Here also he raced against time. He joined a famous coaching school which had completed more than half the normal term. He, however, appeared in the competitive examination and was successful.

Gidney returned to India as an officer in the Indian Medical Service. In 1901 he saw active service in China in the Boxer rebellion. He was mentioned in despatches during this campaign. In 1902 Gidney went to England on medical furlough where he remained for 2 years. During this period he obtained the F.R.C.S. (Edinburgh) and the D.P.H. (Cantab). Towards the end of 1906 Gidney was serving in the new Province of Eastern Bengal and Assam as a Civil Surgeon. It was during the years 1906 to 1910 that he acquired increasing experience as an ophthalmic surgeon. He spent most of his spare time in big game shooting. In 1910 after being given the rank of Brevet Major, he went on a year's furlough to England. This leave was extended by 9 months. During this period he passed the L.R.C.P., M.R.C.P. (E) and the D.O. (Oxon) examinations. In 1911 he was elected Fellow of the

Royal Society (England). He was the youngest man at that time
to be given this high honour. He did fine research work in
Ophthalmology at Oxford and was appointed post-graduate lecturer
in Ophthalmology at Oxford : he held that appointment for about
18 months. Gidney also officiated on the staff of the eye hospitals
of Oxford and London.

Throughout his career in the I.M.S. Gidney came up, repeatedly,
against race and colour discrimination. When he returned to
India, in 1911, he was appointed Civil Surgeon of Kohima in the
Naga Hills. Gidney bitterly resented this appointment, as it was
a deliberate act of professional ostracism, despite his outstanding
qualifications which entitled him to a far more important assignment. The reasons for his relegation were a serious altercation
with the Governor and the rancour of a European member of the
I.M.S. who had become Inspector-General of Civil Hospitals.
This senior official could not forget that Gidney had killed his
practice in the Dacca district, not deliberately but merely because
of Gidney's demonstrably superior professional ability. Whatever
his defects, Gidney did not lack in spirit and physical courage. He
accompanied an expedition against the Naga head-hunters of
Assam. He was appointed Senior Medical Officer of this force.
On one occasion when the camp of wounded soldiers was attacked
by the Nagas, Gidney's presence of mind saved the situation. He
collected a handful of soldiers and beat off the Naga attack. On
this occasion he showed outstanding personal gallantry in rescuing
a porter who, however, ultimately died of his wounds. In this
expedition Gidney was mentioned in despatches three times. He
was understandably resentful of the fact that his leading part in the
defence of the stockade was singled out for non-recognition. All
those who had served under him to beat off the attack were
promoted and given decorations. Gidney alone failed to get any
specific recognition. This drew from him the bitter comment
that had a European officer done half as well, he would have
got the V.C. or at least the D.S.O. The discriminatory treatment
meted out to Gidney rankled and precipitated the decision to resign
from the service at the earliest possible opportunity. The succeeding Governor of Assam, however, had been so impressed by Gidney's
work that he was transferred from the smallest to the largest
district—Sylhet. There he soon built up a large private practice.

It was while at Sylhet that Gidney submitted his resignation: he actually secured an appointment in the London Eye Hospital.

The Great War, however, intervened. Gidney was posted to Peshawar in September 1914. He saw active service in the North-West Frontier and was Medical Officer to the Rajputs when they suffered heavy casualties on the 19th April, 1915, in their attack on the Shabkadar Fort. Gidney was wounded and given three months' medical furlough. In 1916 Gidney was posted to the 6th Division at Mhow. He was given a triple appointment, namely, Surgical Specialist, Ophthalmic Specialist and Specialist in Public Health. Even for the I.M.S., to serve as a specialist in three subjects was a record. In 1917 he was posted as a Senior Surgeon of a large War hospital and promoted to the rank of Lieutenant-Colonel. At the end of the War, Gidney was invalided from the service.

Gidney's Love Life

In 1904 Gidney married Grace Wignall the daughter of a Yorkshireman who had settled in Agra. There were no children of the marriage which was not a success. After a few years Mrs. Gidney settled in the U.K. Till she died in 1937 Gidney supported her. In public life, anyone who amounts to anything has detractors. Gidney certainly had his fill. His rather flamboyant manner often gave his vilifiers a stick with which to beat him. A connoisseur art collector, Gidney had a connoisseur's eye for beautiful women. A polished performer on the dance floor, this added to his reputation as a lady-killer. Even towards the end of his career, when he was an ill man, Gidney would hold the floor and put to shame much younger exponents of the waltz and the tango.

As leader of the Community and with the increasing eminence he achieved as the unchallenged representative of Anglo-India, Gidney inevitably had his temptations. As he went from centre to centre, meeting the most beautiful and accomplished women in the Community, many of them were attracted to him not only for his eminence but for his innate charm and polish.

Men with strong passions subject to strong temptations often commit great faults. The passionateness which impels to achievement by overcoming seemingly insurmountable obstacles not seldom leads to romantic episodes. Much that was said or written about Gidney was often deliberately false and sheerly malicious. Gidney undoubtedly had the capacity to inspire blind devotion in some women. During his public career three women shared his work and his burdens.

A sparkling raconteur Gidney could not only give but take in the field of wit and sarcasm. To the delight of many of his listeners he recounted a series of his alleged romantic escapades. This often supplied further ammunition to his ever-ready vilifiers.

Gidney was served for many years by one V.J. Ayyar. Starting as assistant in the office, Ayyar became the Pooh-Bah of the Head Office of the All-India Anglo-Indian Association. Ayyar was Gidney's private secretary, stenographer, and, in fact, the chief executive in the office. Gidney always had the magnanimity to bow to Ayyar as the architect of some of the most effective representations and memoranda produced during Gidney's unremitting fight for the Community. With much relish Gidney told a story of an irate old Anglo-Indian lady, who had apparently been indoctrinated with considerable anti-Gidney propaganda. This old lady accosted Gidney and said he ought to be ashamed of himself as he did not hesitate even to go on tour with an Ayah (maid servant). Gidney's irrepressible sense of humour made him bow to the lady: he added to her horror by offering to introduce her to his 'Ayah'. He then called for V.J. Ayyar, a very masculine person, and introduced him to the righteously indignant old lady: dumbfounded, she left muttering something under her breath.

Enters Public Life

After retiring from the I.M.S. Gidney set up private practice in Bombay. He opened a large private eye hospital and achieved immediate success. Within a year his practice rose to Rs. 10,000 a month and reached the Rs. 20,000 mark. This was in 1918.

In spite of his lucrative practice Gidney was soon drawn into public life. He had his first taste in the Bombay Corporation. In 1918 he was elected President of the Bombay branch of the Anglo-Indian Empire League, an organisation which had been founded in 1908 by Charles Palmer. Incidentally, Palmer was a member of the well-known Hyderabad family which had founded the Palmer Bank in Calcutta and at one time made a loan of 10 million rupees to the Nizam of Hyderabad. In 1919 Gidney was elected Vice-President of the Central Council of the Empire League. At the end of the same year, in a rather bitter election he beat by one vote J.H. Abbott, who had been the President of the League for many years. Abbott represented the Community in the then Imperial Legislative Council. From then on Gidney devoted himself increasingly to the leadership and organisation of the Community. There were at least 5 organisations representing Anglo-Indians in different parts of the Country including Gidney's League. On the 9th April, 1926, there was a conference between representatives of these organisations from Bombay, Bengal, Madras, Allahabad and Burma. The object was to seek amalgamation. Madras and Allahabad preferred to plough their own, dissident furrows. Bengal and Burma leaned towards amalgamation and unity. Gidney then became President of the Bengal Organisation. Into this he fused his own organisation. The Anglo-Indian and Domiciled European Association, All-India and Burma, was registered in 1926. In 1929 Allahabad also came under Gidney's banner. By his energy, organising ability and relatively outstanding capacity Gidney ultimately wrested the crown of Anglo-India and became its accredited leader.

This was not to say that Gidney did not face opposition. He bitterly commented not only on the base criticism but the evil vilification to which he was often exposed. In Bengal the opposition was kept alive by two prominent Anglo-Indians. One was H.A. Stark, who had achieved not inconsiderable distinction as an educationist, and later wrote commendable histories of the Community. While Stark had none of the flair nor the capacity for All-India leadership which Gidney possessed, he had a not inconsiderable following in Calcutta. Spare in stature, Stark reflected austerity. Instinctively he seemed to resent the 'grandeeism' that strongly characterised Gidney. Stark never lost an opportunity of satirising Gidney. In Stark's journal, the 'Anglo-Indian Citizen', Gidney's monocle and button-hole came under Stark's whip-lash writing. The 'I-Specialist' was a favourite epithet coined by Stark and hurled repeatedly at Gidney.

Gidney constantly inveighed against disunity in the Community. "Disunity has been our greatest curse" was a constant theme.

In The Legislature

With the introduction of the Montague-Chelmsford Reforms the Central Legislative Assembly came into being. The Community had been granted one reserved seat to be filled by nomination. Gidney's growing stature in the Community resulted inevitably in a contest with J.H. Abbott. The two men acted typically. Abbott was preoccupied getting signatures. The dynamic Gidney scorned such pedestrian methods. He toured the Country not once but twice in a short space of four months. The Community was scattered through the length and breadth of the Country and located not only in the main cities but in colonies in almost every railway centre in the Country.

Gidney's almost aggressive character led him to beard Abbott in his home town of Jhansi. He challenged Abbott to appear on a common platform. Gidney's incomparably greater capacity and polish brought him overwhelming victory over Abbott even in Jhansi. As a result of the decisive support of the Community throughout the Country, Gidney was nominated by the Viceroy to the Legislative Assembly and took his seat in the House in September, 1921.

Gidney had no real political background or training. As a medical man, he did not have the background attributes which often contribute to success in the political field. Gidney, however, represented a striking and, indeed, a refreshing departure from his predecessor. Abbott had been, more or less, a silent hanger-on of the European Group and of European policies. Gidney had to feel his way. The House consisted of two main elements that could be broadly designated as radical and liberal. At that time the attitude towards the Anglo-Indians even of the liberals was not only unfriendly but even hostile. Gidney joined the European Group, perhaps with the intention of not making a too sudden break with the past conventions. Gidney was never, however, happy with the European Group. He resented their patronising attitude. In spite of his rapidly increasing influence in the House, they were not prepared to accept him even in the position of a Deputy Leader of the Group. With his aggressively independent spirit and his capacity to more than hold his own, both intellectually and socially, Gidney represented a type of Anglo-Indian whom the European Group often resented. As a nominated member, Gidney could not vote frontally against the Government. Usually nominated members are not supposed to criticise, much less speak against, the Government.

From the beginning, however, Gidney did not hesitate to express his disapproval of Government policies whenever he felt that criticism was necessary. Gidney had the disability of an un-resonant, even thin voice. But with experience and practice, he became a facile and often, when inspired by emotion, a moving speaker. His speeches did not have any special literary or scholarly quality. Gidney was not able to enter the lists in matters which required a legal background. Yet, he was one of the most active and vocal members. In time he came to be regarded as an authority particularly on railway and army matters.

Gidney had considerable social charm. He was considered perhaps the ace raconteur not only of the Legislature but of Delhi society. He had a fund of inexhaustible stories. There was a characteristic tang in Gidney's story-telling. On more than one occasion when about to regale the House with one of his tit-bits, he would be warned by the President to reserve those of a risque character for the lobby. Gidney's ready wit often extricated him from a difficult position in the House when under attack by some outstanding debater or speaker. He also had a not negligible ability for punning, which he used to the discomfiture of an interrupter or a malicious opponent.

Both Mohammad Ali Jinnah and Gidney had a rather theatrical manner. They were both persons with a considerable self-conceit. Both were impeccable dressers. Both sported monocles. Their similarities, however, seemed more to repel than to attract. On one occasion when Gidney got up to speak immediately after Jinnah, referring to Jinnah he said, "The Hon'ble Member who has just sat down has not only got the bull by the horns but the cow by the udder end." The House greeted Gidney's pun with uproarious applause.

Anglo-Indians In The Services

Anglo-Indians in the services owed a great deal to Gidney's tenacious, unremitting championship. Inevitably, a large part of Gidney's attention was devoted to the position of Anglo-Indians in the Railways. Sometimes the criticism was made that the

Association was virtually a railway trade union. In fact, this criticism was not fair. A preponderant section of the Community had for decades found a place in the Indian Railways. Past British policy of deliberate discrimination and the steady economic emasculation of the Community combined to make the Community almost pathetically dependent on Government service. While throwing a few crumbs to the Community by giving it an almost special niche, in a subordinate capacity, British Imperialism served first its own interests by filling strategic positions in the key services with Anglo-Indians on whom they could rely in times of crisis.

From the beginning Gidney took a leading part in the discussions in the Legislative Assembly on the Railway administration. Both in the House and outside he underlined the difficulties of the Community in the Railways. One of Gidney's most difficult tasks was to maintain the recruitment strength of the Community in the Railways. When Gidney entered the Assembly there were approximately 11,000 Anglo-Indians employed on the Railways. In ten years the number increased to about 14,000. Shortly before he died in 1942 there were signs of deterioration and the number of Anglo-Indians had declined to about 12,000. Shortly after his debut in the Assembly Gidney was confronted with a definite anti-Anglo-Indian psychology. The reasons were complex. Some of the causes were certainly not of the Community's making. The Community itself was uncertain of its political and even legal position. For purposes of employment Anglo-Indians were referred to as statutory natives of India, for purposes of defence, and more especially for enrolment in the Indian Defence Force later known as the Auxiliary Force, they were classified as European British subjects. Yet they were completely barred from recruitment to the British Army. Anglo-Indians thus found themselves virtually in a politico-legal vacuum. Gidney had to resist deliberate attempts to squeeze the Community out of the services on the plea of Indianisation which was interpreted as implying de-Anglo-Indianisation. Gidney fought an unremitting and largely successful fight against that misguided policy. The British authorities were not only lukewarm but, often from a misguided sense of offering a sop to clamorous 'Indian' political opinion, they were prepared to sacrifice the Community at the altar of expediency.

Gidney's career and his leadership of the Community were marked by a theme which ran through them like a Greek chorus. This was his consistent fight against race and colour discrimination. One of Gidney's major assignments was his appointment, in 1929, as a Member of the Royal Labour Commission more popularly known as the Whitley Commission. Gidney's memorandum to the Commission and his questions were directed to exposing the discrimination practised as between European and non-European employees. By cross-examining members of the Railway Board and General Managers he exposed the fact that while an Anglo-Indian Ticket Collector received Rs. 33/- a month, from which he had to pay from Rs. 10/- to Rs. 12/- on account of house rent and electricity, leaving him Rs. 20/- to support himself and his family, an uneducated and often completely illiterate British soldier was recruited as a Guard on an initial salary of Rs. 125/- a month.

As a member of this Commission Gidney drew attention to what appeared to be chronic grievances on the Railways, such as, the over-working of the loco and traffic employees for periods ranging from 10 to 20 hours at a stretch. He also strongly criticised the summary and high-handed manner in which the higher authorities disposed of appeals.

Gidney also took up the cudgels on behalf of members of the Community employed in the Posts and Telegraph Department. In this he was handicapped by the consistent non-cooperation and often open opposition of the Indian Telegraph Association. This Association was founded in 1908 by Harry Barton. Barton was a poor lad who had been educated at the Lawrence Military School in Lovedale in South India. In many ways, Barton can be regarded as the Father of Indian Trade Unionism. He was a fearless and determined fighter and did not flinch from arrest or imprisonment. Without either the education or the polish that Gidney possessed, Barton was nevertheless an able organiser and a doughty fighter. Unfortunately, he was one of Gidney's consistent opponents and together with Stark formed the spearhead of the opposition to Gidney in Calcutta. When Gidney had served on the Rangachari Committee in 1923 the Indian Telegraph Association was led by Barton. Unfortunately when Gidney moved in the Assembly, in 1929, for the appointment of a committee to investigate the grievances of the telegraph workers, the Indian Telegraph

Association took up a hostile attitude. When Anglo-Indians were faced with fierce, brutal retrenchment recommended by the Varma Committee, Gidney, who was in London in 1931, represented the matter immediately to the Secretary of State. There is no doubt that Gidney's intervention served largely to blunt the viciousness of the Varma Committee's assault on the Anglo-Indians in the Telegraph Department.

The Indian Medical Department (British cadre) owed a very special debt of gratitude to Gidney. The department, which was attached to the British Army in India, consisted entirely of members of the Community. It gave to the medical service, attached to the British forces, their Assistant Surgeons with Warrant Officer rank, and in the senior ranks of the service a certain number of officers. Gidney had originally entered this department, forging on the way brilliant and perhaps unequalled records of academic and medical distinction. Gidney, however, never lost his attachment for the I.M.D. His dogged representation of their service conditions led, in his life-time, to a vast and almost unrecognisable improvement. The I.M.D. (B.C.) scales of pay were doubled and so also were the pension rates. The Royal College of Surgeons in Britain was opened to members of the I.M.D. (British cadre).

The 1925 London Deputation

Gidney's restless energy chafed increasingly at the unsatisfactory political and legal position of the Community. A reference has already been made to their trinity of status, namely, Natives of India for the purpose of employment, European British subjects for certain defence purposes, and non-Europeans vis-a-vis the British Army. Gidney felt that the time had come for a deputation to the British Government, backed by the whole strength of the Community. It will be recalled that John Ricketts carried a well-known petition, in 1830, which was placed before the British Parliament. In spite of the rather formal and cool reception which Ricketts' petition received it did help to attract the attention of the British Parliament to the then unsatisfactory position of the Community. After that there would appear to have been other representations or even deputations, but they were not publicised : apparently they were not only unsung but virtually still-born. A deputation seems to have gone to England in 1897. Nothing is known as to the character or composition of that deputation or what it sought to achieve.

In November, 1923, Herbert Stark waited on Peel, the then Secretary of State. This would appear to have been a very single-handed effort of which little, if any, notice was taken. Gidney, however, with his flair for organisation, orchestrated his move with plenty of publicity. At that time, unfortunately, there was a multiplicity of Anglo-Indian organisations. Be it said to their credit that they rallied behind Gidney. Allahabad, Bengal and Burma gave their full support. Only the Madras organisation, which preened itself on its ancient lineage and apparently was content to rest on its crutches, stood aside. Gidney was accompanied by Charles Griffith of the Bengal Legislature. In London the deputation was increased to include A.B. Kunning, President of the London Anglo-Indian Association and H.A. Gibbon, its Secretary. The deputation was given 4 days' notice of its meeting with Lord Birkenhead, the Secretary of State. Gidney was at his best in periods of stress and urgency. He engaged relays of stenographers and worked from early morning to early next morning. Ultimately his memorandum was ready for submission to Birkenhead. With Birkenhead were Lord Winterton, Sir Arthur Hirtzel, Sir Campbell Rhodes and officials of the India Office. Birkenhead was known for his domineering and even supercilious manner. At the beginning of the meeting there appeared to be signs of a clash between two men with almost equally aggressive outlooks. Incidentally it is interesting to note that the former F.E. Smith had as his crest the polished Latinism, 'Faber Meae Fortunae', 'The Smith of my own Fortune'. The Anglo-Indian leader who had forged his fortune against much greater odds had for his motto, 'The Impossible is Possible'. Birkenhead wanted an assurance from Gidney that the proceedings would be treated as completely confidential. Gidney, however, maintained that in fairness to his Community the memorandum, which was virtually a public document, should not be kept secret. Birkenhead relented and agreed that a communique would be issued and invited Gidney to help in its formulation. The memorandum emphasised the special difficulties of the Community with regard to its political and legal position in the Country, the threat to its employment in the services, its economic and cultural well-being and to several other important items.

One feature of the memorandum underlined Gidney's own difficult position. As a leader Gidney was not able to move far ahead of the Community psychologically. Among his political opponents, particularly Abbott and Stark, there was always the tendency to accuse Gidney of abandoning their British heritage. There has always been a strong section in the Community which flaunts a pathetic and almost pathological nostalgia for the green fields of England which most of them have never seen. Because of this, we find in the memorandum an attempt to secure recognition for the Community as a group of permanent British settlers. This claim was received with perplexity by the India Office and evoked well-merited ridicule in India. The slow-moving machinery of the India Office and of the Government of India took three years to digest the memorandum and to produce a reply. The most important result of the deputation was that the legal and political position of the Community was recognised and found expression in a communique issued by the Home Department of the Government of India. The right of the Community to preserve its cultural and social identity was recognised and also its right to freedom from any kind of discrimination in recruitment to the services as Natives of India. The plea of the deputation for an Anglo-Indian military unit and also for a training-ship was rejected. Apart from clarifying the position of the Community and thus allaying the fear of expulsion of the Community from the services, it also helped to make clear to Anglo-Indians the fact that they were part of the Indian nation although entitled to preserve their own cultural and social identity.

The Simon Commission

In his work before the Simon Commission and later during the three sessions of the Round Table Conference Gidney soared to even greater heights. On the announcement of the Indian Statutory Commission, popularly known as the Simon Commission, Gidney made an appeal for a united effort by the Community. Even Barton and Stark came forward to cooperate. Gidney was unwell during the preparation of the memorandum, but left his sick bed to dominate the proceedings of the Association. Finally the memorandum, a bulky document, was produced. In some respects it was rather irrelevant. It was, in many parts, a repetition of the memorandum to Lord Birkenhead. On the completion of the memorandum Gidney had it published. This caused an immediate break with Stark and Barton who accused Gidney of breach of faith. Yet it is difficult to see how the document, which was meant for publication, could have been kept under the table. The memorandum was received by the Indian Press with scathing denunciation. The 'Bengalee' of Calcutta condemned the "Gidney Manifesto" and the "Eternal mendicant attitude towards the Government and the British mercantile class which was the bane of Anglo-Indian politics."

When the Commission returned to India, on its second visit, Gidney did not find a place in the Indian Joint Parliamentary Committee. He resented this exclusion and had to accept appointment as adviser to Sir Arthur Froome, the European Representative. Incidentally, Froome had little, if any, interest in Anglo-Indian affairs. On the 26th November, 1928, the Anglo-Indian delegation consisting of Gidney, the Rev. G.C. Rogers, the Rev. Mr. Hobson, Mr. McGuire, the Rev. Mr. Curtis, Mr. Cameron and Mr. McCluskie met the Commission. Many years later, the Rev. George Rogers reminisced to me on the way in which Gidney towered over the rest of the delegation. He had the latest facts and figures at his finger-tips and was able to reply readily and convincingly to questions put to him by members of the Commission.

On one matter, however, the delegation blundered. Unlike the European Association, which could afford to have the services of an expensive constitutional lawyer, the Anglo-Indian delegation had no such resources at its disposal. When asked to formulate precisely the kind of statutory safeguards, which Gidney was so insistent on, particularly in respect of protection for the Community in the services, of their education and their political representation, no ready-made formula was forthcoming. This was unfavourably commented upon by several newspapers including 'The Statesman'. Needless to say, it was seized upon by armchair critics, of which there are plenty in the Community, as a suitable stick with which to beat Gidney and the Association. Nevertheless when the report of the Simon Commission emerged in the latter part of 1930, it bore ample testimony to the extent to which they had been deeply impressed by the evidence given before them by the Anglo-Indian delegation and more especially by Gidney. The need for the protection of the interests of the Community in respect of service quotas, education and additional political representation in the legislatures was fully recognised by the Commission.

The Round Table Conference

Gidney's performance at the Round Table Conference, which had three distinct sessions, represented perhaps the piece-de-resistance of his record of work for the Community. The All-India Anglo-Indian Association had moved the Government to give the Community representation at the Conference. This demand was, fortunately for the Community, granted. The first session of the Conference was opened in the House of Lords by King George V. The British Prime Minister, Ramsay MacDonald, spoke next. At this formal opening 5 persons were selected to speak from the Indian delegation, among whom was Gidney. Gidney actually spoke on the 18th November, 1930. Inevitably, he stressed the need for adequate protection for the minorities. He underlined the recent increasing experience of the Community of encroachment on its economic position. He also emphasised the services of the Community both to India and to the British administration. According to the London Times, his concluding sentence was the most striking epigram heard at the first session of the Round Table Conference. Gidney concluded, "I want to ensure that a reformed India will not result in a de-formed Anglo-India." The Conference resolved itself into several sub-committees. Gidney was appointed to those dealing with the minorities, franchise, defence and the services. Before the Services Sub-Committee Gidney made such an impassioned appeal outlining the special disabilities, the deteriorating economic position of the Community, that he won a unanimous resolution from all sections of this Committee recommending that "The Public Services Commission should be instructed to give special consideration and employment to Anglo-Indians in the Government services."

It is not possible to give any detailed account of Gidney's work both inside and outside the Conference. Outside he canvassed support from every available quarter. One person deserving of special mention is Lord Burnham. Gidney enlisted Burnham's support to such an extent that, although ill, Burnham lost no opportunity of pleading the case of the Anglo-Indians both in committee and outside. It was a tragic blow to Gidney, when after having arranged to send a special bouquet of flowers to Burnham on a particular morning, for his courtesy and continuing interest, Gidney opened the papers to find the announcement of Burnham's sudden death. Gidney attributed Burnham's death to the fact that only a day before, although ill, Burnham had pleaded with great emotional fervour that the European Association should support the Anglo-Indian case. Up to that point the European Association members had evinced little, if any, interest in the Anglo-Indian case. On his return to Bombay in March 1931, as a mark of Gidney's ceaseless and valuable efforts the Viceroy sent him a telegram of congratulation. Higher recognition was yet to follow. In June, 1931, a Knighthood was conferred on him in the King's Birthday Honours List. A few months later at Buckingham Palace Gidney had a private audience with the King after his investiture. One of his reminiscences was that the King smiled when Gidney, talking to him of the Anglo-Indians, referred to them as "my people", and then quickly corrected himself by saying "Your Majesty's people and my Community".

It is a sad and, for the Community, a discreditable reflection that Gidney's work at the first Round Table Conference, which was to bear such full and requiting fruit for the Community, was marred by a malicious attack on him by a leprous clique of Anglo-Indians who gave their mushroom association the high-sounding designation of the Loyalist Legion. They went around passing resolutions of no confidence against Gidney. That discreditable conduct on the part of a few malicious people, unfortunately had an unsavoury reaction even on the Anglo-Indian Association. At its Annual General Meeting some of the members put Gidney a series of questions in the form of a questionnaire. Although Gidney satisfactorily answered all their questions to the extent that even the questioners joined in passing a unanimous vote of confidence in him, yet the ignorant and the malicious often referred to this unfortunate incident.

The second session of the Round Table Conference was perhaps the most important as it was attended by Mahatma Gandhi. The Congress Party had withdrawn its civil disobedience movement and agreed to participate in this second session. Hindu-Muslim differences were inevitably the central issue. There was a danger that the problems of the smaller minorities would be relegated to the background. Gidney entered into the fray and did his best to bring about some kind of communal rapprochement. The Mahatma was prepared to concede a dominant position to the Muslims in those States in which they formed the majority, particularly in Bengal and the Punjab. His one precondition was that there should be joint electorates. Gidney opposed the idea of joint electorates, as, in his opinion, it would lead to the dissolution of the minorities. The Sikhs were also implacable in their opposition to the Muslims being given a majority vote in the Punjab Legislature. When a position of complete stalemate had been reached Gidney persevered with the other minority community leaders and ultimately a minority report was submitted which formed the background of the British Prime Minister's Communal Award. Gidney claimed that he was, in fact, the father of this minority report. This second session of the Round Table Conference lasted from September to December, 1931.

The third and the last session of the Round Table Conference was comparatively short. As usual, it saw Gidney using every conceivable occasion to plead the case of the Community for the protection of their education and their position in the services. The most important result of Gidney's work at the third session of the Round Table Conference was the acceptance of the Irwin Committee report on education and of the need for according special protection to Anglo-Indian education.

After the conclusion of the third session of the Conference Gidney had to await the White Paper, which was to embody the recommendations. On this would be based the new Act and also the deliberations of the Parliamentary Joint Select Committee, which was to meet to consider this White Paper. When the White Paper was issued Gidney had every reason to be gratified. There the recommendation of increased political representation for the Community. Four seats were to be granted to it in the Central Assembly and one in the Council of States (the Upper House). There was also the recommendation of statutory protection for Anglo-Indian education. Gidney, who was one of the few Indian delegates to be included in all the three sessions of the Round Table Conference, was associated with the work of the Parliamentary

Joint Select Committee. As a matter of fact, he adopted the unusual procedure of offering himself for examination and cross-examination by the Committee, so that he would have the greatest possible opportunity of placing every aspect of the Community's case before the Select Committee. Even after his return to India Gidney continued to maintain the closest contact with the members of this Joint Select Committee and more especially with Lord Hardinge and Sir Reginald Craddock. At Gidney's instance Hardinge submitted to the Committee a special memorandum on behalf of the Community. As a cumulative result of Gidney's efforts the Government of India published a resolution of the Home Department dated the 4th July, 1934. This resolution undertook to secure for the Community an overall 8% of all those posts with which the Community was then associated.

Statutory Safeguards

In the meantime the report of the Parliamentary Joint Select Committee was published. While it contained a sympathetic reference to the Community, there was no recommendation for any statutory provision with regard to protection of the Community's service interests. Gidney was understandably disappointed. He was not prepared to entrust the fate of the Community to resolutions or to Instruments of Instruction issued to the Viceroy or to the Governors. In his opinion these Instruments of Instruction, in the case of minorities, usually operated as instruments of destruction. Gidney immediately moved the Viceroy and the Secretary of State, but evoked nothing more than a stereotyped acknowledgment of his protest and request for statutory protection. In the British House of Commons, Sir Reginald Craddock, on Gidney's insistence, moved an amendment for the incorporation of a provision in the Government of India Bill that at least when making appointments of Anglo-Indians to the Railways, the Customs and the Posts and Telegraphs, due consideration should be given to their past association with these services. The amendment was discussed in the House of Commons in April 1935. Colonel Applin, President of the London Anglo-Indian Association, unfortunately pressed the amendment to a division. This would appear to have been bad tactics as the Secretary of State had replied that he would give further consideration to this amendment. When Applin's amendment was pressed the matter was closed against the Community, so far as the House of Commons was concerned. All this happened while Gidney was champing at the bit in India. His ardent and emotional nature had to endure seeing what he regarded as a vital safeguard for the Community gradually being effaced from the legislative anvil. Typically, he suddenly made a decision to dash to London. His public enemies and even the Governing Body of the Anglo-Indian Association felt that he was embarking on a wild-goose chase. With the rejection of Craddock's attempt to get a special provision in the Government of India Bill to protect the service position of the Community, it was considered completely illusory on Gidney's part to hope to achieve anything when the Bill was being considered by the House of Lords. At this supreme moment Gidney lived his motto, 'The Impossible is Possible.' On his arrival in London he immediately had a discussion with Lord Hardinge. He then saw R.A. Butler, Parliamentary Under-Secretary of State for India, who gave him a sympathetic hearing. Gidney now decided that what was known as the Diehard Party was his last chance, though obviously a slim one, for getting an amendment moved in the House of Lords. He went to the committee room of this party and was met by the Secretary who listened courteously to Gidney's complaint.

The Secretary then went into the adjoining room where the members of the party were in conference. There was only a thin partition between Gidney and this room. What was said could be overheard in the conference room. When the Secretary came to him and regretted the inability of the party to meet Gidney, as they had no time, Gidney's pent-up emotions erupted. He said he found it difficult to believe that any body of Englishmen would deny him a hearing when he had travelled 7,000 miles to present the demand of a Community which had special claims on the British. Gidney urged that the party should hear him even for a few minutes. The Secretary retired and came back to inform Gidney that they would give him a hearing. Among those present were Lord Rankellieur, Chyde and Lady Atholl and the Marquis of Salisbury. Gidney being master of his brief, and inspired by emotion, poured forth his case precisely but surcharged with feeling. The Secretary of the Party was asked to draw up a brief for Lord Lloyd. Gidney then phoned Lord Lloyd who agreed to move the amendment. Lord Lloyd entered the House of Lords and, because of lack of time, handed a manuscript amendment to the Lord Chancellor. Lord Hailsham, the Lord Chancellor, announced that he had received an amendment from Lord Lloyd on very short notice and, according to the procedure, asked if the House was prepared to accept it. Lord Zetland, the Under-Secretary of State for India, complained that he had received no notice, but did not oppose the amendment. Less than an hour after the handing in of the manuscript amendment, it was reached on the order list.

Lloyd got up and made a brilliant and moving speech on behalf of the Community. To quote only a few sentences from his speech : "I beg your Lordships to protect them if only in memory of their wonderful past services, and of the great sacrifices they made for us in the war. There was no Community who fought better for us in different parts of the world.......... If I have spoken a little strongly, it is because I feel very deeply about the Community. We had created them; they are our own blood; they are the result of our civilization there."

Lord Zetland rose apparently to oppose Lord Lloyd's motion, but before he could catch the Lord Chancellor's eye Lord Hardinge rose in his seat and was called. Hardinge made an even more brilliant and moving speech than Lord Lloyd. There was a visible change in the atmosphere, for many of the members, in increasing numbers, nodded their heads in approval. It would appear that Hardinge had swung both the Government and the Opposition benches in support of the motion. Zetland was in a difficult position. He sensed the feeling of the House. He knew that if he pressed it to a division, the Government would lose and the Prime Minister had made it clear that any defeat would be accepted as a censure motion. Zetland replied that he did not think that the amendment would carry the position of the Community much further, but that he would redraft the amendment and make it more definite. On this assurance Lord Lloyd withdrew his amendment on the understanding that he would introduce a redrafted amendment later. After that Gidney met the Diehard Party Committee.

Finally there emerged the draft, which appeared later as Section 242 of the Government of India Act of 1935. This amendment was accepted unanimously by the House of Lords. It then came back to the House of the Commons. Sir Austen Chamberlain and Mr. Butler gave their complete support to the amendment and it was accepted. Gidney's last-minute and seemingly hopeless effort had succeeded beyond the wildest dreams of many of the Community's most ardent well-wishers. Lord Wolmer was constrained to write to Gidney, "It is I and all of us who should congratulate you on your signal triumph in getting such an important series of amendments carried at the last moment. This is indeed a notable achievement which I think is without parallel in our parliamentary annals and I do most heartily congratulate you and your Community on the result." It took the Government of India several years before they issued the resolution, Home Department No. 14/5/38, dated May 1st, 1939. This resolution was in amplification of the Government of India resolution of July, the 4th 1934, and carried out the intention of Section 242 more precisely and completely. According to this resolution the Community were to have reservations of $2\frac{1}{2}\%$ of the direct recruitment to the superior railway service, 40% in the telegraphist cadre, 3% of all vacancies in the Appraiser Department of the Customs which were filled by direct recruitment, and 8% on the Railways in posts with which the Community had past association. As hitherto, there was a 50% reservation for the Community in the Preventive cadre of the Customs service.

Gidney also had a last-minute amendment moved in Parliament with regard to the educational guarantees for the Community. This amendment also was submitted in manuscript form. It sought to confine the benefit of the grants for the Community only to those who satisfied the definition of the term 'Anglo-Indian' in the First Schedule of the 1935 Act. The Marquis of Zetland opposed this amendment by saying that while the Governor-General and the Governors would ensure that the interests of the Community would be adequately protected, these schools catered not only for the Anglo-Indian Community, but for Europeans, Jews, Armenians and, at that time, about 20% of other Indian communities. The grants, except for the indigent grants, given ad hoc to Anglo-Indians, were to go to the schools for the benefit of all the children in those schools.

In Gidney's continuous struggle to maintain and, if possible, strengthen the position of the Community, the provisions of the

Government of India Act were his strongest and best weapons. They enabled him to resist the constant pressure in the Legislature directed against the employment of the members of the Community. While the safeguards were intended to provide a minimum of employment for the Community, the D'Souza Report submitted on the railway administration showed that while in the Company-owned Railways more than 8% of the Community used to be recruited, on the State-owned railways this 8% was interpreted as a maximum, and not as a minimum. These guarantees also enabled Gidney to resist the constant pressure on the Community particularly during the regime of Sir Gurunath Bewoor, Director-General of Posts and Telegraphs, who seemed to transpose his personal hostility to Gidney against the Community in the Telegraph Department.

Education

A criticism has been made, although not quite fairly, that Gidney did not take a sufficient interest in Anglo-Indian education. This criticism has to be assessed in the context of the conditions which governed Anglo-Indian education during Gidney's public life. In about 1934 there were approximately 362 schools which were known by the designation Anglo-Indian. Of this number 153 were controlled by Roman Catholic orders with about 34,000 pupils; 79 were run by the Anglican orders with about 12,000 pupils; other religious bodies administered 23 schools with about 3,000 pupils; there were 21 non-denominational schools with a little over 2,000 pupils; 76 Railway schools with about 5,000 pupils; there were also 10 Government-owned Anglo-Indian schools with about 1,500 pupils. There was thus a total of 362 schools with about 55,000 pupils, and about 43,000 were shown as belonging to the Anglo-Indian and European communities. It will thus be seen that the education of the Community was preponderately in the hands of the clerical orders. These orders were fanatically jealous of their autonomy and denied any kind of place to the Community in the direction of Anglo-Indian education. Except for one or two institutions, even where lay educationists were appointed all the upper posts were reserved for Europeans.

Gidney did his best to break down this European caste hegemony in Anglo-Indian schools, but was up against a blank wall of race and colour discrimination.

Gidney also attacked both the race and colour discrimination which was rampant in many of these schools. He complained bitterly of the numerous instances of this discrimination which he contantly saw for himself or which were brought to his notice. Among the teachers there was generally a false sense of values. Europeans had little, if any, identity of interest with their pupils. Even the best of them, because of the social scheme in India, served only to inculcate an inferiority complex in their pupils. The Anglo-Indian teachers also, in many institutions, sedulously tried to escape from the fact that they were Anglo-Indians. With this escapist complex they were hardly the proper psychological mentors for their impressionable wards. Gidney tells of an instance, which in his opinion was not untypical, when a group photograph was taken not only of the staff but of the pupils, the darker members were deliberately kept out of focus. Although the education was in many respects good and better than that available in the best schools run by other communities, the underlying purpose of education of making a person true to himself was overlooked or even perverted. Few, if any, Anglo-Indians emerged from these schools with their values in proper perspective. Thus Gidney tells of an occasion when during a tour of South India he visited a school. He asked the Anglo-Indian boys as to who is an Anglo-Indian. One replied that he is a half-caste and the other a Domiciled European. Gidney bitterly commented that the basic purpose of education was thus not served in most of these schools. The pupils were indoctrinated, if not with contempt for themselves with contempt for things Indian.

Nevertheless, in his own way, Gidney fought strenuously for the strengthening of Anglo-Indian education. He realised that these schools, whatever their psychological shortcomings, represented the nerve centre of the cultural existence of the Community. Before the Simon Commission he devoted a large part of his evidence and his memorandum to the need for proper safeguards.

Anglo-Indian Education

The Hartog Committee, which was an auxiliary of the Simon Commission, made a valuable survey of Anglo-Indian education. Under the Montague-Chelmsford Reforms Anglo-Indian education was a reserved subject in the provincial sphere. This meant that the legislature could vote on the grants but the final decision rested with the Governor who could, if a cut was imposed, restore it. It had been suggested by Stark and submitted as a recommendation to the Simon Commission that Anglo-Indian education should be a central subject. It was strongly felt that if this was conceded then, at any rate, the Anglo-Indian schools would have to deal with one and not several legislatures. The Hartog Committee, however, found against centralisation of control.

Gidney also resisted all attempts to hand over Railway schools, which were administered from the Centre, to the States. He did not wish these to fall victim to the different and often conflicting policies in the different States. As already mentioned, Gidney's outstanding achievement at the third session of the Round Table Conference was the appointment of a Committee known as the Irwin Committee to examine and report on the subject of Anglo-Indian education. The Committee consisted of Lord Irwin as Chairman, with Sir Hubert Carr, Sir Campbell Rhodes, Mr. Jayakar, Sir Mohammad Iqbal and Gidney as members. The Report made three notable recommendations. Anglo-Indian grants could only be reduced by a 3/4ths majority vote of the total number of members in the Legislature. The constitution of the Legislatures and the large majority required made it virtually impossible for a reduction to be effected. According to another recommendation, the Government was asked to set up Statutory Boards of Anglo-Indian education in the States. A vitally important recommendation was the setting up of the Inter-Provincial Board for Anglo-Indian and European Education. Although Gidney's plea for centralisation of control had been rejected, yet through this Board a great measure of coordination and uniformity was hoped to be achieved.

Understandably, Gidney had always fought for a reasonable measure of control of Anglo-Indian education being in the hands of the Community. But this was implacably resisted by the religious orders. The unfortunate intensity not only of religious but of denominational feeling was exhibited at the time of the setting up of the Advisory Boards on Anglo-Indian Education. The religious orders resented the setting up of these boards, as they felt they would lead to the intrusion by the Community in the direction of Anglo-Indian education. Not only did they resist the appointment of

Anglo-Indians, but they also engaged in a regular dog-fight for deno-minational representation. The Viceroy held a private meeting in order to settle the constitution of these boards. In Gidney's words, "I was the only 'Brownie' against a phalanx of British Kodaks."

Regrettably, both the European and the religious interests won. The Community was reduced to a minority and the retrograde principle of denominational representation was virtually accepted.

Gidney always resisted the plea by the clerical orders that the Community had no right to intervene in educational direction and policy. He based the claims of the Community on the fact that at least half of the expenditure in a school was met by the fees received from Anglo-Indian parents; at least another one-third of the expenditure was met from Government grants given for the benefit of the Anglo-Indian Community. He, therefore, argued that, even from the financial point of view, two-thirds of the school expenditure came from or on behalf of the Community. Another glaring commentary on the racialism practised in education at this time was Gidney's deliberate exclusion from the Inter-Provincial Board for Anglo-Indian Education. Gidney was anxious to be the Chairman of the Board. Instead, unfortunately because of the pressure by the then Metropolitan of India, an obscure European was nominated to the Board and became its first Chairman.

Gidney was always anxious to give some kind of financial stabi-lity to the position of Anglo-Indian education. It was to the Simon Commission and later to the Irwin Committee that Gidney made the plea that 50 lakhs should be funded for the benefit of Anglo-Indian education. These pleas were rejected on both occasions. When the Archbishop of Canterbury issued an appeal in 1938 for raising funds for Anglo-Indian schools, Gidney supported this appeal very strongly. Incidentally, the scheme was, later on, sponsored by the Duke of Gloucester. It is interesting to note that a previous appeal had been made in 1911, with the blessings of the King. The target of the 1911 appeal was £250,000. In fact only £90,000 were collected, the major portion being donated by Sir Robert Laidlaw. The response to the 1938 appeal was very much less. Gidney's complaint was that while Britain could raise millions of pounds for the Jews and give the Assyrians 250,000 pounds for a national home, it was unwilling to raise even 300,000 pounds for a community of its making and to which it owed so much.

Unemployment

The evil of unemployment has always bedevilled the Community. There has always been a certain residuum of unemployment in the Community. As in all communities a fraction of the residuum has been the unemployable: but the major part of the unemployment in the Community has been a reflection of the utterly backward economy of the Country. Unemployment in India has perhaps hit most fiercely the middle and the lower-middle classes. And the Community falls predominantly into these strata. The two most acute periods of unemployment in the Community were after World Wars I and II. In his own way, Gidney did his best at least to palliate the incidence and the appalling consequences of unemployment in the Community. The worst period after World War I, when unemployment in the Community reached its most distressing peak, was perhaps in 1923. Gidney sought to focus attention by a letter which was published in 'The Statesman' of July 1923. In that letter he gave a graphic, if heart-rending, description of the conditions prevailing in Calcutta, where there was the largest concentration of the Community. Also in Calcutta there has been the acutest manifestation of unemployment in the Community. "Take a stroll", he wrote, "through the New Market or Chowringhee and you will be accosted by scores of starving Anglo-Indian men and youths, mostly in rags, showing all the ravages of hunger in their emaciated faces, begging for food. Visit the various parks and maidans after 11 p.m. and you will, at times, see European and Anglo-Indian men, women and children who have in vain tramped the streets all day long in quest of employment, sleeping with the turf as their bed and the sky as their roof. Others wend their way to the business quarters anxiously waiting for returning tiffin boys to whom they readily offer a few pice for the bones and crumbs left over from their masters' tiffins. Take a walk along the bye-lanes of Bow Bazaar Street or of Entally and there you will find even the stables occupied by Anglo-Indian families; starving men, women and children, sleeping alongside the animals in the stables. Visit the neighbourhood of Sealdah or the bye-lanes of Upper Circular Road, where you will find these people living under conditions so gruesome as to defy description.... Here you will see men wearing three or four medals, huddled together and living with their families in indescribable filth, squalor and destitution, their faces bearing marked evidence of utter misery and starvation."

In spite of Gidney's intense emotional involvement in the problem, the picture he painted was not exaggerated. It found confirmation in a series of letters contributed by others interested in the problem and also by unemployed Anglo-Indians themselves.

Gidney formed the idea of establishing employment bureaux in Calcutta, Madras, Bombay and Karachi. Unfortunately, his efforts, both at that time and later on, proved abortive. Gidney, however, continued his attempts, both personal and through the Association, to relieve the problem. As an individual he helped to secure jobs for many persons. Apart from constantly badgering the Government to address itself to the problem of middle-class unemployment, Gidney also resisted retrenchment of members of the Community. Thus he charged the Railway administration with deliberately discharging members of the Community to make way for those whom the administration referred to as 'Indians'. Several Anglo-Indians had in their possession documents in which it was unequivocally stated that they had been retrenched in order to give place to 'Indians'. Thus, one Mr. Fenton, the Chief Transportation Officer of the Great Indian Peninsular Railway, addressed Gidney personally saying that his railway had to discontinue employing Anglo-Indians in order to get cheaper 'Indian' labour.

An unemployment committee was formed in Calcutta consisting of a number of Europeans: Gidney was also on this committee. The Bengal Government had formed a committee of enquiry to investigate the causes of unemployment among the middle classes in Bengal. The terms of reference of this committee were extended, in 1923, to include the question of unemployed Anglo-Indians. A large amount of money was collected by the committee. A soup kitchen was also started, which at one time provided 40,000 meals a year.

In 1930 the unemployment position again became bad. A survey conducted by the Anglo-Indian Youth League, in 1936, showed that the position at that time was also acute.

Colonization And Emigration

Gidney's outlook was tinged with a certain pessimism. Thus he felt that without statutory safeguards the position of the

Community would steadily deteriorate. Gidney always anticipated hostility on the part of the 'Indians', as he called them,
towards the Anglo-Indians. Because of this, every now and then
we find a tendency to seek either an enclave for the Community in
the Country or some kind of homeland. This inclination on Gidney's
part was accentuated in times of depression in the Community,
particularly in the years 1923-24. Gidney acquired considerable
enthusiasm for the idea of colonising the Andamans and Nicobar
islands by the Community. He went to the extent of studying the
agricultural, mineral, timber and other resources and potential
resources of these islands. He even approached Lord Leverhulme,
the soap magnate, who undertook to buy all the copra that could
be produced from these islands. Gidney estimated that copra
alone would bring in a total annual revenue of 4 million pounds.

The idea was developed of sending a batch of Anglo-Indians
as the spearhead of this colonisation scheme. The Ex-services
Association was entrusted with the selection of a team of 12 men.
They also undertook to pay Rs. 30/- a month per person for their
food. The prison barracks in the Andamans were to be used for
the purposes of housing. This scheme aroused ardent enthusiasm
in some sections. When it failed there was a corresponding reaction of bitter disappointment. Much of this disappointment was
ultimately directed against Gidney and the blame for the failure of
this venture was placed at his door. But it was a venture fore-
doomed to failure. The Senior Medical Officer, an I.M.S. man
in the Andamans, warned that the scheme was not practicable.
He pointed out that all previous attempts at colonisation had failed
largely because of a virulent form of malaria, particularly in the
Nicobars. It was estimated that it would cost at least two million
pounds for the drainage of these malaria-stricken areas. In the
next place, there was no purposeful attempt to place adequate
resources at the disposal of these pioneers. Apart from the Rs 30/-
a month for their food, not a single rupee was given to them for
implements and the minimum requirements for any agricultural
scheme.

There have been several attempts at forming colonies by the
Community. Whitefield, near Bangalore, attracted a fair number
of members of the Community. Another settlement was established at Mogra, now known as Clement Town, near Dehra Dun.

Perhaps, the most ambitious colonisation scheme launched was by E.T. McCluskie. McCluskie was at one time a lieutenant of Gidney. When he launched the scheme there was some estrangement between them. A self-made man, who had started from humble beginnings, McCluskie organised the scheme with considerable energy. About 300 families settled in Lapra, which later came to be known as McCluskiegunj. At first Gidney was indifferent, if not opposed, to the scheme. Ultimately, on the death of McCluskie, he was persuaded to become President of the Colonisation Society, which was the controlling body of McCluskiegunj. Gidney acquired a great deal of enthusiasm for McCluskiegunj and in his own way gave them a lot of assistance, particularly in the matter of having a road built to Ranchi. A small colony was started at Salur which met with very little success. Some members of the Community also settled at Jhargram on the then Bengal-Nagpur Railway.

Anglo-Indians In The Armed Forces

Gidney constantly came back to the charge, seeking an adequate outlet for the Community's aptitude in the armed forces. His plea to Birkenhead, later to the Simon Commission and then before the Round Table Conference for the setting up of an Anglo-Indian regiment failed.

It would appear that the British authorities preferred to get the Anglo-Indians to undertake the odious task of internal policing and defence by giving them paltry volunteer allowances. Thus, the Indian Defence Force, as it was originally named, was predominantly drawn from the ranks of the Community. This force of about 30,000 men was later renamed the Auxiliary Force. Gidney often referred to this body of men as representing India's second line of defence. To Nationalist India, however, it was perhaps more appropriately defined as the second line of offence, in the sense that it gave offence to nationalist sentiment. From the security point of view this force of Anglo-Indians served a vital purpose. When India was denuded of military forces in World War I, the I.D.F. was the only body that could be relied on to enforce law and order in the Country. Unfortunately, the Community's position was not only embarrassed but compromised by the fact that this force was used, without any qualms, by the British to suppress any form of civil unrest. The police forces were usually either too weak, too unreliable or too communally partisan for the purpose.

Gidney was never able to break down the blank wall of prejudice which informed British policy in rejecting the claims of the Community for a regular battalion. He recalled that as far back as 1906, 30 Anglo-Indians were sent to the Training Ship 'Humber' with the Royal Navy. Although they were favourably reported on, the Royal Navy refused to accept them after their training. In spite of British prejudice and churlish policies, in times of stress the blind faith of the Community, which made it volunteer without reserve, was accepted with alacrity when the British nation had its back to the wall.

Exodus And Infiltration

Gidney was usually concerned about what he referred to as a leakage from the top and adulteration at the bottom, in the Community. Gidney was not a biologist or an anthropologist. For this reason he was not able to see in perspective this inevitable biological process which has occurred throughout human history in every nation and racial group. A number of members of the Community, particularly those, as Gidney put it, at the other end of the pigmentary spectrum, were constantly merging with the British community. Attracted by the lure of reserved quotas for the Community in the services, Goans especially and Indian Christians were constantly accreting. Gidney was perhaps unduly perturbed by this accretion. The distinction has to be drawn between accretion and assimilation. As long as there is assimilation from socially and culturally acceptable strata, biologists agree that there can be no scientific objection to this process which occurs in every racial group. The cultural and economic objection is valid when accretion is at the lowest level—such types are a drag on the Community and are, in fact, not assimilated to the Community's way of life and thinking. I deal with this question more fully in the chapter entitled, 'The Social and Psychological Pattern'. Kenneth Wallace, Gidney's biographer, tells us that when Gidney was shown those who claimed to be of Indo-Portuguese descent in Cochin, he raised his hands in horror because in Cochin the large majority had completely merged with the labourers in Cochin and were to be seen engaged either in the fields or at their fishing nets. They knew no English, their mother-tongue was the local language. Culturally, linguistically there was nothing to distinguish them from the local labourers and fishermen. This objection could be understood, because these persons, whatever their alleged origin, had lost all traces, if they had any at any time, of cultural and social affinity which could give them any kinship with the Community.

Gidney lost few opportunities to criticise those Anglo-Indians who posed as domiciled Europeans. He referred to them sometimes as "Albino" Anglo-Indians, on other occasions as "Domestic Occurrences" and perhaps, most incisively, as "Rear-Rank Europeans". The British community itself regarded this intermediate class of so-called "Domiciled Europeans" often with ill-concealed contempt.

The impact of this renegadism was amply demonstrated in the census returns. Gidney's estimate was that at least 50,000 members of the Community had been shown, in the 1931 census, in the European electorate.

Connoisseur Art Collector

Gidney was a well-known art collector. As a matter of fact he was a connoisseur. Gidney not only had the grand manner, but he also carried this attitude of the grandee into his domestic life. Wherever he lived, he did so in an atmosphere of colourful amplitude. His residence at 87-A, Park Street, Calcutta, and later on at 122, Prithvi Raj Road, New Delhi, would have eclipsed in many respects the trappings of a British Governor's residence. Gidney had been a not negligible shikari. During his earlier years in the I.M.S. he took full opportunity of his postings in Assam, the hunter's paradise, to pursue the pleasures of a big game shikari. He had to his credit 52 tigers, 2 rhinoceros and 4 rogue elephants. Apart from a right and a left tiger, an achievement that not many shikaris can boast of, he had perhaps a unique record with a right and left rhinoceros. It is believed that no shikari in India has ever yet bagged two rhinoceros with a right and left barrel. His house bore testimony to his shikar days—tiger skins, elephant feet and rhinoceros horns.

Gidney's was perhaps the finest private art collection of antiques in the Country. In 1941 he was elected President of the All-India

Arts and Crafts Society in Delhi. Persian carpets lay on the floor of his residence. There were some excellent pieces of porcelain of the Sung and Ming periods and a bronze vase of the Tang period. Georgian and Napoleon glass were some of his prized possessions and also Napoleon porcelain. There was also a beautiful alabaster vase which was said to have belonged at one time to the Marlborough family. Gidney also had some outstanding pieces of Indian carvings, sculpture and brassware. A prized piece was the Mother Goddess, a 10th century piece of sculpture from Khajuraho, where some of the finest temples exhibiting ancient Indian sculpture and architecture are to be found. He had some fine pieces of Moghul and Rajput paintings and also some old English, French and Italian engravings. A beautiful lampstand from a Jain temple and antique brass not only from India but from Persia and Tibet formed part of his varied collection.

The End

I believe that Gidney, in common with other Indian leaders, never envisaged the rapid developments from 1942 which ultimately precipitated a political stampede bringing the sub-continent to Independence. Gidney called a conference in March, 1942, to consider the approach to be made to the Cripps Mission. This was to be his last meeting with the Community. At this time Gidney was far from well. The political background added immeasurably to his mental and physical burdens. Gidney always contemplated, even under the most advanced conditions, a constitution for India where safeguards for the minorities would be imposed by the British Parliament. When Gidney met Sir Stafford Cripps, in 1942, he met a new kind of political phenomenon. Gidney had been accustomed to dealing with Conservative and Liberal Members of Parliament who had an awareness of the British association with India and also a reasonable awareness of the position and needs of the Community. The Socialist Cripps, however, was in the political context what a person without any social background, tradition and family, would be in the social context. Cripps had no inhibitions with regard to past British obligations. He had no political conscience vis-a-vis British political obligations to the Anglo-Indians. Politically Cripps was 'nouveau riche'. From certain points of view this perhaps made his approach to the rapidly changing conditions in India less complicated than that of a Conservative. So far as the Community was concerned Cripps' attitude was not only indifferent but, to Gidney, callously cynical and brazenly opportunistic. Gidney was staggered by Cripps' refusal to give any kind of hope, much less an assurance, of according any place to the Community in the new constitution. Gidney saw his life's work crumbling before his eyes. That is why he convened the conference for evolving from the collective wisdom of its representatives the best methods of meeting the Cripps' approach. Gidney was deeply worried. He felt that the Community had been cynically betrayed by the British. He sent out an anguished cry to the Community, "We have been betrayed by the British at the altar of political expediency." It was in this frame of mind that he met his end. A visit to Igatpuri in the summer to celebrate the golden wedding anniversary of his brother was the last straw. On his way back to Delhi he suffered an attack of sunstroke. Within a couple of days after his arrival in Delhi he passed away on the morning of the 5th May, 1942.

Gidney's mood of depression towards the end and also his bitterness at the ungrateful and even churlish treatment he had often received from the Community were epitomised in a letter which he had written shortly before his death to Kenneth Wallace, his biographer : "I shall spend all my life working for an ungenerous and ungrateful Community. But let me not complain, for, after all, I feel that God is helping me. My health has certainly given me cause for grave concern, and I feel the daily increasing burden of my responsibility is fast bending me. Anyhow, I would rather bust than rust and so I still have my hand on the Community plough till I am called to my ever rest."

Gidney was buried with full military honours. A detachment of British parachute troops provided the pall-bearers and the firing squad. The Viceroy and the Commander-in-Chief were represented among those who followed the cortege. As a mark of respect the Corporations of Calcutta, Madras and Bombay adjourned their meetings. Messages of appreciation and sympathy were put out by Governors of Provinces and leaders of all shades of public opinion. It is a discreditable reflection that while the Government and other communities paid their last tribute to Gidney, his own Community in Delhi, either from indifference or ignorance, failed to do him proper honour. In other centres, however, throughout the Country the Community, through the All-India Anglo-Indian Association, bowed in homage and, indeed, in reverential respect. Gidney continues to be remembered and honoured. At the Annual General Meetings of the All-India Anglo-Indian Association his motto, 'The Impossible is Possible' is conspicuously displayed. Several institutions and clubs are named after him. His birth anniversary, the 9th June, continues to be observed by the Association as 'Gidney Day'.

Was Gidney A Nationalist

If Gidney's attitude, pronouncements and policies are studied objectively, they will perhaps lead to the conclusion that he was hardly a nationalist in his outlook. Thus, before Birkenhead, the Simon Commission and even at the time of the Round Table Conference, Gidney's speeches and utterances were characterised by the distinction he drew between Anglo-Indians on the one hand and 'Indians', as he called them, on the other. Gidney never referred to the Community as Indians. He spoke of statutory natives of India, nationals of India, citizens of India, but it would appear that on no occasion did he describe the Community as a Community of Indians.

Yet, in many ways, Gidney was a progressive. By many sections of Indian opinion he was regarded as liberal and advanced in his thinking. He was accorded several civic receptions; one at Madras in 1934 and another at Lucknow in 1937. These civic bodies were dominated by members of the Congress Party. At these receptions he was welcomed and honoured as an Indian. On these occasions Gidney showed that he was no narrow communalist. He realised that Anglo-Indians could only find their place in India, if they shed their complexes and inhibitions. Speaking at the Lucknow civic reception he pleaded for a national outlook. He emphasised that communalism is the negation of nationalism. Often in his speeches to the Community he exhorted them to identify themselves with the peoples and the interests of India. Speaking at Bangalore, he said, "Deny the fact that you are sons and citizens of India, disclaim it, conceal it in your efforts to ape what you are not, and you will soon be the 'not wanted' of all. The opportunity is yours today to more closely associate yourselves, from early school life, with the rest of India, to realise that you, with all other communities, have a right to live in this, your Country, and that you are first and last sons of India..... But if there is one thing which you must completely eradicate from yourselves it is the retention of the 'superiority' and 'inferiority' complexes; and you should bring about their replacement with a complex of equality."

A constant theme in Gidney's speeches was his denunciation of race and colour discrimination. Thus he condemned unreservedly this discrimination both in the I.C.S. and the I.M.S. He was unqualified in his condemnation of European clubs and of the snobbery practised in them. It is known that he fought strenuously against the ostracism practised by a European Club in Central India against Indian members of the I.M.S. He indicted European women as being the worst offenders in this respect. He fought against the extravagant allowances given to Europeans by the Lee Commission. He referred to these allowances as the 'Lee Loot'.

There is no doubt that Gidney was a progressive leader in the context of the then obtaining attitudes and complexes of the Community. By persons such as Abbott and Stark he was constantly accused of sacrificing the heritage of the Community. Gidney was also confronted with certain inhibitions in the Community. Gidney's policies certainly represented a striking advance on the position taken up by Anglo-Indian leaders who preceded him. He was unqualified in his emphasis that the Anglo-Indians are nationals of India and could only find their proper place if they moved with and accepted the other peoples of India without the inhibitions and complexes of the past. Gidney was ahead of the hard core of Anglo-Indian thinking. Yet he could not go too far ahead for fear of being misunderstood and misrepresented in his own Community.

CHAPTER VII

WORLD WARS I and II

The Burma Epic

THE AUXILIARY FORCE

World War I

FOR many years the leaders of the Community had agitated for restoration of the position prior to 1791 when Anglo-Indians were admitted freely and without discrimination into the British Army. The subject was mooted as far back as 1879. Dr. E.W. Chambers, the President-Founder of what was then known as the Eurasian and Anglo-Indian Association, had raised this question repeatedly. At a meeting held in the Dalhousie Institute in Calcutta in 1885 under the auspices of the Anglo-Indian Association presided over by the Rev. W.H. Bray it was resolved to apply to the Secretary of State for India to move the British Parliament for early sanction of at least one local Anglo-Indian regiment. In a long and able speech, W.C. Madge, CIE, dealt with the military potential of the Community. He referred to the fact that Col. Wooldridge, who commanded a Legion in the Crimean War and held an important post of observation in India during the Mutiny, had submitted a scheme in 1877 for employment of members of the Community. Among other things Col. Wooldridge observed, "I have made it my business, during a residence of 16 years in this country, to occupy my leisure hours in the study of this much neglected people. I can vouch for their personal courage. Their activity and their intelligence compare favourably with the robust frame of the Europeans and there are, moreover, thousands who, after a few months' training, with regular food and proper exercise, may compete with any soldiers in the world."

After the declaration of war on the 5th August, 1914, J.H. Abbott, President-in-Chief of what was then known as the Anglo-Indian Empire League, wired to the Commander-in-Chief offering to raise a regiment of Anglo-Indians for service abroad as well as a corps of women nurses. This offer was, however, declined by the military authorities. In spite of this rebuff the Community did not sulk into a sense of wounded pride. Thousands sought active service wherever it was available to them. By 1916 at least 8000 Anglo-Indians had joined various British units as Europeans. Thus a large number of Anglo-Indians were enlisted in the Dorset Regiment. In the result their identity and records of gallantry were lost to the Community. The Cavalry and the Royal Artillery attracted the Anglo-Indians more than the Infantry. As an old soldier, Reg Newing, the President for many years of the Mc-Cluskiegunj branch of the All-India Anglo-Indian Association, has written, "As Gym Instructors, Signal and Gunnery Instructors they were as good as the best from Britain. In sports they were certainly superior and in the boxing ring as good as the best soldiers from Britain."

On the 15th March, 1916, the Army authorities, after much dragging of feet, sanctioned the raising of an Anglo-Indian Force as an integral part of the British Army. It was decided that in the first instance two Field Troops of Cavalry, one section of Field Artillery and 16 platoons of Infantry should be raised. This belated sanction was received with mixed feelings by the leaders of the Community, although they welcomed the removal of the colour bar which was the real obstacle. Thousands of the best material in the Community had already entered British regiments as Europeans.

Of the Anglo-Indian units the Anglo-Indian Battery was the most popular. It was located at Jhansi and attached to the 77th Royal Field Artillery. Commenting on the quality of the men Lt. Col. Grove, Commandant, 77th Royal Field Artillery, said, "You have, besides your keenness, shown that you have plenty of stamina and your discipline has been good from start to finish. My opinion is that you as a Battery are equal to most and better than some, and that with very little more training you will be able, if called upon, to go to the front, and render an account of yourselves there."

On the 2nd of October, 1916, the Anglo-Indian Battery left Rawalpindi for the front. They were seen off amidst scenes of enthusiasm at Karachi on Monday, the 23rd October, 1916. The quality of the men was such that although the original decision was to constitute only one Field Section consisting of one Lieutenant and 70 NCOs and men, the number was increased to three Lieutenants and about 300 NCOs and men.

Commenting on the service of the Battery on the fighting front the Adjutant-General of India, on the 8th October, 1917, stated, "The General Officer Commanding Force 'D' has reported favourably on the services rendered by the Anglo-Indian Units employed in Mesopotamia and has stated that he would be glad to have more of them if available." Men from all sections of the Community had joined. Those from the highest rung, socially and educationally, educationists, teachers, graduates, professional and business men worked and fought besides those from the lowest.

Apart from their qualities in the field, they were more than able to hold their own in other competitions. Thus No. I Company secured a record in the British Army shooting competitions. In cricket, hockey, football and tennis their teams were unbeaten.

On the return of the Battery to India, the Adjutant-General wrote to Gidney as follows: "I am directed to inform you that the Anglo-Indian Battery will return shortly from Mesopotamia. The exact date will be communicated to you when known. At the same time, I am requested to convey His Excellency the Commander-in-Chief's appreciation of the good services which this Battery has rendered in Mesopotamia."

The return of the Battery was a red-letter day in Bombay. The schools were closed: business firms gave their employees special leave: railway workshops were closed. On behalf of the Commander-in-Chief and the people of India, Brigadier-General St. John, accompanied by his staff, welcomed the Battery back to India paying a golden tribute to their service in Mesopotamia.

On behalf of the Community, Gidney extended to the men a hearty welcome and warmly eulogised their services.

The Volunteer Artillery Battalion

The Volunteer Artillery Battalion raised in Burma from the Anglo-Indians shared in the siege of Kut and established a proud record which deserves to be at least duly acclaimed. A British unit with half their achievements would have been officially invested with the aura of super-heroes.

Major E.B. Davern, CIE, formerly 2nd Lieutenant in the Volunteer Artillery Battalion, gave the following account of how the Volunteer Battalion helped to keep the Turks out of Kut on X'mas eve in 1915.

"At 7 a.m. the Turkish guns began to range on the fort, front line and back kilns. This was the most intense bombardment that they had yet experienced. Some 26 guns concentrated on the fort alone with a pitiless rain of projectiles. Large pieces of the walls of the Sirmoor Bastion and of the north-east face were falling in. The two guns they had were not permitted to reply to this tornado, so they sought the best possible shelter, but wherever they went the shells searched them out : they poured in from all directions. The din was terrific. One had to shout to his neighbour to be heard."

"At 10 a.m. a shell pierced the roof of the dug-out in which the crew of Freeland's gun were sheltering. Christison, Gilbert, Ingham, Lonorgan and Blazey were wounded, the first three seriously. The dug-out was promptly evacuated and only just in time, as two more shells quickly found their way in completing the disaster."

"It was now clear that the Turks were going to mount the impending attack which had been carefully built up. The Anglo-Indian Battery hastily took out their bayonets so that they could fight. The position assigned to them was the barricade which had been built across the mouth of the Sirmoor Bastion between the wing walls."

"The .... whose dug-outs ran along the north-east face, were very badly shaken by the shelling to which they had been subjected. The O.C. of the Fort was made aware of this fact but steps do not appear to have been taken at the time to relieve them. The Artillery telephone wires from the Observation Posts to the batteries scattered about the brick kilns had been destroyed early : in spite of many gallant attempts to restore communication, fresh breaks in the line kept occurring. They, however, hoped that some of the batteries would assist them at the psychological moment."

"At 11-30 a hail of small arm fire broke out, the alarm whistles shrilled their warning blasts and the men sprinted for their positions. The Anglo-Indians mounted the platform of the barricade, took up positions alongside the bombers of the Oxfords and opened magazine

fire at the advancing tide of Turkish Infantry who were breaking
over the battered outer walls.   The Volunteer Artillery Battalion
took to their new environment like old hands in spite of heavy
casualties.   Lecky, Thompson and Mullerworth dropped dead
without a groan, being shot between the eyes.   McGowan was
shot through the thigh.   About 20 of the Oxfords and the 103rd
were killed outright, most of them being shot through the brain.
Some of the Turks were using a heavy leaden bullet about .577
bore, the wounds from which were   particularly   nasty.   The
wounded were being cleared as quickly as possible, as the space
at the disposal of the men was none too large for free movement
and their movement was impeded by the increasing number of
corpses.   The remnants of the Oxford bombers did great execution,
hurling their deadly missiles with telling effect into the masses of
Turks who were ultimately checked at the broken ramparts.   After
half an hour of bitter fighting the Turks began to retreat.   Then
pandemonium was let loose.   British and Indian troops, drunk
with the lust of battle, leapt to the shattered remnants of the walls
yelling and cursing like men possessed and at the same time discharging a devastating hail of lead as rapidly as their magazine
would permit.   Freeland, with some of the Anglo-Indian unit, ran
along to the gallery on the left from whence they discovered a knot
of about 20 Turks in a ditch under the walls leading to the under-
ground tunnel: these they quickly wiped out."

    "Gradually, the din of battle began to subside and a deathly
calm seemed to prevail punctured only by the groans of the
wounded and the dying.   They discovered that a very critical
situation had prevailed for some time on the north-east face
between them and the river bastion.   Major Anderson, the O.C.
of the Anglo-Indian Battalion, who stayed behind to superintend
the removal of the breach blocks of the guns after having seen this
carried out, collected all the men he could lay his hands on and
hastened to reinforce the Anglo-Indian Battalion when he met the
O.C. of the 119th who shouted out that he was proceeding to report
that his men were retiring to the second line as the enemy was
already in the fort.   Upon this Anderson immediately diverted his
small party to the point of danger: cleaving his way through the
retiring Indian troops with his near-handful of men he evicted the
intruders and inflicted considerable losses on them.   How Anderson

accomplished this feat, he has never been heard to relate. The Rajput Company of 119 who were holding the outlying trench near the river bastion, however, did not retire with the other troops. It was fortunate for the Anglo-Indian Battalion that the Rajputs held their position, as they were able to enfilade the Turkish attackers on the north-east face. The Anglo-Indians at the barrier had no idea while the struggle lasted how near they had been to disaster. The Anglo-Indian guns suffered heavily. Davern had two wheels blown to bits while Freeland had sustained two direct hits."

"While the Anglo-Indian Battalion was undergoing a pommelling, a strong feint had been made against the whole of the rest of the front line to divert attention from the main attack. The other troops had not realised the serious position which was faced by the Anglo-Indian Battalion."

At a dinner given to Gidney at Rangoon, Major Davern who replied to Gidney's speech on behalf of the gathering, paid a singular tribute to the Anglo-Indian Battalion at Kut· of which he had been one of the officers. The report in the January, 1927 Review reads as follows :

"Major Davern, briefly replying next, referred to the splendid work done by the Anglo-Indian lads at the siege of Kut. He mentioned the fact that the officers at Kut had always spoken very well of them. They were, he said, equal to any other unit. Where discipline was concerned, they were superior. There was no doubt about it that the boys did what they were asked to do and did it properly. Major-Gen. Charles Townshend himself stated in his report that if it was not for the Anglo-Indian gunners, they would have lost Kut in December." Kut had been invested by the Turks on the 8th December, 1915. After a siege of 143 days, Kut was captured by the Turks. The British forces which included a number of Anglo-Indians were sent into captivity in Eastern Turkey. When welcoming the Anglo-Indian Battery in Bombay, Gidney referred to the gallantry of the Anglo-Indian Volunteer Battalion from Burma. He mentioned that only one-third had survived their grim ordeal.

Achievements Not Recorded

The Machine Gun Volunteer Corps which distinguished itself against the Germans in Africa consisted predominantly of Anglo-

Indian volunteers.   Many of them were decorated for gallantry.

Fred Peters was awarded the D.C.M. by Gen. Smuts and was recommended for the Belgian Leopold II Class Medal by Gen. Tombeur.   He was also offered a commission twice which offers he turned down because as a Regimental Sergeant-Major on the Colonial scale of pay he was in receipt of higher emoluments than he would have drawn as an officer.   Fred Peters, with eleven medals, was the most highly decorated member of the Indian Contingent that attended the Coronation of King George VI. During World War II he was commanding a prisoners-of-war camp with the rank of Lt. Col.   Fred Peters was, for several years, the Honorary Secretary of the Jubbulpore branch of the All-India Anglo-Indian Association.   The family tradition was maintained when his nephew was awarded the Sword-of-Honour at the passing-out parade of Indian Air Force officers at Poona in September, 1944.   It is significant that at that passing-out parade, of the 15 officers who were awarded their wings, 11 were Anglo-Indians.

The achievements of many Anglo-Indians who joined as Europeans were lost to the Community.   Even through the mists of time, however, some are clearly identifiable.   F/Lt. Lief Robinson who joined the R.A.F. in World War I brought down the first Zeppelin over England : he was awarded the V.C. F/Lt. Warneford also of the R.A.F. accounted for the first Zeppelin over France.   In addition to the V.C. he was awarded the Croix-de-Guerre.   Robinson and Warneford were lads from Bangalore.   Percival Lovery, another Anglo-Indian from Bangalore, enlisted as a gunner and was awarded the V.C.   One of his brothers was a Police Sub-Inspector in Madras and another brother a Jailor in the Mysore State.

Major deMonte, an Anglo-Indian Officer in the Indian Medical Department (British Cadre) which consisted entirely of Anglo-Indians, was awarded the M.C. for gallantry in France.

Assistant Surgeon J.W.C. Lopez, IMD (B.C.) was awarded the Distinguished Conduct Medal for conspicuous gallantry and devotion to duty.   The citation showed that on the 17th and 18th of October, 1917, in German East Africa, "He volunteered to remain back with the wounded when our troops fell back before the enemy : he helped to evacuate the wounded under fire.   On the 8th November, 1917, his ambulance was attacked by the enemy and most of the stretcher-bearers were killed.   He carried a number of the wounded under heavy fire to a place of safety and then returned with water and dressings."

Lord Lloyd, one of the most distinguished of British administrators, speaking in the House of Lords, said, "There was no community who fought better for us in different parts of the world : they served in Mesopotamia, in Basra, up the lines of communication, in the line. No community had a better record than the Anglo-Indian Community."

The Indian Defence Force (the I.D.F.) deserves a special, if brief reference. This Force, later known as the Auxiliary Force (India), was drawn almost entirely from the Anglo-Indian Community. It was recognised as India's second line of defence. Its yeoman, if unpublicised, service to the State was crucial. For at least two years when Britain had her back to the wall and India was completely denuded of fighting troops, the I.D.F. represented the only military personnel on which the Government could and did rely for maintaining law and order in the Country.

About 10,000 Anglo-Indians fought in the various theatres of war. About 25,000 constituted the I.D.F.

The three strategic services, the Railways, the Posts & Telegraphs and the Customs owed their stability to the Anglo-Indian personnel. There were widespread strikes during the most critical period of the war. But for the devotion to duty of the Anglo-Indian staff, the Indian Railways would have been paralysed. Every man, irrespective of age or position, put his shoulder to the wheel. Anglo-Indian railway officers worked at menial jobs in order to keep trains moving. Even schoolboys put their hands to every kind of railway work. In addition, every Anglo-Indian railwayman of Military age was required to do duties of patrolling, keeping guard and maintaining civil order as a member of the Indian Defence Force.

The Anglo-Indian women in the Nursing Service occupied a unique role. Practically the whole of the St. John's Ambulance work was done by Anglo-Indian women.

But tragically and, indeed, ironically the post-war period brought unemployment and disillusionment. Anglo-Indians, who had given up everything in order to fight, came back to cold and indifferent treatment by the Government. Many ex-soldiers, wearing their decorations, were to be found walking the streets, unemployed, hungry and bitter. That recurring British Government complex of welcoming the Community's vital services in times of stress and then casting them off like a trusted but no-longer-needed weapon was once again exhibited with almost time-worn cynicism.

World War II

As in World War I about 75% of the available manpower of the Community joined the different Armed Forces. The Community contributed, comparatively, more to the war effort than any other community not only in India but in the Commonwealth.

The Anglo-Indian's capacity for leadership was exemplified by the high proportion of Anglo-Indian officers in every arm of India's fighting forces. There were hundreds of Anglo-Indian officers in the Indian Army, the Royal Indian Navy and the Royal Indian Air Force. While there appeared some reluctance among other communities to join the Air Force, the Anglo-Indian, with a characteristic spirit of adventure, stormed this youngest and perhaps finest of India's services.

The Adjutant-General, Lt. Gen. Baker, had asked me to secure 1350 Anglo-Indians for recruitment; 900 were wanted for the R.A.S.C., the R.A.O.C. and R.E. for the Middle East, 350 for the R.A.M.C. and 100 for the Madras Coast Battery R.A. (A.F.I.).

The R.A.F. to which recruitment of Anglo-Indians had been suddenly stopped was again thrown open. Air Chief Marshal, Sir R. Peirse, informed me that he required about 200 pilot officers for the R.I.A.F. as it was then known.

In addition to our contribution to the Indian Services, thousands of Anglo-Indians joined the British forces. Many of them were fighting with the British Army in the epic Dunkirk evacuation.

Between 3000 and 4000 Anglo-Indians were serving with the Royal Air Force during the Battle of Britain. Many of them won the most outstanding awards. Manser of the R.A.F., the son of a former member of the Telegraph Department, was awarded the V.C. posthumously. Dyson, D.S.O., D.F.C. and bar, the grandson of J.H. Abbott, a former leader of the Community, established what was perhaps a record for the largest number of planes shot down in single aerial combat. Dyson accounted for 6 Italian planes in 15 minutes during operations in the Middle

East. This achievement was specially commended by Lord Beaverbrook.

Acting Group Captain W.G.G.D. Smith, DSO, DFC, received a bar to his DSO. Gr.Capt. Smith commanded a fighter wing in the invasion of Sicily and operations over Southern Italy. The citation stated that he destroyed in all 14 enemy aircraft and a large number of transport vehicles and locomotives. Gr. Capt. Smith was born in 1914 at Madras and had his home in the Nilgiris.

Pilot Officer J.E. Loughran (267 Squadron) was awarded the D.F.C. The citation stated that this officer at all times set an inspiring example by his courage and devotion to duty.

Daniel, the son of a prominent Anglo-Indian Association worker who was employed in the Government of India, was first awarded the D.F.M. as a Flight Sergeant and then the D.F.C. as a Pilot Officer.

Pilot Officer Parker of Moradabad and Lt. Commander Douglas of the Fleet Air Arm were two more of the many members of the Community, in the Royal Air Force, decorated for gallantry.

Guy Gibson was almost a legend in the R.A.F. Gibson, V.C., D.S.O. and bar, D.F.C. and bar, known as the dam-buster, was reported killed in a sortie over Germany. Guy Gibson was born in Simla: his mother was said to have come from a well-known Anglo-Indian family in South India: the father's family would appear to have been domiciled in India.

The V.C. was awarded posthumously to Frank Gerald Blaker. Although the citation referred to him as a British officer, a senior Indian General, who was educated at the same school in India, described Blaker and his brother as typical Anglo-Indians. The Victoria Cross citation reads: "Blaker charged forward alone to attack a Japanese machine-gun post on the summit of a hill over-looking Taungni in Burma. He was wounded in the arm by a grenade and hit three times by bullets from a machine-gun firing from the strong point he was assaulting. He fell to the ground mortally wounded but, struggling to a sitting posture, exhorted the men of his company to advance with the words, 'Well done, 'C' Company. I am going to die but you will go on, I know.' His men did go on and, before Major Blaker paid the price for his valour, he saw them over-run the Jap position. Before this final assault, Major Blaker had led his men in a wide encircling movement over unknown and precipitous jungle country, a feat of considerable military skill."

Blaker was attached to the 3/9th Gurkha Rifles. His Colonel wrote, "Blaker was a slight young man with an engaging personality and great enthusiasm. When a vacancy arose, he was appointed temporarily to command a company. There his flair for training and his leadership quickly made their mark. He retained his appointment in spite of his comparative lack of seniority. He used his initiative and ingenuity on all occasions: indeed, he even had to be restrained at times. He had a quick eye for ground and for the solution of tactical problems, and he had trained his men to act with speed and resolution. The action in which he was awarded his Military Cross and the attack in which he was killed were typical of his methods."

Such awards as the M.C., the D.C.M. and the M.M. were won by many Anglo-Indians.

Once again the military waters were muddied by the British policy, seemingly deliberate, of encouraging the fairer members of the Community (and some not so fair) to join as European Emergency Commissioned Officers. They were given a King's Commission with much higher emoluments than those who joined with an Indian Commission. At least 90% of the European Emergency Commissioned officers recruited in India during World War II were, in fact, Anglo-Indians.

To give only two examples of Anglo-Indians who were decorated while holding King's Commissions: 'Ginger' Pettengell, a Captain, won the M.C. and bar during the fighting in Africa and Italy.

'Ginger' Pettengell was a lad from Jubbulpore and educated at my old school, Christ Church. His cousin, Edgar Pettengell, is, today, one of our Major-Generals.

John Hartley first joined with a King's Commission: later he transferred to the Indian Army getting an Indian Commission. Hartley won the M.C in Italy. The citation reads:

"On the night 14/15, Major J.C. Hartley was ordered to attack and capture the farm area of Casseti in Italy. His men, under his inspiring leadership, broke into the well-held enemy defences and captured the objective. Major Hartley was able to beat back repeated enemy counter-attacks during which his company suffered a number of casualties. Thanks to his encouragement and organisation of his defences, he was able to beat back successive enemy counter-attacks. When his forces had run out of ammunition, he withdrew his company successfully including his casualties. Throughout the action, Major Hartley's courage and coolness inspired his men and his bravery and powers of command enabled him to control and lead his command of young soldiers, including the withdrawal operation, most successfully. Although his command suffered 40% casualties, Major Hartley's leadership and bravery carried his men through. He was granted an immediate MC by Field Marshal H.R. Alexander." Hartley retired fairly recently as a Brigadier from the Indian Army.

Dubois received the M.C. Vaughan of the Indian Medical Department was decorated with the D.C.M.

Pat Dunn, who was mentioned in despatches and wounded in action during the Burma campaign, was the first Indian officer to command a battalion in the field even before Gen. Cariappa, the first Indian to command the Indian Army, with the then designation of Commander-in-Chief. Dunn, who was 2 IC, took over command after his battalion had been ambushed by the Japanese and many of the officers killed including the O.C. I shall have occasion to refer more fully to Dunn in another chapter.

Bertie Litchfield was awarded the M.C. during the Burma campaign. The citation reads : "Throughout the 1945 campaign Maj. Litchfield commanded the 2nd Indian Field Battery and acted in close support of 1/7th Gurkha Rifles in every action in which they took part. His skilful handling of his Battery on several occasions contributed materially to their success. "

"In particular at Meiktila on the 7th March while under shell fire from a 105 mm-gun he destroyed numbers of the enemy opposing our tanks on the Mahalaing road and produced supporting fire on a hostile position 200 yards from a damaged tank, thus enabling the tank and its crew to be successfully withdrawn."

"Again on the March 26th during the clearing of Meiktila airfield although wounded by a grenade he remained at his post for six hours directing fire of the Div. Arty so skilfully that the enemy position was turned into a shambles and captured."

"Again at Yewe, Sadaung, and especially at Helgu his bold handling of his Battery contributed greatly to successful actions and enabled the position to be taken with the minimum casualties to the Infantry."

"His complete fearlessness, enthusiasm and keenness to destroy the enemy combined with his experience as a Troop Commander in the 1942 campaign were an inspiration to his own Battery and to the troops he supported."

Towards the end of 1947 Litchfield took over as Commandant of the Artillery School and in 1948 he went as Commander, Artillery, Armoured Division. During his service with the Armoured Division he was in the front line in the Hyderabad Police Action. Later he served as Brigadier-General Staff to the Military Government at Hyderabad. He was Director of Artillery when he retired.

Regie Noronha was decorated for gallantry in hard-fought engagements during the Burma Campaign. Then a Major he was awarded, in May, 1944, the Military Cross for holding the line with 'A' Company 4th Battalion (WLI) of the Madras Regiment, against a number of attacks put in by a numerically superior Japanese Force, at the Battle of the Sita Ridge on the Imphal Front. He earned a bar to his Military Cross for heroism in February, 1945, in the Irrawaddy Bridge-head battle preceding the capture of Mandalay. For his strong determination, resolution and coolness in the execution of the various other tasks assigned to him during the period November, 1943, to July, 1945, he was also twice mentioned in despatches. Reference is made to his outstanding service after Independence in the chapter 'Saga of Continuing Service'.

George Jenkins was awarded the M.C. during the fighting in Burma. He is a Brigadier, today, after having held the post of Deputy Military Secretary.

Capt. William Alexander Lopez of the I.M.S. helped to affirm the dictum, not however always valid, 'Like father like son'. Reference has already been made to his father Assistant Surgeon, J.W.C. Lopez, of the I.M.D. (B.C.) who was awarded the DCM in World War I. Capt. Lopez was awarded the Military Cross for outstanding service in Burma. The citation mentioned that he was in charge of the Light Air Section of an Indian Ambulance Unit in a region of heavy fighting in Burma. While his battalion was crossing a river, the enemy opened up extremely accurate fire with guns and mortars. Capt. Lopez immediately collected the wounded, attended to their needs and evacuated them. In spite of considerable danger to himself he refused to take shelter. On arrival at the battalion area on the other side of the river, Capt. Lopez set up his aid post and dealt with all casualties. The battalion area was still being attacked, shelled by guns and mortars, but he set a fine example to all by his determination. The citation concluded, "His devotion to duty in most dangerous circumstances was an inspiration to all."

George Charles, an Anglo-Indian lad of about 20 years of age, was awarded the Military Medal for gallantry in Burma. A few details of his exploits make interesting reading. He was dropped in the rear of the Japanese as a Commando. He and a companion were, after some time, surrounded and captured by the Japanese. One night, when he heard the Japanese soldiers carousing, Charles decided to escape from his shack. He attacked the Japanese sentry with bare hands. Before he succeeded in strangling the sentry, the latter managed to bayonet him and partly disembowelled the lad. His hands were also cut to the bone by the bayonet. After killing the sentry, he got hold of a tommy gun. With this he attacked and wiped out a number of the Japanese soldiers. Wounded severely, hungry and worn out, he wandered in the jungles for 11 days before being picked up by British troops.

Major J.N. Pacheco of the IMD (B.C.) was decorated by Marshal Tito early in 1955 at the Bangalore Residency. He was awarded the Titov Lik. While serving in Italy at a British General Hospital, Major Pacheco also had charge of a large number of Yugoslav partisans. He gradually learnt the language. The letter of citation which Major Pacheco received at the time of the award read as follows:

"We would like to express all our recognition for what you have done for our Jugoslav wounded and patients. We may assure you that all the Jugoslavs who have known you will keep you in their memories. With your unstinted work you have made many friends in Jugoslavia, and at the same time you have helped towards a better understanding between our two countries. Thus you have done your part in cementing a lasting peace. Will you please accept as a visible sign of our recognition the 'Titov-Lik.'"

Major Pacheco is the only Indian Army Officer to have earned this distinction. He was the nephew of the late Thomas Richmond, a well-known Anglo-Indian lawyer of Madras, who founded the Richmond Education Trust for Anglo-Indians in Madras with a gift of fifty thousand rupees.

George Rodrigues—G.C.

In a sense George Rodrigues spanned the period between World Wars I and II.

Dr. George Rodrigues, G.C., entered the IMD (B.C.) in 1904. George Rodrigues was on active service from 1914 to 1918 in Mesopotamia and France and was mentioned in several despatches.

In 1920 during the Arab rebellion he was recommended for the Military Cross. On being repatriated to India in March, 1921, he helped to demobilise the 24th Combined Field Ambulance with which unit he had served in Mesopotamia. After that he was posted to the Station Hospital, Bangalore.

In August, 1921, the Moplah rebellion broke out in the Malabar area. Rodrigues was sent there with the Dorset Regiment and served with the troops till the 22nd February, 1922, when he was posted to West Hill, Calicut, where he was in medical charge of the hospital. While at West Hill he was awarded the medal of the Military Division of the Order of the British Empire for gallant service rendered during the Moplah rebellion. He retired from the Indian Medical Department in 1925 and set up private practice in Calicut.

In 1942, in place of the medal of the OBE Military Division, he was awarded the George Cross. He was an honorary member of the Victoria Cross Association and of the George Cross Association.

Rodrigues practised medicine in Calicut for 35 years. The acknowledged leader of his profession in that area, he had a large and lucrative practice. But money was a lesser consideration. A large number of patients who waited at his clinic, every day, were people who could not afford his fee, but were certain of getting the maximum of care and attention free of charge. With a charming disposition, he was warm-hearted and generous to a fault. In spite of his exacting schedule as a private medical practitioner with a large clientele, he found time for considerable social service. For many years he was the President of the Calicut branch of the All-India Anglo-Indian Association.

Both the sons have followed in the professional footsteps of their father.

The Burma Epic

Burma was annexed by the British Government and became part of India and was administered like any other part of the Country. Because of the experience and efficiency of the Anglo-Indians, the Government had reserved certain cadres for members of the Community. A large number of them held high positions. Some of them intermarried with the Burmans as did many Europeans. There was little, if any, social and cultural distinction between the Anglo-Indians and Anglo-Burmans. In 1937 when Burma was politically separated from India, the official name of the Community was changed to Anglo-Burman although many of them had no Burman blood—they were, in fact, Anglo-Indians. Up till that time there was a branch of the All-India Anglo-Indian Association in Rangoon. The number of Anglo-Indians was about twenty thousand.

The heroism, sufferings and sacrifices of the Anglo-Indians in Burma deserve to be recorded as one of the greatest epics of the historic Burma campaign in World War II. No official publicity was given to the gallantry of the Community in Burma such as that accorded to Burmese tribesmen. But everyone, who stayed there long enough to see the Japanese invasion, testified to the tenacious, unyielding courage of the Anglo-Indians.

While even the officials and others were making a hasty exit from Burma, Anglo-Indian railwaymen and those in the strategic services stood by till the end. Even the girls, working as telephone operators, held on till the last. Many of these were either killed or captured. Anglo-Indians in the Auxiliary Force were embodied and fought gallantly. An Anglo-Indian Anti-Aircraft Battery in Burma shot down 17 Japanese planes in one day—perhaps a world record.

The evacuation from Burma was marked by conduct of which the British have every reason to be thoroughly ashamed. In his book 'Trek Back from Burma', W.G. Burchett, an Australian journalist who had spent some time in Burma, has given something of the inside story. At page 155 of his book Burchett writes, "My

God", he said (my old friend David Morrice) doffing his topee and wiping the sweat from his forehead, "When this war is over, I am going to sit down and write a book. I will call it 'I also Ran' : Jesu : did they run? and the 'Burrah Sahibs' led the race."
.... "Then he told me something of the evacuation of Rangoon. Of officials dropping their work and clambering over each other to get away : of one of his colleagues who tried to take all his furniture with him, including a billiard table, of others who buried their valuables, hoping to come back soon and dig them up. Nurses and doctors were ordered to leave their patients and 'scram'."

Referring to the revolting attitude of superiority of the so-called 'Pucca Sahibs' when he was in Calcutta, Burchett writes, "This uncharitable, superior attitude to the Anglos was sickening. Many of the Anglo-Indians and Anglo-Burmans had done excellent jobs in Burma, staying at their posts when the 'Pukkahs' or Europeans who should have had a higher sense of duty and responsibility, skipped off to save their white skins. The Anglo-Indians provided the vast body of executives and white-collar workers who—never able to occupy the highest positions—carried the main burden of administration and commerce. They kept the trains running, manned the fire-brigades and ambulances. Anglo-Burman and Anglo-Indian nurses and telegraph operators performed service jobs up till the last, and when the collapse came, many of them were left to find their own way out of Burma."

When all hope had been abandoned and the senior British officials had bolted, thousands of Anglo-Indians started on a gruelling trek to India. Through trackless jungle and swamp, thousands of men, women and children battled their way to India. Words fail to describe the harrowing nature of their fierce ordeal. Hundreds of them died by the wayside. Exhaustion, fever and disease took a terrible toll. It would repay the historian to ascertain details of the selfless courage, devotion and camaraderie that characterised the behaviour of these refugees.

During my tours I met thousands of the Anglo-Indian and Anglo-Burman refugees in various parts of India. There was a particularly large camp in Coimbatore. I visited them in January, 1943, and addressed three separate meetings. I met others in Dehra Dun. After I had addressed a meeting in Bombay I was particularly touched by the story of an elderly Anglo-Indian man. He was the sole surviving member of his family. His wife, two daughters and only son had died during the trek from Burma. The irrepressible spirit and, indeed, sheer guts of these people, men, women and children had to be seen to be believed. Theirs was a story not only of incredible heroism and long unspeakable suffering during the trek to India, but also of the most shameful dereliction of duty by British officers and civilians.

The Real Heroes

Commenting on the occupation of Rangoon, in a Colombo paper, dated the 17th May, 1945, a South-East Asia Command Military Commentator wrote, "Life in the city under Japanese occupation was more than grim. It was a reign of terror for the Indian, Chinese, Anglo-Indian and Anglo-Burman population. Food was always short. Tea, sugar and flour had been unobtainable for months. There was no attempt at price control and Japanese invasion currency, which now litters every street, poured forth in a never-ending stream until it was of little value."

"The very suspicion of espionage was enough to bring torture. To own an electric torch was a crime. To be clad decently, to appear to have enough to eat, was to bring down the wrath of the preachers of the Greater Asia theory."

"There is no doubt that the real heroes of Rangoon were the Anglo-Indian and Anglo-Burman communities. They were continually under suspicion. If they did not work, they were accused of getting money from the British. If they did work they were told they were spies."

"Many of the older people never left the streets in which they lived from the time the Japanese entered until they fled. They escaped forced labour by a variety of excuses, and they were the best friends the British prisoners in the gaol had. Whenever possible they passed news, cigarettes, clothings and fruit to them. The sufferings of these people were almost as great as those of the prisoners, but their loyalty never flagged."

The Rev. A. Alessi, S.C., wrote, "Next to the Army which fought in Burma and eventually liberated it, and whose story of heroism and sacrifice is written in the graves of the soldiers which dot the countryside from Imphal to Rangoon, the Empire and

Burma owe their deepest debt of gratitude to the Anglo-Indian and Anglo-Burman Community. During the three years of the enemy occupation of Burma the loyalty of this Community and their love for their Motherland has never faltered.''

"With every new Army Division which has entered Burma we have seen Anglo-Indian youths fighting shoulder to shoulder with the men of Britain, of India and the Empire. We have heard, too, of the thousands of Burma refugees from this Community who are still in India and are so loyal to their Motherland and attached to Burma. But I propose to speak of those of the Community— more numerous still—who could not follow the Army to India and who had to remain behind in the hands of the enemy.''

"I have known thousands of these poor unfortunates during the past three years of bitter suffering. I have shared with them the sorrows and the humiliations of the Japanese occupation, and I have shared with them, too, the rapturous joy of the liberation. And I can testify that for unfailing loyalty and steadfast confidence and courage amid the gravest dangers there is no people in the British Empire who will surpass the Anglo-Indians and Anglo-Burmans.''

"With their education and their experience in the many branches of Government service they might have become the pivot of the new Government, they might have secured the best posts and the biggest salaries with the Japanese, but to a man they remained loyal. Without a thought they chose for themselves hunger and persecution, but they would not collaborate with the enemy.''

"They were systematically suppressed and interned and for no other reason than they were loyal. While members of other communities whole-heartedly collaborated and piled up wealth which they converted into jewels, gold and silver, Anglo-Indians and Anglo-Burmans had to dispose of all their ornaments and all their personal possessions, even down to their last shirt. They were forced to sell everything for a few pies with which to purchase a handful of rice for themselves and for their children. The liberating Army, when it re-entered Burma, found most of the Anglo-Indians and the Anglo-Burmans bare-footed and wearing their last tattered shirts and pants.''

"Only two months previously one who lost her husband and all her children but one said to me, 'Father, today I am selling the last thing I cherished, a coat of my youngest darling dead child. I will carry on with that for two months and then—I will die'.

"Elderly gentlemen who had once held responsible positions in Burma were obliged to earn their daily handful of rice by drawing water, chopping firewood and making rice cakes for sale in the streets. One, a famous barrister, well-known all over Burma, spent three years in a wild and dirty village carrying heavy buckets of water daily, washing the family clothes and doing his own cooking."

I received the following unsolicited tribute from a European evacuee from Burma.

"While I was in no way connected with the Railways in Burma, I was in a unique position to know, to watch and to see for myself what the Anglo-Indian drivers and firemen did in those stirring times. They, at least the majority, stuck to their posts: further, they were called to take up duties when, poor fellows, they could hardly stand on their feet with fatigue."

"I lift my hat in admiration of the deeds of devotion to duty of these Anglo-Indian lads."

"One of the most amazing things about it all was that they were expected, in fact, were depended upon to stick to their jobs to the last, when most if not all the rest had cleared out."

Our Women

The contribution of Anglo-Indian women to the war effort was without comparison. Anglo-Indian women contributed more to the war effort than all the women of all the other communities in India put together.

Anglo-Indians constituted about 80 per cent of the Women's Auxiliary Corps. Some of them rendered signal service. A.V. Hubbard, a girl from Kharagpur, was mentioned in despatches for outstanding service in the Middle East. The Indian Military Nursing Service and the Auxiliary Nursing Service drew about 70 per cent of their strength from the Community. These women served in almost every theatre of war. Captain E. Berneys, Liberal National M.P. for Bristol, after a tour of the Indian battle-fronts, said, "During our visit to Indian hospitals we were gratified at the care that is being bestowed upon the patients and many tributes have been paid to the Anglo-Indian nurses." India's fighting men, irrespective of caste or creed, owed an irreparable debt to the Anglo-Indian nurses. The Women's Voluntary Service also consisted predominantly of volunteer workers from the Community. Addressing me on the work of Anglo-Indian women, Lady Bird, the chief organiser of the Women's Voluntary Service, paid a tribute to "The many devoted and reliable Anglo-Indian workers in the different Provinces."

Helen Rodriguez—G.M.

The services of Miss Helen Rodriguez, Matron, Civil Hospital, Taunggyi, symbolised the courage and devotion to duty of the Anglo-Indian women. The citation of the George Medal award reads as follows.

"The King has been graciously pleased to give orders for the following award:

"The George Medal.

"Miss Helen Rodriguez, Matron, Civil Hospital, Taunggyi.

"When Taunggyi was attacked by two waves of Japanese bombers, Miss Rodriguez displayed the utmost courage and devotion to duty. The military hospital was bombed and in the absence of stretcher-bearers, Miss Rodriguez carried patients on her back to places of safety. While performing this heroic task she was bombed and machine-gunned. She returned to the Civil Hospital and herself performed many operations, remaining on duty with practically no sleep for four days and nights. Her courage, initiative and complete disregard of her own safety were in the highest traditions of the Nursing Service."

Miss Rodriguez came from a Bangalore family: her father was Major Rodriguez of the IMD (B.C.).

Civilian Services

But for the ready and complete response of the Anglo-Indian Railwaymen, the Indian Railways could never have stood up to the unprecedented strain suddenly imposed by a vast and un-expected war effort. Long before 1939, those conversant with railway conditions had warned the Government that owing to the outworn and inadequate rolling stock the railways would collapse under the impact of war conditions. Only those who actually ran the trains could speak adequately of the almost superhuman effort that was required to keep them, and consequently the war effort, moving in India. The Railways were literally the wheels on which India's magnificent contribution to the war, in men and material, moved. This crucial service was only made possible by the running staff having to work, very often, for unbroken periods of 20 to 30 hours at a time. The disturbances of August, 1942, made the position critical. Murder, arson and the uprooting of railway track were the order of the day. In the areas around Bihar and through which the troops and supplies, necessary to resist the Japanese invasion, had to be carried, conditions were chronic. But for the Anglo-Indian Railwaymen and also for their military service in doing patrol and sentry duty, as members of the Auxiliary Force, the war effort would have been completely paralysed for a considerable period.

To the Posts and Telegraph Department also the Anglo-Indians made a vital contribution. In the face of unprecedented strain and unrest, Anglo-Indian personnel kept this strategic service intact and efficient.

Even during the war the almost perverted British sense of ingratitude and discrimination persisted against the Community. I had to fight it repeatedly. I have already referred to the hundreds of Anglo-Indians who had joined the different branches of the British Army as a result of a special appeal made to me by the Army authorities. Four years after they had joined the Royal Engineers, 77 Anglo-Indians had their conditions of service withdrawn on the plea that they had been mistakenly enrolled and that, if they wished, they could re-enrol under the Indian Army Act. When I pointed out to Gen. Deedes, the then Adjutant-General, that there were a number of cases of Anglo-Indians wrongly commissioned as King's Commissioned Officers, the reply I received was, "The case of Anglo-Indians wrongly commissioned as K.C.Os was somewhat different. There were special considerations affecting them and as compared with other ranks, their number was small." This was a deliberate perversion of the truth. As I had repeatedly pointed out in the Central Legislative Assembly (the predecessor of Parliament) more than ninety per cent of the so-called European Emergency Commissioned Officers from India were, in fact, Anglo-Indians.

The Auxiliary Force

The Auxiliary Force was constituted by the Auxiliary Force Act of 1920. This Force was the successor to the Volunteer Forces which in 1917 gave place to the Indian Defence Force.

On the 1st July, 1939, the approximate strength of the Auxiliary Force including the reservists was 29,346. The Auxiliary Force which was disbanded with effect from the 14th August, 1947, had a long and proud record. To mention a few of the units : the Bihar Light Horse, the Calcutta Light Horse, the Surma Valley Light Horse, the Assam Valley Light Horse, the Northern Bengal Artillery & Auxiliary Force, the 1st Calcutta Field Brigade, the IVth Cossipore Field Brigade, the Agra Field Battery, the Cawnpore Field Battery and the Infantry Units which were originally formed of the Eastern Bengal Railway Battalion, the Great Indian Peninsula Railway Regiment, the Bombay, Baroda and Central India Railway Regiment, the Bengal and North-Western Railway Battalion, the South Indian Railway Battalion, the Madras and Southern Mahratta Railway Rifles, the Bengal Nagpur Railway Battalion, the Nagpur Rifles, the Punjab Rifles, the Simla Rifles, the Bangalore Battalion, the Allahabad Rifles, the Dehra Dun Contingent, the Sind Rifles, the Eastern Bengal Co., the Poona Rifles, the Kolar Gold Field Battalion, the Calcutta Scottish, the Delhi Contingent, the Coorg and Mysore Co., the Yercaud Company, the Cawnpore Contingent and the Karachi Corps.

In all there were 24 Cavalry and 48 Infantry Units.

During World War II some of the Cavalry units were embodied with the Madras Coast Battery. This Battery, which had been raised on the 1st January, 1879, from the Madras Volunteer Guards was designated the Madras Artillery Volunteers : it was redesignated as the Madras Coast Battery, RA, on the 25th November, 1941 : it was administered as part of the Madras Contingent from the 1st April, 1933, to the 15th January, 1942. It was embodied for service with the Regular Army from the 25th May, 1940, to the 31st March, 1946.

The Bombay Coast Battery, RA, which was formed as the Bombay Volunteer Artillery on the 6th June, 1887, became the 4th (Bombay) Group Garrison Artillery on the 1st April, 1917, and No. V (Bombay) Field Brigade on the 1st October, 1920. One Battery was redesignated as the Bombay Coast Battery, RA, on the 15th April, 1941, and embodied for service with the Regular Army from the 25th May, 1940, to the 31st March, 1946.

No. 3 (Bombay) Fortress Company, RE, which had been raised on the 1st April, 1903, from the Bombay Volunteer Artillery, was embodied for service with the Regular Army from the 25th May, 1940, to the 1st May, 1946.

No. 1 (Madras) Signal Company, RCS, which had been raised from the Madras Artillery Volunteers, became No. 5 (Madras) Field Company on the 1st October, 1920: it was disbanded and reconstituted with the then designation on the 23rd June, 1928, and was embodied for service with the Regular Army from the 10th May, 1941, to October, 1946.

The Calcutta and Presidency Battalion, which was formed on the 3rd February, 1863, as the Calcutta Rifle Corps, was reconstituted as the 1st Battalion, Calcutta Volunteer Rifles, on the 24th March, 1898, and became the 5th Calcutta Battalion on the 1st April, 1917, and the Calcutta Battalion on the 1st October, 1920. 'A' Company was embodied for service with the Regular Army from the 7th June, 1941, to the 31st March, 1946.

The Dehra Dun Contingent which had been formed on the 24th July, 1871, as the Mussoorie Volunteer Rifle Corps and the Thomason College Volunteer Rifle Corps, which was formed on the 19th August, 1872, and the Mussoorie Volunteer Reserve Corps, formed on the 13th August, 1889, were incorporated on the 4th March, 1901. All these units became the 9th Mussoorie Battalion on the 1st April, 1917, and were amalgamated with the Dehra Dun Detachment, U.P. Horse and the Meerut Detachment, No. 5 Company, M.G. Corps and reconstituted as the Dehra Dun Contingent on the 10th July, 1925. They were embodied for service with the Regular Army in January, 1942.

The Bombay Battalion, which was raised as the Bombay Volunteer Rifle Corps on the 15th August, 1877, became the 15th Bombay Battalion on the 1st April, 1917. 'A' Company was embodied for service with the Regular Army from the 22nd March, 1941, to the 31st March, 1946.

The Nilgiri Malabar Battalion was raised as the Nilgiri Volunteer Rifles on the 29th October, 1878. The Coimbatore Volunteer Corps was formed on the 7th August, 1885, and incorporated on the 4th January, 1892. The Malabar Volunteer Rifles was formed on the 14th August, 1885, from the Calicut and Tellicherry Volunteer Corps and was amalgamated as the 29th Nilgiri Malabar Battalion on the 1st April, 1917. 'A' Company was embodied for service with the Regular Army from the 31st May, 1941, to the 31st May, 1946.

The Hyderabad Rifles was formed as the Hyderabad Volunteer Rifle Corps on the 7th July, 1882, and became the 26th Hyderabad Rifles on the 1st April, 1917. 'B' Company was embodied with the Regular Army from July, 1945, to 1st August, 1946.

The East Coast Battalion was raised as the Godavari Rifle Volunteers on the 9th June, 1885, and was amalgamated with the Vizagapatam Rifle Volunteers raised on the 10th October, 1885, to form the East Coast Rifle Volunteers on the 14th October, 1890, and became the East Coast Volunteer Rifles on the 14th October, 1903, and the 38th East Coast Battalion on the 1st April, 1917. 'A' Company was embodied for service with the Regular Army from the 31st May, 1941, to the 30th June, 1946.

The Bangalore Contingent, which included the Bangalore Armoured Car Co. and the Bangalore Battalion, was embodied for service with the Regular Army from April, 1944, to the 1st June, 1946.

The Madras Guards, which had a proud, historic record, was raised on the 2nd July, 1857, as the Madras Volunteer Guards, became the 1st Madras Guards on the 1st April, 1917, and No. 7 platoon was embodied for service with the Regular Army on the 25th May, 1940. The balance of the Unit was embodied on the 10th May, 1941, and the Guards were disbanded on the 31st May, 1946.

From the point of view of continuity the Madras Guards was the oldest Corps in India. It was, I believe, the only Volunteer Force which had the honour of carrying the Queen's colours. Madras City had reason to be grateful to the Madras Guards. During World War II Japanese ships had been sighted off the coast: there was a tremendous flap: most of the officials, led by the then British Governor, evacuated Madras: the Madras Guards alone stayed put.

In December, 1947, I received an interesting letter from Col. Douglas Reid, the last Commandant of the Madras Guards, from his home, Green Gates, Holt, Norfolk. Col. Reid wrote, "I have just received the October number of your journal and write to tell you how much I have appreciated it. There is an air of realism, boldness, commonsense and uprightness coupled with self-sufficiency which was rather lacking in the Community in the past. I worked and hoped for this attitude in the years during the war when I commanded the Madras Guards. The great moment of our service was when Frank Anthony addressed the troops in the inner barrack square from the ancient staircase and visualised what has come to pass."

Compulsory enlistment in the Auxiliary Force was a precondition for employment of Anglo-Indians in the Railways. The Railway Battalions formed the backbone of the Auxiliary Force. Apart from being called out to protect railway property against arson and looting by strikers the Auxiliary Force was also called out for military duty to quell communal riots. By doing duty as the second line of defence and auxiliary to the standing army many crores were saved to the Indian exchequer each year.

From 1928 the striking strength of the Auxiliary Force was at least 32,000. At least two-thirds of these were Anglo-Indians: the rest were the so-called Domiciled Europeans or Europeans. Even here the official British policy of imperial arrogance and discrimination manifested itself. In spite of the preponderance of the Anglo-Indians only about 110 were given Commissions. The contrast was highlighted by a comparison with the Indian Territorial Force which was reorganised in 1927. In that Force every officer, except a Commandant and an Adjutant, was an Indian.

The history of these Forces, which merged into the I.D.F. (The Indian Defence Force) and then the A.F.I. (The Auxiliary Force-India), is probably unique in the annals of Volunteer fighting forces.

CHAPTER VIII

MY GRIM TASK

Final Betrayal

MUCH of what follows is of an autobiographical nature. This, perhaps, is inevitable, because since 1942 the anxious, often grim, burden of finding a place for my Community in the New India has fallen upon me.

Gidney's work and achievements were synonymous with the position of the Community in India for a period of over 20 years. The news of Gidney's death was flashed over All-India Radio on the 5th May, 1942. The Community was stunned. There was a tangible Community trauma. The question was repeatedly asked, 'After Gidney what'. So greatly had Gidney towered over any other person purporting to speak for the Anglo-Indians, that the Community found it difficult to believe that it could produce, particularly at this critical juncture, a leader of sufficient capacity and vision who could achieve a position at all comparable with that which Gidney had secured in India's public life.

The Annual General Meetings of the All-India Anglo-Indian Association represent the focal point of Anglo-Indian public life. Anglo-Indian leaders and representatives from every part of the Country congregate to discuss the Community's problems and to devise ways and means to promote its well-being.

Gidney's Successor

I entered public life at the rather early age of 26. A busy, practising lawyer, I nevertheless took a deep interest in the affairs of my Community. I was nominated by the then Central Provinces Government to represent my Community on the local Municipal Corporation. At the age of 26 I was elected President of the branch of the All-India Anglo-Indian Association at Jubbulpore which had one of the largest concentrations of the Community in the Country. That was in 1934. Because of my professional pre-occupations, I had not been able to attend the Annual General Meetings of the Association. In January, 1942, Gidney visited my home town. Although I had met him often this was his first visit to the branch during my eight years' tenure of office as the branch President . Before asking Sir Henry to address the crowded meeting, I made an introductory speech. 'The Anglo-Indian Review' of February, 1942, reporting the meeting contained these strikingly prophetic words: "Sir Henry Gidney said that in all his 25 years' political experience he had never heard an Anglo-Indian speaker of the same ability. He conjured up a picture in which he could see that as the romance of Henry Gidney ends, the romance of Frank Anthony begins." It was typical of Gidney's irrepressible spirit that he regarded a hard, uphill, often thankless, task as a romance. Gidney insisted that I should attend the Annual General Meeting to be held that year. For the first time, in March, 1942, I attended such a meeting. At that meeting representatives of the Community from every part of India had gathered. Vital matters were discussed. I played a not negligible role in those discussions. Barely two months later Gidney passed away. His successor was chosen by a process of election throughout the branches in India. There was a contest. As a result of the election, Gidney's mantle fell on my shoulders. Gidney was 69 years of age when he died and, in many ways, had achieved an outstanding position in the public life of the Country. For a person 34 years of age, albeit a practising lawyer, the prospect of assuming Gidney's responsibilities, in what was perhaps the most critical period in the history of the Community, was not entirely reassuring.

Gidney had not been too well for some time and was, therefore, unable to tour the branches of the Association. Although the spokesman of numerically perhaps the smallest minority in India, the leader of the Community represents, from the territorial point of view, easily the largest constituency in India. In fact, the Anglo-Indian constituency is conterminous with the sub-continent. At that time the branches of the Association stretched from Karachi to Bombay and again from Multan to Trivandrum.

The political portents were fairly clear to those who could read them and understand. I felt that time was running out. I was convinced that political steps towards Independence would not only be initiated, but perhaps finalised within the next few years. Fortunately, being a bachelor I had no family financial commitments.

Abandoning my law practice, I undertook tours at a blistering pace. The result was reinvigorating, even electrifying, for the Association. A wonderful tonic effect surged through the whole organisation expressing itself in new branches, new membership everywhere. It was the Community's heartening response to my call to mobilise for the fight for survival that would now face us.

After my election to the leadership of the Association, I was nominated by the Viceroy in August, 1942, as the Community's sole representative in what was then known as the Central Legislative Assembly. I was also nominated as a member of the National Defence Council which was presided over by the Viceroy and helped direct India's war effort. I remember rather vividly my first meeting with the Viceroy, Lord Linlithgow, as one of his guests at lunch. Lord Linlithgow, always a complete gentleman, was unable, however, to suppress his surprise as I shook hands with him. He remarked, with due apology, that I looked like a boy. My personal reaction is not printable, but I hope that the record of the past two and a half decades will show that in the fierce, tumul-, tuous testing times that crowded in on me from the very beginning the Community had not, indeed, sent a boy on a man's errand.

Clear Policy

From the beginning I was very clear in my mind that the Community could no longer stand on two stools. It could no longer express a political dichotomy. Making my first major address to the Community at the Annual General Meeting of the Bombay branch in September, 1942, I said to the Community, "We are Anglo-Indians by Community. Of that fact we have every reason to be proud. We have forged a history, in many ways notable, of which any much larger community anywhere in the world could be justifiably proud. Let us cling and cling, tenaciously, to all that we hold dear, our language, our way of life and our distinctive culture. But let us always remember that we are Indians. The Community is Indian. It has always been Indian. Above all, it has an inalienable Indian birthright. The more we love and are loyal to India, the more will India love and be loyal to us." That statement was acclaimed by the leaders of India as some kind of a new gospel for the Community, but condemned by some of the older leaders of the Community as utterly heretical, as a gospel for 'Hinduising' the

Community. I regret to say that the political and, indeed, the mental arteries of some of these older leaders had hardened along parochial, reactionary lines. There was a special flutter in the Association dovecots at Lahore. At the following Annual General Meeting there was an attempt to get me out of office unless I undertook to declare that our policies were not only pro-Government but pro-British. I treated this suicidal myopia with the public whipping it deserved. I reminded the oppositionists of the perfervid declaration of the good old Dr. Wallace of the high-sounding Imperial Anglo-Indian League that 'Britishers we are and Britishers we will always remain'. The only reward for his exaggerated loyalty was the publicly expressed sarcasm of the arrogant Curzon. Fortunately, I was able to mobilise the overwhelming majority of the leaders who had enough vision and imagination to reject the old absurdities which would have meant extinction for the Community. I have never had occasion to deviate from that announcement in the past 26 years. It became, in fact, the greatest single instrument by which I was able to mollify not only the suspicion but ill-concealed hostility of many of the prominent leaders. It became the instrument by which I was able ultimately to secure recognition and, indeed, salvation for the Community.

The attitude of the successive Anglo-Indian representatives in the Central Legislature marked the evolution in the psychological attitude of the Community. Before Gidney the Community's representatives were an avowed appendage of the European Group in the Central Legislature. Pathetically, sometimes ludicrously, they hung on to the political coat-tails of the European Group. They seldom, if ever, spoke in the House and always voted with the European Group. Gidney also joined the European Group. But Gidney's was not only an independent but a rebellious spirit. In spite of the fact that he towered in ability over most of his colleagues in the European Group, the Clive Street mentality, which was an incurable affliction of the European business community in Calcutta, dominated the Group. That mentality made even Gidney the object of ill-concealed condescension. Gidney rebelled and wisely left the Group.

When I entered the Legislative Assembly, I had no intention of joining the European Group. Gidney's almost last tragic cry to the Community, shortly before he died, rang constantly in my ears.

The Community's betrayal by the Cripps Mission, the denial of recognition of the Community in the Cripps' formula of 1942, had provoked what was almost Gidney's death cry, "The Community has been betrayed by the British at the altar of political expediency." While I hoped for the best I realised that in this context of the betrayal of the Community, in the context of a history of constant, recurring betrayals, I dared not place its life in the basket of British promises. And I was not reassured by what I saw and had to fight increasingly.

Discrimination Attacked

In and outside the House I lost no opportunity of attacking the official policy of discrimination. After my first speech on the Finance Bill, the Government Whip approached me to vote with the Government. It was taken for granted that as a nominated member I would vote with the Government. I expressed my inability to do so, because of the continuing policy of rank discrimination against the Anglo-Indians. With ill-concealed horror on his face the Government Whip asked me to go into the lobby to meet the Secretary of the Legislative Assembly—a good Secretary but a dyed-in-the-wool representative of reactionary British officialdom. When I told him that I had no intention of voting with the Government on the Finance Bill, he was dumbfounded. His silence expressed more eloquently than any words that he regarded my attitude, not only as a nominated member but as the Anglo-Indian representative, as rank political heresy. I may mention here that my continuing criticism of Government policy led ultimately to my being summoned by the Viceroy. The Viceroy informed me that my record of speaking and voting was such that Government was reluctant to renominate me. I had committed what was regarded by British officialdom as an unpardonable political crime. But I was able to say to the Viceroy that I was there in a completely representative capacity and that when I spoke, I spoke with the authority of that representative capacity. Be it said to his credit that at least the Viceroy had the sporting sense to recognise my representative capacity and to renominate me.

That has been my strength throughout my public life, the strength drawn from the strength of the Association which is a uniquely representative body. No person without the strength of his community behind him, no person depending for his nomination on Government charity dared to say what I have said and continue to say. The measure of that strength, drawn from the Association, has been reflected down to today in the unusual spectacle that as a nominated member I sit not only in the Opposition but in the front rank of the Opposition in India's Parliament. Because of the strength of the Association only a deliberately dishonest Government could refuse to nominate its leader to represent the Community in Parliament.

Speaking on the Finance Bill in March, 1943, I castigated the Government for the discrimination which it continued to practise against the Community. Among other things I said, "The military authorities, if anything, are today practising this discrimination in a flagrant way. My hon'ble friends do not realise the nature of this discrimination. They are not aware of the nature of the differential scales of pay and allowances that are offered to European Commissioned Officers on the one hand and Indian Commissioned Officers on the other. This is a matter which affects us all in this Country to whichever community we may happen to belong. It is a case of flagrant racial discrimination translated into economic practice. Members are not aware that a married Captain on the European scales gets Rs. 775/- as against Rs. 610/- drawn by an Indian Commissioned Officer: a Major gets Rs. 1105/- as against Rs. 850/- drawn by an Indian Commissioned Officer : a Lt. Col. gets Rs. 1450/- as against 1105/- drawn by his Indian counterpart. And this discrimination becomes more and more marked as the seniority increases. Is there any justification for this discrimination? Economically, there is no justification, morally, it is indefensible."

"I make this assertion on the floor of this House and I challenge the military authorities to investigate my assertion. They will find that what I say is true. I say that ninety-nine and nine-tenths of the so-called British Emergency Commissioned Officers who are domiciled in this country are Anglo-Indians. But because they choose, wittingly or unwittingly, to make a false declaration they are recruited as Europeans : without any investigation whatever, the military authorities give them a differential and higher scale of pay. The utter irony of this position is brought out by the fact that I know of not one but several Anglo-Indian families from which the lesser-educated sons, because of their lack of education, have made a false declaration. The military authorities have given them the enhanced European Commissioned Officers' scales of pay. The better-educated sons have got the reduced scales of pay because they have refused to deny their parentage or their Community. The whole position is thoroughly immoral. The British authorities, today, as they have done in the past, are placing a premium on dishonesty and cheating. If a man lies and makes a false declaration, they pay him more : if a man has the courage of his convictions, they penalise him by giving him a lower wage. I am not asking Government to lower the wage of the British Emergency Commissioned Officer, but I do ask them to increase the level of income and allowances of the Indian Commissioned Officer. As I have said, ninety-nine and nine-tenths of the British Emergency Commissioned Officers who are domiciled in India are Anglo-Indians. They are of Asiatic domicile. They are drawn from the same cultural and economic stratum as the Indian Commissioned Officer. What possible justification, economic or moral, can there be to differentiate in this matter of pay unless it be on obviously communal and racial grounds? I do not blame these persons so much for making these false declarations. I blame much more your Government policy which places a premium on racial discrimination, which offers a mess of pottage to the man who is prepared to deny his Community. Most men have their price."

Continuing I said, "It is this policy which has adversely affected and emasculated the Anglo-Indian Community. It has enabled the British historian to filch the names of Anglo-Indians and falsely to include them in the pages of British achievement. In spite of the fact that in this War, as in the last, 80% of the available manpower of my Community is serving in the different theatres, this discrimination is continuing unchecked. Over 10,000 Anglo-Indians are serving, today, in every theatre of War: 20,000 are in the various Auxiliary Forces. My Hon'ble friend Sir Edward Benthall, the Minister for War Transport, should acknowledge the invaluable service rendered by Anglo-Indian Railwaymen, who form the predominant part of the Auxiliary Force, in preserving the stability and strength of the Railway Administration. Yet in spite of these services the allowances granted to the Auxiliary Force have been recently decreased. There are about 4000 Anglo-Indian lads with the Royal Air Force in Britain. Yet the Anglo-Indians have

suddenly been disabled from offering themselves for service in the
Royal Air Force in India. These 4000 Anglo-Indians, by going
to England, have escaped from this policy of discrimination. The
irony of it is that while they are not permitted to enrol themselves
in India, they go to England and are in the vanguard of achievement there. It is a boy from this Country who holds the record for
the largest number of planes brought down in single aerial combat.
Dyson, the grandson of a former Anglo-Indian leader, shot down
6 Italian planes in 15 minutes."

"I wonder what the Country would do without the many thousands of Anglo-Indian girls who constitute the Nursing Services?
Even as regards our women, this policy of discrimination is there.
It is with the deepest regret that I have to draw the notice of the
House to the unfortunate position that prevails in the Women's
Auxiliary Corps. I have spoken to many scores of Anglo-Indian
girls on this subject. I have received the same general complaint,
that ranking and promotion are determined according to community. In spite of the fact that Anglo-Indians form the overwhelming majority of the personnel of the Corps, it will be interesting to
know how many of them hold commissioned ranks. I have been
told by every Anglo-Indian girl I have talked to that promotions
to warrant officer and commissioned rank are not determined by
education, specialised knowledge, ability or character but by other
and less worthy considerations. There are many girls in this Corps,
who are most highly qualified, who will never be considered for
officer rank because their only crime is that they are Anglo-Indians.
There are many Anglo-Indian girls with the finest of social antece-
dents who are prepared to join the Corps. They refuse to do so
because of this discrimination. There are many girls, today, who
are eager to do their bit but decline to join this service until the
conditions are changed."

"The same is the story with regard to the Indian Army Ordnance
units. Anglo-Indians are no longer certain of their position. One
technical officer says that they are eligible as British Other Ranks
and then another technical officer disqualifies them because they
declare themselves as Anglo-Indians. Some of these lads have even
deliberately been asked to make a false declaration that they are
Europeans. I have brought these matters to the notice of the Adjutant-General. But he has maintained a guilty silence. The only

conclusion that I can draw from this silence is that he is at least conniving at the muddle-headedness and discrimination that is being practised by his underlings."

I concluded my speech with these words, "Today there are many thousands of Anglo-Indian men and women who are serving in the various theatres of War. Today, not only the sons of India and Britain but the daughters of India and Britain are serving the same cause, fighting the same fight. Is it too much to expect from Government to give up this policy of discrimination? Is it too much to expect that from the present crucible of suffering and blood, equal sacrifice and equal heroism, equality of treatment in India irrespective of caste or creed or community will emerge triumphant?"

I fought similar battles in the National Defence Council, presided over by the then Viceroy, Lord Wavell. My Indian colleagues in the Defence Council were shocked when I told them that although about 80% of the Women's Auxiliary Corps was Anglo-Indian of 49 senior Commanders only one was an Anglo-Indian. I had for some time in the Central Legislature attacked the differential scales as between the so-called European and Indian Commissioned Officers. I remember how Wavell tried to justify it on the ground of the British officers having to maintain two establishments and the necessary higher needs of the British Commissioned Officers. How amused and happy were my Indian colleagues and how equally debunked and unhappy was Wavell when I produced a list of a number of so-called European Commissioned Officers on the one side and Indian Commissioned Officers on the other. In one list were the Anglo-Indians, Indian Commissioned Officers : in the other list were their brothers. One list was of those who refused to deny their parentage and their Community and the other was of renegades, rejecting their parentage and their Community, with a financial premium being placed on their renegadism. No longer could the Government justify differential emoluments between brothers. Ultimately not only the Anglo-Indians but officers of all communities were the beneficiaries. The scales were equated.

Envisaging the initiation of steps by the British Government for handing over power, I prepared, in October, 1944, a White Paper for presentation to the British Government and Members of the British Parliament. I also prepared a White Paper for presentation to the leaders of the Country. In 1944 when the Gandhi-

Jinnah talks were in the offing, I watched the developments with understandable anxiety. After the talks failed, through 'The Review', the journal of the All-India Anglo-Indian Association, I addressed the Community and defined what should be our attitude towards Jinnah's Pakistan and the two-nation theory. I underlined the fact that vivisection of the Country would be injurious not only to the Anglo-Indian Community, but more particularly to the other minorities and that it would not solve any of the minority problems.

The Sapru Committee

Early in 1945 what was known as the Sapru Conciliation Committee was formed. Its Chairman was Sir Tej Bahadur Sapru, a former Law Member to the Government of India, who had achieved a special position of eminence not only as a lawyer but in public life. He commanded universal respect and confidence. All important elements in the Country were represented on the Committee, which had the blessings of the majority party. I believe that the invitation to me was a gesture to the policies that I had first announced and pursued through the Association.

I submitted a memorandum on behalf of the Community to the Sapru Conciliation Committee. I opposed the idea of Partition. That part of my memorandum proved to be tragically prophetic. I stated, "I am in the completest sympathy with the legitimate claims of the different minorities. I also feel that everything reasonable should be done to allay misgivings on the part of different minorities. I am, however, emphatically of the opinion that the concession of the Muslim League claim to Pakistan would not only not solve the minorities' problems but would also be fatal to the best interests of the Mother Country. Briefly my reasons for being unable to agree to the Muslim League claim for Pakistan are:

"(1) Under the C.R. formula, Pakistan will only take in 17 out of 30 Districts in the Punjab and 16 out of 28 Districts in Bengal in addition to Baluchistan, the North Western Frontier Province and Sind: a large part of Bengal and Assam as a whole would not fall within Pakistan. Even under the most sweeping claims made by the Muslim League, Pakistan will include, presumably, the whole of the Punjab and Bengal together with Baluchistan, the North

Western Frontier Province, Sind and Assam. Even under this latter claim, Pakistan will comprise a total Muslim population of 55.60 millions leaving 23.74 millions of Muslims as minorities in the various Provinces in Hindustan. Further, there would be about 34.1 millions of Hindus, 3.89 millions of Sikhs and 3.2 millions of others as minorities in Pakistan. The minorities' problem after the division of India would be as acute, perhaps much more acute, in both Pakistan and Hindustan than it is today."

"(2) The Muslim League claim would lead to the Balkanising of India. A potentially powerful India will be emasculated as an international power.

"(3) The analogy of Europe does not apply, as India, unlike Europe, is a geographical entity undivided by real physical barriers such as are to be found in Europe. Further, in spite of differences, Indians have achieved a basic ethnic and cultural unity."

"(4) The division of India will lead to the probability, if not the certainty, of war between Hindustan and Pakistan and to the propagation of narrow and fanatical economic and political ideologies."

When the Committee's Report was published, it was regarded as one of the most important constitutional documents in the political evolution of the Country. It took its place with the Poona Pact and the Motilal Nehru Report. The Sapru Conciliation Committee Report was of special significance as it was endorsed by most of the leaders and parties in India and more especially by the Congress Party. For the Community the findings of the Sapru Conciliation Committee contrasted vividly with those of the Motilal Nehru Report. The Community had not been invited to participate in the framing of the Motilal Nehru Committee Report which was drawn up in Gidney's time. In fact, the Motilal Nehru Report had consigned the Community to oblivion. Three decisions of the Sapru Conciliation Committee Report affected the Anglo-Indian Community vitally.

(1) In the first place while the Cripps' proposals, of 1942, had not given the Community a single representative in the Constitution-making body, the Sapru Conciliation Committee, while recommending that the Cripps' proposals regarding the constitution should be accepted, also recommended that at least 2 representatives of the Anglo-

Indian Community should find a place in that body.

(2) So far as the Union Legislature was concerned, the Community was given recognition as a separate and definite entity: the other small minorities such as the Parsees and Europeans were all lumped together by the Conciliation Committee for the purpose of representation in the Union Legislature.

(3) The most vital achievement was the recognition by the Conciliation Committee of the right of the Anglo-Indian Community to a definite place in the Union Cabinet. Never before was this position recognised.

Unaided we had forged an Indian instrument of recognition.

The Hon'ble Dr. M.R. Jayakar, formerly a Member of the Judicial Committee of the Privy Council, an ex-Judge of the Bombay High Court, and one of the most distinguished members of the Sapru Conciliation Committee, was good enough to send me a letter appreciating my work. He wrote,

"If I may make a personal reference in this matter, may I say that before the Sapru Committee you fought your case very well with firmness not devoid of courtesy and persuasion. It was a contrast to the way the representatives of some other minorities fought their case. I had formed some idea of your methods of work from reading the debates in the Legislative Assembly, but could never imagine that your gifts could make you so irresistible an advocate of your community's claims."

An Interlude—Verdict On A Mental Guttersnipe

The April, 1945, number of the journal of the Association reproduced my speech in the Central Legislature on Beverley Nichols' book 'Verdict on India'. Commenting on the speech the special representative of the Hindustan Times of New Delhi wrote,

"Mr. Frank Anthony entertained the House with a brilliant denunciation of Beverley Nichols. He called the author of 'Verdict on India' a 'mental guttersnipe' and attributed the deliberate distortion and vilification of India to smug British racial arrogance. His retort to Mr. Nichols' remarks about Anglo-Indians being half-castes was that the British were the most hybridized nation in the world."

"But the most exciting moment in his speech was when Sir Sultan Ahmed, Information Member, interrupted him to deny that the Government of India had anything to do with the author of this shameful book. The whole Opposition seemed to jump to its feet to challenge Sir Sultan. Nichols had been chaperoned throughout his stay in Madras by the National War Front leader and Mr. K.C. Neogy remarked that Dr. Spears of the Information Department had been the friend and philosopher of Mr. Nichols. He added that Nichols' book would not have been published in India with such promptness but for the paper specially supplied by the Government of India. Cries of 'Shame, Shame' rang from the Opposition benches and Sir Sultan Ahmed discreetly kept silent, hanging his head to let the storm pass."

The special correspondent of the Indian Nation commenting on my speech wrote,

"The best speech of the day, however, was made by the Anglo-Indian representative Mr. Frank Anthony, whose verdict on Beverley Nichols was a masterpiece of satire, sarcasm and cynicism. Mr. Anthony's speech was also brightened by passages of great eloquence which was appreciated by all sections of the House. Indeed, Sir Sultan Ahmed appeared to cheer Mr. Anthony more often than anybody else."

In my speech I addressed the European Group as a proud half-caste speaking not only to half-castes but to polygenetics. Replying to me the leader of the European Group, Sir Henry Richardson, spoke as one polygenetic to another!

N.M. Jog, the well-known Bombay journalist, replied to Beverley Nichols in his book entitled 'Judge or Judas'. A whole chapter in the book was a reproduction of my speech.

The Simla Conference

A press release of the 10th June, 1945, indicated the exclusion of the Community from the proposed Simla Conference to be convened by the Viceroy. I was on a summer vacation at the time. I immediately wired and wrote to the Viceroy protesting against this exclusion and stating our case. I then sought an interview with Lord Wavell and discussed the position with him on the 21st June. In effect, the Viceroy told me that if the Conference was to deal with general constitutional matters, the Community would have been represented, but as the discussions were to be confined to the forming of an interim Executive Council, His Majesty's Government felt that owing to the numerical smallness of the Community a separate place could not be given to it. As some kind of a sop the Viceroy mentioned that even the Indian Christians, who were about 7 million strong as compared with about 250,000 Anglo-Indians, had not been invited to the Conference : the Parsees also who were of the same strength as the Anglo-Indians had not been invited. I replied that the Sikhs who were smaller in number than the Indian Christians had been invited, the moral being that unlike the Indian Christians the Sikhs were more united and also more troublesome politically. I was not satisfied by the Viceroy's reply and issued a press statement. I underlined that the Community received the news of its exclusion with shocked surprise and bitter disappointment. I pointed out that the strength of the Indian members of the proposed Executive Council was fixed as 15, which would appear to be a desirable number and no reasonable party would object to the smaller minorities being accorded 2 seats between them.

Among other things I said in my statement, "It has become conventional for the British authorities to regard the Anglo-Indian as an inveterate subordinate. Because we have not had representation in the Central Government in the past, it is sought to be argued that we are not entitled to it now. Another argument which is not justified by political theory or justice is that we are too small a Community, numerically, to be granted a seat in the Government."

Continuing I said, "If His Majesty's Government had desired to repay its debt to the Community, it could not only have invited a representative of the Community, but laid down that the Community shall be granted a place in the Executive Council, and I am certain that not a single party except perhaps the Muslim League would have made the slightest objection. But politics has always essentially been inspired by opportunism which seeks to satisfy the vocal or the wealthy." Continuing, I said, "I cannot help feeling that the exclusion of the smaller communities was a concession to the Muslim League policy. It was the original position of the Muslim League to claim parity of representation as between the Muslims on the one hand and all the communities on the other. Since the Wavell proposals predicated parity as between Muslims and Hindus only, the League endeavoured to secure the assurance that the smaller minorities would not get weightage or recognition in the Executive Council.   Their plea to the Viceroy was that if the smaller minorities also received representation, the Muslim League would only get 1/3rd of the total representation.   It is, indeed, unfortunate that the League policy should translate itself into resistance to the claims of the smaller minorities."   I further stated, "It is known on good authority that the Congress are not opposed to a place being granted to the Anglo-Indian Community on the Executive Council. The Sikhs and the Indian Christians are also in favour of the Anglo-Indian right to a seat.   It is all the more unfortunate, therefore, that His Majesty's Government did not think it fit to try and repay, partially, an irreparable debt to the Community by so framing the proposals as to ensure a seat to the Anglo-Indians on the Viceroy's Executive Council.   If anyone owed us an obligation to grant us this place, it was His Majesty's Government."

I concluded, "The obvious lesson which we are compelled to draw from the Simla Conference is that the British Government was not prepared to go out of its way a hair's breadth to do anything to assist the Community."

On the 3rd July, 1945, I sent a cable to the Secretary of State for India which among other things stated, "Exclusion from the Simla Conference bitter blow and incomprehensible because of status of Community recognised by Indian leaders."   Continuing, I said in the cable, "Request His Majesty's Government not to deny us what Indian leaders are prepared to grant.   Sapru Conciliation Committee consisting of most eminent Indians recognised the right of the Community to a seat in the Central Government because of our recognised importance and services to the Country.   Sapru Report acceptable to majority of Indian parties including the Congress Party.   Past history and present war effort entitle the Community to representation on the Executive Council."   Continuing, my cable read, "Auxiliary Force drawn from Community maintained Administration in two World Wars.   Railways would have been paralysed but for Community's effort.   Anglo-Indians nearly 35 per cent of Officer cadre of Royal Indian Air Force and 20 to 30 per cent of Royal Indian Navy and many hundreds in the Army.   Anglo-Indian women contributed more to War effort than all the women of all other communities put together. Anglo-Indian services during Campaign in Burma recognised epic'." The cable went on, "Representation on Executive Council vital to protect economy which dependent on Central Services. Greater right to seat than numerically larger communities whose services to the State and war effort nothing like ours. If His Majesty's Government denies us place which is recognised by Indians will be tragic requital for present and past services."

In the meantime there was landslide victory for the Labour Party in the British General Elections.

In September, 1945, Wavell announced a plan for consulting the opinion of Indian leaders and then forming the Constituent Assembly. The formula was vague and I was unable to secure from the Viceroy any clarification or assurance that the Community would be invited to those consultations. I was not prepared for a repetition of the Simla Conference betrayal. I convened an emergent meeting of my Governing Body and placed before them certain stark and even unpleasant facts. I pointed out that one of the greatest obstacles the Community had always to face and fight was not only the ignorance but, above all, the prejudice of the senior British civilians in India towards the Anglo-Indians. The Indian leaders had always been more ready to accept our case. Substantial proof was given by the Sapru Conciliation Committee. I felt that if we were to enlist the support of the British Government, then we could only enlist it through the British in Britain. I pointed out to the Governing Body that it was the Briton at home who had shown some appreciation of the Community's services. I reminded them of what had happened in respect of the safeguards granted to us under the Government of India Act, 1935. When the 1935 Bill was formulated, the British Indian Government completely refused to accept our plea for statutory protection. It was only through the intervention of politicians in the British Parliament that our position had been ultimately secured.

London Committee

The Congress maintained the India League in London as a permanent propaganda medium on their behalf. The Muslim League had fairly recently set up their own organisation in England. At that time I wrote words which proved to be prophetic. I said in 'The Review', "I look further ahead. It is my opinion that the

the Constituent Assembly will not meet. The Labour Government, in view of its repeated promises to India, cannot afford to stand still with regard to the Indian question. It is my opinion that even after the constituent body fails to meet, His Majesty's Government will probably propose a new Constitution for India. It is not unlikely that the outlines of this constitution have already been considered. Under these circumstances unless His Majesty's Government is made fully aware of the rights of the Anglo-Indian Community, this Constitution will probably overlook our whole position and will result in our political and consequently economic extinction."

I arrived in England at the end of October, 1945. My experience in the U.K. confirmed my worst fears. I found that the War had created a complete void so far as the Community was concerned. The old friends of the Community, such as Lord Lloyd, Lt. Gen. MacMunn, Sir Reginald Craddock, Col. Wedgewood, M.P. were dead. Others had retired from public life. At the beginning I was confronted with a dense atmosphere of sheer ignorance concerning the Community. The process of trying to make new contacts and finding fresh friends was not only difficult but almost heart-breaking. My first contacts were with some of my former colleagues at the English bar who had been students with me at the Inner Temple, such as Quintin Hogg. They were then members of Parliament. From my conversation with them I was convinced that Indian affairs and, above all, the affairs of the Anglo-Indian Community held no interest for them. I then spent practically all my time in the House of Commons. I listened to the debates and formed my own impressions as to who were the most active members with regard to India. In fact, I found that Indian affairs attracted comparatively very little interest in Britain. If the leading papers carried four lines of news with regard to India, it represented a great deal of interest. The people in India were not aware of the general blackout of Indian news in the English papers and the almost complete lack of interest in Indian affairs. Britain was preoccupied with her own formidable domestic problems and also with international issues. I then set about making personal contacts. I met and ultimately developed cordial relations with Arthur Henderson who was then the Under-Secretary of State for India. Sir David Monteath was another person with whom I became friendly; he was the head of the Civil Service and permanent Under-Secretary of State for India.

During my conversations in London with the leaders of the Labour Party and more especially with Arthur Henderson, I was given the impression that the Labour Cabinet, while sympathetic towards the Anglo-Indians, was convinced that the Community would not be recognised in the New India. Arthur Henderson told me he felt that neither the Anglo-Indians nor the Europeans would get recognition. I told him that this might happen to the Europeans only because of the myopic policies which had been dominated by the Clive Street representatives. Had Europeans like Sir Frederick James, who understood Indian psychology and conditions better than either the British officials or the European commerical community, been allowed to direct European politics, the attitude in India might have been very different. I told Arthur Henderson that so far as the Anglo-Indian Community was concerned, I felt that my nationalist policies, often bitterly criticised by uninformed members of my own Community and misunderstood by the British officials, would perhaps stand us in good stead with the Indian leaders.

Eventually I met and had long discussions with Lord Pethick Lawrence, the Secretary of State for India, and Sir Stafford Cripps. I addressed both Winston Churchill and Attlee. Churchill specially deputed Mr. Richard Austin Butler to meet me and discuss the position of the Community. I was fortunate in Churchill's choice. By a coincidence RAB Butler had been born in Madhya Pradesh (then the Central Provinces) my home State, when his father was the Governor of that Province. Over drinks in the House of Commons I discussed with him at considerable length the whole position of the Community. I found in him not only a sympathetic listener who knew a good deal about the Community but one who was prepared to use his influence on our behalf. He told me that, if necessary, he would raise the question of the position of the Community in the House of Commons when he considered it appropriate. The other leading members of the Conservative Party who I met were Col. Oliver Stanley, M.P., Sir Stanley Reed, M.P., Deputy Chairman of the India Committee of the Conservative Party, and Lord John Hope, Secretary of the India Committee of the Conservative Party.

I realised, however, that it was vital that I should make contacts with members of the Labour Government.   Hitherto all our contacts had been with the Conservative Party.   Some of those whom I met and who assisted me were Reginald Sorensen, Tom Smith and Harold Laski.   I was surprised by the knowledge that Harold Laski had not only of Indian affairs but also of the Community.   He mentioned that he had been gratified by my speeches in the Central Assembly.   He felt that the British Government had dealt shabbily with the Community.

Through these members I was able to address the Commonwealth Group of the Labour Party in the House of Commons which consisted of over 150 M.Ps.   Among the most interested members of this group was Major Woodrow Wyatt, M.P., and the Earl of Listowel, a member of the Government who was formerly Under-Secretary of State for India and later Secretary of State for India. Attlee was in the United States, but I wrote to him on several occasions and he sent me three personal letters, mentioning that he had asked for a very full report on my conversations with the India Office and that he had studied my letters setting out the position of the Community not only with considerable interest but with sympathy.

In the few weeks that I was in London, I also met several persons outside Parliament who I felt might be useful to me in my work. I decided to try and establish a Liaison Committee of the All-India Anglo-Indian Association in London.   I was largely helped by a grand old man who was at that time 84 years of ago.   He was Bishop Eyre Chatterton.   By a happy coincidence he had confirmed me when he was the Bishop of Nagpur.   I found in him an ardent and dauntless champion of the Anglo-Indians.   He had written several pamphlets on the Community.   He was responsible for the inauguration of the fund to help Anglo-Indian Education, and secured the support for this purpose of the Archbishop of Canterbury, Lord Linlithgow and others.   I believe he raised about £ 100,000 to assist Anglo-Indian Education.   He told me that the collections would have been much larger but for the sudden outbreak of the War.

Ultimately, I was able to set up an influential London Committee of the Association consisting of the following members.   Sir Harry Haig, a former Governor of the U.P., was the President: the Secretary was Eric Pound, an Anglo-Indian, whose family had settled in England, and who was working in a responsible position in India House. The other members were,

Lord Hailey,

Dr. Phillip Lloyd,	Bishop of St. Albans who had been Bishop of Masulipatam in India.
Bishop Eyre Chatterton,	who was Bishop of Nagpur when he was in India.
Sir Geoffrey Clarke,	one of the most influential businessmen of the City of London and who had recently been President of the London Chamber of Commerce.
Sir Frank Brown,	a member of the editorial staff of the London Times.

Sir Stanley Reed, M.P.,
Major Woodrow Wyatt, M.P.,
and Miss M. Tyrwhitt-Drake.

Eric Pound was, in fact, the only Anglo-Indian on this Committee.

I lost no opportunity of publicising the case of the Community in London and received friendly editorial comment from the London Times.

Association Captures Every Seat

I returned to India on the 7th December, 1945, and immediately plunged into Association and Community work which, in the context of impending events, proved decisive. At that time the Community had reserved seats in the Provincial Assemblies, to be filled by election in the Community. Elections to these Assemblies were to take place early in 1946. I realised that on the result of these elections would depend the character and ability of our representative in the Constituent Assembly, if we were granted representation. I repeatedly addressed the Community through our journal that it was of vital importance for Anglo-Indians throughout the Country to vote for the candidates put up by the All-India Anglo-Indian Association. I pointed out that the Community owed its position in the Country entirely to the Association. Among other things I said, "In the event of a Constituent Assembly meeting, the representatives of the Anglo-Indian Community will be elected by our 12 provincial representatives." I further said, "It is absolutely vital that in the future we have a co-ordinated policy throughout the Country."

The chapter on Gidney's work shows how he had largely forged unity in place of disunity and had brought the different Anglo-Indian Associations under the banner of the All-India body. Only one organisation in the South continued to stay out, to plough a lonely, dissident and completely ineffective furrow. Its claims were based on its alleged ancient character and little else. Throughout Gidney's struggle and achievements for the Community it had not helped and, indeed, could not help. It lost no opportunity, however, to attempt to stab Gidney in the back. The same policy was continued after I assumed Gidney's place. In all the critical phases through which the Community passed, it never raised its voice. But it came to my notice that, furtively, whenever a memorandum was submitted by Gidney or me a dissident note would be struck by this body.

Quite frankly, I could not understand Gidney's attitude towards this dissident but ineffective organisation which could only act in a manner subversive of the Community's best interests. Gidney had offered them every conceivable consideration to come in and join the All-India Body, but petty, parochial considerations prevailed. I also made every conceivable gesture, but I found that parochial interests always took precedence to the larger interests of the Community. Gidney had adopted an attitude of non-intervention in the case of certain dissidents. The results had not been happy for the Community. In Bengal there was the demoralising if not degrading spectacle of the Anglo-Indian representatives going into opposite lobbies and often speaking against one another.

I realised that the very existence of the Community now depended entirely on the All-India Body sweeping the dissidents out of existence. I also knew that 99% of the Community were, in fact and in spirit, behind the All-India Body. From the 11th January, 1946, I undertook a lightning tour of our branches in the South. I took the buttons completely off the foils with regard to the candidates put up by the so-called South India Association. I pointed out that they had never been able to lift a finger to achieve anything on behalf of the Community. All that they had done from time to time was to seek to undermine the position of the only organisation and its head to whom the Community, including the Community in South India, owed everything. I mentioned that while I was pleading the cause of the Community both in India and in Britain, this organisation sent a telegram to the Viceroy questioning my statement on the Community's case. In effect, I said that an organisation which did not know anything of what was really happening in the political field, of what took place before the Sapru Conciliation Committee, of my efforts in respect of the Simla Conference, an organisation which was helpless to raise a finger to assist the Community, yet spent its time in trying to destroy the efforts of the only organisation to which the Community owed everything, deserved no quarter.

In Bengal which holds the largest concentration of Anglo-Indians in the Country, a body of independents set themselves up against the Association's 4 candidates. I did a lightning tour also of Bengal. In March the results of the Provincial Assembly elections were announced. Every seat in every Legislature was captured by the candidates set up by the All-India Body. For the first time in its history the Community presented complete, unique cohesion.

For the Community these developments proved to be providential, as my interviews with Gandhiji and more especially with Sardar Patel, a few months later, will show.

As part of the steps towards constitutional changes, the British Parliamentary Delegation came out to India in December, 1945. I met the delegation formally in the Viceroy's House on the 7th December, 1945. On the 11th December I invited the leader of the Delegation, Mr. Richards, and Mr. Woodrow Wyatt, M.P., who was also a member of the London Committee of the Association, to lunch. After lunch I placed before the delegation in some considerable detail the history of the Community, its War record and its political and economic position. I underlined the need for the British Administration at least to accept the recommendations of the Sapru Committee which had, in turn, been accepted by the major parties in India including the Congress Party.

Speech Against Discrimination,

Among the several speeches I made in the House during the Budget Session, that delivered by me on the 25th March, 1946, on the Finance Bill recaptures, to some extent, the position of the Community at that time, the odds that we were fighting against and also the discrimination that continued to inspire the policies of the Administration.

"Mr. Frank Anthony (Nominated Anglo-Indian) Mr. President, Sir, in the few minutes at my disposal, I propose to make a plea on behalf of the smaller minorities in India, more particularly on behalf of the Anglo-Indian Community in view of the momentous discussions which are now going on. There may be a tendency at a time like this for the two main protagonists, the two huge communities in India, to occupy and to monopolise completely the political arena. I would appeal to them and to those responsible for conducting the discussions not completely to overlook the rights of the smaller minorities in India."

"Speaking for my small but important Community, let me make it very clear that I heartily endorse the sentiments expressed by Pandit Malaviya. I hope, more than that I pray, that these discussions will result in India being given her rightful place among the comity of free and great nations."

Encouragement Of Renegadism

"On behalf of my Community, I wish to make an emphatic protest. Discrimination is not so definite or obvious as in the days of Valentia, but it is as real, if more insidious, today."

"For instance, my Community is, today, a community several hundred thousand strong. But if you look at the official census figures of 1941, you will see that we have been listed as 140,422. What is the reason for this official estimate of a Community which, at a conservative estimate, is closer to half a million? It is the result of a deliberate official policy of emasculating my Community. In 1931, 15 years ago, the Census Commissioner said that the Anglo-Indians were about 200,000 strong. Fifteen years since then, suddenly, a community which was accepted by him as being a virile and prolific community has instead of increasing been reduced by 39 to 40 per cent. The truth is that Anglo-Indians are being encouraged deliberately to practise renegadism. Anglo-Indians are being encouraged to return themselves on the European electoral rolls. I have no quarrel with my European friends. I wish them well and I do hope that they will continue to play a great part in the future India. But I wish to point out that this renegadism has resulted in swelling the number of Europeans and bringing them inflated representation in the different Provincial Legislatures. I also have a grievance against the European Association. They deliberately encourage people whom they know not to be Europeans to join the European Association. It is an avowed policy."

Mr. C.P. Lawson: "Will the Hon'ble Member quote chapter and verse in support of his statement and prove that it is true?"

Mr. Frank Anthony: "I will give you one instance. I shall refer to the Punjab. According to the official census figure of 1941, there were about 6000 Anglo-Indians of whom about 3,000 were adult literates and should have been on the electoral rolls. Instead of this you find 503 on the electoral rolls: and of this number 300 appear also on the Europeans electoral rolls."

Mr. C.P. Lawson: "Who did it?"

Mr. Frank Anthony: "You did it. You encouraged people during the war. I was addressing the European Group through you, Sir. The Administration has encouraged this deliberately, I am sorry to say, during the war. I protested over and over again to the military authorities that their recruiting officers deliberately encouraged and even compelled Anglo-Indians to register themselves as Europeans. I can cite case after case. When a lad would go to a recruiting officer and say, 'I am an Anglo-Indian,' the recruiting officer would say, 'Go back. Think over it and come back tomorrow and enrol yourself as a European.' He went back and the next day he was recruited as a European. I say you have deliberately emasculated my Community. You do it in order to inflate your electoral rolls in order to get inflated representation in the Legislature."

Mr. C.P. Lawson: "That is nonsense."

Mr. Frank Anthony: "It is absolutely true. You have done it over and over again and it is part of your official policy. There is no use in trying to resist my argument by saying that this is nonsense. I can quote chapter and verse in support of my statement."

Mr. P.J. Griffiths: "On a point of information."

Mr. Frank Anthony: "I am not giving way. At the beginning of the war there were differential scales of pay. Indian Commissioned Officers were given one scale: the so-called European officers recruited in India got a different and a higher scale. What was the result? Because of these differential emoluments Anglo-Indians were encouraged to make false declarations. I gave not one but scores of instances to the military authorities. One brother, because he was not prepared to deny his parentage and his Community, got the scales of the Indian Officer. The other, the renegade, the cheat and the liar, because he made a false declaration, was getting the higher scale of the so-called European. This is all part of your policy, an insidious policy of preventing a person who has the courage of his conviction from achieving a position commensurate with his ability and thereby encouraging renegadism in my Community. I can give the House numerous instances where persons have been members of the Viceroy's Executive Council, Governors of Provinces, famous military commanders, who were all Anglo-Indians, but they would not have been allowed to reach those positions if they had called themselves Anglo-Indians. They were made and encouraged to call themselves Europeans."

An Hon'ble Member : "Define the term 'Anglo-Indian'."

Mr. Frank Anthony : "I am glad this question has been put to me. Even the most highly placed official does not appear to know the definition. The Government of India Act of 1935 has defined this term. My Hon'ble friends of the European Group are under a misapprehension as regards the connotation of this term Anglo-Indian. A person of European descent in the male line whose parents are habitual residents of India is an Anglo-Indian. If I may give an example, my Hon'ble European friends sitting there on the front benches, according to the definition, if their parents are habitual residents of India, they may claim to be of the purest European descent tracing their ancestry from the remotest Kings of England, but if their parents are habitual residents of India and they were born in this country, then they are Anglo-Indians."

The Hon'ble Sir Archibald Rowland : "Don't point at me. I am a Welshman."

Mr. Frank Anthony : "I am not pointing at anyone. If your parents are habitual residents of this Country and you were born here, then you are an Anglo-Indian, whether you like it or not. My Hon'ble friends of the European Group want me to quote chapter and verse. In all the Government official communiques and in all Government records they deliberately encourage people to call themselves Domiciled Europeans. There are not more than about 200 Domiciled Europeans in the whole of India. Yet look at the official figures. What was done during the war? We Anglo-Indians are a small Community. During the last war we won V.Cs but the recipients were all classified as Europeans. In this war, too, you denied the Anglo-Indian Community the credit of their achievements. In this small Community you have drawn a division. You have lumped the so-called Domiciled European and the European together. I maintain that 99 per cent of the so-called Europeans born in India and in the Armed Forces are Anglo-Indians. Yet the Government has tried to filch the credit from us. I am sorry to have to address the European Group in this way, but they are morally responsible for it. They aid Government in the continuance of this policy. They have done irreparable injury to my Community. They have fostered this renegadism in my Community. Why do you use this term 'Domiciled European'? The other day, one of my Hon'ble friends on the other side put a question as to how many Indians and how many Europeans there were in a particular department and the Hon'ble Member in charge of the department gratuitously said there were so many Indians, so many Anglo-Indians and so many Europeans. I say an Anglo-Indian is an Indian by nationality. But the Government maintains this artificial division between us and the other communities in India. Further, why do you also continue this term Domiciled European? It is misnomer. If a Pole settles down in America, does he call himself a Domiciled Pole? No, he becomes an American. Similarly when a European settles down in India, he must become an Indian. Why does he call himself a Domiciled European?"

Mr. President: "The Hon'ble Member has dealt with this point at sufficient length. He will take up other points, because his time is being taken up only by this point."

Mr. Frank Anthony: "This is the most important point and that is why I have taken up so much time. I do wish to be allowed some more time if necessary to elaborate this point. As I was saying, Sir, why should people from my Community be asked to classify themselves as Domiciled Europeans? I admit that we have had renegades in the past. Thank God owing to the policy pursued by my predecessor-in-office and myself, 99 per cent of my Community, today, are proud to call themselves Indians. But as a result of this official policy pursued by the Government and by the European Group, you tempt some of the Anglo-Indians to become renegades. I ask again, why do you continue to use the term Domiciled European ?"

"There is another aspect which I should like to point out to the members of the European Group. A Domiciled European is not a native of India. When you encourage an Anglo-Indian to return himself as a Domiciled European you deliberately encourage him to commit economic 'hara kiri'. It is very likely that an Indian Government will exclude Domiciled Europeans from employment in this Country, as they are not natives of India. You deliberately encourage the members of my Community to call themselves Domiciled Europeans without making them realise the implications of such a step."

An Hon'ble Member : "No : No."

Mr. Frank Anthony : "You have deliberately done it over and over again."

Mr. President : "The Hon'ble Member's time is over."

Mr. Frank Anthony : "I wish to be given ten minutes more, Sir."

Mr. President : "The Hon'ble Member will have to finish in five minutes."

Mr. Frank Anthony : "There was this renegade complex in the past. I do not apologise for it, but these were the reasons. We have through our schools contributed vitally to the national life of this Country. I hope this will be appreciated by all sections of people in this Country. We have given to India through our schools a system of education which other schools have nothing to offer by way of comparison. But I have been a bitter critic of the psychology in some of these schools. The European has hitherto largely controlled education in these schools. My Community has been made to look away from India. But thank God we are slowly bringing back these schools under the control of Anglo-Indians. I hope, Sir, my Hon'ble friends of the European Group will not feel aggrieved at what I have said. It is entirely the result of their own policy that they have so few friends in India who will tell them the truth. I say to the Europeans, in all sincerity, that we, the Anglo-Indian Community, after all, are able to under-stand the European better than any other community in India. We understand also the people of India better than any European could ever hope to do. But it is very difficult for me to make a

European appreciate this. It is because the European has sealed himself off in a highly insulated social system that he is unable to get to understand the real feelings and emotions of Indians. A European may serve in this Country for 30 or 35 years: he may give the best years of his life, he may put in selfless service to the cause of Indians in this Country, yet I say that 99 per cent of the Europeans in this Country, after having put in a long and even brilliant career of service, fail completely to understand the psychology of the people of this Country. There is this psychological void. You do not understand the peoples of this Country. If you had willed it, you could have allowed us to fill that void. But if I talk to a European about the bitterness of India in the matter of racial discrimination you do not understand. The reason is not far to seek. A Britisher in his own country is perhaps the finest European in the world. But what happens to him the moment he crosses the Suez Canal, I do not know. I feel that the main causes of bitterness in this Country are social causes. The Europeans have no social contacts with the people of this Country. The European women in India unfortunately have done a criminal disservice to their own people in England."

Mr. President: "The Hon'ble Member's time is over."

Mr. Frank Anthony: "I would make a final appeal to the European Group not to regard what I have said in a spirit of resentment, because I do believe that if only the Europeans would offer the hand of friendship to the other peoples in this Country, in return the people of India will extend to the Europeans real friendship."

Final Betrayal

On the 10th April, 1946, I interviewed the Cabinet Mission. I had taken the precaution of preparing a memorandum setting out fairly fully the position of the Community and its claims in any proposed constitutional pattern. On the 12th April, 1946, the Hindustan Times, the leading nationalist English daily in New Delhi, wrote the following editorial.

"The awakening of patriotism among Anglo-Indians has been more recent, but they, too, have nearly fallen into line. The difficulties of this small Community are many. In its origin, it was an alien and almost hostile element, but through the pressure of circumstances and wise leadership it has come to feel that it should throw in its lot with the people of India as a whole. The All-India Anglo-Indian Association, in the course of their reply to the questionnaire of the Sapru Committee bitterly complained of the false position in which the Anglo-Indians had been placed through wrong education and step-motherly treatment. 'All manner of absurd prejudices have been current in the socio-economic structure of Indian life. The European has affected and canalised an attitude of superiority to Indian and Anglo-Indian alike. The Anglo-Indian has been guilty of affecting an attitude of aloofness to his Indian brother. By way of retaliation, our fellow-Indians have regarded us with mistrust and unfriendliness'. The memorandum concluded with the words, 'We cannot be blamed for the fact that our mother-tongue is English and our culture is a culture derived from the West. The history taught us in our schools has been British history. But, today, the Anglo-Indian Community has awakened to the fact that it is one of India's communities, and that the hopes and aspirations of India are also our hopes and aspirations'."

"We are glad that Mr. Anthony, their able spokesman, told the Cabinet Mission that the Community had completely entered the nationalist fold and would be content with such safeguards as it could obtain from its countrymen on grounds of reason and justice."

"It is worthy of notice that Mr. Anthony pleaded for a strong Centre. As in the case of separate electorates, there is a mistaken belief that a strong Central Government will benefit the majority community. The only danger to minorities is from local prejudices and animosities getting exaggerated importance through passion and propaganda. Just as under responsible Government the influence of minorities is considerably lessened by separate electorates, statutory protection to the minorities through fundamental rights and other means is weakened if the authority to enforce it in practice is completely decentralised and vested in the units. A strong Centre, in the legislature and executive on which the minorities will be duly represented, will be a valuable protection against the exploitation of communal passions by local vested interests. The case for the widest provincial autonomy rests on the need for providing the maximum possible expression to linguistic and cultural groups, and in India these groups cut across religious and communal frontiers."

'The Statesman', a widely read and influential English daily, one of the few then British-owned, on the 11th April, wrote the following editorial.

"That the Anglo-Indian Community had entered the Nationalist fold and did not seek privileges or preferential treatment, but would work with other small minorities for the recognition of certain rights, was one of the points stressed in a memorandum submitted by Mr. Frank Anthony, President of the All-India Anglo-Indian Association, to the British Cabinet delegation today."

"It is understood that the memorandum presented by Mr. Anthony began by outlining the history of the Anglo-Indian Community, which is of Indian nationality and has throughout contributed largely to the national life of India. It then urged that the smaller minorities, including Anglo-Indians, should be given adequate opportunity of stating their case in the Constituent Assembly where they should have not less than a specified number of seats. In any interim arrangement at the Centre, there should be a composite Executive Council on which they should be represented. These points are also part of the Indian Christian case."

"The Anglo-Indian memorandum went on to urge that there was a danger not only of the principle of weightage for minorities being misapplied but also of this misapplication being extended. Weightage was intended to protect smaller minorities' interests, but if it was given to huge communities, smaller minorities might be squeezed out and the principle perverted."

"It was also stated that a comparatively small community like the Anglo-Indian scattered in various provinces likely to be under Congress or Muslim League control, could not be expected to take sides actively on the question of the division or unity of India. As a nationalist community they had no sectarian leanings but desired to see India a great Country. Anglo-Indians felt, however, that the best interests of the Country would be served by political unity with as strong a Centre as possible. Before any decision was taken on a division of India, it should be submitted to a plebiscite of adult inhabitants of the areas concerned."

"The memorandum expressed the belief that the future Government or Governments of India would welcome the Anglo-Indian

Community on account of its proved qualities which included discipline and civic stability. After referring to Anglo-Indians' services to the Country in the armed forces and the great departments the memorandum added, 'We shall give to the future administration the same loyalty and steadfastness that we have exhibited in the past.' It was pointed out that Anglo-Indians in the police force had already shown during 1937-39 that they would serve popular Ministries with their customary efficiency and loyalty."

I immediately reported back to my Governing Body my impressions of my interview with the Cabinet Mission.

In my report to my Governing Body I pointed out my fears with regard to the attitude of the Cabinet Mission. I had spent more than an hour and a half in discussions with the Cabinet Mission and had also gone through my memorandum with them. I found Lord Alexander a well-meaning person but one who appeared to have no conception of the Indian scene and still less of the real position of the Anglo-Indian Community. So far as Lord Pethick Lawrence was concerned, he was certainly well-meaning towards Indian aspirations, but had no real knowledge either of the history or the services of the Community. Perhaps, inevitably, the person whom I found to be the most informed was Sir Stafford Cripps. He asked me many questions which were indicative of a keenly analytical, legal mind. The trend of his questions showed perhaps a logical but also a mechanical approach to the position. He underlined the numerical smallness of the Community and emphasised that giving representation in the Constituent Assembly would mean giving unprecedented and almost fantastic weightage. I pointed out, however, that our case was not posited on any mathematical or mechanical formula : our position represented an amalgam of historical and political facts which had, only recently, been accepted by the Sapru Committee, whose recommendations had been endorsed by the largest party in the Country, namely, the Congress Party.

I did not hide from my Governing Body, however, my anxiety as to the results of my talks. I drew attention to the fact that Cripps had a bad record so far as the Community was concerned. In 1942 the Cripps' formula had completely ignored the Community and had given it no semblance of a place in the proposed Constituent Assembly. The Cripps formula of 1942 gave the Community no opportunity even to present its case to the framers of the Constitution. The Cripps proposals in 1942 had been described by Sir Henry Gidney, the then accredited leader of the Anglo-Indians, as a cynical betrayal of the Community. I, however, felt that my request for minimum representation, that is, at least one seat in the Constituent Assembly to enable the Community to state its case before India's constitution-making body would be accepted, particularly as the Sapru Conciliation Committee had recommended that the Community should be granted at least 2 seats in such a body.

In one respect the representatives of the Labour Government started with certain advantages. Unlike members of the Conservative Party, they had no association with British rule in India and, therefore, no background of any preconceived notions or what may even be described as political inhibitions. For a Community like the Anglo-Indians, however, this advantage could easily turn into a calamitous disaster. As I mentioned to my Governing Body, I had pleaded our case before people who might be described, without any offence, as 'political parvenus'. They had no real background association with conditions in India and the special position and difficulties of the minorities and more especially of the Anglo-Indians.

On the 16th May the Cabinet Mission's plan was announced. No place was accorded to the Community in the proposed Constituent Assembly. An Advisory Committee, however, was proposed in which the Community would receive representation, but the quantum of such representation was not defined.

Letter To Viceroy

On the 30th May I addressed a letter to the Viceroy, Lord Wavell.

Inter alia, I said,

"There are certain features of the Cabinet Mission's recommendations which are not clear so far as they affect my Community. I shall, therefore, be most grateful if these points could be clarified as there is certain understandable apprehension on the part of my Community about the exact implications of these items."

"I had sincerely hoped that a minimum of representation for the smaller minorities, in the Constituent Assembly, would be prescribed by the Cabinet Mission. For instance, in the proposed house of about 200 members for British India, I feel certain that none of the Indian leaders would have objected to at least 2 or even 3 seats being granted to my Community."

"Further, it is not clear as to what the constitution, functions and powers of the proposed Advisory Committee will be. From the statement of Sir Stafford Cripps it would appear that this Advisory Committee is to be set up with the specific purpose of securing effective representation of the interests of the smaller minorities particularly of the Indian Christians and Anglo-Indians."

"I shall be grateful for a clarification as to how this effectiveness is to be secured to the recommendations of this proposed Advisory Committee."

"What guarantee is there that the Advisory Committee must be brought into existence? Further, what representation, to be considered adequate, is to be granted to my Community on this Advisory Committee?"

"Lastly, in what way is this representation to be made, that is, what is the procedure to be adopted for securing the representation of my Community on the Committee?"

I received a reply on the 8th June, 1946. Among other things the Viceroy said,

"The constitution functions and powers of the proposed Advisory Committee were left to be determined by the Constituent Assembly. The Cabinet Mission certainly expect, however, that the Committee will be a powerful and influential body. It will be for the Constituent Assembly to accept or reject the recommendations of the Committee, but clearly a Committee of this sort will carry a great deal of weight, and its report will attract publicity all over the world."

Quite frankly, the proposals came as a shock to me. I realised that the Advisory Committee, as its name suggested, could only be a recommending body. There would be no Anglo-Indian in the Constituent Assembly to urge the acceptance of the recommendations which the Advisory Committee may make in favour of the Community. The Cabinet Mission proposals left the Community without even a single advocate of its cause in the Constituent Assembly. I knew that even with a representative our position would be inordinately difficult in the Constituent Assembly. There would be blank walls of prejudice, if not of hostility, to break through in the Constituent Assembly. Without a powerful advocate in that forum, there was little, if any, hope of the Community receiving any kind of recognition much less of representation in the future political set-up.

Meetings With India's Leaders

I then decided to meet Gandhiji, Jawaharlal Nehru and Sardar Patel. I met Gandhiji on Friday, the 10th June. At that time he was staying in what was known as the 'Bhangi' (Sweeper) Colony. He gave me a long and patient hearing. This was the first time that I had the occasion to meet Gandhiji. Since my assumption of office, most of the political leaders had been in prison. I gave him a brief survey of the position and needs of the Community. He was frank with me and said that but for the policies that I had pursued during the past 4 years, there would have been little hope of the Anglo-Indian Community receiving any consideration from the leaders of Indian opinion.

Gandhiji asked me why the Community wanted recognition as a separate entity: it was an Indian community and Christian, and he felt that it could take its place as part of the Indian Christian Community. I explained to Gandhiji, at some length, that this would mean the destruction of the Community. The Anglo-Indians, in fact, are the only real racial-cum-linguistic minority in India. Over a period of 300 years we had evolved into a distinctive, homogeneous entity with our own way of life, our culture and our language, English. I pointed out that the Anglo-Indians would regard any de-recognition of our position as a distinctive minority as a blow at our very existence, which could not be acceptable to the Community.

I told Gandhiji that apart from the historical and political factors that combined to make the Anglo-Indians a distinctive and distinctly recognised community, this position also had statutory sanction. Apart from the definition of the Community specifically embodied in the Government of India Act of 1935, I said that the Indian Succession Act of 1925 had defined the 'Indian Christian' as a native of India of unmixed Asiatic descent and who professed any form of the Christian religion. This statutory definition of

'Indian Christian' did not include the Anglo-Indian.

More than once, Gidney had been challenged by hostile members in the Central Legislature. He was asked why he claimed separate identity from the Indian Christians. Once Gidney was asked, "Are you not an Indian?" Gidney replied "Yes". He was then asked "Are you not a Christian?" Again Gidney said "Yes". To the assertion "Then you are an Indian Christian," while rather indignantly repudiating the suggestion, the usually quick-witted Gidney for once had no rational reply. Not being a lawyer, he was perhaps unable to elucidate both the constitutional and the statutory position.

Gandhiji then asked me what representation I felt would be adequate. I had not come prepared to meet such a question specifically. I, however, mentioned that I felt that since the Sapru Committee had recommended 2 seats, 3 seats would be adequate. Gandhiji said that so far as he was concerned, he would be prepared to recommend 3 seats for the Community in the Constituent Assembly.

I met Jawaharlal Nehru on the 11th June. This was also my first meeting with Nehru. Quite frankly, I had wondered what his attitude would be. In his Autobiograhy, Nehru had made some unflattering references to the arrogance of the Anglo-Indians and their overbearing attitude towards other Indian communities. I wondered whether he would be conditioned by that thinking. Actually, I found Nehru very charming. I put the position of the Community to him much more briefly than when I had met Gandhiji. I found that Nehru was not concerned with details. He asked certain questions which were not unduly pertinent to the constitutional or political position of the Community. I remember distinctly his asking me whether his relative's children were Anglo-Indians. As it happened, the relative in question, B.K. Nehru, who was later our Ambassador in Washington and is currently the Governor of Assam, had been a contemporary of mine at the Inner Temple, London. I mentioned that I knew him well and that although he had married a European woman, under the definition of the term 'Anglo-Indian' the children would not be Anglo-Indians: I said that biologically they might be Anglo-Indians but not legally since the definition postulated European descent in the male line.

I then met Sardar Patel. This, also, was my first meeting with the Sardar. In the popular mind he had been invested with an awesome aura, as the 'Iron Man' of India. That nom de guerre suggested not only a hard but even ruthless approach to administrative and political problems. As a practising lawyer I had got into the habit of trying to study those whom I met and of forming an estimate of their qualities. As I sat down, I scrutinised the Sardar. His heavy-lidded, half-closed eyes and sphinx-like manner did not help in my assessment. I stated the case of the Community before him rather fully, setting out the historical and political position and also the special economic needs of the Community. Beyond a few non-committal, monosyllabic grunts he did not interrupt me. I wondered how much he had taken in. To my surprise he then put me a series of staccato questions which no other leader had asked. I realised then, what further contacts and subsequently increasing close association only helped to confirm. Here was a man with a crystal-clear mind who could see to the core of a problem within the shortest possible time. He asked me how many seats I wanted. I said 3. He asked me how many votes in my opinion would be required to return 3 candidates to the Constituent Assembly. I said that my estimate was that, on an average, it would require about 4 votes in each Provincial Assembly to return one representative to the Constituent Assembly. I made it clear, however, that except for Bengal where we had 4 seats, we could not, on our own, return an Anglo-Indian representative to the Constituent Assembly. He asked me how many seats we had in all the Provincial Assemblies. I said 12. How many of these representatives, he asked, would vote according to my direction. I said all 12. He was a little incredulous that I could command the vote of every Anglo-Indian in every Legislature, but I assured him that this was a fact. He then said that since we had 12 seats in the Provincial Legislatures, he would be prepared, on my assurance of their voting solidly at my direction, to recommend 3 seats for the Community in the Constituent Assembly. He said that the Anglo-Indians would have to vote in support of non-Anglo-Indian Congress candidates in States where no Anglo-Indian representative could be returned, but that from three Provincial Assemblies he would ensure, by giving us the necessary number of Congress votes, that 3 Anglo-Indians were returned to the Constituent Assembly.

I followed up my interviews by writing fairly comprehensive letters both to Gandhiji and the Sardar. The position with regard to the Constituent Assembly had been clarified. In my talks with them I had not laid particular emphasis on the need for representation in the Executive Council, the Indian counterpart of the British Cabinet. In my letters I did place this emphasis.

Congress Recommends Anglo-Indian For Interim Government

In the meantime active steps had been taken to form an Interim Government. I was anxious that the Community should find a place in the Interim Government. I realised that in this matter I could get no assistance either from the Viceroy or the British Administration. The Simla Conference and the Cabinet Mission's proposals had illustrated that abundantly. With the seal that had been placed on our position by the Sapru Committee we had an excellent case for representation in the Interim Government. I felt strongly that with an Anglo-Indian in the Central Cabinet the chances of the Community finding a place of recognition in the future Constitution would be vastly enhanced. I also felt that once the principle of representation of the Community in the Government was accepted, it would grow into a convention and would give the Community an established place in the highest councils of the Nation. I also realised that, here again, I was up against the die-hard attitude of the British officials who surrounded the Viceroy. Further, I had some misgivings as to the personal attitude of Wavell. I had on more than one occasion crossed swords with him when he was the Commander-in-Chief and I was a member of the National Defence Council. Unfortunately, I had also been obliged to criticise Lady Wavell's handling, when she was acting head of the Corps, of the policies in the Women Auxiliary Corps which had created so much resentment among the Anglo-Indian members. I took the precaution, therefore, of writing to the Viceroy and informing him that in pleading the case for the inclusion of the Community in the Interim Government I sought nothing for myself. All I wanted was the principle accepted of giving the Community representation in the Interim Government. I said that the Governing Body of the Association would recommend an Anglo-Indian, if necessary other than myself, for a place in the

Cabinet. I then wrote to Gandhiji and the Sardar. In my letters I mentioned that I was not pleading for a place for myself. I saw the Sardar once again. He, however, said that if the Congress recommended an Anglo-Indian, they would only recommend me.

Gandhiji sent me a long letter much of which was of a personal character giving advice to the Community and commending the policies that I had pursued. The following extract with regard to the representation in the Interim Government was significant. "The Sapru Committee's recommendation was correct. But please remember that this is an interim affair. If the Constituent Assembly were to ignore you then it would be a dangerous thing. But this must not happen. As matter of fact, if the Congress could have had its way, which it has not, you would have been in the Interim Government too."

The Sardar sent me the following reply to my letter dated the 18th June.

Dear Friend,

I have received your letter of the 18th instant. We tried our best to accommodate all the minorities, including the Anglo-Indian Community, in the formation of the provisional National Government. Unfortunately, Mr. Jinnah and his League took an attitude from the beginning of not allowing any minority representation except that of the Sikh and Christian Communities. He insisted on the limitation of 12 seats, of which, on a parity basis, he claimed 5 and agreed to allow 5 to the Congress. We pressed for increasing the number so as to enable us to accommodate representation for the Anglo-Indians, Parsis and Women."

We also pressed for more representation for the Depressed Classes. But the League would not agree to any increase. It was with great difficulty that we succeeded in getting the number increased to 14, in which a Parsi was nominated by the Viceroy without our knowledge. I am enclosing herewith a press-cutting from which you will see our attitude regarding your Community. Whenever in future any occasion will arise, we will see that justice is done to the Anglo-Indians. You can be sure of that so far as the Congress is concerned.

Yours sincerely,
Vallabhbhai Patel

Frank Anthony, Esq., MLA, Barrister-at-Law,
President-in-Chief,
The Anglo-Indian Association,
New Delhi.

The press-cutting which the Sardar enclosed was from the
Hindustan Times. It was as follows.
"Hindustan Times,
New Delhi,
Sunday, 10th June.

Majority Of Congress Nominees Accepted By Mission

"The statement of the Cabinet Delegation and the Viceroy
regarding the Interim Government has been well received by
political quarters. The main reasons for this attitude are:

"There is no Congress-League parity.

"The Muslim League are 5 out of 14 instead of 5 out of 12 as
demanded by Mr. Jinnah.

"The names of Sardar Baldev Singh and Dr. John Mathai
recommended by the Congress have been accepted."

"There is a specific pledge that the composition of the Interim
Government will not be treated as a precedent for the solution of
any other communal question."

"Out of 14 names, 11 are those recommended by the Congress".

"The changes made are Sir N.P. Engineer, Sardar Abdur Rab
Nishtar and Mr. H.K. Mahtab. It is said that the Congress recommended Mr. Frank Anthony of the Anglo-Indian Community,
since the Parsi Community has had representation in the Executive
Council. The working Committee had also proposed that Dr.
Zakir Hussain should represent Independent Muslims. It was
proposed by the Working Committee that Mr. Sarat Chandra Bose,
leader of the Congress Party in the Assembly, should be in the
Cabinet."

Mala Fide

Not satisfied with the calculated exclusion of the Anglo-Indian
Community from representation in the Constituent Assembly,
Viceroy Wavell, with almost malicious deliberation, resisted at
every step the inclusion of a representative of the Community in
the Viceroy's Executive Council. The enormity of this crowning

disservice has to be measured against the fact that the Community was fighting for its very existence—an ultra-microscopic minority seeking to find a place among the hundreds of millions of India's other communities. In spite of the odium that our services to the British had attracted towards us, I had succeeded, in the space of 4 years, in largely effacing that odium. Fortified by the Sapru Committee recommendations, I had secured from the leaders of India specific recognition of the Community's place as one of the important, politically recognised minorities in India. The Government's own plan originally was to have 12 seats for the Viceroy's Executive Council or Interim Cabinet. The 12th seat was to be filled either by an Indian Christian or an Anglo-Indian. This meant that if the number was raised to 13 an Anglo-Indian was bound to have been selected. But even when the number was raised to 14 the Anglo-Indian Community was singled out by the Viceroy for exclusion.

In the list of nominees submitted by the Congress Party to the Viceroy there was a representative of the Anglo-Indian Community. While the Viceroy accepted all the other nominees of the Congress Party, he went out of his way to ignore the Anglo-Indian nominee and instead selected Sir N.P. Engineer. Engineer, however, possessed no representative capacity even in his small community, the Parsis. He was a servant of the Crown being the then Attorney-General. Perhaps British officialdom felt that Engineer's appointment was an adequate 'quid pro quo' for his prosecution of the Indian National Army personnel. Even then the Congress did their utmost to secure a place for the Anglo-Indian Community. They approached the Viceroy to increase the number of seats from 14 to 15 as they did not wish to insist on N.P. Engineer's removal so as to suggest any kind of hostility to the Parsis. Once again, the Viceroy, almost with deliberate malice, refused.

The Congress leaders pointed out to him that there was no possible justification for adhering to the Viceroy's formula of 6 representatives of the Congress, 5 of the Muslim League and 3 of the minorities as announced by the Viceroy on the 16th June. They pointed out that there was no object in adhering to the formula since the Muslim League had, at that time, not agreed to join the Interim Government. It was also made clear to the Viceroy that should the League join the Interim Government, the Congress nominees would resign and a fresh Cabinet formed. But all arguments with the Viceroy failed. His only purpose seemed the continuing, deliberate exclusion of the Community from the Central Cabinet. And that the seeming animus of the Viceroy was directed not against me, but against the Community, was clear from the context of what actually happened. As mentioned earlier, I had written to the Viceroy making it clear that any Anglo-Indian and not myself could be included in the Interim Government provided he had the approval and the confidence of the Governing Body of the All-India Anglo-Indian Association.

The British seemed to resent that we had achieved so much on our own. They seemed to resent that our fellow-Indians were prepared to give us what the British had never deigned to give us throughout British Indian history.

I convened an Extraordinary General Meeting of the Association on the 22nd June, 1946, to consider the gratuitous disservice done to the Community by the Cabinet Mission's proposals concerning the Constituent Assembly and the exclusion of the Community from the Interim Government. Vehement speeches were made by the younger elements, urging direct action against the Government in every possible way. I, however, counselled moderation in spite of my appreciation of the justification for the indignation and bitterness. A resolution was then unanimously adopted expressing the Community's incredulity and bitterness at the criminal disservice done to the Anglo-Indians, when we were fighting for our existence, by the Cabinet Mission and the Viceroy. It was also resolved to call upon the Community to resign from the Auxiliary Force.

The bitter and widespread resentment of the Community against these successive acts of cynical and conscienceless betrayal first by the Cabinet Mission and then by the Viceroy was demonstrated by the way in which the members of the Community in every part of the Country, at the call of the Association, submitted their resignations from the Auxiliary Force. This was no light or easy decision. For generations the Anglo-Indians had an almost traditional loyalty to the Government. In the Auxiliary Force they had represented India's Second Line of Defence. In fact, for the Anglo-Indians on the Railways membership of the Auxiliary Force was made part of their contract of employment. When the Community, through the Association, decided to resign, the

Railway Administration immediately took up a menacing attitude. Anglo-Indian railwaymen were threatened with instant dismissal. They were told that their resignation from the Auxiliary Force meant a breach of contract. I pointed out to the Railway Board that this was nothing of the sort: that under the Auxiliary Force Act if an Anglo-Indian had completed 4 years' service or had reached the age of 45, he had the absolute right to resign. I further pointed out to the Railway Board that the compulsion on Anglo-Indians to join the Auxiliary Force, as a condition precedent to their employment, was illegal. The Anglo-Indians being Indian nationals could not be singled out from all the other Indian nationals for compulsory service. Every pressure, overt and covert, was, however, brought to bear by the European Railway officers on Anglo-Indian railwaymen. They realised that the undisturbed running of the Indian railways was not worth a day's purchase without Anglo-Indian support. There was also perhaps a personal element in the attitude of European railway officials. Many of them were officers in the Auxiliary Force and they did not view with equanimity the sudden termination of their opportunities to play at soldiering. The sheer cynicism of the Administration was underlined by the fact that while the Wilcox Army Reorganisation Committee had recommended, early in 1946, that the Auxiliary Force should be disbanded, suddenly the Government, while initiating measures for Indian Independence, decided to maintain the Auxiliary Force and to insist on the Anglo-Indians serving in it.

The wanton disregard of the interests of the Community could not have been underlined more clearly. At a time when the Community was fighting, literally, for its existence in the New India, when both the Cabinet Mission and the Viceroy had rejected the position which the Community had achieved vis-a-vis Indian public opinion, yet the Viceroy and his Government insisted on Anglo-Indians continuing in a force that would have been used at any time not only to break strikes on the railways but called out to suppress any political demonstration and, if necessary, to shoot down their fellow-Indians. The courage displayed by the Community at this time made even the cynical British Administration rethink its position. When I made it clear that any attempt on the part of the Administration to victimise the Anglo-Indians for resigning from the Auxiliary Force would be suitably answered by the Community, the Government decided to accept the resignations of members of the Community and to make membership of the Auxiliary Force voluntary. This order was issued in August, 1946.

The apparently calculated cynicism of the Cabinet Mission towards the Anglo-Indians was highlighted by the insidious way in which they sought to give the Europeans fantastic weightage in the Constituent Assembly. While the Anglo-Indian Community had been denied even a single seat, the Cabinet Mission's proposals would have resulted in the Europeans, because of their artificially large representation in the Bengal Legislature, being able to return between 6 and 8 representatives to the Constituent Assembly.

I saw through this device and exposed it in the press. I also mentioned it in my talks with Sardar Patel whom I met frequently. When this device was brought to their notice, the Indian leaders reacted strongly and insisted that the Europeans should not only have no seat in the Constituent Assembly, but should not even be allowed to exercise their votes to elect representatives from the Provincial Assemblies to the Constituent Assembly.

I am almost certain that if the Cabinet Mission had acted in an open-handed, fair manner prescribing specific representation for all the minorities and had also granted about 2 seats to the Europeans, there would have been not a single dissenting voice in India. But it was regarded as sheer political jobbery for about 20,000 Europeans in the whole of India to be granted, in a tortuous way, between 6 and 8 seats in the Constituent Assembly. The result of this attempted political nepotism was gratuitously to antagonise the Indian leaders and ensure the complete exclusion of the Europeans from the Constituent Assembly.

Changed Attitude Of Indian Leaders

The rapid change in the attitude of the Indian leaders, at this critical juncture, was eloquently demonstrated by the address to the Community of the Chief Minister of Bombay, Bala Saheb Kher, one of the oldest and most respected leaders of the Congress Party. Addressing the Annual General Meeting of the Bombay Branch of the All-India Anglo-Indian Association in July, 1946, he said, "One of the striking features of your Community life and its activities is its great cohesion. No other Community has such a well-knit organisation to see to or represent its interests. It is no wonder, therefore, that the Association has succeeded in getting all the Assembly and Council seats in the Country filled by its candidates. I should like to congratulate you on this and assure you that the cooperation of your representatives will be needed, and will be much appreciated in the Assembly which will frame Free India's Constitution."

Continuing Bala Saheb Kher said, "You have some special talents. You have been outstanding in certain fields of service. These qualities will always stand you in good stead. There is much need for your courage, your sense of duty, your managing ability, your cheerful outlook, your mechanical aptitude. There is much room for the employment of your great organising ability."

Critical Phase

The delicate and often dangerous position in which the Community was placed at this fluid but decisive period in Indian history was illustrated by the tight rein that I was required to keep on the policies which some of our MLAs, perhaps unwittingly, pursued.

The Anglo-Indians in Bengal and those who represented the Community in the Bengal Legislature were not entirely to blame. They were, in a sense, the victims of local circumstances. European politics not only in Bengal but in India had been dominated by the Clive Street mentality, that is, the mentality of the English business tycoons. Because of this reactionary mentality and their complete ignorance of the psychology of the Indians, the Europeans, in the penultimate stage, threw away their opportunities with both hands. Personally, I would like to have seen the Europeans get some sort of representation in the Constituent Assembly in order to place their very real case before that body. If really experienced European politicians, such as Sir Frederick James, had controlled the policy of the European Association and not the reactionary, politically short-sighted European businessmen, the attitude of Indian opinion towards the Europeans would, almost certainly, have been quite different. Seemingly bereft of political imagination, the British businessmen-politicians continued to live and move in their isolated world of reactionary illusion. The British representatives in the Legislature were suspected of having a secret alliance with the Muslim League.

Even after I had succeeded in securing representation for the Community in the Constituent Assembly, the conditions in the Country continued to be critical and of a highly volatile character. The political set-up already highly complicated was made even more difficult and complex by the increasing tension between the two major political parties. The Anglo-Indian representatives had to walk with a constant wariness on which depended the very existence of the Community. There was always the danger that our representatives in some of the Legislatures might commit themselves to policies, determined by narrow provincial and parochial considerations, and which would have calamitous All-India repercussions on the Community. The position of the Anglo-Indian representatives in the Punjab and Bengal was particularly difficult. While in Bengal the Muslim League had a working majority, the opposition was powerful and vocal. In the Punjab, the cornerstone of the Pakistan claim, the Muslim League, although the largest single party, was unable to form the Government. Through speeches and articles in our journal I kept before our MLAs the vital need not to be stampeded by any temporary or local issues or to do anything which would antagonise the largest party, the Congress. I pointed out that the Congress Party was in a majority in 9 out of the 11 provinces. Three-fourths of the Community, I underlined, were resident in the Congress provinces. Above all, I emphasised the fact that we are an All-India Community not only in the sense that we are scattered throughout the Country, but because 80% of the life and economy of the Community was tied up with and dependent on the Central Administration. With its overwhelming majority in the Constituent Assembly the Congress could, if our provincial representatives gratuitously antagonised this party, deprive the Community of its economic life-line in the Central Services and also destroy our whole educational system. It was only by dint of keeping a constantly tight rein on some of our provincial MLAs that they were prevented, because they were unable to see the picture whole, from acting in a manner that might have gravely compromised if not destroyed the position of the Commu-

nity. Although the Anglo-Indian MLAs in Bengal had been returned on the Association ticket and were loyal to the Association,
a quite misguided parochial assessment of the political situation
made them believe that Bengal, including Calcutta, would fall into
Pakistan. I was equally emphatic that Calcutta and a large part
of West Bengal would never be included in Pakistan. Because of
this misguided assessment, and from a desire not to antagonise the
Muslim League, our MLAs, on a vote of no confidence which had
been tabled by the powerful Congress Party in Bengal, voted with
the Muslim League Government. Immediately a bitter cry of
condemnation went up from the Indian nationalist dailies. Thus
the 'Hindustan Times' of New Delhi, which was then perhaps the
most influential daily in the Country, published a scathing indictment of the action of the Anglo-Indian MLAs in Bengal. 'The
Amrita Bazar Patrika', the most influential nationalist English daily
in Bengal, in an editorial in the month of June insisted that not only
the Europeans but the Anglo-Indians also should have no vote for
or a seat in the Constituent Assembly.

In the same way, the Anglo-Indian MLA in the Punjab pursued
a course which promised to antagonise both the Congress and the
Muslim League. Although the Anglo-Indian MLAs had been
returned because of the Association's support and were enjoined to
pursue an independent policy this MLA accepted the position of
Private Parliamentary Secretary to the Chief Minister of the Punjab
(Khizar Hayat Khan) who belonged neither to the Congress nor
the Muslim League party.

Sardar Patel phoned me and protested against what he regarded
as the opportunism of our M.L.A. in the Punjab. To undo the
damage, I convened an extraordinary meeting of the Governing
Body of the Association, to which our representative in the Punjab
was summoned. At my request, Sardar Baldev Singh, who later
became the Defence Minister, attended the meeting and explained
the critical position of the minorities in the Punjab. After hearing
our Punjab M.L.A., the Governing Body decided to expel him from
the Association.

Realising that these actions of our MLAs might very well not
only endanger but destroy the whole position that I had built up,
I wrote a very strong page in our journal (The Anglo-Indian Review) for their future guidance. I pointed out that our MLAs

owed a supreme responsibility to the Community throughout the Country and that in the critical context in which we were moving, we were bound to observe policies that were balanced in terms of the good of the whole Community.

Be it said to the credit of the Anglo-Indian M.L.As in Bengal that they resisted all attempts by the Muslim League Ministry to seduce them politically. Offers of a Ministership and other blandishments were rejected because of their allegiance to the larger interests of the Community as defined by me.

Those were, indeed, grimly critical days. During that fateful period I had to tread a political razor's edge. One false step would have meant not only political decapitation for the Community, but the destruction of its schools and economy.

CHAPTER IX

THE MIRACLE OF OUR CONSTITUTIONAL SAFEGUARDS

IN accordance with the assurance given me by the Congress leaders, the Congress Party assisted in the election of 2 out of the 3 Anglo-Indian representatives to the Constituent Assembly. The number of votes required to ensure the return of one candidate from the Bengal State Legislature to the Constituent Assembly was 4. As it happened, there were 4 Anglo-Indian representatives in the Bengal Legislature. I did not require any Congress support for my return, as the 4 Anglo-Indian representatives voted for me.

It is an interesting sidelight that votes were fetching fantastic prices. It was known that certain candidates to the Constituent Assembly were prepared to pay at least Rs. 30,000/- for a vote from a Provincial Assembly representative. It was also alleged that on the morning of the voting in Bengal for the Constituent Assembly at least one vote had been bought for Rs. 30,000/. It was fortunate that the Anglo-Indian Community's representatives who were returned on the Association ticket were persons of unimpeachable integrity. The other 2 Anglo-Indian representatives were returned from the Madras and what was then known as the Central Provinces Legislatures. Since the Community had only 1 representative in each of these Legislatures, the Congress Party gave these 2 representatives the necessary first votes from their party members in those two Legislatures to enable the other 2 Anglo-Indians to be returned to the Constitutent Assembly.

The Constituent Assembly

In October, 1946, I was selected as one of India's principal delegates to represent the Country in the first delegation from Independent India to the United Nations. The leader of the delegation was Mrs. Vijayalakshmi Pandit. I returned to India before the rest of the team as the work of the Constituent Assembly was to start on the 6th December, 1946, and I was deeply anxious for the fate of the Community.

On the opening day the Constituent Assembly did me the honour of unanimously electing me as Deputy Chairman.

One of the most important non-official committees to deal with the work of the Constituent Assembly was formed shortly afterwards. It was known as the Advisory Committee of the Congress Party. This Committee was to advise the Congress Party on all matters arising in or which had to go before the Constituent Assembly. It was a sort of steering committee. Although I was not a member of the Congress Party, I was invited to join it. Throughout the framing of the Constitution the membership of this Committee enabled me to express, in what was virtually a decision-making body of the majority party, my views on many vital matters which came up, later, for decision before the Constituent Assembly. On this Committee were Pandit Nehru, Maulana Azad, Sardar Patel, Pandit Pant, Acharya Kripalani, Khan Abdul Ghafar Khan, Mrs. Sarojini Naidu, Dr. Rajendra Prasad, Mr. Rajagopalachari, Mr. S.C. Bose, Mr. Rafi Ahmed Kidwai, Dr. Jayakar, Dr. Shyama Prasad Mukherjee, Mr. Jagjivan Ram and four or five others.

The Final Political Stage

On the 20th February, 1947, Prime Minister Attlee announced in the House of Commons that the transfer of power to India would be made not later than June, 1948. If anything, the position of the minorities and, in a particular way, of the Anglo-Indians had become even more difficult and delicate. Because of the already acute and growing tension between the Congress and the Muslim League, the position of the minorities was anything but enviable. The tendency on the part of the major parties was one of almost blind intolerance. There was a tendency to think in terms of black and white. A party or a group or leader was either for or against. No allowance was made for independent or objective thinking on the part of the minorities.

In this atmosphere, surcharged with communal suspicion and

bitterness, I once again sounded a warning of the disastrous consequences to the Community if any of our M.L.As. allowed their conduct to be determined by parochial considerations.

Lord Mountbatten—Last Viceroy

Shortly after he assumed office as Viceroy of India, I sent Lord Mountbatten the following letter:

"Your Excellency,

I address you on behalf of the Anglo-Indian Community. I met Your Excellency when I was a Member of the Viceroy's Defence Council. My reason for addressing Your Excellency is to request that, in this final stage of transfer, nothing will be done by the British authorities which may injure the interests of my Community. Few Europeans are aware of the real history of my Community and of the vital part we have played in the development of India's strategic services and in the maintenance of the stability of the Administration.

Our numerical smallness makes our position in the political field extremely difficult. Our services to the British Administration have added to our difficulties. We were regarded by other communities as the standard-bearers of British Imperialism. We had earned the right to expect that in the final stage the British authorities would not lose sight of the position of my Community. We did not ask for or expect any favours.

The Cabinet Mission did a serious disservice to my Community by excluding us completely from the Constituent Assembly. Fortunately, this disservice was remedied by the Congress Party. An equally serious disservice was done to my Community by Lord Wavell when he ignored the recommendation of the major political party that my Community should be granted a seat in the Interim Government. My Community had hoped that the British might have helped us to strengthen our position. Instead, we were shocked when so far from rendering us any assistance Your Excellency's predecessor struck us a gratuitous blow by deliberately ignoring the recommendation of the major political party. The Community, is, today, straining every nerve to see that its rights are recognised. We sincerely hope that the Administration will do nothing, as was done in the recent past, to hamper or injure us in our present struggle for our very existence.

Allow me to wish Your Excellency a successful and happy tenure of office.

With my kind regards,

Yours sincerely,
Sd/- Frank Anthony."

H.E. Rear Admiral,
The Right Hon'ble the Viscount
Mountbatten of Burma, K.G.,G.M.S.I.,
GCVO, KCB, DSO, ADC,
Viceroy's House, New Delhi

The Viceroy sent me the following reply.

The Viceroy's House,
New Delhi.
29th March, 1947.

"Dear Mr. Anthony,
Thank you for your letter and good wishes.

I think that the subject matter of your letter is so important that I should like to discuss it with you in person and have asked my Secretary to arrange an interview.

Yours sincerely,
Sd/- Mountbatten of Burma."

Frank Anthony, Esq., MLA,
President-in-Chief,
The Anglo-Indian Association,
Hindustan Times Building,
New Delhi.

I met Lord Mountbatten on the 7th April. I gave him as fully as possible the background with regard to the Community and my efforts to secure it a place of recognition in the New India.

I do not know to what extent Mountbatten understood the real position of the Community. He was concerned with coming to some arrangement with the major political parties. In any case, there was little, if anything, that he could now do since the machinery of the Constituent Assembly had already been established and the process of beating out a constitution was committed to that Assembly with which the Viceroy did not interfere.

About Lord Mountbatten's personality, however, I formed a pleasant impression. He had a charm and naturalness which, I knew, would present a striking contrast to the attitude of rigid protocol that infected most of the former Viceroys. With him disappeared the usual laboured procedure of heralding a person into the presence of some demi-god, the demi-god having already taken up an appropriate posture of pseudo-deification. Lord Mountbatten, however, met me at the door of his office and greeted me with a warm, friendly handshake. As I neared his table, he took up a chair and brought it for me to sit in. Had a die-hard British civilian been present, he would have died of some kind of official apoplexy at Mountbatten's complete informality and, according to sundried officialdom's standards, very unViceroy-like behaviour. I realised, then, that whether Mountbatten possessed the necessary political education or experience would not matter, as he had with him many Advisers with a considerable political background. I thought to myself that with his charm and informality he would immediately break down the barriers of reserve and even resentment that generations of British priggishness and artificial codes of racial snobbery had erected. Above all, Mountbatten could afford this informality. The British civilians were, at best, middle class representatives. Mountbatten represented the bluest of the blue blood from Britain. Whatever he did could not be stigmatised even by the British wives as declasse. In fact, whether it was deliberately conceived or not, one of the master-strokes of British diplomacy was to send out a person who was a British Maha Brahmin (Great Brahmin) to deal with the Brahmin representatives of India. Mountbatten's freedom from artificial social inhibitions was worth cohorts of political experts in breaking through the walls of Indian sensitiveness and resentment reared, over decades, by the self-styled aristocracy of British officialdom. At this critical stage, a Viceroy who yielded to the deadening hand of crusted officialdom, who dragged his feet in deference to the mumbo jumbo of a perverse social code, might easily have failed where Mountbatten succeeded.

Edwina, Lady Mountbatten

About a fortnight later I met Lady Mountbatten. I expected to be one of several invitees. When I arrived, however, I found that I was the only person invited to have tea with her. Few people could have resisted Lady Mountbatten's complete naturalness and unaffected charm. She evinced a deep and intelligent interest in the women of the Community. She mentioned that her long association with the Nursing Services had given her a special interest in Anglo-Indian women who at that time represented the overwhelming majority of the nurses of India. She remarked on this phenomenal position of Anglo-Indian women and said that during her inspection, both private and official of several hospitals, she was struck by the fact that practically every nurse was an Anglo-Indian. She spoke highly of the excellence of the Anglo-Indian nurses. In spite of the fact that, by and large, Indian hospitals were hopelessly under-staffed, they could, in her opinion, compare with the highest standards obtaining in the West.

Lady Mountbatten was interested in my analysis of the social system. I mentioned to her that in my view more bitterness had been created in India by an artificial, stupid social system the greatest architects of which were the British women in India, than by anything else. She appeared not unimpressed by what I regarded as the genesis of this social system. I explained to her that before the opening of the Suez Canal in 1835, comparatively very few British women came out to India and that, in fact, almost up to the end of the 19th century even British wives were usually not allowed to accompany their husbands. At that time 80 to 90 per cent of the British officials, both civilian and military, married Anglo-Indians and, in my view, they had done very well. The Anglo-Indian women were among the most beautiful in the world. I mentioned to her that Dupleix, the French political genius, had married an Anglo-Indian and so also had Warren Hastings. She was interested in my account of Catherine Worlee, the Anglo-Indian beauty who first married Grant, a member of the Viceroy's Council and, later, proceeding to Europe, married Taleyrand, Napoleon's Foreign Minister, and as Princess Taleyrand was an acclaimed international beauty of her time. My analysis was that when the unattached British women who came out to India, which represented an increasingly attractive marriage mart, with the avowed purpose of finding suitable husbands, they ran into a blank wall of competition represented by the often very much lovelier Anglo-Indian women. Self-preservation, the most powerful of all motives, made them evolve a social code which eliminated this uneven competition. A social taboo was erected. This was enforced, progressively, with all the refinements of which only the feline species is capable. Lady Mountbatten appeared not only amused but interested. I do not know whether she was convinced. But she was provoked into a mildly sarcastic reference to the inhibitions of the British women in India. She mentioned that on her way to Delhi, she had visited a hosptial in Karachi. The European Matron of the hospital almost dropped dead when Lady Mountbatten insisted on shaking hands with the domestic staff. Such a thing was unheard of in the hide-bound code of protocol. Lady Mountbatten was, however, happy especially when she was told, later on, that many of the staff had said that they would avoid washing their hands for as long as possible so that they could retain the honour of the handshake with the Vicereine of India. She also mentioned how utterly horrified some of the wives of the senior British officials in Delhi were when they first saw her call the sweeper into her lounge to attend to some necessary chores and also talked to him.

My first impressions of the Mountbattens were vindicated by later developments. Much of Indian resentment and suspicion dissolved under the impact of the Mountbatten charm and friendliness. In the years that they were to spend in India, Lady Mountbatten found a special niche in the affections and esteem of peoples of all classes. That she was generally referred to as Edwina was the measure of her charm and popularity. It would not be inappropriate to refer to her as the Greatest Ambassadress of Goodwill that Britain had ever sent to India.

Partition

By accepting the Viceroy's plan, as announced on the 3rd June, 1947, the Congress Party and the Muslim League accepted the Partition of India. Commenting on this, I addressed the Community through the President-in-Chief's page of the Anglo-Indian Review of July, 1947.

"The division of India has come. British India will be divided up into India and Pakistan. As I had anticipated, the Muslim League has got very much less than it was given by the Cabinet Mission's statement. Instead of the control of the whole of Bengal and Assam, the League flag will now only fly over Eastern Bengal and Sylhet. In the North-West area, also, instead of the whole of the Punjab, only the western area has been included in Pakistan". Commenting on the implications for the Community, I wrote : "Fortunately, the Community has been saved from vivisection. As it is, only about 5,000 Anglo-Indians in the Punjab, 2000 in Sind and another 1,000 in East Bengal will fall into Pakistan." Continuing I said, "All the resistance to our quotas in the services has invariably come in the Central Assembly from the Muslim Community. Educationally and economically the Muslims are, on an average, more backward than the Anglo-Indians, and have been largely dependent on Government service. They have always looked with longing eyes on the Anglo-Indian quotas. The fiercest attack that Sir Henry Gidney had to face was from the Muslim representatives in the Central Assembly in 1932. Subsequently, the Hassan Report asked for the reduction, if not the abolition, of the Anglo-Indian quotas. The Post and Telegraph Department, today, is illustrative of Pakistan in action. Unabashed, brazen and fanatical communalism has led to the pitchforking, over the heads of others, of unqualified Muslims in the Post and Telegraph Department. Fortunately, with the reformation of the Central Government this process will now be stopped." Continuing I said, "With division political issues have clarified. At least 95% of the Community will be in the Indian Union. We shall now have to deal with only one effective party, namely, the Congress. The nationalist policies of the Association, criticized by some morons and would-be politicians in the Community, have saved us from extinction. With the seats in the Constituent Assembly granted to us by the Congress we are fighting to secure the future of the Community. Further, we shall have a strong Centre. With partition the Cabinet Mission's plan for a weak Centre is dead. The Congress Party and the Constituent Assembly are evolving details that will give to India a strong centre. Our organisation, highly integrated, will be in a position, even better than before, to protect the interests of the Community throughout the Country." I concluded on this note, "Never before have we faced a more testing time in our history. Fortunately, wherever I have gone, signs are abundant that the Community has at last awakened to the stark realities that face us. Monster meetings and a rapid influx of membership are indicative of the realisation, late though it may be, that this is the last chance Anglo-Indians have of uniting under the banner of the only organisation to which they owe everything and on which their future will depend. I realise intensely that the task we are facing is a titanic one. Political forces will tend to squeeze minorities into a difficult position. We shall have to fight, with all the resources at our command, in order to secure what we regard as our legitimate interests and in order to ensure what we regard as a minimum guarantee of our culture, our language, our way of life and a reasonable degree of economic standards. I can only hope, and pray, that my task will be crowned with success. On that result depends the future of the Community, and, equally, the future of every Anglo-Indian in the Country.''

Framing Of The Constitution

One of the first tasks which faced me was to get adequate representation for the Community in the Advisory Committee on Minorities' Rights which was to be set up under paragraph 20 of the Cabinet Mission's formula.   The Advisory Committee was to deal with fundamental rights and the rights of the minorities and the tribals. All manner of conflicting interests had to be accommodated. There was strong opposition by the representatives of certain minorities, and particularly the Indian Christians, to the Anglo-Indians receiving more than one seat on this important body. The Indian Christian spokesmen argued that while the Indian Christians, who were over 6 million in number, had been accorded only 4 seats in the Advisory Committee, it would be grossly unfair to give the Anglo-Indians, who according to the official census were 140,000 in number, more than one seat. I flatly refused to accept this proposal and underlined the fact that, according to me, the official explanation by Sir Stafford Cripps made it clear that the Advisory Committee had been set up with the specific purpose of giving the minorities, and particularly the smaller minorities, an opportunity of securing necessary guarantees in the Constitution. After a long discussion it was agreed to give us 2 seats in the Advisory Committee. This also I declined to accept. Ultimately it was agreed to give us 3 seats. The Sikh representatives also fought strenuously for the maximum of representation in this Advisory Committee, but since the Indian Christians were satisfied with 4 seats, the Sikhs, numerically somewhat smaller than the

Indian Christians, had ultimately to accept the same number.

The 3 representatives for this Advisory Committee were selected by the Governing Body of the All-India Anglo-Indian Association.

In all, 72 persons were appointed to this body.

A Minorities' Sub-Committee of the Advisory Committee was also set up consisting of about 20 members. I was also a member of this Sub-Committee. Matters referring to the Minorities and Fundamental Rights went first to this Minorities' Sub-Committee.

Memorandum To The Constituent Assembly

In April, 1947, I submitted a carefully prepared Memorandum to the Constituent Assembly on the Anglo-Indian Community. It was a printed brochure of 18 pages. Among other things it dealt with the history of the Community, misconceptions and misunderstandings, our contribution to India's development, fundamental rights, education and instruction in our mother-tongue, English, and our contribution to the future of India.

The Constituent Assembly started its work in December, 1946, but it was in August, 1947, that the real fight for the existence of the Community began. Addressing the Community through 'The Review' I said: "We are in the throes of the most critical period in our history. It is a challenge to the character and moral stamina of every Anglo-Indian." Before August the Constituent Assembly had already adopted a draft model Constitution. According to that model Constitution we had set out certain basic demo-cractic principles. We had accepted the principle that so far as representation in the Central Legislature was concerned, it would be on the basis of one seat for approximately one million persons, and so far as representation in the State Legislatures was concerned we had accepted the principle that there would be one seat in respect of approximately one hundred thousand persons. The Constitution was posited on adult franchise and these basic democratic principles. In the face of that model Constitution, because of our ultra-micro-scopic size, the case of the Community appeared to be not only seemingly impossible but utterly hopeless. The Constitution was being framed on the basis of the 1941 Census. According to that Census we did not have a sufficient number in a single State to justify even a single seat. According to the 1941 Census the largest Anglo-Indian population was in West Bengal, namely, 29,000: in Madras it was 18,000, in Bombay 14,000, in the U.P. 13,000, in Bihar 5,000 and in what was then known as the C.P. 4,000. It will thus be seen that on the basis of our model Constitution we were not entitled to any representation anywhere.

In The Minorities Committee

Sardar Patel was the Chairman of the Advisory Committee on Minority Rights, which was a limb, so to speak, of the Constituent Assembly, and also of the Minorities Sub-Committee of the Advisory Committee. As mentioned earlier, I was a member of both the Advisory Committee and the Sub-Committee. The communities were divided into three groups : the 'A' Group consisted of the two smallest communities, the Anglo-Indians and Parsees who, according to the 1941 Census, had about the same strength, and would not be entitled to any political representation. The 'B' Group consisted of the Sikhs and the Indian Christians, each Community being about 5 to 6 million in strength. The 'C' Group consisted of the Muslims and the Scheduled Castes, each Community being between 40 and 50 million in strength. The Minorities Sub-Committee started first with the case of the Anglo-Indians. Immediately I was opposed by Sidhwa one of the two Parsee representatives. He said that he would oppose any Anglo-Indian representation as a nationalist Parsee, whatever that may have meant. He further said that if the Anglo-Indians were given representation, it would not only mean fantastic weightage but it would encourage the Parsees also to seek similar representation. The fight was long, grim and bitter. The case of no other minority occupied so much time. Every section of the Sub-Committee was opposed to giving the Community any representation, because they said it could not be justified either by principle or logic. For two days I argued and re-argued, and then K.M. Munshi, a leading member of the Drafting Committee and one of the principal spokesman of the Congress Party, made me an offer of 2 seats in the Centre, 1 in Bengal, 1 in Madras and also 1 in Bombay. He pointed out that even this offer was ultra-generous, as it meant giving us 2000 per cent weightage in the Centre, 300% weightage in Bengal, 500% weightage in Madras and even more in Bombay. As against this he pointed out that the Indian Christians with a population of over 40,000 in the C.P. were not claiming a single seat. I, however, expressed my inability to accept this offer.   I remember being called upon by Sardar Patel to reply to the debate, in the Minorities Sub-Committee, at 4 o'clock in the evening.   He told me that a vote would be taken by 6 p.m.   I know that sometimes some Anglo-Indians think that I am inclined to speak for an inordinately long period on Anglo-Indian affairs.   It was a good thing on that occasion that I had this capacity.   Rapidly I arranged my points.   I knew that there was no hope in the Minorities Sub-Committee.   I knew also that I had to beat the clock.   At 6 p.m. I was still arguing the case for the Community. That night I pleaded with Sardar Patel to allow the Anglo-Indian case not to be decided by the Minorities Sub-Committee, but to allow it at least to go to the Advisory Committee.   The next day when I resumed my speech, I asked for the case to be remitted to the larger Committee.   Sardar Patel supported my request and the matter was referred to the Advisory Committee.

How The Nominations Were Secured

In the Advisory Committee the discussion on the Anglo-Indian case started on the 28th August.   I do not mind mentioning that the bitterest opposition to our case came from the Indian Christian representatives led by Dr. H.C. Mukherjee, the de facto leader of the Indian Christians.   He asked how they could give fantastic weightage to Anglo-Indians : it would mean, he said, offending the very democratic basis of the Constitution.   I stated my case briefly, because I knew that my reply would have to be detailed, carefully planned in order to meet the attacks from every section of the House.   As a politician and a lawyer, I knew that I had to leave some room for bargaining.   Therefore, I proposed my resolution that the Anglo-Indians be given 3 seats in the Centre, 3 in Bengal, 2 in Madras, 2 in Bombay, 1 in the U.P. and 1 in the C.P. My claim was torn to shreds by every section of the House.   It was dubbed as fantastic.   It was pointed out that the Sikhs with a population of 23,435 in the U.P. did not claim a single seat; yet the Anglo-Indians with a population of 4,000 in the Central Provinces were claiming 1 seat.   It was also pointed out that the Indian Christians had given up all claim to representation in the U.P. where they were 1,31,327 and they were also not claiming any representation in Bengal. Mr. Munshi then repeated his offer of 2 seats in the Centre, 1 in Bengal, 1 in Madras and 1 in Bombay. Once again I expressed my inability to accept it. My old friend, Pandit Pant, then proposed the formula that while there could be no specific reservations for Anglo-Indians and Parsees because they were too small in number, but where they failed to secure representation in the Legislature, the President or the Governor shall have power to nominate their representatives. At this stage Sardar Patel intervened : he suggested that only the Anglo-Indians should be given special representation by nomination. His suggestion was accepted by the Advisory Committee. Thus emerged the present provisions contained in Articles 331 and 333 of the Constitution. They were differently numbered in the draft Constitution.

Our Quotas And Educational Grants

But there were yet the service quotas and the educational safeguards to be considered. Speaking for the Parsees, Sir Homi Mody said that they did not want any reservations in the services, but if the Anglo-Indians were given reservations then they would also claim a similar concession. The Sikh representatives fought long and hard for reservations which they had hitherto. The Muslims asked for reservations on the basis of their numbers. Dr. Ambedkar put forward certain specific demands for the Scheduled Castes. The Muslims' case for reservations in the services was put to the House and voted down. I was then asked to state my case. I was called upon to speak at 5 p.m. I pleaded not only for reservation in the services, but also for our education grants. This time also I would have been able to beat the clock, but there was general, unanimous opposition to the Anglo-Indian case. The feeling was that we had already been treated ultra-generously by being given special representation. At 5.45 p.m. someone moved a closure and my resolution for service quotas and the continuance of education grants was put to the vote. Every member voted against my resolution. The 3 Anglo-Indians were in complete isolation. I confess, without shame, that immediately after the vote I broke down and wept, for I saw all my work on behalf of the Community crashing around me. My colleagues were not only frustrated but gave up hope. One of my ablest colleagues was Stanley Prater a man of considerable experience and ability who had represented the Community for 17 years in the Bombay Legislature. He asked me to advise the Community to leave the Country, because he saw no hope of survival. I refused to accept this advice: I told my colleagues that this was not only a counsel of despair but of suicide for the Community: there would always be tens of thousands of Anglo-Indians who would not or could not leave the Country. At 10 o'clock that night I phoned Sardar Patel. He expressed deep sympathy for me, but said that nothing could be done as the decision was by a unanimous vote of the Advisory Committee. I not only pleaded with him but insisted on seeing him. He then asked me to see him at 5 o'clock the next morning. For more than an hour I walked with him in his garden. Perhaps I pleaded the case for the Anglo-Indian Community with greater passionateness than ever before and with an earnestness born of desperation, because I realised that if the decision stood, then everything I had sought to achieve on behalf of the the Community would come to nothing. All my attempts over several years to find a place of recognition for the Community would mean nothing. I also knew the Sardar well. I knew that he could never be intimidated or coerced, but I made it clear to him that if the decision stood, then the Anglo-Indian representatives would have no alternative but to leave the Advisory Committee, as we could not be a party to a decision which spelt our destruction. Fortunately, the Community and the Anglo-Indian representatives spoke with one voice. Unlike every other community, we were the only community which was completely united. Sardar Patel was as usual his undemonstrative, monosyllabic, sphinx-like self. All that he emitted was in the nature of monosyllabic grunts. My colleagues said that I should expect nothing. But I was not without hope, because I had worked, often very closely, with this 'Iron Man' of India. But even I was not quite prepared for what followed the next morning. The next morning as he arrived in the Advisory Committee he announced to the House that he had promised to reconsider the whole Anglo-Indian case because of certain new facts that I had placed before him. He said that he had given me his word and that he knew the Advisory Committee would honour his word. He, therefore, proposed that the case of the Community should be considered by a special Sub-Committee.

He asked me what I had to say in the matter.   I immediately moved a resolution to the following effect, "Owing to the complete
dependence of the economy of the Anglo-Indian Community on
their position in certain services and their existing educational
facilities a sub-committee consisting of the following members,
report on these matters,
    "Pandit Pant, K.M. Munshi, Mrs. Hansa Mehta, Mr. Prater
and myself."

The Education Grants

For several weeks this Sub-Committee sat and considered our
case.   I did not have very much trouble with regard to the quotas.
The proposal, as I made it, was accepted and later embodied in
Article 336 of the Constitution.   But I had much more difficulty
with the educational grants.   K.M. Munshi suggested a formula
by which the gap between the percentage of the approved expenditure paid by the Government to Anglo-Indian schools and the percentage of the approved expenditure to similar schools of other
communities should be done away within a period of a few years.
I expressed my inability to accept this.   I pointed out that there
was no definite interpretation of the term 'approved.'   The
Government approved expenditure in respect of boarding in Anglo-
Indian Schools, whereas this was not an approved item in the non-
Anglo-Indians schools. The formula based on the term 'approved'
would have led to the wholesale immediate reduction of our grants.
Ultimately, I proposed that the present Central and Provincial
grants to Anglo-Indian education may be reduced by 10% at intervals of 3½ years provided that the amount in no case would be below
the per capita grant to similar schools maintained by other communities and that the matter should be reviewed at the end of 10
years. The non-Anglo-Indian members of the Sub-Committee
insisted on cutting down the period from 3½ to 3 years. This proposal was then accepted by the Sub-Committee and went back to
the Advisory Committee on Minority Rights.
    The proposal with regard to our quotas went through without
much opposition in the Advisory Committee on Minorities' Rights.
But when the formula with regard to our educational grants came
up for discussion, I was suddenly faced with strong and general
opposition. M.S. Aney, formerly a member of the Central

Government and Leader of the House, objected to the word 'review'. He felt that all the inequalities and privileges should automatically cease at the end of ten years. This opposition raised a hornets' nest. Prof. K.T. Shah, who was known for his anti-Christian sentiments, wanted our special grants to cease immediately. He made a bitter denunciation of missionary schools. He asked whether Government was going to subsidise institutions which covertly, and sometimes overtly, were nothing but agencies for conversion. He made a powerful appeal to the sentiments of some of the members who very near to the surface were always bitterly anti-missionary and certainly anti-conversion. And on this issue not only the caste Hindus, but the Scheduled Castes are agreed. To this I replied that I was not pleading for missionary institutions : that it was only an accident that some of them were Anglo-Indian schools. I was pleading for the Community and the Community is not a community interested in conversion, because we are Christians by birth and origin and not by conversion. I could feel the sense of the House steadily rising against me. Once again Dr. H.C. Mukherjee, the Indian Christian leader, got up. Even at that time he was rather old. He was then about 75 years of age and yet his memory reaching back 60 years was still bitter. He said that when he was a boy, he had been refused admission into an Anglo-Indian school. In answer to this, my reply was that I had been the bitterest opponent of the racial and anti-Indian complexes in some Anglo-Indian schools. But I realised that if a vote was taken, our grants would go. So I got up and said that I was prepared to accept the provision with the word 'review' removed, but that I would ask for the word 'may' to be retained. Sardar Patel, without putting it to the vote, said that he took it that since I had made this concession the House would accept the provision without the word 'review', and he declared the provision to be unanimously adopted. My resolution, as amended, later appeared as Article 337 of the Constitution.

Restoration Of Quotas

Although the Advisory Committee had accepted my proposal to continue the quotas that the Community enjoyed in the Railways, Posts & Telegraphs and the Customs, the Constitution had not been finalised. The Government of India Act and with it the safeguards for the Community had been rescinded by the India Independence Act which had been passed by the British Parliament in 1947. Consequently our quotas were no longer being given to us. I addressed Sardar Patel pointing out that the Government had accepted the principle of the continuance of the former quotas and that even a temporary lapse would adversely affect the economy of the Community. On the 29th March, 1947, I was informed by the Home Minister, Sardar Patel, that the Government had decided to restore the reservations in favour of the Anglo-Indians in the Railway, Posts & Telegraph and Customs Departments.

A Tribute

Stanley Prater, M.L.A., O.B.E., J.P., C.M.Z.S., was one of the ablest representatives that the Community has ever produced. He represented the Community for 17 years in the Legislature of the then Bombay State. In the Constituent Assembly he was my principal lieutenant. More than anyone else, he was aware of the hard, almost impossible, road that had been traversed in order to secure the provisional acceptance of the guarantees for the Community.

Welcoming me at a meeting of the Community in Bombay, Prater said, "Before I say anything else, I wish to welcome our President-in-Chief to Bombay and to say how happy we are to have him with us this evening."

"Mr. Anthony comes to us fresh with the laurels of his work in the Constituent Assembly. What that work was and what it implies to the Community, Mr. Anthony will tell you presently. I, who was associated with him in the task, can tell you something about which he will not speak. The more I worked with him through those difficult days, the more I came to realise how deep was his devotion to the Community; how unyielding was his purpose and determination; how tireless his labours in our cause. In all its long and chequered history never has the Community faced so grave a crisis—a crisis involving its very existence. No Anglo-Indian leader has ever had the odds so heavily cast against him. Yet Mr. Anthony won through. His far-sighted policy, his genius and ability have won for the Community a breathing space—a vital necessary period in which it can adjust itself to the radically changed conditions in the India of today."

"Sir, from the bottom of our hearts we thank you for all you have done. May God bless and prosper your work."

It is a sad thought that before the Constitution was finalised, Prater persuaded himself that there were mounting signs of Hindu revivalism and implacable resistance to the provisional safeguards for the minorities. In the belief that I was bound to fail in the final run, he resigned from the Constituent Assembly and migrated to the U.K. Although over twenty years my senior, while he worked alongside of me Prater gave me not only highly informed co-operation but unswerving loyalty.

Prater was a typical Anglo-Indian. On hearing in the U.K. of Gandhiji's murder, he wrote me a deeply moving letter. In his words, he wrote that letter with tears not only in his eyes but in his heart.

I had occasion to meet Prater on my subsequent visits to the U.K. He was never happy in the U.K.: in fact, psychologically he was deeply unhappy. He had achieved an outstanding position in his own profession as the world-famous curator of the Bombay Museum. Before he decided to leave India, I had secured for him the offer of the Headship of the Government of India Museum in New Delhi. In the U.K. he could find neither recognition nor respect for his abilities. He had to accept a post as a humble clerk in some office. For a year before he died, he suffered from a form of melancholia and would not talk to anyone. I believe he died as a broken-hearted exile.

An Interlude—Mehr Chand Khanna

Towards the end of November, 1947, I was asked by the Prime Minister Jawaharlal Nehru whether I would proceed to Peshawar in order to defend Mehr Chand Khanna, the ex-Finance Minister of the N.W.F.P. No Hindu lawyer dared go to Peshawar and perhaps no lawyer belonging to any other community. At first I thought the Prime Minister wished to engage me in my professional capacity. When I met him, I quoted what I regarded would be a reasonable fee. The Prime Minister, however, told me, quite frankly, that he was asking me to do this as a personal favour. When he put it to me in that way, I accepted his request. A special chartered plane was placed at my disposal. The only occupants were myself, B.M. Kaul, an official in the External

Affairs Ministry and later our Ambassador in Sweden and my servant. When we arrived in Peshawar, we were met by Pakistani officials who drove us to the leading hotel. I was provided with an armed escort. After a bath and breakfast I asked Kaul to contact the Governor, Sir George Cunningham. I spoke to the Governor and asked for an interview which he promptly gave me. At the interview I pointed out to the Governor that I felt that the charges against Khanna were of a trumpery character. Khanna was being prosecuted under the Arms Act for the possession, without a licence, of a cartridge refiller. I emphasised the fact that the charge would be farcical but for the fact that the sentence which Khanna was facing was seven years' rigorous imprisonment. I also pointed out that Pakistan had only recently introduced an Arms Act. Under the Indian Arms Act, although the provisions requiring a licence for guns were rigorous, there was no provision which required a licence for a cartridge refiller. To apply such a requirement in the N.W.F. Province was, in my opinion, to pull the political long bow unduly. I pointed out to Cunningham that in the N.W.F. Province not only cartridge refillers but arms of all kinds were openly carried and without any licence. He confessed to me that there was little he could do and that Khanna's arrest and impending prosecution were nothing short of a political vendetta on the part of the Chief Minister, Abdul Qayum Khan. I pointed out to him that he was supposed to be the trustee of minority interests and that at least in this case he should exercise his trust on behalf of Khanna who was a member of the minority Hindu Community. Cunningham, however, regretfully expressed his inability to do anything.

I then asked Kaul to contact Qayum Khan. I had known Qayum Khan for several years, when he and I were both members of the Central Legislature. He was, at one time, the Deputy Leader of the Congress Party in the Central Legislature. That was before the Muslim League had reached a peak of political power. Qayum Khan ultimately went over to the Muslim League. Like many converts, political and religious, he exhibited greater fanaticism than those of the original faith. My recollections of Qayum Khan of the former days were pleasant. He was an easy mixer and a person with a bluff, friendly manner. Kaul, acting as my Secretary, contacted Qayum Khan's Secretary twice or three times. On each occasion he got the same message that the Chief Minister was busy. Qayum Khan obviously knew that I had come on behalf of Mehr Chand Khanna. I then tried to contact Qayum Khan personally. His P.A. repeated the stereotyped reply. I was then convinced that Qayum Khan was stalling and that he was deliberately evading a meeting with me.

I drove straight to the Secretariat and went to the Chief Minister's room. I was stopped outside by Government minions who asked whether I had an appointment. I told them that I did not, but that I was a very old friend of the Chief Minister and had come to see him on an urgent matter. I sent in my card. I was wondering whether Qayum Khan would find an excuse for avoiding an interview with me. In a way I was surprised when he literally burst out of his office and came forward to meet me in his typical warm-hearted manner.

Inside his office he was all hospitality and began to recall the days when we were colleagues in the Central Legislature. I found him as likeable as ever. I then came straight to the question of Mehr Chand's arrest. He asked me not to discuss it. I told him that I had been specially deputed not only by the Prime Minister but by Sardar Patel to do my utmost to get Mehr Chand Khanna released. Qayum Khan was nothing if he was not forthright. He told me that he had no intention of releasing Khanna. In fact, he intended that he should get the maximum sentence. With all the seriousness I could command I then told Qayum Khan precisely what I been told by the Sardar, that if Mehr Chand Khanna was not released the Sardar would be obliged to treat in a similar manner leading members of the Muslim League who were in India. I strenuously pleaded with Qayum Khan not to add further bitterness to an already deeply embittered position. I pointed out to him that this was a game at which both sides could play; there were many more hostages to be found among the millions of Muslims in India. I could see that the threat of Sardar Patel had clearly weighed with Qayum Khan. He then insisted that I should have lunch with him. Jocularly I expressed the hope that there would be no poison administered with my lunch. After lunch he asked me to accompany him on a short tour that he was undertaking. I asked him the nature of it. He was quite frank. He said that he was organising the tribesmen to go into Kashmir; that he regarded the Kashmir problem as a personal fight between himself and

Jawaharlal Nehru, he being a Kashmiri Muslim and Nehru a Kashmiri Hindu. Naturally, I declined the invitation.

I had already seen Mehr Chand Khanna immediately on my arrival to get the facts from him. He was extremely dubious about ever getting out of Peshawar. He emphasized that the charge against him was entirely trumpery; he did not even know how many guns he possessed, but he had licences for all of them. After my lunch with Qayum Khan I went back to see Mehr Chand who was locked up in the Peshawar Jail. I remember standing in the doorway of his cell talking to him when he suddenly pulled me down on to his bed. He said that standing in the doorway I offered a provocative target to some trigger-happy tribesman. I told him about my interview with Qayum Khan and expressed my belief that he would be released. The same day I left Peshawar.

Immediately after my arrival, I drove to the Prime Minister's residence and told him precisely what had happened. I then drove to see Sardar Patel and gave him a first-hand account. Shortly afterwards Mehr Chand Khanna was released. I have little doubt that the Sardar's promise of reciprocity of treatment had a salutary effect. Mehr Chand later became the Minister for Rehabilitation and Refugee Relief in the Central Cabinet. He has always been deeply appreciative of my role in securing his release. He was primarily responsible when he was a Minister in the Union Cabinet for getting me the land on which the Frank Anthony Public School, New Delhi, stands. One of the four Houses in the school is named after him—Khanna House.

Mahatma Gandhi's Assassination

I had secured provisional acceptance of certain guarantees under conditions which represented nothing short of a miracle. On the 30th January, 1948, Mahatma Gandhi was assassinated. I realised immediately the consequence of that senseless crime. There was a tremendous revulsion of feeling against any form of separate representation to the minorities. Unfortunately, the Sikh leadership was at that time particularly militant. Certain of the prominent Sikh leaders were demanding a separate Sikh State. This gave a perfect handle to the communalists from the majority community to demand, under the guise of nationalism, the withdrawal of all minority safeguards. The whole question of the minorities was thrown back into the melting pot, at any rate so far as re-presentation was concerned. Although the draft Constitution had given representation to the minorities on the basis of reservation of seats in a system of joint electorates, the whole question was reopened.

Every other minority except the Anglo-Indians was divided in its approach and in its policies. I approached Jawaharlal Nehru and Sardar Patel and told them that so far as we were concerned, we could not accept a position which meant resiling from what had already been granted to us provisionally and after a great deal of careful and detailed consideration. The matter was raised before the Advisory Committee on Minority Rights and it was decided that all representation for the minorities should be abolished. Before the resolution withdrawing representation to the minorities was put to the vote, I got up and sought a clarification from both Pandit Nehru and Sardar Patel. Both Jawaharlal Nehru and the Sardar made it clear that this resolution would not affect the provisions accepted on behalf of the Anglo-Indians for their representation was specially granted to them by nomination.

Many newspapers, however, reported that the resolution adopted abolishing the reserved seats for all the communities except the Scheduled Castes involved the abolition of the provisions on behalf of the Anglo-Indian Community. These wrong reports led to near confusion and dismay in the Community. I was inundated by messages of indignation from Anglo-Indians. I immediately issued a statement clarifying the position, pointing out that the Anglo-Indian provisions had not been affected as we had been singled out for exceptional constitutional safeguards.

16th June—1949

The 16th of June, 1949, marked a red-letter day in the history of the Community. On that day the Constituent Assembly finally adopted Articles 297 and 298 as they were then known. These were later numbered as Articles 336 and 337, giving the Commu-nity quotas in the services and guarantees in respect of education. But until the actual adoption by the Constituent Assembly of these Articles I could not be certain of the position. About 20 leading members of the Constituent Assembly, mostly from the Congress Party, had given notice of amendments ranging from complete abolition to at least a serious whittling down of these provisions. Fortunately, I was a member of the Consultative Committee of the Constituent Assembly, which was a Select inner Committee, consisting of a limited number of leaders. I also canvassed the members of the Drafting Committee and certain of the other front-rank leaders of the Congress Party. As a result of this behind-the-scenes activity I was able to persuade all the members who had given notice of their amendments, to withdraw them. On the morning of the 16th June the Articles were formally moved by Dr. Ambedkar: the 20 odd members withdrew their amendments. I intervened to make a short speech. I thanked the members of the House for their generosity and understanding.

25th August—1949

On the 25th August, 1949, the Constituent Assembly finally adopted the two remaining provisions relating to the Anglo-Indians namely, Articles 293 and 295 (now renumbered as Articles 331 and 333) referring to the nomination of Anglo-Indians to the House of the People and the Provincial Legislatures.

A Further Safeguard

Just before the adoption of the Constitution on the 26th November, 1949, in its finalised form I was able to get an addition to the guarantees on behalf of the Anglo-Indian Community. The 4 provisions already adopted only referred to what was formerly known as British India. There were no guarantees for Anglo-Indians in the former Princely States. It was fortunate for the Country, and especially fortunate for us, that before the third reading stage of the Constitution the Princely States decided to integrate and to surrender their powers to frame their constitutions to the Constituent Assembly. Once again, I approached my friends in the Drafting Committee to make two amendments. In one Article I had the words 'Raj Pramukh of the State' added. This was the Article providing for nomination to the State Legislatures. Up till then the only word used was 'Governor'. By adding the words 'Raj Pramukh' the Anglo-Indians of Mysore, Hyderabad and Travancore-Cochin would get representation.

The position facing the Community in the different Princely States was indicated by the attitude of the Mysore Constituent

Assembly. In the Mysore State, which includes Bangalore, there was a comparatively large concentration of Anglo-Indians. Yet the Mysore Constituent Assembly, before integration, had decided not to give the Anglo-Indians any guarantees in respect of employment or education and also not to give the Community any kind of political representation. I also got another amendment put into the provision with regard to educational grants. Up till then this provision only referred to the 'Part A' States, that is, to those States which formed part of British India. I had the expression, 'Part B' added to this amendment, so that the Anglo-Indian schools in the former States of Hyderabad, Mysore and Travancore-Cochin would continue to get grants.

The Lesson Of Unity

The supreme lesson of those critical days was the lesson of our survival because of our unity through the Association. Every other community failed, because the spokesmen of every other community spoke with divided voices. The Parsee representatives, Sidhwa and Homi Mody, opposed each other. The Indian Christians, in my view, never counted for anything at any time. They asked for nothing and they got nothing. All that they seemed to be interested in was to see that the Anglo-Indians got nothing. The Sikhs were divided: the Scheduled Castes were divided: the Muslims were divided. We survived in a unique way because, and only because, we were completely united. The 3 Anglo-Indian representatives were all nominees of the All-India Anglo-Indian Association: my two colleagues worked with me loyally: they allowed me to speak on behalf of the Community and they supported every word and action of mine. What we lacked in numbers we made up for in cohesion. The 'Christian Democrat', a well-known Indian Christian journal, commenting on the safeguards that I had been able to secure, said, "Union is strength. It is also something more. Union is—above all things—union, and now more than ever at any other time, we (Indian Christians) run the risk of succumbing to the poison contained in the saying that if we do not hang together, we shall hang separately. And, what is more, it is true. If proof was needed of the necessity, nay the effectiveness, of a single authoritative body to represent as well as to advocate individual claims, the achievements of the Association that represents the microscopic community of Anglo-Indians need only be quoted. Here we have an Association that would have suited our purpose admirably. It is well organised, well conducted and well run. It is moreover an all-India organisation and has, within the limitations of its present scope and objectives, secured for its members as well as for the members of its community, advantages unparalleled in the history of like Associations in India. Unfortunately, the provision of its constitution, and the name by which it is known, exclude all others but the Anglo-Indians and the Domiciled Europeans from its list of membership."

Representation In Legislatures Extended

Article 334 of the Constitution is a composite provision prescribing the period for which the special representation by nomination for the Anglo-Indians and the special reservations of seats for the Scheduled Castes and the Scheduled Tribes would continue. Under the original Article the special representation to these groups would cease to have effect on the expiration of 10 years from the commencement of the Constitution. The Constitution having come into effect in 1950, this meant that our special representation would cease in 1960. Because of the then forthcoming mid-term elections in Kerala, the question of amending this Article became urgent. If an amendment was acceptable to Government, it had to be passed not only by the end of 1959 but as early as possible, as under Article 368 of the Constitution any amendment which affects representation of the States in Parliament has to be ratified by the Legislatures of not less than one-half of the States before the amending bill is presented to the President for his assent.

I discussed the whole question of the extension of our safeguards with Pantji, the Home Minister, in 1959. I counted Pantji as one of my real friends. Our relations were most cordial. Seldom, if ever, did he refuse me any reasonable request. Unfortunately, because of developments on the language front our relations became strained. Pantji was the Chairman of the Joint Committee elected in 1958 by both Houses of Parliament, under Article 334(4) of the Constitution. It was known as the Parliamentary Language Committee. In another chapter I have referred to the fact that to the report of the Committee I wrote the only minute of dissent. All the other members, including the members from the South such as Sir Ramaswami Mudaliar, had signed the report which had accepted, in effect, the effacing of English from the official language pattern of the Country by 1965. This was a period of deep anxiety for me. Pantji had asked me, more than once, to see him in an effort to get me to withdraw my minute of dissent and to join the others in signing the report. Much as I respected Pantji, I informed him that it would be impossible for me to do so. For him it would have been a unique achievement to secure a unanimous report from members representing all the States and the major linguistic groups. I knew that by standing out and by resisting every pressure to sign the report, I would perhaps be creating bitter political hostility. I knew that within a short time I would have to approach the leaders, especially Nehru and Pant, if I wanted the continuance of our Constitutional safeguards which were due to expire in 1960. I knew also that by holding out on the language issue I would be putting in jeopardy the continuance of our safeguards. All these factors had to be carefully weighed by me before I decided to stand out, alone, on the language issue.

I concluded that it would be pointless to get the continuance of our representation in the Legislature, the continuance of our quotas in the Services and the continuance of our educational grants, if English was to be banished from the official language pattern by 1965. The effacing of English would mean the destruction of our schools, in which context any educational grants would be not only meaningless but a mocking irony. Representation in the Legislature would be meaningless because there would be nothing to represent. Without our language, without our schools, it would be only a question of time before the Community was destroyed as a recognised or recognisable entity. Apart from the position of the Community, I have always believed that if English is removed as a link language in higher education all semblance of national integration will disappear. In that event India will represent merely a geographical description. I, therefore, stood out alone on the language issue. It was in this context that I had to approach both Nehru and Pant for the extension of our safeguards.

Nehru never harboured any kind of personal animus. At the same time, he was not unduly interested in any particular minority except the Muslims. With his sweeping, I will not say amorphous, concept of secular democracy he felt that such safeguards tended to perpetuate sectarianism.   He did not have the time or perhaps the inclination to study the special needs and difficulties of a community like the Anglo-Indians.

During my meetings with Pantji, I sensed a certain bitterness. I could not resist the conclusion that he had not forgotten or forgiven my lone resistance in the Parliamentary Language Committee and my solitary minute of dissent.   He made it clear that he at least would not be prepared to recommend the continuance of our Constitutional safeguards: as Home Minister he would have to pilot an amending bill.

I then submitted notes to the Cabinet with regard to the extension of our safeguards.   I proposed to the Government certain amendments to Article 336 which dealt with our quotas.   I asked that instead of the word 'shall' the word 'may' be substituted, so that at an interval of two years there may be a reduction of 10%.   It would thus be within the discretion of the Central Government whether to reduce our service quotas or not.   I pointed out that there was still large-scale unemployment in the Community.   I also mentioned that the continuance of Article 336 would merely mean giving to the Community the quotas which, in fact, we should have got during the past ten years.   I referred to the fact that there had been a considerable gap between the reservations and the vacancies filled.   I also underlined the notable services that the Community had rendered in building the great national assets of the Railways, the Telegraphs and the Customs during the difficult pioneering days.   I pointed out that the Community had developed certain special aptitudes for these services over a long period.   Above all, I stressed that the recruitment of members of the Community would give to these services continuing stability and ballast.

In my note with regard to the continuance of educational grants I pointed out that our schools, under the guidance of the Inter-State Board for Anglo-Indian Education, had taken their place in the vanguard of the general educational pattern of the Country. Anglo-Indian schools were the first to subscribe to the three-language formula.   Above all, I underlined the fact that without our indigent grants a large number of less fortunate Anglo-Indian children would be without education.

Pantji was, however, not disposed to accept any of my pleas

with regard to the continuance of our safeguards in respect of the services and education. He, however, gave me the assurance that if it was decided to continue the special safeguards for representation of the Scheduled Castes and the Scheduled Tribes, the Anglo-Indian provisions with regard to nomination to Parliament and the State Legislatures would also be continued.

I kept in close touch with the Congress Parliamentary Committee which was appointed to go into the question of the continuance of the special representation for the Scheduled Castes and Scheduled Tribes. On several occasions, I met the Chairman and other members of the Committee. The Congress Parliamentary Committee recommended the extension of the period of the safeguards for only 5 years. Strong pressure was, however, brought to bear to extend the period by 10 years which was accepted.

In my further discussions with Pantji, he asked me to accept certain modifications to the Anglo-Indian safeguards so that the number of the nominations to the State Legislatures would be fixed. The reason he gave was that the Central Government wanted to ensure that no State Government from mala fide motives could nominate a large number of Anglo-Indians in order merely to maintain itself in power. I saw nothing unreasonable in this and agreed.

The Constitution (Eighth Amendment) Bill, 1959, was introduced by Pantji in the Lok Sabha. It contained three clauses: the first was merely the enacting clause and the long title: the second clause sought to make an amendment in Article 333 to the effect that not more than two members of the Anglo-Indian Community would be nominated in the case of West Bengal and in the case of any other State one member of the Community: the third clause sought to substitute the period "20 years" for "10 years": this was because the 10-year period expired in 1960 and the 20-year period would mean that the special representation would carry on till 1970.

Under the proviso to Article 334, the period would, in fact, terminate in 1972 as the sitting members nominated in 1967 would continue for the full legislative term of 5 years.

When the amending bill came before Parliament there was not inconsiderable opposition to the continuance of the provisions for the Anglo-Indians. From the Congress Party, Thakur Das Bhargava, a senior member, opposed the continuance of the Anglo-

Indian nominations. Another leading member of the P.S.P., S.N. Dwivedy, also joined in this opposition. Hiren Mukherji, a leader of the Communist group, who as a person I like very much indeed, also opposed the provision for Anglo-Indian nominations. Hiren Mukherji made the criticism that the Community had not yet adjusted itself and did not deserve the continuance of this special safeguard. Replying to him, I said that whatever the Community's failings, which we had in common with the other communities, it had made and continued to make a contribution to the progress of the Country out of all proportion to its size. I referred among other things to the outstanding and indeed decisive role of the Anglo-Indian fighter pilots in the Kashmir campaign. I mentioned that the need for the continuance of representation was to watch over, especially, the educational interests of the Community.

The Communists sought, through an amendment introduced by T.C.N. Menon, to amend Article 333 so that the nominations would not rest with the Governor, but would be made in pursuance of the recommendations of the leader of the majority party or that of the biggest single party in the State Legislature.

Speaking in the House, I strongly opposed the Communist amendment. I pointed out that the provisions were given to the Anglo-Indian Community and were not meant for the benefit of any political party in power. I mentioned that in Kerala, where there was a Communist Government enjoying an extremely precarious majority, they deliberately ignored the needs of the Community and the representative character of the person recommended for nomination. I mentioned that I had secured the original provision in the Constitution placing nomination in the hands of the Governor, because the Governor was supposed to exercise this power as part of his discretionary powers: he was supposed to ensure that the person or persons nominated represent the Anglo-Indian Community and not the party in power or any political group.

Pantji also declined to accept the Communist amendment. When the voting was taken there were not sufficient members present in the House to secure the required majority. Article 368 of the Constitution requires a Constitution amending bill to be passed in each House of Parliament by a majority of the total membership of that House and by a majority of not less than two-thirds of the members of that House present and voting. The Speaker postponed the voting to the following day.

The Communists, after hurried consultations with S.N. Dwivedy, suddenly decided to oppose Clause 2 which referred to Anglo-Indian representation in the State Legislatures. From their audible deliberations it was clear that they were under the impression that if they opposed Clause 2 and the requisite majority was not forthcoming, the Anglo-Indian Community would get no representation in the State Legislatures. The voting was taken. Because of the opposition by the Communists and others Clause 2 was defeated as there was not a sufficient number in the House to carry the Government proposal. In an attempt to explain away their motives, T.C.N. Menon rose in the House and said that the Communists were not in fact opposed to the Anglo-Indian nominations to the State Legislatures, but they were opposed to it in its present form, because they wanted the nominations to be in the hands of the ruling party and not with the Governor. Quite obviously, T.C.N. Menon and his fellow-Communists had not understood the significance of their opposing Clause 2. All that Clause 2 sought was to limit the number of nominations of Anglo-Indians to two in West Bengal and one in the other States. When it came to Clause 3, which was a general clause, namely, that for the word "10" in Article 334 of the Constitution, the word "20" shall be substituted, the Communists dare not oppose it because this affected not only the Anglo-Indians but the Scheduled Castes and the Scheduled Tribes. All the parties pay competing lip-service to the needs of the Scheduled Castes and Scheduled Tribes. Their solicitude is not uninfluenced by the voting strength of the Scheduled Castes and Scheduled Tribes who, today, number about 140 million. With the passage of Clause 3, the Anglo-Indian nominations were automatically extended.

The net result was that while the Communists intended to throw out the Anglo-Indian nominations to the State Legislatures, by voting against Clause 2 they, in fact, restored the Anglo-Indian nominations to their original form, namely, that the Governor will nominate to a State Legislature, and the number is not fixed but rests in his discretion.

There were many members in the House who were also under the same impression as the Communists and sought to commiserate with me on the loss of the Anglo-Indian nominations to the State Legislatures.

I promptly explained to them that not only was there no loss, but the Communists, without intending it, had given the Anglo-Indians the continuation of their nominations in the State Legislatures without any limitation. When I explained the significance of their actions to the Communist members in Parliament, their chagrin was obvious.

If the Communists had not joined to defeat the Government proposal contained in Clause 2, the Anglo-Indians would only have got 2 seats at the most in West Bengal. But because Clause 2 was defeated, the original position was restored and the Community has continued to have 4 members nominated by the Governor to the West Bengal Legislature.

With regard to this matter of nominations, I am bound to pay tribute to the democratic sense of the Congress Party. In this respect they have compared favourably with the British authorities who, despite their many shortcomings, had a basic sense of democratic decency. Although some British members of the Viceroy's Executive Council hated my political guts because of my constant criticism of their policies of discrimination, they recognised the uniquely representative character of the All-India Anglo-Indian Association; they recognised the fact that I was the undisputed leader of the Community. The Congress Government at the Centre has unhesitatingly accepted this position and nominated 2 representatives of the Community to Parliament on the recommendation of the All-India Anglo-Indian Association. Both of us sit in the Opposition and, for many years, I have sat in the front rank of the Opposition.

The Communists, however, have never been worried by democratic niceties. In Kerala the Communist Government once nominated a person who was an avowed Feringi. In West Bengal, the Communist-dominated Government, with Ajoy Mukherjee as a front, deliberately and, indeed, dishonestly, side-tracked the Association in 1967. In West Bengal, the All-India Anglo-Indian Association is particularly powerful : in fact, there is no other Anglo-Indian Association in West Bengal. The Communist-dominated Government resorted to a device which is typical of Communist techniques : they insisted on the Anglo-Indian nominees signing a bond of allegiance to the ruling party. This was something unheard of in the history of our nominations. After having secured the bond, they nominated persons who, except for one, represented no one but themselves. Two of them were members of the All-India Anglo-Indian Association. They were promptly expelled by the Association for having accepted nomination against the Association's nominees. The way in which the Communists have stultified and, indeed, prostituted our solemn Constitutional guarantees is an ominous portent of what the smaller minorities may expect from their totalitarian and unprincipled methods.

The Governors, who made the nominations on the dictation of the Communist and Communist-dominated Governments, cannot also escape their share of blame. When I had these provisions put into the Constitution I had deliberately asked that the responsibility should vest in the Governor who would exercise this power as part of his discretionary powers. A responsible Governor would then be able to ensure that the Anglo-Indian nominees are really representative of the Community and not pawns or stooges in a game of unprincipled power-politics.

By abdicating their discretion and becoming rubber-stamping agencies, some Governors also have to be blamed for the stultification of the guarantee by Communist-dominated State Governments.

On two occasions at least, once in Kerala and more recently in Uttar Pradesh, the Governors did not allow the Communists or some motley political combination to stultify the Anglo-Indian guarantees. They exercised their discretion to nominate the person recommended by the All-India Anglo-Indian Association, which is the only body representative of the Community throughout the Country.

CHAPTER X

THE SPORTSMEN AND THE SPORTSWOMEN OF INDIA

Builders Of Key Services

IN spite of its numerical smallness the Anglo-Indian Community bestrode the sporting world of India like a Colossus. For many decades the Community maintained a towering superiority in the field of sport.

Hockey is the national game par excellence. As recently as May, 1968, A.F.S. Talyarkhan, the internationally famous sports commentator, wrote in The Times of India: "India's hockey grew thanks to the greatest hockey-playing entity the world will ever know, the small Anglo-Indian Community of the Country. Not only this, but the stands all over India were largely patronised by members of the same Community, whole families turning out to cheer their favourites. Nor was this in any way communal frenzy, for the simple reason that most of the stupendous pioneering clubs, composed of Anglo-Indians, were the great nurseries of the world's hockey: the famous railway centres were nothing but Anglo-Indian, and even new hockey clubs and private teams could never have come up but for the guidance, the talent and the enthusiasm of this microscopic Community. This was one great reason why a tournament like the Aga Khan in Bombay was such a world-famous attraction and much the same applied to Calcutta's Beighton Cup event—the clubs, the players community-wise and the supporters."

No one has cared to maintain a record but here are some available facts.

The Calcutta Hockey League, one of the premier tournaments of India, was, in the 20 years between 1905 and 1924, won on 17 occasions by Anglo-Indian teams.

The Aga Khan tournament of Bombay, perhaps the queen of

all-India tournaments, was lifted year after year by an Anglo-Indian eleven. Teams drawn from other communities from every part of the Country were brushed aside. This was in spite of the fact that the Anglo-Indian team was formed from a restricted field, either a school, a railway workshop or a mofussil area consisting of barely 500 to 1000 Anglo-Indians.

Not infrequently the final was played between two Anglo-Indian teams as in 1926 when the Customs of Bombay met the Christ Church School Old Boys, Jubbulpore. These two teams won the Aga Khan trophy year after year. Again in 1927 the Aga Khan final was an all-Anglo-Indian affair : Christ Church Old Boys, Jubbulpore, beat the BB & CI Railway team from Ajmer by the only goal secured in the match.

A team drawn from 40 or 50 apprentices of the Ajmer workshop generally swept everything before it. Year after year this eleven, consisting of little more than schoolboys, wrested the All-India Scindia Gold Cup, one of the most coveted trophies of India's hockey world.

The Calcutta Customs hockey team had an enviable record of beating on the way the best hockey teams that the Country could produce. In spite of the fact that World War I saw the mass enrolment of Anglo-Indians in the different departments of the Armed Forces, the Anglo-Indians continued to sweep everything before them in the world of Indian hockey. The Bengal Nagpur Railway hockey team, the Port Commissioners, Calcutta, carried all before them, the Winter League, the 1st and 2nd Division Leagues and the Beighton Cup which, like the Aga Khan trophy of Bombay, was regarded as the blue ribbon of Indian hockey.

In 1926 some one conceived the idea of sending an Indian Army hockey team to New Zealand. That team was carefully selected from 50 battalions of India's fighting men and 500 British officers. After being carefully trained, they played a few test matches in India. One of the tests was played against a scratch team of Anglo-Indians from the North-Western Railway. The railway team was recruited from the local Anglo-Indian railway-men. The result was a thorough trouncing for the carefully selected and equally carefully trained Indian Army hockey team.

In 1927, the Telegraph Club, Agra, which team consisted entirely of Anglo-Indians, won three successive hockey tournaments at

Agra, Bharatpur and the Scindia Gold Cup, Gwalior, all in the space of one month. The final of the Scindia Gold Cup was played between two Anglo-Indian teams—the Telegraph Team and the Jubbulpore Gymkhana, G.I.P. Railway.

In the South, Anglo-Indian teams swept everything before them. The Anglo-Indian Sports Club was the first civilian team to win the M.C.C. tournament. It was the leading team in the South in the Twenties. The M. & S. M. Railway team, consisting entirely of Anglo-Indians, was outstanding. In later years the supremacy of Anglo-Indians in hockey in the South remained undisputed, the Telegraph Recreation Club, another Anglo-Indian team, winning all the major hockey tournaments.

In 1928, India sent a hockey team to take part in the World Olympics. It covered itself and the Country with unprecedented sports glory. They swept everything before them scoring 29 goals against their opponents, and without a single goal being scored against themselves. Of the 11 playing members, 8 were Anglo-Indians. Of the 3 spares, 2 were Anglo-Indians. The Manager of the team was also an Anglo-Indian, A.B. Rosser. The team, as finally chosen was,

Goal—Allen (Bengal)

Backs—Michael Rocque (C.P.) and Hammond (U.P.)

Half-backs—Kehr Singh (Punjab), Penniger (Punjab) and Cullen (U.P.)

Forwards—Gateley (Punjab), Feroze (Punjab), Dhyan Chand (U.P.), Marthins (U.P.) and Seaman (U.P.)

The general utility players were Shaukat Ali (Bengal) and Rex Norris (C.P.)

The reserves were Boodrie (Punjab), Lal Shah (Punjab) and Deefholts (Bengal)

Jaipal Singh, at present a member of Parliament, joined the team as Captain; he was an Oxford Blue in the U.K. He did not play in many of the matches and Penniger, the Vice-Captain, had to stand in most of the time.

About their performances in their preliminary matches, a famous British sports commentator wrote, "Hockey, as played in India, came as a revelation to the hockey enthusiasts in England. Lovers of this great amateur game had no idea that hockey could attain such a high standard of proficiency and science. The Indian players have been likened to the professional soccer players. They have a wonderful knowledge of position play: they are fleet-footed and expert exponents of the first time and through pass. They are most unselfish in their methods; have a wonderful eye; their stick-work is deft and polished and they are great believers in stopping the ball with the hand to make sure of the next movement."

A commentator of international repute said after the game against the Hockey Association XI, at Folkestone, "The play of these Indians is the creme de creme of what first class hockey should be. One and all were impressed with the tackleback. Nothing like it has ever been witnessed in England."

On their return the conquering heroes were given a tumultuous welcome. From the Viceroy downwards they were sent messages and telegrams of congratulations. On behalf of the Community Gidney sent the following message, "On behalf of the Anglo-Indian Community I welcome you home and congratulate you on world-famed achievement. We are particularly pleased and proud that 9 Anglo-Indians with their Indian colleagues won the final in Olympic tournament. We are doing our utmost to refund excess expenditure." The Governor of Bombay sent the following letter to Penniger, who was the acting Captain:

"Dear Mr. Penniger,

I am extremely sorry that I shall not be in Bombay myself, and consequently unable to take part in any of the welcome to you and the members of your team, but I am sending this letter by Captain Seymour-Williams who will represent me.

I desire to offer you a very sincere welcome back to India and also to offer you my whole-hearted congratulations on the great success which your team has attained in Europe. I think I am justified in saying that this success is without precedent and, while you and every member of your team must naturally feel pleased, there is, at the same time, no one in India or who has any connection with India, who does not feel proud of your achievements.

Yours sincerely,
Sd/- Leslie Wilson."

It is no exaggeration to say that the Anglo-Indian Community could have produced at least 6 equally good teams. Before they left India, the all-conquering 1928 Olympic team played a scratch team of Anglo-Indians in Bombay and was beaten. They played a return match with this scratch team after their triumphal return. This time they beat the scratch team, but sports commentators drew attention to the fact that the scratch team had no opportunity of practising before they played the return match. The names of the members of this scratch team are worth recording: Ogden (Captain), Massey, Mackenzie, Brewin, Abreo, Smith, Milne, Muller, Long, Willis. It was mentioned that Potts of the Customs might also play.

Over the years the number of Anglo-Indians in the Indian Olympic team has progressively decreased. The 1932 team had 7 Anglo-Indians; Allen, Tapsell, Hammond, Brewin, Penniger, Carr and Sullivan. In 1936 there were 6 Anglo-Indians; Allen, Tapsell, Cullen, Emmet, Michie, Gallibardy. In 1948 there were 4 including Claudius and Jansen. Patrick Jansen won his spurs in hockey in the Calcutta Port Commissioners, another Anglo-Indian hockey team which became a legend in the Indian hockey world. Playing as inside-left Jansen achieved the position of being the top scorer of the side. In 1948, India retained the title of hockey champions of the world.

In 1952 there were 2 Anglo-Indians and in 1956 and 1960 only one, Leslie Claudius. Claudius has also been described as one of the greatest half-backs the world has ever seen. Actually Claudius' first love was football. He was introduced almost by accident to hockey by the great Dickie Carr. Claudius was selected by Carr to play in the 'A' team for the Beighton Cup in 1946. Those were days of the almost fabulous Anglo-Indian figures of Carr, Tapsell, Gallibardy and Gerry Glacken to whose help and guidance Claudius owed much.

Some of those great and unequalled Anglo-Indian hockey players deserve special mention. Rex Norris of Jubbulpore, the gnarled weather-beaten veteran, is still going strong. From 1954 to 1956 he was the national coach to Holland. In 1960 he went in the same capacity to Italy. The latest reports show that Rex Norris, one of the world's greatest hockey coaches, is at present training the Mexican team for the Olympic Games to be held in October, 1968.

Among India's finest sportsmen and sportswomen were the sons and daughters of Rex Norris. I shall refer to them in their appropriate places. Rex Norris was perhaps the greatest centre-half of world hockey: Penniger had an almost equal reputation: Allen was described as the world's greatest goal-keeper,

Michael Rocque and Hammond as among the greatest full-backs.

With the exodus of some of the best sporting talent in the Community, India's loss has been the gain of the countries to which Anglo-Indians have emigrated. In future it will be interesting to scrutinise the Commonwealth hockey teams, especially from Australia, New Zealand and the U.K. More and more Anglo-Indians will be found in them, accounting for the new-found hockey prowess of these Commonwealth teams. Thus in the quarter-finals of the Rome Olympics in 1960, India beat Australia by a solitary goal. The two opposing captains who met for the toss were both Anglo-Indians: Leslie Claudius of Calcutta, captain of the Indian team, and Kevin Carlton, a St. Joseph's (Naini Tal) boy, the Australian captain.

Recent reports show that Eric Pearce, of the famous hockey-playing family, may carry the Australian flag this year (1968) at the Olympic Games in Mexico. Eric Pearce will be representing Australia at the Olympics for the fourth time. His other brothers Gordon and Julian have also been selected to represent Australia in Mexico. The Pearce brothers hold the world record for the number of members of a family selected to represent a country at the Olympic Games. Since 1956 there have always been at least 2 Pearce brothers representing Australia at the Olympic Games. There are 5 brothers in the Pearce family and each has represented Australia at least 3 times. In 1958, the 5 brothers were in the same State side (Western Australia), thus making up practically half the team. An Australian paper has mentioned that it is strange that despite their excellent record in Australian and international hockey not once has a Pearce been asked to captain an Australian side. The Pearce family came from Jubbulpore. Their father was, in his time, a hockey enthusiast in India. The family migrated to Australia in 1947.

Boxing

Boxing was introduced in India by the British Army. Anglo-Indian Schools took to this sport early in their existence, and Anglo-Indians dominated the Indian boxing scene year after year. Anglo-Indian boxing champions from the Auxiliary Force over and over again beat the best men from British regiments. There have been many well-known Anglo-Indian boxers. Reference may be made to a few.

Edgar Brighte of Bombay was for many years the champion Lightweight boxer of India. Milton Kubes was another outstanding master and exponent of boxing. No British regimental boxer could be found to stand up to him. Illustrative of this is the interesting fight in Bombay, in 1926, between Kubes (10 st. 10 lbs) and Gunner Melvin (12 st. 4 lbs.) of the R.F.A. Kirkee, Light Heavyweight champion of Western Command. In spite of having to give away so much weight, Kubes beat his formidable opponent on points. For sheer blood and thunder veterans recall the epic fight between Milton Kubes and Kid D'Silva.

Kid D'Silva was in his time the idol of the boxing fans in Calcutta. He was one of the most scientific boxers that India has ever produced. His thin, almost emaciated, appearance belied his uncanny powers of endurance and capacity to punch. On one occasion he was sent to Australia where he held his own against the best Australian boxers. He was described in Australia as "The Hindoo Giraffe with the punch of a Mule." Duncan Chatterton, Secretary for many years of the Jhansi branch of the All-India Anglo-Indian Association, was the Middleweight champion from 1934-1937. He was also the undefeated All-India Inter-Railway Light Heavyweight champion from 1930 onwards. In an exhibition bout, he knocked out the British Army and Air Force Middleweight champion. In the following year, although giving away considerable weight, he knocked out the British Army Light Heavyweight champion in the second round.

Arthur Suares was a boxing legend in the thirties and forties. At the early age of fourteen he won the coveted 'Green Howard Cup' for the South Indian Bantamweight Championship at Madras. Even before his coming of age he fought professionally, scoring victories over great boxers like Jack deSouza, the Light-Weight champion of Western India and Harry Bell of Australia. In the course of his career he had spectacular victories over Al Rivers, Dixie Kidd, Seaman Nobby Hall, Gunner Melvin, Milton Kubes, Duncan Chatterton and Johnny James to mention a few. He even beat the great Gunboat Jack, the American Negro who made India his home: according to many experts Gunboat Jack should have annexed the Middleweight championship of the world had he remained and fought in America.

At the top of his career Suares embarked on foreign tours to Ceylon, Burma, Malaya and Singapore. He fought many leading international boxers including Frank Malino, Tiger Freeman, Seaman Youngman, Champion of the Burma Fleet, Bill Brady, and the most outstanding Ignatio Fernandez who was then rated as world class.

Suares turned down a contract for boxing in the U.S.A. and returned home. On the declaration of World War II Suares enlisted in the R.A.M.C., where he continued his boxing career generously donating his purses to the War Fund.

While posted with the Middle East Forces at Iraq, Suares achieved the impossible of a triple knock-out in one night, earning for himself the title of Light Heavyweight Champion of the P.I.I. Forces (Persia, Iraq and Iran).

With the cessation of the War he joined the Hyderabad State Army as a boxing instructor. When that unit was disbanded, he joined the Artillery Centre at Nasik Road. After retirement in 1962 he joined his family in Bangalore and spent his time in coaching youngsters in boxing and athletics. He was extremely proud of his young nieces and nephews whom he personally coached. Deanna Syme, Minette Suares, Arthur Mark Suares, Milford Hennessy and Lincoln Suares were among the few who have hit the headliness.

Dusty Miller was from 1942 the 'Middleweight King' of the R.I.N. In spite of the emigration of some of our best boxers, the Anglo-Indians continued to dominate the boxing arena. After a lapse of about 5 years the Northern India Boxing Championship was revived in 1951. Dusty Miller was matched against Capt. Campagnac of the 3rd Gurkha Rifles. Although Campagnac fought gallantly and weighed thirty-one pounds more than Miller, the latter proved too good for him. Dusty Miller added the Northern India Heavyweight Championship to his existing title as Lightweight and Heavyweight Champion of Ceylon. Incidentally, Campagnac today is a Colonel. During the Indo-Pakistan conflict he commanded the 3rd Gurkha Rifles. His grandfather fought as a civilian in 1857 during the Lucknow siege.

At the 1951 meet, Major Roach of Western Command captured the Middleweight title. He proved too good for 'Killer' Khem Bahadur Thapa of the 8th Gurkhas.

Maurice Monnier won the Northern India Light-Heavyweight Championship.

World War II gave a fillip to boxing in India, when the Americans added to the popularity of this sport. The most memorable tournament staged during World War II was the China-Burma-India Championship at the Monsoon Square Gardens at Calcutta. The coloured American fighters had things very much their own way. The Anglo-Indians were the only boxers from India who won their respective crowns. Dusty Miller punched his way to the championship of the Middleweight Division.

Aaron Joshua emulated this performance in the open Featherweight Division. Joshua's greatest victory in this meet was over Roy Ankarah of the Gold Coast: Roy Ankarah, otherwise known as the Black Flash, was the leading contender for the world title at a later stage.

Veterans of boxing refer to the fight between Dennis Barbaro and Private Lewis of the South Wales Borderers as perhaps the best they can recall, and that between Ron Wilmer and Ralph Janz of Ceylon as the next best for scientific boxing.

In the 1952 Olympiad at Helsinki there were practically only Anglo-Indian names in the galaxy of well-known Indian boxers.

Ron Norris, champion son of a champion father, was quoted as 'world class'.

In 1949, Ron Norris annexed the Madhya Pradesh Lightweight championship. In 1952 he hit the headlines in the All-India Championship held in Calcutta. His most spectacular fight was with Havildar Janardhan of the Bombay Police, then the reigning Western India Champion. Norris outfought the crafty, experienced Havildar. In February of the same year an Indian boxing team was invited to Ceylon to take part in the Colombo Championships. In the semi-finals of the Welterweight Championship Norris beat Parker of the British Royal Navy. In the finals he beat the Ceylon Welterweight champion, O.M.V.D.Pereira, and annexed the Welterweight title of Ceylon.

In the selections for the Indian team to represent the Country at the Helsinki Olympics, there was a return bout between Norris and Janardhan. On this occasion Norris proved in an even more convincing manner than before his superiority over Janardhan. Norris was one of the 4 selected to represent India at Helsinki.

Capt. Oscar Ward, the Captain of the team, was another well-known Anglo-Indian boxer. Norris was the only member of the team, however, to have the spotlight focussed on him at Helsinki. Fighting against Battilla of Canada, he hammered the Canadian champion into submission in the third round. In the quarter-finals he was pitted against Jer Johnson. Norris fought a great fight. The verdict of points was given, however, to the Dane. There was considerable comment in the press against the verdict. On his return to India, Norris met Gopal Krishen, the Madras Middleweight, and scored a spectacular victory by knocking him out in the third round. In Calcutta he put on the gloves against Anwar Pasha, the Olympic representative of Pakistan. Pasha was knocked out within two minutes of the first round. Norris then represented India against the Japanese. The Japanese were fast and had terrific stamina. They literally stormed through the Indian side mowing down the opposition until they met the Anglo-Indians. Norris brought them to a stand. In his first encounter he beat Onuki the 'Human Hurricane'. Norris then beat Kaji, K.O. Kaji as he was known in India. Isaacson, another Anglo-Indian, also beat his Japanese opponent.

Rudy Hourigan, a product of St. Joseph's College, Calcutta, began to show his ability as a boxer while in school. Ultimately, his name was included in the list of boxers summoned for trials preparatory to the choosing of the Indian team which was to participate in the World Olympiad to be held in London in 1948. In the final bout Hourigan was opposed by Bhattia of Bengal. Throughout the fight Hourigan dictated terms, on one occasion dropping Bhattia for a short count. When the decision was awarded to Bhattia, pandemonium broke loose; the police had to intervene to save the judges and the referee from being manhandled. Despite the protests from the press and the public, Bhattia represented India at the Olympic Games and met with little success. Hourigan made his appearance again in Ceylon where he beat the reigning Ceylon Featherweight champion. In 1944 Hourigan joined the Indian Air Force where he soon annexed the highest boxing titles. He decisively beat the famous Lal Bahadur Thapa of the 8th Gurkha Rifles who had been the unbeatable national champion since 1945. He then annexed the Featherweight title of the Services. In the All-India Championship at Bombay he even beat the well-known

Havelock Norris, the Western India champion, and became the National Featherweight Champion at the early age of 19.

Athletics

In athletics also the Anglo-Indians established a dominant position.

The first Indian to win a medal in world athletics was N.J. Pritchard, an Anglo-Indian teacher from Lucknow. Pritchard was second, five meters behind J.W.B. Tewkesbury of the United States, who won the 200 metres. This was over 60 years ago, at Paris, in the second of the modern series of International Games.

In the 1948 Indian contingent for the Olympics there were several Anglo-Indian athletes. They included Eric Philips the sprinter, John Vickers the hurdler, Nuttall who captained the boxing team and, perhaps the most outstanding, Henry Rebello.

A Bangalore boy, Henry Rebello jumped to international fame. He made his way in the Mysore Olympic meet by creating a new provincial record in the Hop, Step and Jump of 42'-9". As a result of long and strenuous practice, by 1944 he cleared 44' in the Hop, Step and Jump and 21' in the long jump. By 1945 he had increased the distance to 46' and 21'-9" respectively. In 1946 he again won the Hop, Step and Jump event in the Mysore Olympic meet clearing 46'-6¾". He then went on to win the event in the Indo-Ceylon Athletic Meet the same year, clearing 46'-11". He then got bogged down at the 47' mark. He eventually decided to lay off for a while and concentrate on sprinting and hurdling. In the 1948 Mysore Olympic Athletic Meet he made a stupendous jump of 49'-7". He then went on to shatter the Indian record at the All-India Athletic Meet the same year with a distance of 50'-2". This performance found him a place in the Indian team which participated in the World Olympiad of 1948. Sportsmen throughout the Country had their thoughts centred on the Indian Hockey team and on Henry Rebello for world honours. There was much joy when during the practice jump before the Games he cleared 52'-1½" at Motspur Park. This joy turned into despair, however, when the tragic news was received that during the practice he had pulled a muscle and would not be able to take part in the Games.

The Sutton brothers were famous names in Indian sport in 1930. W. Sutton represented India in the Olympic Games at Los Angeles in 1932. He ran neck and neck with Lord Burghley, the famous British hurdler.

Ken Powell of the Kolar Gold Fields and an all-round sportsman is one of India's most famous athletes. In March, 1964, at the All-India Open Athletics meet, Powell equalled the National and Asian record for the 100 metres by clocking 10.6 seconds. Earlier in May, 1963, at the Mysore State Olympics Powell achieved the title of the fastest man in India and Asia with a record timing of 21.3 seconds in the 200 metres dash. In November, 1963, Powell was selected to represent India at the International Athletic meet at Nairobi (Kenya) to celebrate Kenya's Independence Day. He won the 220 yards but lost the 100 yards.

In June, 1964, Powell was selected to represent India at the Olympic Games at Tokyo for the 200 metres and the relay team for the 4×100 metres. In July, 1964, Ken Powell and Deanna Syme, an outstanding Anglo-Indian woman athlete of Mysore, toured West Germany for training-cum-competition along with an Indian team consisting of 12 members. At Poona in March, 1965, Powell and Barry Ford, another Anglo-Indian, broke the Indian record for the 100 metres and set up a new record of 10.4 seconds in the 100 metres and 21.4 seconds in the 200 metres.

It is interesting to recall that Derek Boosey, also of the Kolar Gold Fields, covered 49' and 4" in the Hop, Step and Jump bettering the 15 year old record of Henry Rebello. By winning the National Championship in 1960, Boosey equalled the record of his father, Leslie Boosey, who had won the National Championship about 20 years earlier.

Football

Football does not attract the same interest as hockey in India. But for many years Anglo-Indian schools have devoted increasing attention to this sport. Football is played with considerable skill and enthusiasm in almost every Anglo-Indian school. The Durand Cup was the premier football trophy. In pre-Independence days British regimental teams usually claimed this trophy, but very often Anglo-Indian elevens would reach the final beating on the way some of the best British regimental teams. In 1927, the East Indian Railway team, consisting only of Anglo-Indians, reached the final. [In 1929, the Great Indian Peninsular Railway team, consisting again only of Anglo-Indians, won the All-India Railway Football tournament. After this they reached the final of the Durand tournament; they lost by one goal to a crack British regimental team.

Cricket

Cricket is also not played in India with the same enthusiasm as hockey. Anglo-Indian schools, however, have turned out some really good cricketers. After leaving school these lads have little, if any, opportunity of developing their sporting talent further. The prowess attained by the Anglo-Indians can be illustrated by a provincial cross section of Anglo-Indian achievement. For instance, in the Central Provinces (now Madhya Pradesh) the Quadrangular Cricket tournament was, for many years, won by the Anglo-Indians: the name of the tournament was derived from the fact that four teams—the Anglo-Indians, Europeans, Hindus and Mohammedans—competed. The European team was usually strong, being drawn from several British battalions in the Province. In one year, either 1924 or 1925, the Europeans fielded an exceptionally fine team. There were four British County bats in the team: yet this team was beaten in the final by the Anglo Indian eleven. Some of the latter were boys drawn from Christ Church Boys' School, Jubbulpore. In passing, it might be mentioned that this School claims to hold a world record in cricket. The school team once played an eleven drawn from a well-known British Regiment— the Hampshires. Incredible as it may sound, this regimental eleven was dismissed for an inglorious blob. The eleven members of the British team were not able to make or sneak a single run. They were not even fortunate enough to secure a bye. This perhaps unique achievement can be verified by an inspection of the official score sheet duly framed and hung up in the school hall.

First Indian World Champion

While writing about the men I would refer last, but not least, to Wilson Jones. He was the first and, so far, the only Indian to win an individual World Championship title. He won the Indian Billiards title in 1950 and held it for three successive years. He regained the Indian title in 1954 and retained it for two years. He was again the Champion in 1957, 1960 and 1961, and held the Indian Championship title from 1963 till his retirement in 1967.

Wilson Jones represented India in the World Billiards Championship in 1951, 1952, 1954, 1958, 1960, 1962 and 1964 and in the World Snooker Championship in 1963. He not only reigned for 12 years as the Indian Billiards Champion, he also won the all-India title for Snooker in 1948, 1952, 1954, 1958 and 1960. In 1958, he won the coveted crown of the World Billiards Champion. In December, 1964, at Auckland, New Zealand, Jones regained the title of World Billiards Champion, being the only player to finish the tournament.

When Wilson Jones won the World title in 1958, both the then President and the Prime Minister were so impressed by his success that he was honoured with an audience and earned the privilege of playing an exhibition game of billiards at Rashtrapati Bhavan. In March, 1963, Wilson Jones was given the Arjuna Award by the President Dr. Radhakrishnan at a function held at Rashtrapati Bhavan. In 1965, he was awarded the Padma Shri.

Sportswomen

Anglo-Indian girls excel in all kinds of sport, especially athletics. Until recently they did not have serious competition except, perhaps, in tennis, from girls of other communities. For years most of the Women's Provincial Athletics Championships were won by Anglo-Indian girls. In hockey the Anglo-Indian girls dominated the game, as much as the Anglo-Indian men. The Provincial and National Championships were swept by the Anglo-Indian teams. Usually, the final was fought between two Anglo-Indian teams. Calcutta, Bombay, Madras, Jubbulpore, Delhi, the U.P.—all produced Anglo-Indian girls' teams that were unbeatable in their respective areas.

In 1953 a team was sent to the U.K. to take part in an international hockey tournament. Among the members were Betty Catchick (Captain), Vanda Williamson, Mary D'Sena and Doreen Stephenson : all four were from Bengal. Also in the team were Yvonne Smith and her sister, Dorrel Smith, both Jubbulpore girls, and Philomena Norris, one of the daughters of Rex Norris.

In 1956 another Indian team was sent to take part in an international hockey tournament in Australia. The Captain, this time, was Yvonne Smith : Wendy Norris, another daughter of Rex Norris, was also in the 1956 team. Yvonne Smith was as good a hockey player as she was handsome. She captained the Madhya Pradesh's Women's Hockey Team from 1947 to 1957 during which period the team often swept everything before them in the National Championships.

The Women's National Hockey Tournament held in Bhopal in 1961 was an all-Anglo-Indian affair. The Madras State Team went down narrowly in the final to the star-studded Mysore State Team.

Ann Lumsden, who typified the athletic and yet beautiful Anglo-Indian girl, was the first woman hockey player to get the Arjuna Award : that was in 1962.

The Delhi Olympic meet held in February, 1951, illustrated the continuing domination of athletics by the Community. In Delhi, at that time, there was a total population of not more than three or four thousand Anglo-Indians including the children. At the Delhi meet the team fielded by 'The Anglo-Indian Youth' team of Delhi swept the board, both in the Men's and Women's sections. Ivy Scott won the title of Champion Girl Athlete, Senior Section, and also Champion Woman Athlete, Open Section. Christine MacInnis won the Champion Girl's Trophy, Junior Section, and broke the State record for the high jump, open section, with a jump of 4'-2-5/8".

The 400 metres relay race was won by the young Anglo-Indian boys and the girls' relay team romped home a lap ahead of the team which found second place.

Ivy Scott won seven first places in the meet, a performance which has never been equalled by a girl or woman in the Capital. She easily won the 50 metres, 100 metres and long jump events in the Senior Girls' Division and by winning the 50 metres, the 100 metres and long jump events in the Women's Open Section, she annexed the championship trophies in both divisions, while her final quarter in the women's relay was practically a solo affair. She broke the tape far ahead of the others and enabled the Anglo-Indian Youth team to annex the trophy for the third year in succession.

Deanna Syme, another outstanding Anglo-Indian sportswoman, showed her versatility by shining in the Mysore University both as a student and as an athlete. She was also a first class hockey player, being a member of the Mysore State Women's team in the Hockey Championships held at Poona in 1958. In the same year

Deanna won the Inter-University Championship at Jubbulpore. In April, 1961, the Mysore University Sports Committee gave her a special prize as 'The Outstanding Athlete'. In the National Athletics in 1957, Deanna became the long jump champion with a leap of 17 ft. 4½ ins. She retained her title the following year at Calcutta, lost it in 1959 and regained it in 1960. Deanna Syme has followed in the footsteps of her aunt, Miss Marjorie Suares, who won the National championship many years ago.

Betty Davenport, who was for some time the P.T. Instructress in the Frank Anthony Public School, New Delhi, has been for several years the undisputed National champion in the Javelin and the Discus throw.

Christine Forage of Bombay has been described as 'India's Wonder Sports Girl'.

Christine, who was born on the 27th January, 1946, had by the age of 17 piled up a dazzling array of achievements and trophies that might well have turned the head of many an older sportswoman of international repute. Breaking into athletics at the age of 12, she made her debut at the National Games in Trivandrum and secured second place in the high jump, somewhat to the surprise even of those who knew her. After doing exceedingly well in the Bombay State Championship, Christine collected 2 gold medals in the National Championships held at New Delhi in 1960. In 1961, she created an all-time record in the Maharashtra State Senior and Junior Games by sweeping the board in 9 events, thus establishing a record which would be difficult, if not impossible, to equal. Despite a bad knee she was in a class by herself in the National Athletic Championships at Jullundur in 1961. She swept the board in the under-sixteen events, apart from establishing a whole series of new records. She won 6 gold medals and narrowly missed the seventh.

In the National Games at Jubbulpore in 1962, she dumbfounded even the most ardent prophets by taking part in 9 events and winning a medal in each. She won 6 gold medals, 2 silver and one bronze.

A tribute to Christine's versatile and yet consistent athletic genius was the National Award for Physical Efficiency. In a two-day competition held for the first time in 1962, she collected 3,392 points beating to a complete frazzle all the competitors from 12

States and 3 Union territories. It is significant that no awards were made to the Seniors as they did not measure up to the minimum standards.

Sportsmen and sportswriters acclaim Christine as one of the rarest combinations of outstanding capacity in track and field events. She is in a class by herself being equally at home in sprints, hurdles, the jumps and throws.

What kind of a person is this teenage Anglo-Indian wonder sportsgirl? Essentially, she is shy and admits to being nervous before any race. She is completely unspoilt and has the interests of any average Anglo-Indian teenager, including jazz. Apparently she prefers Elvis Presley to the top Anglo-Indian pop-singer Cliff Richards. Apart from the necessary physical attributes, Christine has the prerequisites for championship in any walk of life—the will and the capacity to work hard and to keep to a rigid schedule. Christine, today, is a star the like of which has not yet shone in the Indian athletic firmament. Whether she places India on the map of world athletics will depend on whether those who have anything to do officially with the promotion of athletic talent in the Country ensure that she gets the necessary opportunities and the proper training. In 1962 Christine was invited to Russia for further training.

Reference to our sporting women would not be complete without mentioning Jenny Sandison. For many years she was the undisputed queen of All-India tennis. Her talent took her to Wimbledon. But playing conditions being very different, she did not do as well as was expected. She, however, had the satisfaction of beating Betty Nuthall, the reigning British champion.

Shikaris

Some of the best-known shikaris in the Country have been Anglo-Indians. This perhaps was inevitable because the majority of Anglo-Indians were interested in shikar. Youngsters were brought up to the use of the shotgun and the rifle from a very early age. The names of some Anglo-Indian shikaris, who also have books to their credit, are household words, such as, Jim Corbett of Naini Tal, Anderson of Bangalore, and Powell of Mussoorie. A recent book written by Pat Stracey entitled, 'Reade, Elephant Hunter' is worth reading. In his book Stracey describes Lovel Reade as "The

Jim Corbett of Elephants." Stracey points out that, like Corbett, Reade was of humble origin. Reade, whose grandfather was a European, started life as a clerk, was transferred to the Agriculture Department being first an Inspector and then rose to official status. Reade shot his first elephant in 1928 at the age of 38 and his last in 1967, at the age 76. Reade had a phenomenal bag of 220 raiding elephants most of which he shot on foot.

Although an Anglo-Indian, Reade appears to have identified himself with the Khasis of Assam among whom he is a legendary figure. Stracey points out that Reade has not achieved the fame of Corbett because he functioned in a distant, inaccessible part of India and also, perhaps, because unlike Corbett he did not have the patronage of persons in high places. Stracey himself is no mean shikari. He retired as Chief Conservator from the Imperial Forest Service after 30 years of service. He is one of the highly successful Stracey brothers to whom I refer in a later chapter.

I should imagine that over the years there have been hundreds of Anglo-Indians who have shot more than a dozen tigers apart from panther, bear, bison, wild buffalo and elephant. Thus an uncle of mine, William Anthony, who retired from the Imperial Forest Service, although not a fanatical shikari had 57 tigers to his credit. He and Col. Leake, a European and Chief Medical Officer of the then Bengal-Nagpur Railway, were great shooting companions. Leake was an ardent big-game shikari apart from being the only living double V.C.—that was between 1920 and 1930.

I remember a story my uncle told me about Leake and himself. My uncle was then Conservator at Balaghat, a fine shooting district in the then Central Provinces. The Governor was Sir Montague Butler. Butler, who was very friendly with my uncle, asked him to arrange a really good shoot, which was done. A number of tigers came out in the beats, but apparently the Governor and his party were indifferent shots. They were able to bag only one tiger between them. My uncle felt that Leake would like to join him as the beats had shown a large number of tigers in that area. After about a fortnight, he and Leake went over the same area. Between them they bagged 4 tigers. On that occasion my uncle got a right and left using his trusted .500 bore double-barrel rifle.

The average Anglo-Indian shikari could always produce some

hair-raising stories of narrow escapes.   One, which my uncle told me, is worth repeating.

He and a Gond shikari were walking through the jungle when, suddenly, a tiger appeared in the bend barely thirty yards away. One of the pieces of advice that my uncle gave me, when I first started shooting, was never to fire at a tiger if he was looking at you. His theory was that even if the tiger was hit with the heaviest of bullets, in the heart, if he was at a distance of thirty yards, he would be able to kill the shikari before collapsing.   On this occasion he apparently forgot his own advice : he brought his rifle to his shoulder and pulled the trigger.

Apparently, Providence was with him.   He had a misfire. Hearing the click, the tiger charged coming to a stop, within a few feet, snarling and lashing his body with his tail.

My uncle said that his immediate reaction was one of cold terror. This was partly due to the Gond shikari being immediately behind him.   The Gonds of Madhya Pradesh are fine shikaris and usually full of pluck. A good tracker, that shikari was, however, notorious for being extremely fleet-footed at the first sign of danger.   My uncle was terrified that he would bolt, which would have meant the tiger killing them both.   Fortunately, the Gond belied his reputation.   Standing behind my uncle he followed his example and stared at the tiger.   He even went one better : he growled out the imprecation, "Sala bap ko nahin pehchanta (You so-and-so, don't you recognise your father!)."   The tiger snarled, lashed his sides with his tail and moved away.

Some of us, as youngsters, shot our first big animal at the age of twelve or thirteen.   Many Anglo-Indians started their bag of tigers in their teens.   Shirley Forrester, who comes from an old Central Provinces family, qualified for the I.C.S. doing his examination in London.   When he appeared for his viva voce interview, among the questions he was asked was whether he had done any shooting since he came from one of the best shikar areas in India.   He said, 'Yes'. When pressed as to whether he had shot any tigers, he again said, 'Yes'.

When asked how many—he was still a college student—he said, 'Eleven'. The examiners must have thought that the young Anglo-Indian student was trying to pull the long bow.

Shirley Forrester had, in fact, shot almost all his tigers on foot.

Several years later when he was District Magistrate at Hoshanga-bad, 2 tigers were apparently swept across the flooded river and lodged themselves in the nearby public garden or the garden of the 'Burra' Club. When they were spotted, there was general consternation and arrangements were started to get a posse of police to deal with them. As soon as Forrester heard the news, he went down to the spot and stalking the tigers shot them both.

The best shot that I have ever seen was Tyrrel Hawkins. The son of a senior railway official who left him a substantial legacy, Hawkins was able to indulge in his penchant for shooting. He had a fine armoury including guns made by Holland and Holland. On one occasion when he visited the U.K., Hawkins was invited by the management of Holland and Holland to a pheasant shoot at a well-known ducal estate. At the end of the shoot the other members of the party were dumbfounded by Hawkins' shooting: his bag was more than that of all the other guns put together.

Hawkins often formed one of our party at the time when I used to shoot in the Madhya Pradesh jungles almost every week-end. Some of us preened ourselves on our shooting, but with Hawkins about we suffered almost from an inferiority complex. Quite literally, I never saw him miss whatever the bird, from jungle fowl and partridge to duck and snipe. And the bird always fell in the centre of the pattern and dropped dead.

Hawkins was equally good with the rifle. On one of our shoots I watched him pull down a running boar at a distance of at least 250 yards. It would have been a good shot if the boar was standing. As it happened, the boar had broken from the beat and was bolting through an open space in the fields. Hawkins brought the boar down using a Springfield with a peep sight. On another occasion when we were beating for the usual sambhar, cheetal and pig, we were all on the ground sitting on our respective canvas stools. At the end of the beat after some of us had fired shots at different animals, Hawkins suddenly called out telling us to stay put as he had fired at a tiger. It was winter, the jungle was dense and it was not a pleasant thought that a wounded tiger might charge from any direction. After a while Hawkins called out that everything was all right. We went up and found a stone-cold tiger. Hawkins had taken him while he was slinking through some bushes offering a most difficult shot. Once again using a Springfield, he had dropped him dead with a bullet placed at the junction of the neck and the shoulder. Personally, I would not use a Springfield for tiger. Although I have shot almost everything from Chinkara to Himalayan bear and tiger with my .350 Rigby Magnum, when deliberately going after a tiger I use my .450/400 d.b. hammerless ejector.

On one occasion Hawkins was driving his car through the jungle while I sat beside him. I noticed some jungle fowl on his side and pointed them out to him. Hawkins, while still driving the car, loaded his .12 bore and put it out of the car window. Two jungle fowl rose and flew almost parallel with the car : still driving, using one hand, Hawkins brought them both down with a right and a left. It would have been a fine shot with the shikari standing and using both hands!

I have shot with Karni Singh, the Maharaja of Bikaner, who is a member of my Group, the Independent Parliamentary Group in the Lok Sabha. A few years back my wife and I were the guests of the Maharaja and the Maharani at an Imperial grouse shoot in Bikaner. After an overnight stay at the famous Lalbagh Palace we were driven to Gajner, which is 20 odd miles from Bikaner, to the 'country' Palace, so to speak, of the Maharaja. In the afternoon we did a short duck shoot over the nearby lake where there were a few birds. In an hour's shoot, between six guns, we bagged about 120 duck. Using a .20 bore Bikaner brought down his birds without missing a single shot.

Next morning after a bath and breakfast, we drove about two and a half miles to the butts where the first droves of Imperial grouse were expected. This was my first Imperial grouse shoot. For several days in advance the local watchers had been out. They are so highly skilled in this business that they are able, literally, to count the number of birds when in flight. It was estimated that there were about 12,000 grouse in the vicinity. We took up our positions in our respective butts at about 7 a.m. This was the famous shooting ground of the former Viceroys of India. To Gajner went every Viceroy at the invitation of the ruler of Bikaner for the well-known Imperial grouse shoot.

This was a real Maharaja shoot. The habits of the birds had been carefully studied. At 7.30 every morning they flighted in thousands over the butts to a large stream of water. This was the

part of the flight that we were lined up for.   The butts were interesting structures: in this particular line they were of wrought-iron,
circular in shape, and with metal lattice-work around them.   Inside
each butt were two swivel stools.   We had been in position for
about 20 minutes when Bikaner called out, "Here they come".
I was using my 25 inch cylinder barrels and was loaded with No.
6 shot.   In the distance I saw a long thin line of what looked like
a wisp of smoke stretching against the skyline.   This line gradually
took on a firmer and larger shape and then I realised that it was
the first flight of Imperial grouse as they came at us.

The Imperial grouse flies at about 60 miles per hour, if not
faster.   The first batch flew straight at me.   I waited for them to
whizz past and then took a right and a left.   My luck was in and
two birds plummetted to the ground.   There were five of us in
the first line.   Bikaner was shooting away and so also were the
other guns.   Then the pace got faster and more furious.   Batches
of 20 and 30 kept swooping down in all directions going over to
the drinking spot which was about a mile behind us.   In the next
few minutes while my barrels grew hotter my average was not so
hot: in fact, it was becoming progressively colder.   We finished in
about forty minutes and then the beaters, who were to pick up the
birds, started coming in all directions.   They collected about
100 odd birds.   Bikaner was shooting with a .28 bore and yet
his performance was first class.   He got the largest number of shots
and also the best average.

We collected to discuss our gains and our losses.   I confessed
that I could not understand how my average was not better.
While I regard myself as a very average, indeed, a poor duck shot,
the fast flight of the Imperial grouse was much more in my line of
quick shooting.   On a good day I have averaged 7 out of 10 in
snipe and 8 and even 10 out of 10 in partridge.   Bikaner felt that I
was making a mistake by allowing the birds to pass me before taking
the shot.   I admitted that this was correct, as I preferred to take
my birds on a side swing.   He pointed out that it is difficult to shoot
Imperial grouse in this way as they carry a tremendous amount of
lead and should be taken coming head on.

When we arrived at the next site of butts, I changed to my 28"
choke barrels and took the birds from the front.   Instead of carrying
two or three shotguns, I have a .12 bore with interchangeable sets

of barrels. In the next half an hour to forty-five minutes we did nothing except to blaze at the oncoming flights of grouse. I had shot about 40 birds in this second venture and was feeling quite pleased with myself when I suddenly heard a shout from the line of shikaris. My shikari jerked my hand towards a line of on-coming birds and shouted "Pintail, Maro!" Bikaner called out to me and said, "You must get it." I did not know whether I was going to get it, but I tried to pick out the pintail who was flying high and coming straight overhead, raking him with my barrels from back to front and pressing the trigger as I covered his head, I continued to swing. In an overhead shot this continuance of the swing, which is vital, is fairly easy. There was a howl of delight from the shikaris as the pintail folded up and fell. One would have thought that I had bagged a rogue elephant or a predatory man-eating tiger! Bikaner mentioned that the pintail was a rare trophy as one pintail in a bag of 1000 Imperial grouse was about the average. That pintail, stuffed and mounted, is among my trophies.

The beaters brought in altogether over 500 birds. We posed with only some of the birds as it was felt that in the New India, with increasing vegetarian sentiments, it would not do to be photo-graphed with the full bag!

After an excellent lunch we got ready for the Houbara shoot. The Houbara is also known as the lesser Indian bustard. This was also my first experience of shooting Houbara. I got into a convertible Chevrolet driven by one of the A.D.Cs., popularly known as Jimmy. Two guns were put into each car. Bikaner had told us that Houbara shooting can lead to accidents as cars have to travel between 50 and 60 miles an hour, chasing the bird, and if the gun in the back seat loses his head he could easily shoot one of the occupants in front. He reminded us that this had happened on a previous shoot when the gun in a back seat had blown off the elbow of the person in front. The other gun in my car was a Brigadier of the British High Commission. Bikaner told us that we would be lucky if we could get one or two Houbara per gun. We set out in our car and the others went in different directions. After we had gone about three or four miles the shikari, who accom-panied us, told us to cross into the fields. The terrain was flat and covered with shrub jungle. After we had gone about a mile winding through the shrub jungle, Jimmy spotted a Houbara and speeded the car to about 50 miles dodging bushes and trees in the process. I was interested to see this bird, which was the first time for me. He is about three or four times the size of a stone-plover, is grey flecked, has long legs a long neck and the male bird has a fine ruff. Incidentally, my attention was not concentrated entirely on the Houbara. Jimmy, the A.D.C., must have been the world's prince of trick drivers. As we swirled around bushes and trees in the direction of the Houbara, which by this time was taking a run in order to get air-borne, Jimmy swerved around a bush and told me to shoot, which I did. This kind of snap shooting was like mother's milk to me: I had done this type of shooting for years in the old Central Provinces jungles—of course without the speeding car. With a right and a left from my .28 inch barrels the Houbara's airborne career was abruptly ended. I then got into the back seat and allowed the Brigadier to sit in the front for his shot. In a little while we saw another Houbara and the Brigadier did his stuff. After the Brigadier had missed a couple of shots, Jimmy suggested that we should not take shots by turn but the person quicker on the draw would take the bird.

Brought up to shoot with instinctive coordination of eye, hand and gun, I was able to poop off both barrels while the Brigadier was still bringing his .12 bore to his shoulder. On one occasion in his desire to catch up on a male bird, Jimmy speeded up to about 70 miles an hour and how we avoided a tree I still do not know. As he avoided the tree, I took a crack at the Houbara through a bush while he was taking off. We were pleasantly surprised to see him drop dead. It was a beautiful male bird with a lovely ruff.

We tore around in the area, picked up 8 Houbara of which number I accounted for 6. With Jimmy swerving around on two wheels, dodging bushes and trees, it was quite a thrill. Jimmy was fulsome in his tributes to my shooting : I was even more fulsome in my tributes to his driving! When we got back we found that ours was easily the best bag. The other cars had between them shot altogether 5 Houbara. Bikaner told us that ours was a record bag as even 4 Houbara to one car was regarded as excellent. Incidentally, the Houbara is very good to eat.

Bikaner, is India's ace shot in clay-pigeon and skeet and has represented the Country for several years at the World Olympics. In many ways he is an extraordinary shot. Yet I do not think that in a jungle he would be as effective as Hawkins, from jungle fowl to a tiger slinking through the bushes or a bolting boar at 250 yards.

Bob Woods, a dental surgeon in Jubbulpore, has over 30 tigers to his credit. Today, he runs one of India's premier shikar firms.

As bird shots, too, Anglo-Indians have produced some outstanding shikaris. A young Anglo-Indian policeman, Ainsworth Harrison, was always included in the Viceroy's duck and bird shoots. A deadly shot, he could be relied upon to ensure a record bag. In Delhi, today, George O'Brien is still known as an excellent shikari and fisherman. He often shot with Vizianagram and one day he bagged 4 tigers. Even, today, although he has undergone a serious eye operation, he still shoots. Leslie Johnson of the I.C.S. told me an interesting story. Johnson himself is no mean shikari, having accounted for a number of tigers and brown Himalayan bear. He swears by his Springfield and uses nothing else. Johnson mentioned that when George O'Brien goes out for a duck shoot nowadays, he always keeps a shikari standing near him as he is unable to see the birds in flight. The shikari warns him that a couple of birds are coming towards him, tells him on which side they are. George O'Brien shoots instinctively and still gets a right and a left when, as Johnson puts it, a person with the best of eyesight and at the height of his powers would find it difficult to do so.

Anglo-Indian women and even girls, especially when I was a youngster, did their share of shooting. A girl cousin of mine, Edith Webb, was barely eighteen when she shot a tigress. Recently, I met an Anglo-Indian family by the name of Carberry, who have a large farm near Dehra Dun. Mrs. Carberry, who comes from the Powell family, has shot many tigers in her time.

Builders Of Key Services

The Railways

After the middle of the 19th century, the Anglo-Indians along with pioneering Britons laid the first railway sleepers in India. These Anglo-Indian pioneers were scattered all over the Country. They lived under the most difficult conditions, having to hack their way through jungle and swamp and without any medical, much less social amenities. They were, usually, separated from their families for a period of 4 to 5 years. Because of the inhospitable, dangerous conditions under which work had to be done in those pioneering days up to 1920, members of the other communities were not forthcoming except for the lowest categories. With over a hundred years' intimate association with the building and working of the Railways, Anglo-Indians developed an almost hereditary aptitude for Railway Service.

In 1960, I led a deputation to meet Jawaharlal Nehru. We met him in the large interview room of the External Affairs Ministry. When I walked in with the deputation Nehru remarked that it was more an invasion than a deputation. I had called a special meeting, in New Delhi, of the representatives of the Community and Anglo-Indian Schools to discuss the continuance of Anglo-Indian guarantees in respect of education and quotas in the Services especially the Railways.

During the discussion I pointed out to Jawaharlal that employment on the Railways had become almost an economic necessity for the lesser-educated Anglo-Indians. For generations fathers, sons and grandsons had entered certain departments without having to show any high paper qualifications. It was because of their near-heroic service that the Railways had been built to their present size and importance. I underlined the fact that with the raising of the educational qualification even for the lower categories of posts, the sense of duty, the efficiency in the Railways had rapidly declined. Graduates and undergraduates, obsessed with their paper qualifications but with no background of loyalty or family service to the Railways, were being increasingly employed. To Nehru's amusement I related what I had been told by an Anglo-Indian mail driver. That driver had taken his son for employment. The family had served the Railway from generation to generation for a period of almost a hundred years. But the son was refused a fireman's post because he had not completed the High School or Senior Cambridge. The father complained bitterly to me that instead a weedy, pigeon-chested youth, who had done his Intermediate, had been chosen. He put me a rhetorical question: "What comparison could there be between such a youth and his son, powerfully built, a boxer and an athlete, from whose veins, if they were cut, steam engines would emerge!"

Up till about 1920, practically every engine-driver, guard, station master and permanent way inspector was an Anglo-Indian or a Domiciled or Covenanted European. Anglo-Indians, usually of the fairer variety, reached the positions of Agents, now known as General Managers, Chief Engineers and General Traffic Managers. In order to break through the British wall of colour discrimination they had to masquerade as Europeans or at least as Domiciled Europeans.

The stability and progress of the Railways depended on the Anglo-Indians. Strikes were short-lived because of the sense of duty not only of the Anglo-Indian railwaymen but of their families. Thus, in 1923, there was a major strike on the then Eastern Railway when even the Anglo-Indian schoolboys came to the rescue of the Administration and cleaned railway carriages. In 1927, the then Bengal-Nagpur Railway was faced with a serious strike. Once again, the Anglo-Indian Community kept the wheels moving and prevented the strike from spreading to the other Railways. In 1928 there was another strike on the East Indian Railway when the Anglo-Indian railwaymen served beyond the call of duty in order to keep the goods and passenger trains moving.

Up to 1925, 50% of the superior service vacancies were filled by promotion from the subordinate grades. In that year the Railway Board passed the order that only 15% were to be promoted to the official cadre. The channel of promotion hitherto open to the Community was thus severely restricted. In 1926 the Anglo-Indians held 8% of the superior posts, the other communities about 21%, and Europeans about 70%. In the same year, out of a total of 762,553 railway employees 14,007 were Anglo-Indians. Gidney was able to get the Anglo-Indian quotas protected by the incorporation of Section 242 of the Government of India Act of 1935. I was able to get a similar guarantee put into the Constitution of Independent India : that was Article 336 of the Constitution. Under that Article appointments of members of the Community to posts in the Railway, Customs, Postal and Telegraph services of the Union were to be made on the same basis as immediately before the 15th day of August, 1947. During every succeeding period of two years, the number of posts reserved for members of the Community was to be less by 10% : at the end of ten years from the commencement of the Constitution all reservations were to cease. This provision ensured that in the posts with which the Community had been associated in the past, such as, Fireman rising to the Driver and beyond that to the official grade; Guard rising to Station Master and beyond that to the official grade; Assistant Permanent Way and Permanent Way Inspector rising to Engineer, Assistant, District and Divisional, the Community had a reservation of approximately 8%. This guarantee wasted out by 1960.

In their private moments even the most ardent advocates of the egalitarian principle will admit that with the decline in the employment of Anglo-Indians, the sense of discipline and service in this great public utility concern has steadily and even precipitately fallen. Even today, the Anglo-Indian railwaymen are among the comparatively few who can be relied to do their duty and, indeed, more than their duty and not to hold the Country to ransom by going on strike at the drop of a cap by some irresponsible trade union or would-be trade union leader.

Indian Telegraph Department

For over 50 years the Anglo-Indians did the major part of the pioneering work in the building of the Telegraph Department.

Up till 1916 the percentage of the Anglo-Indian employees in certain categories of the Telegraph Department was $66\frac{2}{3}$%; by 1920 the number had fallen to about 50%; and by 1928 it had come down to 40%. This percentage was, however, only in certain cadres, as the Anglo-Indians did not enter the class IV categories. Even up to 1928 the Community enjoyed a large share of the superior appointments reserved for promoted subordinates and also a large share of appointments in the superior traffic services. One of the best known Directors-General of the Post and Telegraph Department, Sir Geoffrey Clark, paid repeated tributes to the Anglo-Indians. He said that the Telegraph Department of India would not have been administered efficiently but for the Anglo-Indian employees. Many Anglo-Indians rose to the highest positions on the engineering and the traffic side. Carlton Cunningham, who entered the superior service by competition, was after Independence the Senior Deputy Director-General of Posts and Telegraphs.

Customs

From its inception in 1915 till 1920, the Preventive Branch of the Customs Department, in Calcutta for instance, was entirely staffed by Anglo-Indians and Domiciled Europeans. The employment of Anglo-Indians in the Preventive Branch was a tribute to their special aptitude for the work. They had the special responsibility of preventing contraband articles from entering and leaving the Country. There was also an Appraiser Branch of the Customs. Up till 1909 this branch was also exclusively staffed by Anglo-Indians and Domiciled Europeans. Under the guarantee provided in Section 242 of the Government of India Act of 1935, the reservations in favour of Anglo-Indians worked out to about 75% in the Preventive Branch and 50% in the Appraiser Branch. Section 242 (3) provided that in framing the rules for the regulation of recruitment to posts in the Customs, Postal and Telegraph services, the Governor-General or person authorised by him in that behalf shall have due regard to the past association of the Anglo-Indian Community with the said services, and particularly to the specific class, character and numerical percentages of the posts previously held in the said services by members of the said Community and to the remuneration attaching to such posts. Article 336 of the Constitution provided that as with the Railway and Postal and Telegraph services so also with the Customs, the appointment of members of the Anglo-Indian Community shall be on the same basis as immediately before the 15th day of August, 1947. As with the Railways, that special guarantee wasted out in 1960.

The recommendations of the Simon Commission, as it was popularly known, referred to the fact that some time prior to 1916 appointments to some of the provincial and higher services were made by nomination of suitable Anglo-Indians and members of other communities. Anglo-Indians were required to hold a Senior Cambridge examination certificate because, as pointed out by the Simon Commission, they did not have the same difficulty with regard to English as it was their mother-tongue. Members of the other communities were required to possess a University degree.

The Commission paid a tribute to the fact that the Community had helped to build the Roads, Railways, River Transport and the Telegraph system. The Commission also referred to the fact that the Anglo-Indians were among the pioneers to develop such departments as Excise, Salt, Opium, Forests, Survey, but from these latter departments they had been practically eliminated.

Police

For many years Anglo-Indians were employed in appreciable numbers in the police departments of the various States. Most Provinces had a Sergeants' cadre which was reserved for Anglo-Indians. Many rose to Inspectors, Deputy Superintendents and Superintendents, but seldom beyond that. In many States, the Anglo-Indians formed the back-bone of the civil police. The discipline and impartiality, especially during communal trouble, were due largely to the Anglo-Indian personnel. Unfortunately, their service during the civil disobedience and non-cooperation movements was often held against the Community. After Independence, although the reserved cadres disappeared, the Anglo-Indians who had joined in pre-Independence days reached the highest of positions. Many were awarded the coveted police medal for outstanding or courageous service.

Not In Fact Privileged

Because the Community was given certain reservations in certain categories of departments such as the Railways, Posts & Telegraphs and the Customs, the accusation was often hurled against the Community that it was specially privileged. That accusation was demonstrably fallacious. Admittedly, Anglo-Indians were predominantly employed in the pioneering departments but only because members of other communities were not prepared to accept the original hardships and dangers. The Anglo-Indians were the pioneers but it is erroneous to suppose that they were handsomely paid. A Telegraphist started on Rs. 27/- a month. He was given 33% more subject to his liability to serve anywhere in India or Burma : he thus had an initial total salary of Rs. 35/- a month. When the pioneering Anglo-Indians accepted these posts, there were no transport facilities, no medical services and no social amenities. They had to travel by whatever primitive means of transport were available. It often took 4 and usually 8 weeks to reach their destination. Several died of malaria. The employees had often to swim across swollen rivers or negotiate fever-infested swamps. Many of them became chronic invalids for the rest of their shortened lives. It was the same story on the Railways. The young Anglo-Indian started in a workshop on 4 annas a day. After a year or two he rose to 6 annas and gradually worked his way up to the position of a Driver, Foreman or an Engineer. There is perhaps not a railway bridge in any part of the Indian Railways that has not been traversed by the sweat, toil and often blood of the Anglo-Indian railwayman. The graveyards in the farthest outposts of Assam and Burma and in the deserts of Sind and Rajputana are hallowed by the memory of Anglo-Indian fathers, sons, mothers and daughters. It was only after the roads, transport facilities; medical and social amenities had become plentiful that the other communities began to accept and seek employment in these departments.

The I.M.D. (B.C.)

The Indian Medical Department (British Cadre) as it was generally known was the junior medical service doing duty with British troops : it came into regular existence in about 1890 and was known as the I.S.M.D. (The Indian Subordinate Medical Department). In a sense the precursors of the I.M.D. (B.C.) were the Apothecaries of the British Army. The Apothecary recruits were selected by officers commanding British regiments from the sons of British soldiers : they had the option of receiving their pay either in sterling or in rupees and to retire in England if they so wished. With the formation of the I.S.M.D., however, a four-year course of training was introduced and the pay and status was raised. Only Anglo-Indians or Domiciled Europeans were eligible for the Department. In 1920 a five-year course was introduced and only those with the Senior Cambridge or equivalent qualification were admitted as Military medical pupils. Between the period 1890 and 1920, many changes for the better took place. The name was changed to I.M. D. (B.C.) : the suffix B.C. or British Cadre was made to distinguish it from the I.M.D. (Indian Cadre) to which members of other communities were recruited but who did not have to serve with the British Army.

Men of outstanding ability were trained in the different colleges, but they only received the diplomas of D.M.C. (Calcutta), M.D.C. (Bombay) and D.M.C. (Madras). While these diplomas entitled the holders to recognition as qualified medical men in India, they were not recognised in Britain. Because of this the Government raised the training period from four to five years and the M.M. F. (Membership of Medical Faculty of Bengal) was granted in place of the old diploma. Although the members were employed primarily for duty with British regiments, a certain percentage was for some time employed in the various Provincial Civil Medical Services as also in the jails and asylums.

The quality of men who entered this Department was often outstanding. Many of them held their own with the British officers of the R.A.M.C. and I.M.S. The Department produced some of India's most eminent medical men. Among the galaxy of brilliant members of the Department were Sir Patrick Hehir, K.C.I.E., K.C.B., Sir John Tytler, Col. Mulrowny, Col. Sykes, Col. O' Gorman and many others: they ultimately entered the I.M.S. by competition; Gidney was a distinguished product of the I.M.D. (B.C.).

Col. A.D. Baptist, M.B.E., played a notable part in establishing the high reputation of the School of Tropical Medicine, Calcutta, and the All-India Institute of Hygiene and Public Health.

Many of the members of this Department, after retirement, were in the front rank of the profession in different parts of the Country. Thus my father, Dr. Richard John Anthony, after having been wounded in World War I was invalided out at a comparatively early age with a special military pension. He was then barely forty years of age. He set up practice in Jubbulpore and within a few years dominated the profession. His clientele was drawn from members of all communities–Europeans, Hindus and even ladies from the Muslim zenana and, of course, the Anglo-Indians. With a reputation as a brilliant physician, with an uncanny skill in diagnosis, he was sought after for consultation by leading members of the I.M.S. and R.A.M.C. As a tribute to his eminence in his profession and the respect he commanded among all communities, the Jubbulpore Corporation, after his death in 1950, named one of the principal roads in the Civil Station after him.

Charles Bamford died in Bangalore, in 1959, at the age of 62, when he was at the height of his fame as a surgeon and gynaecologist. As a member of the I.M.D., he saw active service in France during World War I. Later, Bamford went to the U.K. where he did his M.R.C.S. and L.R.C.P. He was appointed lecturer in surgery in the Salem Medical School and after that R.M.O. at the Bowring Hospital, Bangalore. During World War II he was appointed surgical specialist to many of the British hospitals in the Country.

Paul Van Ross, who joined the I.M.D. in 1935, was commissioned in the I.M.S. in 1943. He retired from the Navy in 1948 and then set up private practice in Bangalore and is, today, in the front rank of the profession.

The Department consisted of about 500 members. They served with the British Army in every theatre of war. In World Wars I & II many of them received the highest awards for gallantry. Some of them rose to the highest positions. Thus Major P.F. D'Mellow was appointed, during World War II, to the Indian Medical Service. He rose to be the Principal Medical Officer of the Royal Indian Navy (as it was then known). He was decorated with the M.B.E. for zeal and devotion to duty and was commended for distinguished service during the Bombay Docks Explosion in 1944. D'Mellow was the Anglo-Indian representative in the Mysore State Legislature. He had developed into a competent politician.

Members of the I.M.D. (British Cadre) started as British Warrant Officers in the regular land forces of the British Army. They started as fourth class Assistant Surgeons. For purposes of discipline they came directly under the Army Act and not under the Indian Army Act. Gidney fought tenaciously for improvement of the conditions of his former Service. He pointed to the discrimination between the salaries of those who were recruited to the Indian Unattached List and those in the I.M.D. The members of the I.U.L., as they were known, required no special qualifications and yet their emoluments were higher. The Warrant Officers of the I.M.D. were given precedence over every British Warrant Officer and yet received lower emoluments. The British Military Hospital nurses who took their orders from the Military Assistant Surgeon of the I.M.D. were in receipt of twice the salary and emoluments of the 4th class Military Assistant Surgeon of the I.M.D. As Gidney pointed out, a British Staff-Sergeant in the Indian Unattached List, which consisted of such departments as the Indian Army Service Corps, Indian Army Ordnance Corps, etcetera, and who were promoted from the ranks and usually had little education, received in salary and allowances about Rs. 380 per month, more than the salary of an Assistant Engineer in the superior Railway services and almost double the salary of the 4th class Military Assistant Surgeon in the I.M.D. After about eight years of service a British Staff-Sergeant in the I.U.L became a Major with total emoluments of Rs. 1,100 as compared with Rs. 700 of a Major in the I.M.D. Ultimately, Gidney's fighting was responsible for the removal of much of this discrimination. The revised scale given to the I.U.L. was, however, only made available to the I.M.D. on the 1st October, 1927. From the rank of a British Warrant Officer, the I.M.D. men rose to the ranks of Lieutenant, Captain and Major. They could not rise beyond the rank of Major.

Many of them went overseas and secured the highest British qualifications. Before Independence members of the I.M.D. were regarded by Gidney as the elite of the Community. That was the time when for an Anglo-Indian to aspire to the rank of Major was regarded as a pinnacle of achievement. British official policy saw to it that Anglo-Indians, as Anglo-Indians, could not move beyond Upper-Subordinate status in Government service or beyond the 800 rupee per month mark in British firms.

Even while the war was on, I had to fight the twisted complexes of British officialdom. On the 24th November, 1944, I addressed General Hance, the Director-General of Indian Medical Services, about the very unsatisfactory position of the I.M.D. (British Cadre). I pointed out that no promotion roster had been maintained. Because of this a man who was a Lieutenant in the I.M.D. before the war and had been seconded to the I.A.M.C., retired on the pension of a Lieutenant although he may have reached the rank of a Major in the I.A.M.C. I further pointed out that if the promotion roster had been maintained then according to the procedure in the I.M.D., such a person would become a Captain in 1½ years and a Major in another year, retiring on the pension of a Major in the I.M.D., which was Rs. 200 more than the pension of a Lieutenant.

In May, 1945, as a result of questions by me in the Central Legislative Assembly (as it was then known) I extracted a disclosure which came as a bolt from the blue to the Community. The War Secretary informed me that the authorities had scrapped the I.M.D. (B.C.) from 1941 and not merely discontinued recruitment to it. In my letter to the Commander-in-Chief I pointed out that the Department had been in existence for almost a hundred years and that it had a long record of proud and distinguished service with the British Army. As long as the British Army continued in India there could be no reason why the I.M.D. (B.C.) should be destroyed. I also pointed out that by being seconded to the I.A.M.C. the senior members would lose considerably in pay and emoluments. Many of them were retiring on a rank and a pension much lower than that to which their service normally entitled them.

Ultimately, in 1946, as a result of discussions with and representations by me to the Commander-in-Chief several members of the I.M.D. who had retired on the pension of Lieutenant were granted pensions according to the length of their service as Majors and Captains. The members of the I.M.D. had rendered particularly distinguished service in World War II, when during the acute shortage of trained personnel they formed the back-bone of the Indian Medical Service. But they never got the terms given to the usually uneducated British members of the I.U.L. This was, indeed, the last kick. I saw Sardar Patel. I gave him the history of the I.M.D. (B.C.) I pointed out that not only educationally but officially they were superior to the I.U.L. While the mustering-out terms for the I.U.L. were more than generous, those given to the I.M.D. were not only niggardly but deliberately discriminatory.

Generously, Sardar Patel said that if the British medical and military authorities recommended equal mustering-out terms, he would see that the I.M.D. (B.C.) got those terms. But I regret to say that I could not get the British authorities to do elementary justice. It would have cost them nothing. I got little comfort from the fact that a very senior Irish officer in the Medical Directorate worked almost day and night to help me get justice for the I.M.D. personnel. When I failed that Irishman remarked that it was just another instance of typical British ingratitude and perverted sense of race and colour discrimination!

Incomparable Nurses

Dr. A Lakshmanaswami Mudaliar, Vice-Chancellor of the Madras University, presiding over a mass meeting addressed by me on the language issue in October, 1963, at Madras, said that while India owed much to the Anglo-Indian Community it could never repay the debt it owed on account of the "Devoted and glorious service" rendered by the Anglo-Indian nurses. The record of the Anglo-Indian nurses is perhaps unequalled. 80% of the Nursing Services were, for decades, drawn from the Anglo-Indian Community which along with the Parsis is the smallest recognised minority in the Country. The Indian Statutory Commission of 1928, commonly known as the

Simon Commission, paying a tribute to the Anglo-Indian nurses said, "They have given of their best in tending to the sick of all races and have thus done something towards meeting one of the foremost and most urgent needs in Indian society."

Free from the caste and other inhibitions of the women of other communities, the girls and women of the Community were responsible for maintaining, in hospitals, standards comparable with those of the most advanced countries. The girls who took to nursing had a sense of vocation. They built up a tradition of selfless service, indeed, of dedication to their profession. Many of them came from the finest of homes where they had every comfort and, indeed, luxury. They were well-educated and refined. The beauty of some of the Anglo-Indian nurses was proverbial. Many of them married the most highly placed Europeans. They took to the nursing profession at a time when the emoluments were not only niggardly but scandalously inadequate. Even, today, the emoluments are grossly inadequate.

Comparisons tend to be odious, but the objective observer will agree that with the steadily decreasing number of Anglo-Indian nurses and, indeed, their disappearance from many of the leading hospitals the standards in these hospitals have declined. Where, today, there is still an Anglo-Indian matron or even a small stiffening of Anglo-Indian nurses the standards are usually better than in hospitals where there is no element of Anglo-Indian nurses.

. The dominant role of the Anglo-Indian nurses continues to be indicated by the fact that since Independence the post of Chief Principal Matron of the Indian Military Nursing Service has been held by an Anglo-Indian. Immediately after Independence the Chief Principal Matron was Col. (Mrs.) Dorothy Howard. The post has been redesignated and is now known as Matron-in-Chief with the rank of Brigadier. The present Matron-in-Chief is Brigadier (Miss) Dulcie Zscherpel. During the Indo-Pakistan conflict the Matron-in-Chief was Brigadier (Miss) Joyce Staggs.

The Florence Nightingale Medal is awarded every two years to nurses who have rendered service of exceptional merit. The awards are made by a special Commission of the International Red Cross Committee in Geneva. The names of Anglo-Indian nurses have appeared over and over again among the recipients of this coveted nursing award. I refer to only a few of the recipients: Col. (Mrs.)

Dorothy Howard, the first Chief Principal Matron after Independence; Col. (Miss) Dorothy Davis, who succeeded her as Chief Principal Matron : Dorothy Davis was the recipient also of the Cross of Jerusalem and the Royal Red Cross award; Col. (Miss) Florence St. Claire Watkins, who is at present Command Principal Matron (Southern Command) : a recipient of the Florence Nightingale Medal she was also awarded a certificate for outstanding service in the Middle East during World War II. There were many Anglo-Indian nurses among the recipients of the Florence Nightingale Medal in pre-Independence days. I recall the name of Winifred Grace McKenzie. The award was conferred on her because she had displayed outstanding devotion to duty at the Indian Military Hospital in Ferozepore in 1945 during an outbreak of Cerebro-spinal Meningitis.

Among recipients of the Royal Red Cross award were Col. (Miss) Olga Mylan and Col. (Miss) Winifred Gardiner. Col. (Miss) Loucielle Braganza, at present Command Principal Matron (Western Command) was awarded a certificate from the Commander-in-Chief of the Middle East Forces for outstanding service during World War II.

Dr. Lakshmanaswami Mudaliar was, indeed, right when he said that India owed an irreparable debt to the incomparable Anglo-Indian nurses.

CHAPTER XI

POST-INDEPENDENCE BATTLES

The Menace Of Hindi Imperialism

I HAD hoped that after a long, unremitting fight, over a period of several years, for the existence of the Community, I could have sat back and rested somewhat on my oars. But for the leader of a microscopic minority confronted, inevitably perhaps, by all manner of pressures this was not to be. As we faced or surmounted one problem, another took its place. I have always been of the view that without its language, English, and without its schools, the Community cannot survive, because essentially we are a Community based on language and a way of life which give us our distinctiveness and distinctive recognition. That is why one of the constant preoccupations of our Association has been not only the preservation of Anglo-Indian education but to strengthen it at every stage. The Association has kept vigil on developments not only at the Centre but in every State.

Mysore Recommendation

The attitude of some State Governments against the Anglo-Indian Schools and instruction through the medium of English was exemplified by the recommendation in February, 1953, of the Educational Reforms Committee appointed by the Mysore Government. That Committee recommended that the Anglo-Indian Schools should be allowed only a reasonable period of transition for a change-over from English to the regional language as the medium. I promptly wrote the following letter to the then Chief Minister of Mysore, "No. Ed/53 7th March, 1953.

My dear Hanumanthiah,

I have seen a report in the Deccan Herald dated the 27th February, 1953, with regard to the recommendations of the Educational Reforms Committee.

I have received an urgent message from my Community in Bangalore. It is seriously perturbed by the recommendation that the Anglo-Indian Schools should be allowed a reasonable period of transition for a change-over from English to the regional language. I do not know whether the Committee was aware of the guarantees contained in Article 30 of the Constitution. Under this guarantee every minority, whether based on language or religion, has been given the fundamental right to establish and administer educational institutions of its choice. When the provision was on the Constitutional anvil, I moved an amendment after the word choice, namely, through the medium of its mother-tongue. No less a person than Jawaharlal Nehru said that this was redundant as 'choice' meant choice and a minority based on language, such as the Anglo-Indians, would naturally choose to teach through the medium of its mother-tongue, which is English.

This position has been accepted by other States. At the same time, as Chairman of the Inter-State Board for Anglo-Indian Education, I am aware of the need for adapting the curriculum in these schools to changing social, economic and cultural conditions. Because of that Anglo-Indian Schools are, perhaps, in the vanguard in this respect among the schools maintained by minority communities. The standards of teaching of the regional language and Hindi are being progressively upgraded. But as I have already said, the Anglo-Indian Community, which is one of the recognised Indian minorities and whose mother-tongue is English, has, under Article 30, the permanent and inalienable right to administer educational institutions of its choice carrying the clear implication of teaching through the mother-tongue of the Community, namely, English.

I believe that the local MLA, Mr. Thomas, and Mr. Corbett, the President of the Bangalore Branch of the Association, with a deputation, will be waiting on you and the Minister for Education to clarify this position.

With my kind regards,

Yours sincerely,
Sd/- Frank Anthony."

Shri K. Hanumanthiah,
Chief Minister,
Mysore Government,
Mysore-2

As a result of my intervention with Hanumanthiah, who has proved to be a good and continuing friend of the Community, this proposal was put into cold storage by the Mysore Government. Ultimately, we had to face this issue in Bombay.

Opposition To Linguistic States

At every stage, I opposed strongly, and usually alone, in Parliament the proposal to reorganise the States on a linguistic basis. In August 1952, speaking in the Lok Sabha, I registered a strong and unqualified protest against the motion for the formation of linguistic States.

I quote some of the more important extracts from my speech.

"Belonging to a linguistic group or sub-group, I can understand the motive of genuine fear which inspires many of these claims for linguistic provinces. There is fear and there is good basis for fear in the minds of linguistic groups. I say this with all respect to my friends who are seeking to propagate Hindi overnight. Hindi has been accepted as the official language. I say that it can be the official language of this Country. But what is happening, Sir? We see that the intolerance and aggressiveness on the part of Hindi fanatics are creating a corresponding resistance characterized by this increasing demand for linguistic provinces. The more the Hindi fanatics will parade this demand for Hindi being imposed overnight, equally will this cry for linguistic separatism be accentuated. The other motive, as I see it, is the motive of ill-concealed communalism. I know that in making this plea for linguistic provinces, people will not only deny, but indignantly deny, that their motives are even remotely communal. I say this with all respect, that many of those who are pleading the case for linguistic provinces, that spiritually they are akin to the former Muslim Leaguers, and that the motives which underlie their claims for linguistic provinces are indistinguishable from the motives of the Muslim Leaguers. Stripped of verbiage, what are these motives? The motives of many of those who are claiming linguistic provinces are to create enclaves, cultural enclaves, administrative enclaves, and political enclaves, which the predominant group will make a happy hunting-ground for the privileges of that particular group. In effect, while the Pakistan demand was based on a two-nation theory, I submit that the demand for linguistic provinces is based equally on a multi-nation theory."

"Indian history has shown us that through the centuries parochial, regional or State loyalties have more often than not outweighted or overborne national loyalties. I say this with all seriousness that we are still trying to, in the formative stage—trying to be one nation. We are not a nation as yet—and we have yet to build, firmly, the various constituents of nationhood. If, in this incipient stage, we accept even in principle linguistic provinces, then I say we will revive and inflame regional loyalties to such an extent that they will destroy and consume our nascent national loyalties."

"As I was saying, Sir, the first great surrender, the first great retreat that the Congress beat was when they accepted, against the advice of Mahatma Gandhi, that the official language of this country should be Hindi instead of Hindustani. I say that.... (Time bell rings) that was the first great retreat they beat. Today, the Congress party is faced with another language challenge. The Congress has not yet stopped beating a retreat on the language front. If on this particular issue, Sir, the Congress makes another surrender, then I say it will be releasing into the political arena opposing linguistic armies which will make Pakistan and the Muslim League theories pale into insignificance. I say that you will not have partition of the Country into two parts, but you will have partition, but-chering of the Country, into multiple parts, as great in number as you will have linguistic provinces. I see my friend (referring to Dr. Katju the Home Minister) shaking his head. I hope the shaking of his head does not represent the considered opinion of his party. I say that the only approach to this problem is the approach from a rational linguistic point of view. Jawaharlal Nehru has done well in tackling communal political bodies. That is an issue with which he has joined battle, but he has failed today to join battle with the new communalism, the communalism represented by this new phrase—coined by K.M. Munshi—linguism. I say it is a new communalism which is hydra-headed. It has a greater potential for danger than the old communalism with which Jawaharlal Nehru has battled in this Country. And the only way in which the Congress party can deal with it is by applying itself—it is long overdue—to the problem of language."

Bitter Opposition To Formation Of Andhra Pradesh

In August, 1953, practically alone I opposed bitterly the bill for the formation of the Andhra State. Commenting on the debate, the special representative of The Statesman, New Delhi, dated the 28th August, 1953, wrote, "In a debate which will certainly echo for a good many years in India, Mr. Anthony's speech was a courageous one, as Mr. P.D. Tandon remarked. In the context of economic distress in the country he described the present concern with linguistic States as an 'utter perversion of priorities'. The argument that it represented the fulfilment of a Congress promise he dismissed with the reply that many other promises remained unfulfilled—such as that to separate the judiciary and the executive. The concession of a linguistic State to Andhra, he said, was a 'hostage to disintegration.'"

I reproduce my speech: it recaptures not only my unhappy conviction that we were giving irrevocable hostages to disintegration but also my ominous predictions which as time has shown were tragically prophetic.

"Shri Frank Anthony : (Nominated Anglo-Indian)

"Mr. Deputy Speaker, I perhaps am going to enjoy the uniquely unenviable position of being the only person to oppose this bill outright. I know that my attempt is going to be a lone and a forlorn one. But I am not without the hope that people like me may ultimately attract the saner elements in the Country into resistance— people without any political axe to grind, without any motive of personal self-aggrandisement—may attract them into an awareness of the unlimited dangers of the policy to which the Home Minister has committed this Country. May I say this, Sir, that I was convinced more than ever, after hearing the Home Minister, that the Government had conceded the Andhra State in a mood of weakness or vacillation or even in a mood of political opportunism. (Some Hon. Members. No. No.) I listened to the Home Minister, for as long as I could; I heard him for 25 minutes. During all that time what the Home Minister did was to regale the House with details as to why the Andhra State should not have been brought into existence at this particular juncture.

What The Urgency Of This Measure

"I would like to ask the Home Minister this. What was the particular urgency for this measure in the context of the economy of the Country? Would the Andhras have been exterminated? Would our economy have disintegrated and fallen to pieces if this malformed, deformed and truncated State had not come into existence on the 1st of October? (Interruptions) I am sorry, I have not got the time; if I had, I would reply to every Hon. Member categorically. Those of us who are outside the arena—I am outside the arena so to speak and it is an axiom that the onlookers see most of the game— many of us—feel strongly that Government has been stampeded into this, beaten a retreat in the face of political blackmail, by fasts, riots and violence."

"Another line of argument, and perhaps categorically emphasised, was that this promise was made by the ruling party about 30 years ago. We were given the impression that here is a ruling party which is not only sensitive, but tremulously sensitive to all its promises, and it is honour bound to implement them. I say, with all respect, this line of argument struck me as being so much political cant and hypocrisy. What about other promises, equally vital promises by the ruling party, promises which affect not a small area like the Andhra State but the whole Country? What about the separation of the Executive from the Judiciary? Your motive here, I am sorry to say, is a political motive; it does not suit you to separate your power-drunk executive from the judiciary; something which will give real meaning and significance to Independence. You forget about that much more vital and much more sacred promise, but from political motives you constitute this malformed State. Our only problem is the economic rehabilitation of the Country and that alone should have absorbed all our energies."

"What does Indian history show over and over again? History has a way of repeating itself. What are the forces and bonds which have united India? The three bonds which still keep Indians more or less as a single nation are the unified administration introduced by the British, secondly the person and personality of Jawaharlal Nehru, and, thirdly a common medium of expression between the leaders of the Country. The first two are extremely transient. Already the mortar of unity of the administrative machinery is crumbling under the impact of regionalism. A vote-catching competition is going on among all the political parties for the services to be regionalised. Unfortunately Jawaharlal Nehru—I am sorry to say he is not here—has been unable to resist that.

Then there are the language fanatics, who without the wisdom and statesmanship and capacity first to substitute in the place of the common medium of expression some single national language, are wiping out English.

Seth Govind Das: Remember the Constitution.

Hostage To Disintegration

Shri Frank Anthony......and I regret that you are giving this hostage to disintegration. What has my hon. friend the Home Minister said? In his pontifical way he asked Mr. Gopalan to accept this as a solemn act. Mr. Gopalan has used it to initiate a still greater process of disintegration. My Hon. friend the leader of the Communist Party has threatened you in so many words that this is only the beginning of your trouble. You have gratuitously perpetrated a man-made problem for this Country. Who is it going to satisfy? Those people who are engaged in an unseemly controversy for the spoils of office. It is going to satisfy the unemployed element in your legislatures. They see in their own legislature an opportunity for more lucrative and more permanent employment. It is going to satisfy the unabashedly communal elements in Andhra, who think in terms of the loaves and fishes of office. (An Hon. Member: "No, No."). My Hon. friend says "No." What is sauce for the goose must be sauce for the gander. Why, when Mr. Hukum Singh asked for a Punjabi-speaking State, did somebody raise his hands in horror. Why, when the Sikhs make that demand do you raise your hands and say: "This is a communal demand." Why—I am not pleading anyone's case, I am only arguing by analogy—why when 16 million Muslims in Uttar Pradesh do not ask for a separate State but only ask for a small measure of cultural autonomy to teach their mother-tongue, once again you call it a communal demand." "But when your co-religionists ask for a separate State you endow it with noble and lofty motives. When your co-religionists demand it, it assumes the refinements of a natural, irrepressible and cultural urge. That is what is happening."

"If you really want to serve the linguistic minorities set your face against linguism. The greatest guarantee for a linguistic minority is not a linguistic State but a multi-lingual State. Whenever you place one language in a position of unchallenged supremacy, then the people whose mother-tongue happens to be that language will oppress and destroy the real linguistic minorities. It is happening in Uttar Pradesh. It will happen in Andhra and it will happen in every linguistic State. This means not cultural autonomy for the linguistic minorities—it means cultural death."

"One of our poet friends with typical poetic hyperbole referred not in lyrical but hysterical language to what he described as a festival of culture being ushered in by linguistic States. Fortunately, neither poets nor madmen are the best judges of hard-bitten political or administrative problems."

"What was going to happen to the Andhras if they did not have a linguistic State? Were they going to be physically exterminated? This is so much political cant and hypocrisy. Telegu is one of the major regional languages. The Telegus have already achieved cultural autonomy. They have their schools and colleges. This is not a cultural but a political cry."

"Today the Country is bleeding to death. Millions and millions of people are starving or are near starvation. Every penny we have we should have spent on food, clothing and housing. Today you are indulging in cheap political tomfoolery. What is going to happen? You are going to spend crores of rupees on Andhra. You will not only drive national unity into the background but into ultimate oblivion. (Seth Govind Das: "No. No."). My Hon. friend says "No. No," but let him face facts. When Andhra comes in, my Hon. friend will not be able to go to Madras. The Dravida Kazhagam will drive him out. When you are canalising your emotional feelings into narrow regional tendencies you will drive out all thoughts of one nation and one language. That is what is going to happen. I pray to God that I may prove to be a false prophet."

"Mr. Justice Wanchoo has calculated the Andhra State as a deficit State. He has calculated the deficit as Rs. 5 crores. Today, the political bandwagon represents a rake's progress. When all of your politicians get into the saddle, you will see more and more expenditure, which the British never even dreamt of—all the pomp of imperial times and the paraphernalia of so-called democracy, the importing of hordes of Ministers, Deputy Ministers, Parliamentary Secretaries, hordes of gilt-braided chaprassis. Let your political "nouveau riche" get going. Let them have all their political sops and your deficit in Andhra will not be 5 but 15 crores. There is this utter perversion of priorities in this Country. The Finance Minister is here: one of the wickedest acts he perpetrated was to take away the food subsidies: he made the food of the people dearer just to save 15 crores: yet without batting an eyelid we are prepared to waste as many crores in starting an unnecessary, deformed State. You are performing not an act of folly but an act of treason. Fifty years from now the Home Minister will be indicted by posterity and be damned. His effigy will be either hanged or burnt. He won't be there; he has a facile manner of dismissing a problem by a wave of the hand; but by oversimplifying it, he won't be there to exculpate himself even partially."

"I blame all the parties, the Praja Socialist, the Communist and others: they are all playing the same game. They know it is a problem of language—a highly emotional problem. It is like the Muslim problem of 'Islam in danger'. It is an irrational problem. They know that an emotional, irrational problem can be exploited by political adventurers as a vote-catching device. I am sorry the Leader of the House is not here. I have got a very great regard for him. I did expect that he at least would have said: "Let us stop this disintegration and disruption of the Country", but in a moment of weakness he has agreed to this."

"Privately, at any rate, all parties will admit that they should not release these centrifugal forces. But publicly they all engage in vote-catching. That is what is happening. You do not have the strength, you do not have the statesmanship, the courage to say: "Let the Communists vote-catch as much as they like. Let the Praja Socialists compete with them. We will, at this stage at any rate, stop any tendency to encourage centrifugal forces. We will concentrate on one thing, and one thing only, and that is to give our starving people some food, our naked people some clothes, our homeless people some shelter." (Speech Ends)

An interesting sidelight during my speech was that Dr Katju, the then Home Minister, walked out of the House in protest when I said he would be indicted and damned by posterity, his effigy hanged or burnt for what he was doing.

I received many letters of congratulation. They showed that there was a strong element in the Country that had not lost vision, indeed sanity, on basic issues. Unfortunately, the correspondence also showed that the thinking elements in the Country have more and more receded into a position of political impotence. Political power has filtered down increasingly into the hands of the demagogues, the opportunists, the little essentially uneducated men, with their petty, parochial horizons. Writing to me from the U.P., a well-known personality said, "Hearty congratulations on your brilliant speech in Parliament in the course of the debate on the formation of Andhra State. Even the ranks of Tuscany could scarce forbear to cheer! You were the one member who was not afraid to face facts."

Fight For Minority Safeguards

Finding that I was practically in a minority of one in Parliament in my resistance to the suicidal political propulsions to disintegration, I addressed myself to salvaging some kind of meaningful safeguards for the linguistic minorities from the welter of confused thinking, the rank opportunism, the mealy-mouthed hypocrisies of even the top leaders. In fact, I fought a long, grim battle from the 2nd of July, 1956, in the Joint Select Committee on the States Reorganisation Bill and the Constitution (Ninth Amendment) Bill till September when the debate in the Lok Sabha concluded.

In the Joint Select Committee I had the majority of the Committee behind me in my several proposals but at that stage, Govind Ballabh Pant, the Home Minister, was not prepared to concede any worthwhile guarantees to the linguistic minorities.

I reproduce my minute of dissent as it has a permanent validity for the linguistic minorities in the Country.

Minute Of Dissent To States Reorganisation Bill

"I append this minute of dissent to the reports of both the States Reorganisation Bill and the Constitution (Ninth Amendment) Bill in a mood not only of disappointment but of sadness. I wish to draw pointed attention to the fact that the States Reorganization Bill and the Constitution (Ninth Amendment) Bill are both disfigured by the complete absence of a single guarantee or safeguard for the linguistic minorities. I use the words 'guarantee' or 'safeguard' advisedly. A guarantee or safeguard carries the implication of the recognition of a right which is enforceable. In both the bills there is not a single sanction or a single enforceable provision given to the linguistic minorities."

Gap Between Promise And Performance

"The Prime Minister, the Home Minister, the Congress Working Committee, the A.I.C.C. have repeatedly proclaimed, in recent months, the need for ample and generous guarantees to the linguistic minorities."

"The absence of a single guarantee or safeguard on behalf of the linguistic minorities marks a sad gap between promise and performance and is a challenge to the conscience of the Government. This lacuna underlines, I submit with respect, the inability of those in power or of those belonging to majority groups to understand the real fears, born of bitter experience, of linguistic minorities. Promises and paper assurances which have no legal or executive sanction are poor comfort to those who, in their day-to-day lives, come up against the stark and cruel realities of discrimination and oppression."

Analysis Of The Two Provisions

"It might be said by Government, in reply, that two provisions have been included for the protection of linguistic minorities—the provision for Zonal Councils contained in Clause 23 of the S.R. Bill and the provision for Minority education in Clause 21 of the Constitution (Ninth Amendment) Bill. I do not wish to decry these provisions. But in the final analysis neither of these provisions is a guarantee or a safeguard. Even a cursory examination of these provisions shows this."

"The linguistic minorities are one of the subjects which fall within the purview of Zonal Councils. I am glad that the phraseology was changed, at my instance, in the Joint Commitee so that any matter affecting the linguistic minorities will be within the purview of a Zonal Council. Under the original language only those matters, concerning linguistic minorities which arose out of the reorganisation of the States were within the competence of Zonal Councils. Even with this change, however, what is the effect of this provision? A Zonal Council shall be an advisory body. There are absolutely no legal or executive teeth in this provision. Even if a linguistic minority right is raised in a Zonal Council the State concerned can refuse to attend the meeting. If it condescends to attend it can treat with undisguised contempt even the unanimous finding of the other member States of the Council. Zonal Councils will be helpless to bring an errant State to order or to prevent the open oppression of a linguistic minority. The provision that Zonal Councils can consider linguistic minority questions is thus not a guarantee or safeguard. This provision suffers from the further defect that only those minorities with political influence will be able to have matters raised in Zonal Councils. Thus the Bengali minority in Bihar will be able to agitate its rights, only because the Bengalis are in a majority in Bengal. The same will apply to the Bihari minority in Bengal. But a minority without political influence in any State will have to suffer in silence."

"Clause 21 of the Constitution (Ninth Amendment) Bill provides the insertion of a new Article 350A to read as follows:

"350A. It shall be the endeavour of every State and of every local authority within the State to provide adequate facilities for instruction in the mother-tongue at the primary stage of education to children belonging to linguistic minority groups; the President may issue such directions to any State as he considers necessary or proper for securing the provision of such facilities."

This provision is also of an advisory character. All it says is that it shall be the endeavour of a State to do a certain thing. We are aware that Article 45 of the Directive Principles of the Constitution has provided, using identical language, that it shall be the endeavour of the State to provide, within a period of 10 years from the commencement of the Constitution, free and compulsory education. The ten years are nearing completion, yet not a single State has been able to implement this direction of the Constitution. Of course, this has been due to lack of financial resources. Similarly, with regard to this new provision, the States are bound to plead that they just cannot provide primary education in the mother-tongue to linguistic minorities because they have not got the means."

"In this provision there is no obligation on the part of a State to provide primary education. The linguistic minorities might have to wait several decades, at least, before this 'endeavour' becomes a reality.

"Thus the only two provisions, one in the States Reorganisation Bill and the other in the Constitution Amendment Bill are purely advisory and not in the nature of a guarantee or safeguard."

S.R.C. Recommendations

"Yet the States Reorganisation Commission considered the problem of the linguistic minorities important and serious enough to devote a whole chapter to it—chapter I of Part IV of the Report entitled 'Safeguards for Linguistic Minorities' (pages 205-216). The Commission has, in this chapter, recorded the fact that it received numerous complaints that linguistic minorities suffered from cultural oppression and economic exploitation. The Commission gave the examples of arbitrary domiciliary qualifications and language tests for recruitment to the services adopted by certain States with the intention of striking at certain minorities."

"The Commission drew attention to the fact that it was strongly urged before it that even the safeguards for minorities, embodied in the Constitution, have proved inadequate and ineffective against the cultural oppression of linguistic minorities and their economic exploitation."

"After giving thought to the matter the Commission categorically recommended that the Central Government must be responsible for linguistic minorities. I quote relevant extracts from the Commission's Report. At page 215 the Commission observes:

"There is no reason, however, why the Governor should not function as an Agent of the Central Government in regard to a matter which is of NATIONAL CONCERN. There is nothing anti-democratic about such an arrangement, because the Central Government will be responsible to the Union Parliament for functions performed by the Governor as its agent. It will amount only to supervision by the larger democracy over the smaller democracies in respect of matters of NATIONAL CONCERN." At page 216, the Commission says, definitely, "The decision of the Central Government should be issued as a directive from the President."

"It is thus abundantly clear that the Commission categorically recommended that the Centre must be responsible for the linguistic minorities, that the Centre should be responsible to Parliament in this matter and that, in the final analysis, directives should be issued through the President which directives shall be binding on the States."

"In the Select Committee there was a strong feeling that the Governor would NOT be the appropriate agency through which the Central Government should act. In my opinion the Governor, as a Constitutional head, should not be embarrassed by bringing him into likely conflict with his State Government. It may also be emphasised that by making him the agency in the State to protect minority interests, he would be constantly approached by minorities with grievances against the State, which would further embarrass his position. Further Governors, who have become accustomed to acting as constitutional heads, would refrain from taking appropriate action even in a case of palpable injustice, because they would be loath to provoke a conflict with the State Ministry. I know that the Instruments of Instruction issued under the 1935 Act, for the protection of minorities, to Governors, who were in the habit of exercising independent and even arbitrary powers, were usually ignored. The reluctance of Governors, even in the days when they were disposed to set one community against another, to act, made the minorities stigmatise these grandiose but still-born Instruments of Instruction as Instruments of Destruction."

"The most serious objection to a Governor acting as the agent of the Centre, under the machinery contemplated by the S.R. Commission, is that when a Governor refuses to move, the Centre will not be seized of the matter and will not therefore be able to issue the necessary directives."

Statutory Minorities Board

"There was strong support in the Joint Committee for my proposal for a Statutory Minorities Board, appointed by the President. The Board might place its report, at such intervals as the President may direct, before Parliament and after the report is debated by Parliament the necessary directives would issue. The arguments of the States Reorganisation Commission that a Statutory Board would encourage minorities to look beyond their borders is, I submit with respect, a political cliche which is a hangover from the thinking in the context of the old religious minorities' problem. It is an argument which has no validity as the Commission itself has accepted the principle of a Central Agency. It is impossible to reconcile the principle with the argument that a Statutory Minorities Board will encourage minorities to look beyond their States. If this is a valid argument, then the Government should not have remitted the question of linguistic minorities to Zonal Councils. The provision in respect of Zonal Councils is almost certain to encourage linguistic minorities to look beyond their borders, in a reactionary and anti-national way. Thus a section of persons, who are a minority in one State, such as the Bengalis in Bihar may, under the Zonal Council scheme, be encouraged to look to the majority in the adjoining State. In fact, the majority in one State may encourage the minority in the adjoining State to make all manner of exaggerated claims and complaints. Thus I can envisage a period of irredentism as between certain States in a Zonal Council. A Central Agency will be the most salutary check to this kind of process and to minorities being encouraged by majorities, across the border, into making extravagant and impossible demands."

"It has also to be remembered that the Commission made its recommendations for minority safeguards when it had no conception of the violent and even vicious turn linguistic passions would assume in certain areas."

"I submit, with respect, that the Government cannot run away from the disagreeable facts of reorganization."

"In my consistent opposition to linguistic reorganisation of the States, I had underlined the certainty of the consequences which have overtaken the Country. Thus Government cannot disclaim responsibility for the tribal passions and linguistic hatreds which have been aroused. Not only have so many more linguistic minorities been gratuitously created, but, for a considerable period of time, in certain areas, they will be reduced to a position of political, cultural and economic helotry. And the Centre alone has the capacity, as it has the duty, to attempt to qualify these conditions of helotry by assuming direct responsibility for the linguistic minorities. The Commission has recognised the principle that the linguistic minorities are of national concern. If the minorities are of national concern, they must be the concern of the Centre. And the Centre can only discharge that concern, if it has powers to intervene where necessary."

"There is no question of encouraging the minorities to look to the Centre. They have the right to look to the Centre as the ultimate custodian of their interests. In my opinion the Centre would only h ave discharged its duty by accepting, in the present context, a provision for a Ministry for linguistic minorities. This has not been done. The lesser provision of a Statutory Minorities Board has also been rejected."

Commissioner For Linguistic Minorities

"I regret to say that even my proposal for a Commissioner for linguistic minorities, appointed by the President, was rejected by Government. I had proposed the inclusion of a constitutional provision according to which there would a Commissioner for linguistic minorities, appointed by the President, who would place his report before Parliament at such intervals as the President may direct: after this report is debated in Parliament, the Centre would issue such directives as it deemed necessary. In spite of the assurances of Government to provide ample and generous guarantees for the minorities, in spite of the recommendation of the S.R. Commission for the setting up of a Central Agency for the protection of linguistic minorities, even this diluted proposal of mine for a Minorities Commissioner was found unacceptable."

"Finally, at least a simple provision giving the President powers to issue directives to the States on behalf of the linguistic minorities should have been accepted as the S.R. Commission had specifically recommended that the President must be given powers to issue directives on behalf of the linguistic minorities. This last proposal of mine was, however, also rejected. If the President is to have powers to issue directives as recommended by the S.R. Commission, then there must be a specific provision in the Constitution. The whole scheme of our Constitution makes this abundantly clear. There is no provision in our Constitution requiring the President to take care that the laws are faithfully exercised, as there is in the American Constitution. Article 257 only gives power to issue directives to the States to ensure that the executive power of the 'Union' is not impeded. Article 339 (2) clearly underlines the principle that the President can issue directives on behalf of the Scheduled Castes and Tribes, since the power is specifically provided. Article 353 shows that even in the case of an emergency, powers to the President to issue directives have been specifically given."

"All that the report, as it has emerged from the Joint Committee, now envisages is that the good offices of the Governors should be used on behalf of the linguistic minorities. This is completely different from and, in fact, opposed to the recommendation of the S.R. Commission. The Commission had recommended a specific safeguard and the taking of specific powers by the Centre to issue directives to the States. This can only be done by setting up the machinery and giving the powers through a specific provision in the Constitution. There is also a suggestion in the report that the question of appointing a Minorities Commissioner will be examined. Even if a Commissioner is appointed, he will be utterly useless to the minorities, as he will have no statutory position and the Centre will not be empowered to issue directives to the States on his recommendations."

"I submit, with respect, that I cannot resist the conclusion that the assurances of the Government to the linguistic minorities, the recommendations of the S.R. Commission, the strong feeling in the Joint Committee have all been ignored because of some theory of State Autonomy. The crux of Government's opposition to any real safeguard appears to consist in the thesis that such a safeguard, with powers to the President to issue directives, will be an encroachment on State Autonomy. I submit, with the greatest of respect, that this approach is completely fallacious and indefensible. It is absolutely correct that the minorities must learn to look to and live among the majority in that particular State. But when we recognise that the minorities have all manner of difficulties, that these difficulties will be accentuated a hundredfold because of the linguistic passions that have been aroused, we must provide adequate machinery at the Centre for their ultimate protection."

"In the final analysis, the S.R. Commission itself has recognised that the minorities are of national concern. They are not exclusively the concern of the States. The Centre has an inescapable duty to look after the minorities. The minorities have an inalienable right to look to the Centre."

"Parliament, also, has an inescapable duty to look after the minorities. And Parliament is the best qualified democratic machinery to ensure justice to the minorities. The provincial and regional prejudices which often bedevil State Legislatures are usually absent from Parliament. Because Parliament is a cross-section of the whole country it is in the best position to take an objective view of minority problems."

"Finally, surely Parliament and the Central Government can be trusted to exercise their powers with discretion. The Central Government will obviously only issue a directive to a State when the State is clearly in error and refuses to do justice to a minority."

Affiliation Of Educational Institutions

"The inclusion of a provision in the Constitution giving a linguistic minority the right to affiliate educational institutions, administered by it, to a recognised examination, in the language of that minority in any part of the Country is necessary. I consider that such a provision is a natural corollary to the fundamental right, provided in Article 30 (1) of the Constitution giving minorities the right to establish and administer educational institutions of their choice. I have to point out, with regret, that certain minority languages are particularly exposed to deliberate oppression and discrimination. Thus because of the continuing memories of foreign rule the lingering resentment against the Englishman is often transposed against English, which happens to be the language of the Anglo-Indian Community. Thus there have been attempts in some States to destroy the schools of the Anglo-Indian Community, because they are the main purveyors of the English medium. In other States insidious policies to undermine or stifle these schools are current."

"In the same way we know, and those of us who are honest will admit, that the justifiable resentment against Pakistan's policies has, in certain States, transposed itself against Urdu. Urdu, which should be nurtured as part of the rich and varied language heritage of the Country, has in some States been an object of language vendetta."

"Although States may not be able to provide education even at the primary stage to linguistic minorities, I wanted this further provision, at least to prevent States from destroying educational institutions which a linguistic minority may itself provide."

"I am grateful for the small mercy that Government agreed that this provision, which the Joint Committee considered desirable, may after examination by the Central Education Ministry, be put into the Home Ministry circular to be issued to the States. This Home Ministry circular is salutary in indicating the good intentions of the Central Government. But this circular and these intentions will suffer from the vital defect present in all the Central Government proposals. They will only constitute advice. As guarantees and safeguards they are utterly valueless. They will not have a single sanction either statutory or executive. The Central Government will be powerless to prevent a State from deliberately flouting its advice and from deliberately oppressing a linguistic minority."

"I submit, with respect, that in rejecting the several proposals made by me, in rejecting the specific recommendation of the S.R. Commission that the Centre must take powers to issue directives to the States on behalf of the linguistic minorities, the Government has not only not been generous, it has not been just."

Frank Anthony,
Member, Lok Sabha, Div. No. 498
Dated 15-7-1956

My minute of dissent attracted considerable support from leading newspapers in the Country. It also captured the sympathy of the leaders of all sections of the Lok Sabha. When the Bill came before the Lok Sabha, I spoke at every stage and made four speeches. They contained impassioned pleas for a Constitutional safeguard for the linguistic minorities, for at least the appointment of a Commissioner who would report to Parliament on the position of the linguistic minorities.

I led a deputation of senior M. Ps. to the Prime Minister. In fact, I met Jawaharlal Nehru on three occasions. Inch by inch, I was able to advance the cause of the linguistic minorities. In the first stages, the Home Minister, Govind Ballabh Pant, agreed to consider my suggestion for a Commissioner but without any Constitutional provision. Later, in the Lok Sabha, Government agreed to have a provision in the Constitution. Even here, the Home Minister was not prepared to give directive powers to the Central Government.

I pleaded for this final guarantee. The matter was placed before the Cabinet. I moved a resolution in the House. The Home Minister was prepared to accept two-thirds of it, but not the last part giving powers to the Centre to issue directives to the States.

It was as the result of my long, grim fight that Article 350 B was put into the Constitution. That Article provides for the appointment by the President of a special officer for the linguistic minorities who will report to the President and which reports are to be laid before each House of Parliament and sent to the Government and the States concerned.

Then in the third reading stage, during an interchange between Govind Ballabh Pant and myself, he accepted the position that there was no need for a final clause in the Constitutional guarantee as, in the opinion of the Government, the Centre had inherent powers, under Article 355 of the Constitution, to issue directives to the States. I accepted this assurance and wound up by paying a generous tribute on behalf of the minorities to Jawaharlal Nehru and Govind Ballabh Pant.

Commenting on the long debate and the ultimate concessions by Govind Ballabh Pant, the Hindustan Times representative wrote in the issue of September 5, 1956 : "As was expected, it was Mr. Frank Anthony's day. He said all linguistic minorities would be grateful to the Home Minister for what he proposed to do."

Arising out of my demands during my several speeches in the course of the debate, Govind Ballabh Pant laid on the table of the house a memorandum that recognised as a corollary to the right contained in Article 30 of the Constitution, which gives the minorities based on language and religion the right to establish and administer educational institutions of their choice, that all schools and the colleges using minority languages, where it is not possible to arrange affiliation in respect of courses of study to universities and other authorities within a State, should be permitted by the State Government to affiliate to outside bodies. Grants-in-aid and other facilities would be given irrespective of such outside affiliation.

Bombay Schools' Case

On the 16th December, 1953, the Bombay Government issued an order prohibiting the admission of non-Anglo-Indians to Anglo-Indian schools. I only received the full text of the order on the 19th December. On the 21st December I sought to raise an adjournment motion in Parliament on the ground that the Bombay Government's order offended the constitutional guarantees given to the linguistic minorities. The motion was ruled out of order by the Speaker on the ground that Education was a State subject. My resentment against the order was accentuated by the fact that at the meeting of the Central Advisory Board of Education in Delhi held on the 10th November, 1953, I had in a speech underlining the value of Anglo-Indian education to the Country, made a general reference to my fear of the intolerance of certain State Education authorities. At that time I had no definite information of the intention of the Bombay Government. It was a coincidence that in my speech I referred to rumours that the Bombay Government was contemplating an order of the kind which it ultimately issued. Maulana Azad, the Minister for Education in the Central Government, who was in the chair, intervened when I was speaking and put a specific question to the Bombay Government Education Minister. He asked whether there was any basis for my fear and whether the Bombay Government was, in fact, contemplating such an order. The Bombay Education Minister categorically denied that such an order was under the contemplation of his Government. Yet barely a month after, namely, on the 16th December the order was issued. I realised that this form of 'Prohibition' on the part of the Bombay Government meant the certain destruction of Anglo-Indian Education in the State. An analysis of the figures showed that about 60% of the pupils in the Bombay Anglo-Indian schools were non-Anglo-Indians. The proposed embargo would mean the shutting out of about two-thirds of the pupils and the inevitable closure of Anglo-Indian schools.

I addressed the Prime Minister pointing out the flagrantly illegal character of the Bombay Government's order and seeking his intervention. Unfortunately, Jawaharlal Nehru apparently did not have the time to apply his mind to the Bombay Government's palpable violation of the Constitution. He replied vaguely stating that the order must have something to do with the State Government's policy. I then saw Maulana Azad. He promised to write to the Chief Minister of Bombay. But knowing the intransigence of the Bombay Government, especially of Morarji Desai the then Chief Minister, I felt that there was no hope of getting it to retrace its illegal steps.

This was a period of grave anxiety for me. Some office-bearers of the Association were against making an issue of the Bombay Government's order. Some of our office-bearers in Bombay wired seeking to dissuade me from fighting the Government. They felt that the State Government might retaliate by victimising the Community in one form or another. I gave the whole position careful, anxious thought. I realized that this was literally a question of life or death for our schools. I realised, also, that if we did not fight, in any case it would mean extinction for Anglo-Indian education and consequently for the Community. I realised also that if we fought and lost, the same consequences would follow, but if we fought and won then we would have achieved a charter of freedom for our schools. I knew also that some other States, many of which were not unduly friendly to Anglo-Indian education, were watching the Bombay scene. Ultimately, I decided to fight. I proceeded to Bombay and spent a whole month in preparing the case. Several English-medium schools, which faced the same fate, were run by members of the Parsee Community. I sought to enlist their support. But they made no secret of the fact that they were too afraid to fight as they felt that the Bombay Government might oppress their community. The majority of the Anglo-Indian Schools in the State were run by the Roman Catholic Orders. Some of the Orders, especially the Irish Christian Brothers, were prepared to fight. But the ultimate sanction had to be given by the Cardinal. I, therefore, met Cardinal Gracias. I was accompanied by Anglo-Indian State leaders who were Roman Catholics. Unfortunately, the Cardinal expressed his inability to join the fight. I then turned to non-Roman Catholic run schools. Fortunately, I was able to get Barnes School, Deolali, which was run by the Bombay Education Society, to be the main petitioner. Ultimately, the Anglo-Indians fought and fought alone.

On the 11th, 12th and 13th February, 1954, our petition came up for final hearing before Chief Justice M.C. Chagla and Mr. Justice Dixit. Mr. N. Palkhivala, an outstanding advocate of the Bombay High Court, and I addresssed the Court on behalf of the Anglo-Indian Schools. The Advocate-General of Bombay appeared on behalf of the State. On the 15th February the Bombay bench delivered its judgment striking down the Bombay Government's order as being repugnant to the Constitution.

On the 26th April the Bombay Government made an application to the Supreme Court for expediting their appeal which was set down by the judges for hearing before the vacation at the end of May. The hearing in the Supreme Court commenced on the 12th May and was heard by a special constitutional bench consisting of Chief Justice Mahajan and four other judges. The Attorney-General of India appeared on behalf of the Bombay Government.

Palkhivala and I argued on behalf of the Anglo-Indian schools. On the 26th May, 1954, the Supreme Court handed down its judgment which was a landmark in the Constitutional history of India. The principal ratio laid down by the Supreme Court was in the following words: "Where, however, a minority like the Anglo-Indian Community, which is based, inter alia, on religion and language, has the fundamental right to conserve its language, script and culture, under Article 29(1) and has the right to establish and administer educational institutions of their choice under Article 30 (1), surely then there must be implicit in such fundamental right, the right to impart instruction in their own institutions to the children of their own community in their own language. To hold otherwise will be to deprive Article 29(1) and Article 30(1) of the greater part of their content. Such being the fundamental right, the police power of the State to determine the medium of instruction must yield to this fundamental right to the extent it is necessary to give effect to it and cannot be permitted to run counter to it." The Supreme Court judgment vindicated the right of the Anglo-Indian schools not only to teach through the mother-tongue of the Community, English, but to offer instruction through English to any Indian child who wished to avail himself of it. That judgment remains a charter of educational freedom not only for the Anglo-Indian schools but for institutions run by all linguistic minorities in the Country.

The Kerala Education Bill

In 1958 the President of India referred, under Article 143(1) of the Constitution, to the Supreme Court for their opinion certain provisions of the Kerala Education Bill, 1957, which had been framed by the then Communist Government of the State. Mr. D.N. Pritt, a well-known British Q.C., appeared on behalf of the Kerala State Government. The Roman Catholic Schools, of which there is a very large number in the Kerala State, employed leading Indian counsel. I appeared on behalf of the Anglo-Indian schools of Kerala as interveners. The case was argued at length and strenuously. Ultimately, the Anglo-Indian schools were the only institutions completely to win their case. In effect, the Supreme Court held that the various clauses of the Bill were of a restrictive character and offended the rights of the Anglo-Indian Community as guaranteed under the Constitution. In several provisions the Bill sought to regiment not only the management but the education in the schools.

A crucial issue which was not argued by any of the other institutions but which I canvassed elaborately on behalf of the Anglo-Indian schools was in respect of Clause 20 of the Bill. According to that clause, merely as a pre-condition to recognition, the State Government insisted that no fees should be charged in the primary school. According to the definition in the Bill, the primary school extended to class eight. No Anglo-Indian school could exist if it was compelled not to charge any fee in eight out of the ten or eleven classes. Fortunately, the majority of the Supreme Court judges accepted my submissions that it would be a travesty of our fundamental right to establish and administer educational institutions of our choice if we were to be denied the right to charge the necessary fees.

The Gujarat University Case

On the 21st September, 1962, a Constitution Bench of the Supreme Court consisting of six judges, including the Chief Justice, by a majority judgment upheld the judgment of the Gujarat High Court striking down the action of the Gujarat University seeking to outlaw English. The crucial ratio in the judgment was that legislation imposing an exclusive medium was likely to result in the lowering of standards of higher education which fell within item 66 of the Union List and outside the power of the State Legislature or the University. Item 66 relates to the 'Coordination and determination of standards in the institutions for higher education or research and scientific and technical institutions'.

Mr. Nani Palkhivala argued on behalf of the main petitioner and I on behalf of the All-India Anglo-Indian Education Society which had intervened in the Supreme Court. There were also other interveners.

What was involved was not merely the question of the medium of instruction in the Gujarat University but, in effect, the whole position of the link language in the language pattern of higher education throughout the Country. The Gujarat University had outlawed English. Had the Gujarat University and the State Government succeeded in their appeal in the Supreme Court, there can be no doubt that their example would have been followed by a succession of States and Universities. The consequences would have been disastrous not only for the standards of University education but for the larger cause of educational and emotional integration in the Country.

For the Anglo-Indian and English-medium schools the consequences would have been fatal. Without opportunities for University and higher education through the medium of English, inevitably no one would go to English-medium schools.

Apart from the legal issues involved, a general submission made by me to the Supreme Court was that in the context of a bewildering multiplicity of regional languages and the hopelessly disparate stages of their development, the link language, English, is a necessary instrument of co-ordination. In this welter of competing regional languages, utterly disparate in their content and development, to give the right to Universities to outlaw English would be to destroy the only life-line of unity in the field of higher education. Other vital aspects of co-ordination such as the interchange of teachers, the migration of students, would be utterly impossible if the different Universities constituted themselves into watertight linguistic enclaves. I submitted that in this context a developed link language is indispensable for the maintenance and co-ordination of standards at the University stage.

Commenting on the judgment, I wrote, "All those interested not only in the maintenance of standards of higher education but in the unity of the Country must acclaim this judgment as perhaps the greatest single blow struck for preventing a decline into disintegration. I believe, sincerely, that to carve up University education into watertight linguistic enclaves is deliberately to pursue the inevitable disintegration of the Country. This judgment will receive the hearty approval and acclaim of thinking educationists and those capable of taking an objective view of the larger interests of the Country. There can be no doubt that the regional language will be used, increasingly, even at the University stage, but there can also be no doubt that a regional language, however highly developed, cannot, except from motives of language chauvinism and sheer obscurantism, be used as an instrument for outlawing the existing facilities in a world language. I feel that so far as science and technology (including engineering) and professional courses such as law and medicine are concerned, a firm decision should be taken that there should be instruction in a single language. Thus, in the case of my own profession, the law, apart from the sheer babel that would ensue as a result of instruction in a multiplicity of regional languages, overnight the standards of professional knowledge and ability would be struck an irretrievably fatal blow. Today, there are about 52 law reports in English which publish, each year, at least 2,500 cases decided by the Supreme Court and the different High Courts. Many of the High Court judgments are monuments of legal knowledge and examples of finished legal phraseology that has acquired scientific precision through usage and interpretation. Through these law reports the earnest lawyer and jurist has at least the judgments throughout India for his field of study. In fact, through the American and English reports the vast field of jurisprudence throughout the English-speaking world is within his reach. These arguments would apply perhaps with even greater force to the pursuit of higher education in science and technology. Only little men, blinded by ignorance or language chauvinism, will deliberately destroy the opportunities and horizons of those who wish to pursue higher education in its fullest and best sense."

"This historic judgment may well represent an epochal turning point in India's progress towards unity and strength. For ultimately, a pattern of higher education that encourages communion between the best and most active minds throughout the Country is the supreme, decisive instrument of national integration."

The Menace Of Hindi Imperialism

The official language issue is the most important—perhaps the most critical—for the Country as it will determine not only the progress, educational, technological and scientific, but the very unity of India.

I have had not a little to do with this language issue. Circumstances have sometimes placed me at the very centre of the discussions. I make no pretensions to complete objectivity on the language issue. It is not humanly possible for anyone to be completely objective on such an issue, as each one of us is the product of a certain matrix, historical, cultural, linguistic. Each one of us has his mother-tongue and rightly cherishes it.

Unlike the Hindi chauvinists, I have, in my humble way, given many hostages to my bona fides on this language issue. Hindi happened to be the second language that I learnt at school. It was the language through which I had largely earned my income at the Bar in the early days of my profession. As Chairman of the Inter-State Board for Anglo-Indian Education, for more than 20 years, I was responsible for making Hindi a compulsory second language in most of the Anglo-Indian schools throughout the Country.

Desire Of Gandhiji.

During the framing of the Constitution I was on several committees. At that time language was not a live issue. The Constituent Assembly was riding a crest of national fervour and enthusiasm. It was preoccupied with forging a Constitution that would make India strong, united and prosperous, Even then I had misgivings about the language question. I discussed the matter with Jawaharlal Nehru and underlined the desire of Gandhiji that a neutral language, such as Hindustani, should be the official language. With his unerring instinct, Gandhiji realised that in a multilingual State only a neutral language which gave no undue advantage to any particular group and which was not identified with any particular community or religion, so as to make it an instrument of political domination, could be the official language. Unfortunately, Jawaharlal was too preoccupied and felt that there was no distinction between Hindustani and Hindi. I also met Maulana Azad but he was not disposed to oppose Jawaharlal. I expressed my fear that the use of the word 'Hindi' would immediately be seized upon by communal elements in the North to make it a symbol of communalism, even of religion and a negation of secular democracy. During the framing of the Constitution, however, I hoped for the best. I not only strongly supported Hindi being made the official language but made strong speeches in favour of it. I, however, underlined the fact that the official language could develop only by an evolutionary process.

I pointed out that Hindi would grow and be accepted in exact proportion to its tolerance and spirit of accommodation and its readiness to allow the other languages and the languages of the minorities also to grow and flourish.

Unfortunately, and tragically for the Country, my fears about Hindi were justified sooner than I expected. Obscurantism, intolerance and arrogance became increasingly the attributes of the Hindi chauvinists. The greatest single motivation of the Hindi Imperialists has been ill-concealed hatred for English. They have worked to the superstition that if they destroy English-medium schools, which are the nerve-centres of English teaching, they will destroy English. They have deluded themselves into the belief that if they destroy English, Hindi, by some magical process, will take its place.

Attack On English-Medium Schools

I have referred above to the fact that in 1953 the Hindi-motivated hatred for English expressed itself in an order of the Bombay Government intended to destroy the English-medium schools. According to that order English could not be the medium of instruction for any Indians except Anglo-Indians. Indians could be taught through the medium of any language except English. Every form of political hypocrisy was pressed into service by the Bombay Government in an effort to justify that iniquitous order. Even Jawaharlal Nehru expressed his helplessness to intervene to stay such an evil order. Fortunately, first the Bombay High Court and then the Supreme Court struck down that order as illegal.

The Language Commission

The next phase was the appointment, by the President, of the Language Commission under Article 344 of the Constitution in June, 1955. May I say, with great respect, that the overwhelming majority of those appointed were well-known for their Hindi predilections. The recommendations of the Language Commission were a foregone conclusion. Two members had the courage to append minutes of dissent. Dr. Subbaroyan, a well-known figure in the Madras State, and Dr. Suniti Kumar Chatterjee, the famous Indologist from Bengal who has some outstanding works on Hindi to his credit, entered a powerful plea that there should be no haste with regard to Hindi imposition and that the 'status quo' should continue. Their plea was brushed aside with impatience and arrogance by the Hindi chauvinists in their headlong pursuit of Hindi imposition.

Parliamentary Committee

The next stage was reached with the appointment of the Parliamentary Language Committee, in 1958, under Article 344(4) of the Constitution. Twenty members were elected by the House of the People and ten by the Council of States. Once again, an attempt was made to pack the committee by a stringent whip issued by the Congress Party. Fortunately a few Independents, including myself, were able to secure election in spite of that stringent whip. The Committee began its deliberations in May, 1958. The Home Minister, Govind Ballabh Pant, was the Chairman.

I can speak from inside knowledge. At the very outset I asked for the proceedings not to be held 'in camera'. I emphasized that this was a critical issue for the Country and the Country had the right to know the views of the members and the discussions of the committee: it had the right not to have some decisions, taken by a handful of persons behind closed doors, suddenly imposed on the whole Country. I also asked that the Press should be admitted. My proposals were summarily brushed aside. All that the Press got were carefully doctored hand-outs. I had also asked that the Chief Ministers of Madras and West Bengal should be examined as the position in those two States had changed entirely since the report of the Language Commission. The Madras Government had modified its position taken up before the Language Commission and had recommended permanent bilingualism. The West Bengal Legislature had gone further. Both Houses had unanimously passed a resolution that the 'status quo' should continue. The West Bengal Legislature had made it clear that they were not prepared to accept Hindi as the sole official language. That proposal of mine was also brushed aside. The atmosphere in the committee was not only utterly vitiated but utterly foul. It was made so not only by the intemperate but utterly offensive character of the language used by the Hindi protagonists. Sir A. Ramaswami Mudaliar said that he had never, in his long public life, sat in a committee with such a foul atmosphere. A member from Tamil Nad expressed his desire to withdraw. The committee finalised its report in November, 1958. I had gone to the Committee with an open mind as I had done during the discussions in the framing of the Constitution. But the sheer intolerance, arrogance and hate-filled attitude of the Hindi Imperialists made me realise that unless some of us resisted this tide, the spirit of neo-imperialism would lead to the attempted destruction of every minority language, the relegation of every language which is considered to stand in the way of Hindi imposition to second-class status. I appended the only minute of dissent against the blanket imposition of Hindi, from 1965, as the official language.

Plea Rejected

My private member's resolution that English be included in the VIIIth Schedule of the Constitution came up for discussion in Parliament in April, 1959. I made, as far as it was humanly possible, a completely objective plea for the inclusion of English in the VIIIth Schedule : I pointed out that English is my language : that it is the language of a recognised minority, the Anglo-Indians. I referred to the decisions of the Bombay High Court and the Supreme Court which affirmed the position that English is as much an Indian language as the other languages of India. In fact, as pointed out by the Chief Justice of the Bombay High Court in his judgment English is the language of the Anglo-Indians and as much entitled to protection as any other language spoken by any other section or community in the Country. It was further pointed out by that Court, that from the constitutional point of view English was more an Indian language than any of the languages in the VIIIth Schedule : it was the language of the Constitution, it was the sole official language till 1965, it was the administrative language of the Country, it was the official language of the States until replaced by some other language, it was the language of the courts, of the High Courts and the Supreme Court. All laws, orders and notifications had to be in English : it was the only authoritative language of legislation.

Significance Of VIIIth Schedule

I further pointed out that on the 21st February, 1959, the Prime Minister had announced that the Sahitya (Literary) Academy had recognised English and Sindhi in addition to the 14 languages enumerated in the VIIIth Schedule as among the major Indian languages. The Senate of the Calcutta University had, on the 18th July, 1958, resolved that English be included in the VIIIth Schedule.

I underlined the significance of the VIIIth Schedule. The VIIIth Schedule did not purport to exhaust all the Indian languages, because there are, at a conservative estimate, 179 Indian languages in addition to 544 dialects and patois. The VIIIth Schedule only means that in terms of Article 351 of the Constitution, Hindi, so that it may serve as a medium of expression for all the elements of the composite culture of India, should secure its enrichment by assimilating the style and expressions of Hindustani and of the languages of India specified in the VIIIth Schedule. I underlined that both the Language Commission and the Parliamentary Language Committee had emphasized the need for Hindi drawing liberally on English especially in respect of scientific and technological terms. By inclusion in the VIIIth Schedule a language did not become either a regional or a national language.

Human Plea

Apart from the legal and factual position, I entered a final human plea on behalf of my Community. I pointed out that when anybody says that my language is foreign, a stab of pain shoots through me. I repelled the thesis that English is a foreign language. Foreignness is only a question of degree. In a relative sense Urdu is a foreign language, as it was a language forged by conquerors who had come to India. Yet its richness, its beauty and its refinement have been among the great leavening influences on Indian language, thought and culture. In a sense also Sanskrit is a foreign language because it was brought to the Country, although thousands of years ago, by Aryan conquerors. In a relative sense English was also foreign to the British. The lineal ancestors of the English language were the dialects of the Angles, Saxons and the Jutes who went as conquerors to Britain and took their foreign dialects with them. The original dialects of the British were Celtic. The plea of 'foreign' is merely a device of the Hindi Imperialists. Our parliamentary system is foreign : our jurisprudence is foreign, our tanks and jet planes are foreign, but nobody condemns these for that reason. English has become part of the warp and woof of Indian thought, language and culture. It has not been imposed on India. It was at the instance of liberals like Rammohan Roy that it became part of the educational system. Because of and through English there was a tremendous cultural and intellectual renaissance in India. Through English India jumped from mediaevalism into the modern age. Some of India's greatest thinkers and writers have interpreted not only themselves but the ethos of India to the world through English.

Mortar Of Unity

Continuing my plea in Parliament, I said that no one is to blame for the place that English occupies. That is a legacy of history. Many leading thinkers have referred to it as a gift of history to India. The stark fact is that English represents the mortar of administrative unity. It is the mortar of judicial integration. In fact it represents the only instrument of emotional and intellectual integration at least among the educated sections. Without English, today, the people from Tamil Nad and Bengal would be greater foreigners in Delhi than in Europe. All my pleas fell on ears made deaf by hatred. In the words of the correspondent of 'The Mail', "All my pleas including my plea based on humanity were rejected by the Hindi fanatics in Parliament with jeers."

The Nehru Formula

The debate was postponed to August. The then Prime Minister, Jawaharlal Nehru, sensing a resurgence of resistance to Hindi imposition, intervened and announced on the 7th August, 1959, what is now commonly known as the Nehru formula, namely, that English would continue as the alternate/associate language for as long as the non-Hindi speaking people so desired.

Unfortunately even the Prime Minister was not a free agent. He was a prisoner of the compulsions of the political dominance in Parliament of the Hindi chauvinists. There was no answer to the case for the inclusion of English in the VIIIth Schedule. The Prime Minister admitted that on principle there was nothing against the inclusion of English in the VIIIth Schedule. But because even Jawaharlal Nehru was not a free agent politically he dared not do elementary justice to a small minority which was politically helpless because of its smallness of numbers. If we were a larger community or if we were given to demanding our rights through agitation, rioting and arson, no one from the Prime Minister downwards would have dared to insult my Community by referring to our language as 'foreign'.

Hindi Imperialists' Phalanx

On the 2nd, 3rd and 4th September, 1959, the Lok Sabha considered the report of the Parliamentary Language Committee. The public were not aware of the peculiar provisions of the Constitution with regard to the Language Commission and Committee. Although the Parliamentary Language Committee was elected by Parliament, it was not a Parliamentary Committee in the legal sense. The report could not go back to Parliament: Parliament could not modify the report of its own committee. The report had to go, instead, directly to the President to issue his directions. Under pressure, especially from me, the Home Minister Govind Ballabh Pant agreed to place the report before Parliament. It will be recalled that mine was the only minute of dissent to the report which otherwise sought to efface English from the official language pattern by 1965. The Home Minister moved a motion that 'This House takes note of the report of the Parliamentary Language Committee'. I had given notice of 3 amendments seeking merely to concretise the Prime Minister's formula that English shall be the associate/alternate official language. I had reason, increasingly, to doubt the bona fides of the Hindi Imperialists both in the Congress Party and outside. I knew that they hated the Nehru formula and that they had no intention of honouring that formula. Their mala fides became immediately clear as soon as I got up to move my amendments. The whole Hindi phalanx in the House, obviously by preconcerted design, rose to raise objections to my amendments. Unfortunately, my amendments were disallowed as being out of order. The rules of Parliament give every member an inalienable right to move an amendment to a substantive motion. Even the Chair felt some difficulty which was underlined by the request to the Government to change its motion which was, in fact, a substantive motion. No change was made to the motion: nevertheless my amendments were not permitted to be moved.

Sheer Hatred

The sheer fanatical hatred of the Hindi Imperialists had to be seen to be believed. Mr. Barucha, an Independent Parsee member, and Mr. Thangammani, a member from the South, said that they were outraged. The demonstration by the Hindi fanatics in the Congress Party showed that they had no intention to honour the word of their

Party leader, the word of the leader of the Government.

Seeing the resurgence of the resistance created by Hindi fanaticism the Prime Minister intervened once again. On the 4th September, 1959, Jawaharlal Nehru reaffirmed the formula that English would be the associate/alternate language as long as the non-Hindi speaking people so desired. He went a little further : paragraph 34 of the Parliamentary Language Committee report had recommended that there should be compulsory Hindi tests for entry into the Central Services, including the subordinate services. The Prime Minister said that there should be no compulsory tests for entry into Central Government service.

Official Languages Bill—Chauvinists Got What They Wanted

The next phase was represented by the Official Languages Bill which came up for discussion in the Lok Sabha in April, 1963. At the outset I asked that the Bill he circulated in order to give the State Legislatures a chance to consider its far-reaching implications. I pointed out that in framing the Bill the Government had functioned in an atmosphere of unreality and under continuous pressure from the Hindi chauvinists as Delhi is a stronghold of Hindi chauvinism.

No Opportunity Given To States To Study Bill

Even the State Governments had no opportunity to study the Bill. Thus the West Bengal Chief Minister had, in a statement, mentioned that he had no idea of the implications of the Bill. Even when he replied to the debate, the Home Minister, Lal Bahadur Shastri, stated that he had merely referred Clauses 5 and 6, which dealt only with Hindi translations, to the State Governments. Clauses 3 and 4 which were the heart of the Bill, and were carefully evolved instruments for side-tracking both Parliament and the State Legislatures, had not even been considered by the State Governments, much less the State Legislatures. But in their desire to rush the measure through, my plea for circulation was brushed aside.

From the time of the Nehru formula the Government had been under unremitting pressure from the Hindi chauvinists, whose whole desire was not only to dilute but to destroy that formula. I had been approached by a senior Congressman to accept a compromise on the Nehru formula. The Hindi protagonists did not want the words "alternate" or "associate" : they wanted some word like "secondary" "or additional". They did not like the indefinite period : above all, they did not want the matter left to the non-Hindi-speaking people. The Bill was placed before the House after several postponements. It was immediately clear that everything the Hindi zealots wanted had found a place in the Bill.

Backdoor Method

In my speeches during the passage of the Bill, I underlined that if there had been any intention to honour the Prime Minister's assurance the Bill could have been a simple two-line measure, namely, that English shall be the associate/alternate language until otherwise decided by a majority of State Legislature or a certain proportion of members of Parliament. Instead, Clauses 3 and 4 had been carefully, even tortuously, evolved to ensure the blanket imposition of Hindi by the backdoor. Clause 3 provided that English may, from the appointed date, that is, 15 years from the commencement of the Constitution, be used in addition to Hindi. A plain reading of the provision meant that Hindi had first to be used for all the official purposes of the Union and after 1965 English may, or may not, be used. That was even against the recommendations of the Language Commission and the Language Committee both of which had recognised that Hindi would not be sufficiently developed even after 1965 for use for all the purposes of the Union.

There was a good deal of argument about the use of the word 'may'. The Prime Minister obviously had not applied his mind to the matter and was misled by his advisers. I wrote to Jawaharlal Nehru mentioning that the use of the word 'may' in clause 3 reduced the Bill to a travesty of his assurance. He replied to me by letter dated the 18th April that in his view 'may' meant 'shall'. Lal Bahadur Shastri piloted the Bill. Although I had the deepest regard and, indeed, affection for him, I was obliged to fight him bitterly on this issue. Pressed by me for a clarification in the House he admitted that 'may' meant may and was permissive. According to the plain meaning of the language, English may, but it also may not, be used.

Side-tracking Of Parliament

Clause 4 was a calculated provision for side-tracking both the non-Hindi-speaking Legislatures and Parliament. That clause provided for the appointment of a committee after 10 years from 1965 under the guise of reviewing the progress of Hindi. How carefully the procedure to side-track the Legislatures and Parliament was worked out was exposed at the second reading stage. When the Minister of State, Hajarnavis, was on his feet, I put to him the question whether the committee would be a Parliamentary Committee. At first he hesitated, but under pressure he replied that without reservations he could say that it would be a Parliamentary Committee. Fortunately or unfortunately, the Deputy Leader of the Praja Socialist Party, H.V. Kamath, pointed out that if that was so, the report would first come to Parliament and the ultimate recommendations to the President would be that of Parliament. The Home Minister Shastriji, realised what was happening and after hurried consultations, got up to say that although elected by Parliament, it would not be a Parliamentary Committee. I intervened to remark that "The cat was out of the bag" and that Clause 4 was a piece of deliberate political chicanery to by-pass Parliament which was always the intention of the framers of the Bill. As in the case of the last Parliamentary Language Committee, the next one will be packed: its recommendations will be a foregone conclusion taken behind closed doors, and these will go directly to the President for imposition on the whole Country.

Merely A Blind

As a sop to the non-Hindi-speaking people, there was an amendment that the views of the State Governments would be asked for. But this was merely a blind. A State Government, especially one which belongs to the same ruling party as the Central Government, might not even be consulted.

I had given notice of certain amendments. One was that English should be the alternate/associate language until otherwise decided by a majority of three-fourths of the State Legislatures. That was brushed aside. I had given notice of another amendment to the effect that English should be the alternate/associate language until otherwise decided by a majority of three-fourths of each House of Parliament. That was similar to the majority required to amend the Constitution as provided in Article 368 of the Constitution. That was also brushed aside. Kamath, as the Deputy Leader of the Praja Socialist Party, moved an amendment that the report of the Committee should come to Parliament and then go to the President. He was supported by every section of the Opposition except the Hindi chauvinists. Once again, the Congress Party whip cracked : yet the Government could only muster a little over 200 votes in order to steam-roller the 40 odd votes cast in favour of Kamath's amendment. Even Kamath was constrained to observe that those who had voted for Clause 4 had supported the by-passing of Parliament, as Parliament had no power to say by a motion whether it agreed wholly or partly with or entirely disapproved of the report of a committee elected by Parliament.

Fraud On Non-Hindi Peoples

It was claimed by Government that the Bill was a good compromise. The truth was that it was a compromise with the Hindi fanatics and was a complete dishonouring of the Prime Minister's assurance that English would be the alternate language until otherwise decided by the non-Hindi speaking people. The decision would now rest with a handful of picked members who would make their dictated decisions behind closed doors. I was thus obliged at the third reading stage to oppose the Bill in one sentence, "Because the Bill is a travesty of the Prime Minister's assurance given to the non-Hindi-speaking peoples : because it is a calculated scheme for the blanket imposition of Hindi by the back-door : because it is a calculated scheme for side-tracking not only the non-Hindi-speaking Legislatures but Parliament and, finally, because, in effect, the Bill is a fraud in law on the non-Hindi speaking people."

Bitter Revulsion In The South

In furtherance of my campaign against the menace of Hindi Imperialism, I addressed mass meetings in Madras and Bangalore in October, 1963. The tremendous popular response to my speeches was a measure of how strong was the feeling in South India against the imposition of Hindi. An ominous, if unhappy, incident at Bangalore underlined this strong feeling. At the end of my speech to a packed meeting at the Bangalore Town Hall, the National Anthem was being played. Among the audience were men of eminence from every walk of life, Judges of the High Court, lawyers, educationists and doctors. General Thimmaya, a former Chief of the Indian Army, was noticeable standing to soldierly attention.

Suddenly, in the midst of the National Anthem there was considerable commotion in the gallery. The police had to intervene. An enquiry showed that some of the members of the audience, educated men and women, were shouting interruptions during the National Anthem, wanting to convey that the National Anthem was meant to unite the Country, but if it continued to be played in Hindi, or what they considered to be Hindi, in the South it would be resented and would become a symbol of division. This unhappy incident only underlined the deep, bitter, universal resentment in the South against Hindi imposition, which the Central Government, functioning in Delhi in an atmosphere of Hindi unreality, could continue to ignore only at the peril of the Country's unity.

The reaction in the Madras State was eloquently summarised in an editorial in "The Mail", an influential Indian-owned English-medium daily.

"The Mail," Madras, Saturday, October 26, 1963.

English

"Those who attended the public meeting addressed by Mr. Frank Anthony on Friday could scarcely in their experience have listened to a more closely reasoned, eloquent and cogent presentation of the case for English. The stream of orderly and lucid argument, its level surface lashed now and again by gusts of passionate feeling, flowed on unhasting, unresting for over an hour. English has been described by one of its great masters as 'an unsurpassed instrument of human expression'. Mr. Anthony's address illustrates its multitudinous resources. Those whose ears are attuned to the great harmonics of that language will be saddened beyond words by his exhaustive and moving account of the demoniac attempts of the Hindi fanatics to extirpate it root and branch from Indian life where for a century and more it has struck such deep and fruitful roots. The disheartening story is revealed in its entirety. 'Every form of political hypocrisy was pressed into service' not only by the Bombay Government but also by the high and mighty in New Delhi to deprive English of its rightful place."

"Mr. Anthony is the leader of the Anglo-Indian Community on behalf of which, he says, he 'entered a final human plea' when every other had failed. But English is not the monopoly of the Anglo-Indian Community. This only strengthens the case for English, which long ago ceased to be a foreign language and which, in the pregnant phrase of Mr. Rajagopalachari, is 'Saraswathi's gift to India'. It is, as Mr.Anthony pointed out,much less 'foreign' to the educated classes in India than Hindi."

"The conclusive argument for its retention is that, as Dr. Lakshmanaswami Mudaliar said, its abandonment 'would lead to the utter destruction of all possible advance in science and technology'. The cruel paradox of Indian life today is that while the Prime Minister and the Government talk ceaselessly about India emerging into the nuclear age their policies are calculated to put her back into the bullock-cart age. Who believes in earnest that Hindi can take the place of English in the foreseeable future or that its adoption as the official language will not plunge the Country into primordial chaos? The Prime Minister's 'formula' afforded some ground for hope that the present insensate march towards confusion and darkness would, in some measure, be arrested: but by tactics which it is sufficient to term adroit even that formula has been jettisoned. Parliament has been by-passed : the State Governments have been coerced or hoodwinked. All the unanswerable arguments for the retention of English have been put forward again and again by educationists and others who have the best title to speak on the subject, though perhaps they have never been marshalled and presented with such force and clarity as by Mr. Anthony. They have fallen on deaf ears because Reason has ceased to be the decisive influence in Indian affairs. The only hope of the educated people consists in the certitude that English will one day again come back into its own when Hindi will be discovered to have been an agent of ignorance. But a great deal of avoidable hurt would have been inflicted in the meanwhile on the common weal."

Mounting Revulsion Against Hindi

Inevitably, the increasing intolerance, obscurantism and, indeed, overweening arrogance of the Hindi chauvinists created their own reaction. This reaction gained momentum after the passage of the Official Languages Act in 1963. It was realised, increasingly, that the Act was a travesty of the Nehru assurance of permanent bilingualism. In December, 1963, C.N. Annadurai, leader of the Dravida Munnetra Kazhagam, and four others were sentenced to six months' rigorous imprisonment each on charge of a criminal conspiracy to burn the language chapter of the Constitution. Mr. M.C. Chagla, the then Education Minister, did his best to bring sanity and a healing touch to the situation. Repeatedly he pleaded against too much of politics in education: he also urged educationists not to play politics. But nothing could stop the crudity, the vulgarity and the growing Imperial lust of the Hindi chauvinists.

In January, 1964, 27-year old Chinnaswamy burnt himself to death as a protest against the rising tide of Hindi Imperialism. But the Hindi fanatics continued their insane course. In Uttar Pradesh, in February, the Socialists walked out because the Governor, Mr. Bishwanath Das, addressed the joint session in English with a small introduction in Hindi. The then President, Dr. Radhakrishnan, rather than submit to the blackmail by Hindi chauvinists, who insisted that the Presidential address should be first delivered in Hindi, appeared to have decided to undergo an eye operation so that the Vice-President could deliver the address in Hindi.

True to form, Uttar Pradesh, which usually has been the spearhead of Hindi chauvinism, gave a typical demonstration in August, 1964. There was a complete breakdown of any semblance of decorum in the U.P. Vidhan Sabha when 28 Opposition members were suspended or forcibly removed from the House. This demonstration was against a perfectly legitimate Bill which sought to allow amendments to enactments passed in English also to be made in the same language even after 1965.

In the welter of growing language madness, Mr. Chagla, the then Union Education Minister, in October, 1964, called for a realisation of the implications of going ahead with the introduction of the regional languages as media of instruction at the University stage without, at the same time, providing a link language. He dared to plead for two proposals, which have now been killed by the Hindi chauvinists, that education should become a concurrent subject and that an all-India education service be created to maintain some semblance of uniformity in educational policy. Speaking in the Rajya Sabha in 1964, Chagla said that he would not submit to pressure, however great, which would undermine national unity. He underlined that national unity was paramount and that what India required was a bond between different people, universities, courts of law, schools and academicians. He said that he was surprised at the attitude of those who wanted to do away with English in haste.

. Speaking in the Lok Sabha in November, 1964, amidst much badgering by the Hindi zealots, Chagla adhered to his position that
while he did not emphasise the supremacy of English he shuddered
to think of the day when interpreters will be needed at a conference
of Indians.

In the meantime, the antics of the Hindi chauvinists produced
their own inevitable, increasing revulsion not only in Madras but
in the other States. The West Bengal Public Vehicles Department
seized all transport vehicles with Hindi number-plates coming from
Bihar and the U.P. The Department pointed out that the police
found it difficult to enforce traffic regulations as they were unable
to understand the Hindi number-plates. They also complained
that to make matters worse, the communications received from the
Transport Departments of Bihar and Uttar Pradesh were written
in Hindi. All number-plates in West Bengal had to be in international numerals.

In January, 1965, anti-Hindi rallies were held all over the Madras
State. In February, 1965, 24 persons were killed during a State-wide
hartal, which had been launched by the Tamil Students Anti-Hindi
Agitation Council. A peak in this tragedy, provoked by the growing pressures of the Hindi Imperialists, was reached in February,
1965, when two persons, Muthu Goundar and Veerapan, headmaster of an elementary School, burnt themselves to death in a
protest against Hindi becoming the official language. This
brought the number of self-immolation cases to 5.

In Calcutta, in February, anti-Hindi demonstrations were held.
Cinema houses cancelled the screening of Hindi films. The anti-
Hindi flames were spreading steadily to the rest of the Country. In
February, 1965, in Nellore in the coastal area of Andhra Pradesh,
2 persons were killed and 3 injured during demonstrations against
Hindi. O.V. Alagesan, the Minister of State for Petroleum and
Chemicals, submitted his resignation in February, 1965. He under-
lined the need to give real statutory effect to the Nehru assurance
that English will be used as long as the non-Hindi speaking people
want it.

In Calcutta, once again, in February, 1965, the students of
Jadhavpur University protested against the introduction of Hindi
in place of English. The Hindi Resistance Committee of West
Bengal in a communication to the Anti-Hindi Committee of Madras

rejected giving Hindi the position of the official language. All schools and colleges in Calcutta and the districts closed for a week in February in the context of the anti-Hindi agitation. In Cooch-Bihar, students of all educational institutions stayed away from their classes in a protest against the introduction of Hindi as the official language.

On the 17th of February, 1965, the President reiterated the Government's assurance that English will continue as the Associate official language as long as the non-Hindi speaking people so desire.

On the same date, the Kerala Government closed all the schools and the colleges from the 18th to the 22nd February in view of the students' decision to stay away from the classes as part of the anti-Hindi agitation. The All-Kerala Students Action Council called for a State-wide hartal.

Anti-Hindi revulsion erupted again in Hyderabad : 3 people were killed in Hindupur and Anantpur when the police opened fire. In February, 1965, representatives of the students from Mysore, Kerala, Andhra Pradesh and West Bengal met together to concert measures to oppose the imposition of Hindi. The consensus that emerged was that all the languages mentioned in the VIIIth Schedule of the Constitution should be given the status of national languages with English as the official language.

Rajaji continued his campaign in which he underlined that he was not in favour of bi-linguism : what he wanted was the status quo ante.

In the meantime, in the Central Government, which is a hotbed of well-known Hindi fanatics, circulars went out to the effect that Hindi had become the official language of the Union and that the entire work would be done in Hindi. Commenting on the circular issued by the Ministry of Food and Agriculture, Mr. C. Subramaniam, the then Minister, said that some Hindi enthusiasts in the Ministry seemed to have issued the circular.

In February, 1965, 9 Akali members of the Punjab State Legislature walked out in protest when the Governor made his address in Hindi.

Meanwhile, the Hindi Chauvinist bloc, even in Parliament, was not idle. In February, 1965, about a 100 Hindi zealots submitted a memorandum against the introduction of the promised amendment to the Official Languages Act. Some of the signatories were Congress M. Ps. thus underlining the fact that Hindi Imperialism cuts across party affiliations.

The anti-Hindi revulsion continued to simmer in the South: in March, 1965, one person was killed in Ootacamund when the police opened fire on anti-Hindi agitators.

Amendment To The Official Languages Act

In December, 1967, a Bill to amend the Official Languages Act of 1963 was introduced. It took the blood-bath in the South to make the Central Government acknowledge that the 1963 Act was not, indeed, a fulfilment of the Nehru assurance to the non-Hindi speaking people. I give below my speech in Parliament on this amending Bill and the accompanying resolution. Apart from analysing the amendments, my speech serves to recapture the atmosphere of the sheer intolerance and, indeed, the overweening arrogance displayed, even in Parliament, by the Hindi Imperialists.

"Shri Frank Anthony (Nominated Anglo-Indians): Mr. Chairman, Sir, may I say with great respect that there does not seem to have been much attention paid to what is before the House—this amending Bill and the resolution. I propose to confine my remarks to the amending Bill and the resolution.

The Home Minister had mentioned that this amending Bill was a compromise. I agree entirely with him that it is a compromise, it is a compromise between the Nehru assurance and the increasing, the unremitting pressure of the Hindi lobby both in the Congress Party and outside. You may remember that when the original Bill or the original measure was on the anvil I had analysed what became sections 3 and 4. I pointed out that they constituted a calculated scheme for the blanket imposition of Hindi by the back-door. I had summed up my opposition to that original measure at the third reading stage in one sentence. I said that it was travesty of the Nehru assurance, that it was a calculated scheme for the imposition of Hindi by the back-door and that it was, indeed, a fraud on the non-Hindi speaking people.

Sir, I will concede this to the Hindi zealots that they have been consistent, they have been consistent in their intention to ensure that the Nehru assurance is not implemented, they have been consistent in their intention to ensure that the Nehru assurance is both sabotaged and indeed dishonoured (Interruptions). I am only dealing with the Nehru assurance, nothing outside.

Some people, including my hon. friend who has interrupted me, seek to invoke the Constitution; either-—I do not want to be harsh, in the courts I am the personification of mildness and I do not want to impute any motives—they do not choose to understand the plain language of the Constitution or deliberately they seek to distort it in order to suit this Hindi imposition motive. Article 343 is invoked in season and out of season. Equally it is distorted in season and out of season. The Hindi protagonists say, look at Article 343, it sets an absolute dead-line after 1965 for the complete imposition of Hindi as the sole official language. I say, no. I say, look at the whole article, look at clause (3) which is a non-obstante clause. You know, Sir, what a non-obstante clause is. What does clause (3) of Article 343 say? It says:

"Notwithstanding anything in this article,
Parliament may by law provide for the use, after the said period
of fifteen years, of—
(a) The English language, ..."

It says that notwithstanding anything in Article 343, after 15 years, that is , after 1965, Parliament may specify the use for English. In my respectful submission—the Hindi protagonists will not agree— provided Parliament specifies the use, it may say, in terms, that after 1965 English shall continue for all the official purposes of the Union. That, in my respectful submission, is the plain and ordinary meaning of the non-obstante clause. The non-obstante clause effaces everything before it, effaces the reference to Hindi being the official language of the Country.

Travesty Of The Nehru Assurance

As I said, the original Bill, in my respectful submission, was a travesty of the Nehru assurance. I say this with great respect to the Home Minister that this amending Bill is a continuing travesty of the Nehru assurance. All the basic defects, all the basic snares in the original Bill are still continued. You may remember the language used—English MAY be used in addition to Hindi.

Now, Sir, I had written to Jawaharlal Nehru. He had replied to me on the 18th April, 1963. I told him that this language, this permissive language was a travesty of his assurance to the non-Hindi speaking people. He replied to me—I have got his letter, reply,

with me—saying that it was his intention that it should be mandatory
and he had been advised that "may" in that context meant "shall".
That was the clear intention of the Nehru assurance propounded
by Nehru himself, that it will have to be mandatory. But what
happened? When I was seeking a clarification, the then Home
Minister Shastriji—I loved him but I had to fight him on this issue—
said that "may" means "may"; "may" is permissive, and in this
context how will it be interpreted? I do not want to point a finger
at all the members of the Central Cabinet. I believe the Home
Minister wants to try and implement the Nehru assurance. But he
and other people like him—God knows there are only a handful
there—are complete captives of the dominant Hindi chauvinist
bloc in the Central Cabinet itself. In that view of the matter, what
will it mean? It will mean that it is a complete travesty of the
Nehru assurance; that Hindi shall be there for all official purposes,
that will be the interpretation. English may be, or indeed it may
not be, used for a single official purpose. That is what the present
amending Bill means. It is a complete and utter travesty of the
Nehru assurance.

My friends, the Hindi zealots are worked up. Certain sops have
been given. I agree; they have spelt out certain mandatory uses
for the English language. But if you analyse the mandatory uses,
they are an insult to the Nehru formula. You have merely spelt
out certain utterly inconsequential, valueless uses for mandatory
purposes. In my respectful submission, this was not the Nehru
assurance, this was not the assurance of bilingualism.

Then, I would ask you to recall what was section 4, the original
section, which has not been touched. One of my strenuous objections was to the original section 4. It is intact. What is section 4
which remains intact. I had attacked it, because it says that after
10 years, that is, 10 years after 1963, that was the date on which
it was put on the legislative anvil, there will be a committee. I say
that committee will be a mockery because that committee will be
hand-picked, it will be packed; that committee will be picked by
Parliament, but it will be mockery of a parliamentary committee,
because the report of that committee will not come back to Parliament. So, this section 4 is a negation of a parliamentary committee.
The report of that so-called parliamentary committee, Parliament
will not be able to amend it by one single word, Parliament will not

be able to amend it by a single syllable. That report will go directly to the President. He may be an avowed Hindi chauvinist and he will make his recommendations for the blanket imposition of Hindi.

What does this amending Bill do? I am surprised that even my friends of the DMK have not analysed it. A few crumbs, a few crumbs, a few scraps have been thrown from the table of the Hindi masters, from the Hindi Herrenvolk to the non-Hindi speaking people. What are these crumbs? Look at these crumbs—communications between one department of the Government and another will carry an English translation; resolutions, general orders, rules, notifications, contracts between one department and another, they will also carry an English translation. Is this the assurance of bilingualism? It is a negation of the Nehru assurance of bilingualism. It is a garish mockery of that assurance. That assurance was that until the non-Hindi speaking people decide, at least till then, English will be used for all the official purposes, in addition to Hindi.

Is this the assurance? As I said, it is a cynical travesty; this Bill is nothing but a cynical travesty of the Nehru assurance to the non-Hindi speaking people.

The Bill, itself, it contains all the means, all the instruments, this amending Bill, if you analyse it—nobody has bothered about it.—I am doing it as a lawyer—it contains all the means, all the instruments for the blanket imposition of Hindi.

Shri S.S. Kothari : A good advocate for a bad cause, a lost cause.

Shri Frank Anthony : It is not a lost cause. You are destroying the Country.

All that was necessary in order that the Nehru assurance should have been honestly, really implemented, was, as I told Jawaharlal Nehru, an ordinary two-line measure that English shall be used as the associate language, in addition to Hindi, for all the official purposes of the Union, and also alternatively because even the Parliamentary Committee on languages, of which I was a member, said that even after 1965 Hindi will not be sufficiently developed for some of the major purposes, and there English must be used as the principal language. That would have been an implementation of the assurance.

Tortuous Resolution

Now, look at the resolution.

The resolution, with great respect to Mr. Chavan—I do not think he had much to do with it—is even more tortuous; it is even more devious than this amending Bill. It is another surrender to this unremitting pressure by the dominant, clamorous Hindi bloc in the Congress Party and outside.

What does it do? The few scraps, the few crumbs that this amending Bill purports to throw to the non-Hindi helots, like the DMK people, even those are negated and stultified. Look at the built-in devices in the resolution itself for the blanket imposition of Hindi : the imposition of the three-language formula : promotions and confirmations will depend on passing a Hindi test : a multiplicity of media leading inevitably to the quota system, and the quota system meaning what? The largest quota going to the Hindi-speaking people. Why? Because they have the largest number of illiterate heads in the country.

Shri Bhola Nath (Alwar) : Why not? This is a democracy.

Yes, we must enjoy.

Shri Frank Anthony : That is a new interpretation of democracy, that for entrance into the superior services where some education is required you must count the number of illiterate heads. That is quite a new and a devious interpretation of democracy.

The worst feature in this resolution is—it is worse even than section 4—that there has to be an annual review guaranteeing the progressive imposition of Hindi. My objection to section 4 was that, contrary to the Nehru assurance of bilingualism until the non-Hindi speaking people so decide, under section 4 after 10 years you can have the blanket imposition of Hindi by a packed committee, but here by this provision for a review every year, it may not be even ten years. Within a year, within two years or within three years, by the back-door, through this provision, there will be the blanket imposition of Hindi.

Shri Kanwar Lal Gupta : Why back-door?

Shri Frank Anthony : Let me deal with some of the items in the resolution—I should have liked to deal with all. I should like to deal with some briefly.

The Home Minister in his resolution has referred to Article 351 of the Constitution. I agree with him that Article 351 is a directive principle. It casts a duty on the Union to develop Hindi so that it will be—what? You know what it was meant to be—an expression of the composite culture of all the elements. That much the Home Minister put in. He omits—I do not say that he did it deliberately—the second part of Article 351. What does Article 351 in the second part say? It says, "In order to represent the elements of the composite culture of India, Hindi will draw on the forms, the styles and the expressions of Hindustani, on the languages in the VIIIth Schedule and primarily on Sanskrit."

Who has stultified Article 351? The Central Government, apart from the Hindi zealots, has done that. Has Article 351 got any meaning and content today? Every style, every form and every expression in Hindustani—has been deliberately purged from the new Hindi: although it is the commonest language currency, today Hindustani has been driven out not because it is Urdu but because it has an Urdu sound.

I learnt Hindi as my second language. At least I thought it was Hindi. I have earned not a little money at the bar through the medium of Hindi. Today, I am an illiterate because of the new Hindi, because of the artificial monstrosities of All-India Radio. Today we have become illiterates because of the new Hindi.... (Interruptions).

Shri Frank Anthony : People talk glibly. They talk of 2 per cent of the people being English-knowing and 40 per cent being Hindi knowing. Either these are deliberate canards or they are deliberately ignorant statements. I will not talk about the English figures but what are the Hindi figures? Look at the 1951 census and after that the 1961 census. You will find that Hindi which does not constitute even 25 per cent has filched the figures for a whole range of languages which have nothing to do with Hindi. Urdu, Punjabi, Rajasthani—over 70 dialects—have all been included. The census has been doctored to inflate the figure of 25 per cent. ... (Interruptions).

The tragedy with my friends is that they will not argue at a rational level; they sink to vulgarities.

That will not do. No crudity. my hon. friends. You do not understand English.

Shri Hardayal Devgun (East Delhi) : You use vulgar language. You have been using abusive language saying Hindi chauvinists and all that.

Shri Frank Anthony: I can only pity my friend's knowledge of English if he says that 'chauvinists' is a word of abuse.

Sir, the resolution talks of accelerating the development of Hindi. I say 'yes'. I have given a substitute resolution. If the Central Government wants to accelerate it, let it accelerate it at the cost of the Hindi States. Why? (Interruptions). When I speak the truth, they get offended. Today, Hindi is a comparatively new and an undeveloped language. You cannot develop a language by artificial respiration, by throwing away crores of rupees....(Interruptions). The tragedy is that they do not like anybody to make out a case. They want to shout them down. Let them try to understand and counter my arguments.

Shri Hardayal Devgun: Are not words like 'fanatics' and 'chauvinists' abuses? This is an abusive language.

Shri Frank Anthony: What a pathetic commentary on my friend's knowledge of the English language. It is choice language, the quintessence of dignity of language ....(Interruption).

Shri Hardayal Devgun: If this is the dignity of language, we pity you.

Shri Frank Anthony: As a sop to the non-Hindi speaking people, my friend the Home Minister has said that Government will develop the languages in the VIIIth Schedule and Hindi. With great respect to my friend, the Home Minister, may I say that this part of the resolution is the greatest affront to the many Indian languages that are not in the VIIIth Schedule? Some of the languages in the VIIIth Schedule are not regional languages; some of them are not the official language of a State. Now, if you want to insult the other Indian languages, you may insult them but don't insult the official language of a State.

Sir, I argued it in the Supreme Court, whatever my friends may say, and as a result of my argument—let them go and look at the 1954 judgment of the Supreme Court in the Bombay Education Society case; my friends will not probably accept it—the Supreme Court said that English is as much an Indian language as any other language because it is the language of Mr. Anthony's Community. They went on further and affirmed that not only is it equal in status to the languages in the VIIIth Schedule....(Interruptions). I am telling them what the Supreme Court has said and they are shouting it down. Today, the position is much stronger....(Interruptions).

Mr. Chairman : Let him be allowed to proceed. The Supreme Court judgments do stand.

Shri Frank Anthony : The Supreme Court said that English is not only equal in status to the languages in the VIIIth Schedule but it is the dominant Indian language because it is the language of the Constitution, it is the language of the Supreme Court, it is the language of the High Courts and, unlike what Mr. Chavan said, it is the only language of authoritative legislation.... (Interruptions). I am not going to attempt to reply to my friends there. My friend asks me : What is the position today? Today, the position is infinitely stronger. Today, Nagaland has chosen, rightly, to adopt the English language—presumably, Nagaland is an Indian State—as the official language.... (Interruptions).

Shri Kanwar Lal Gupta : So what?

Shri Frank Anthony : So far, you have been insulting my Community because it is a small Community : You have been deliberately insulting us.... (Interruptions).

Mr. Chairman : Will you kindly sit down? Let him proceed.

Shri Frank Anthony : What do you say? You point to my language and you say, destroy it.... (Interruptions). The other day, my wife was insulted—I do not want to bring in such a thing here.... (Interruptions). Is it because we are supposed to be foreigners and speak a foreign language? Today you insult us because you think you can do it. Today, the Central Government says that the Nagas are welcome in spite of the pressures from the Hindi chauvinists.

You cannot both eat your cake and have it too with regard to the Nagas. You cannot say to the Nagas, "Yes, you are welcome, but your language is anathema to us. So far you have insulted this language because it was only the language of the Anglo-Indians. But now you will not be able to say that to the Nagas, not only because it is my language, but because it is an official language, it is a regional language, it has a superior status to many of the languages in the VIIIth Schedule which are neither regional languages nor official languages.

Multiplicity Of Media

Let me now deal with the question of the multiplicity of media. I know that even my friends from Tamil Nad have subscribed to that—multiplicity of media for the examinations for the Central Services. But who has studied the implications? I regret to say this that the Central Government, on vital matters, comes to snap decisions; some momentary political pressure and the most vital decisions having disastrous consequences for the Country are arrived at. Jawaharlal Nehru was angry with me when I fought him and told him about the impetus that he was giving to disintegration when there was that decision about linguistic reorganisation taken on the basis of slogans, which had ceased to have any validity in the new Indian context. (Interruptions). Today, my friends have not analysed the position. I have to analyse it because I know something about it. For the I.A.S. examination, how many examiners are there? There are about 70 examiners, and they have to be changed every 3 years. Multiply them by 12 or 14. We find difficulty to get suitable examiners for the IAS when they have to be changed. Multiply it by 12 or 14. Where will you find suitable examiners in 12 or 14 languages (Interruptions). I am showing the implications.... (Interruptions).

Mr. Chairman: Please allow him to proceed.

Shri Frank Anthony: Then you will have to have 12 or 14 Viva Voce boards, each competing in mark-giving. So far, you had one person standing first in the IAS, but now you will have 12 or 14 persons standing first in the IAS.

Shri Rabi Roy: To kya hua?

Shri Frank Anthony: The 'Kya Hua' will be this that the competition will be not among the examinees, the competition will be among the examiners. That will be the 'Kya Hua'. Then, what will be the further 'Kya Hua'? The further 'Kya Hua' will be this that because of this competition among examiners, my friend Dr. Ram Subhag Singh will put in his whole weight, which is not inconsiderable, behind the quota system and while he puts in his weight behind the quota system, what will happen? (Interruption).

An Hon. Member: Mr. Piloo Mody is here to outweigh him.

Shri Frank Anthony: At present about 3 or 5 per cent of the people who get into the Central Services by competition are from the Hindi States. That cannot be helped. If they have got only 3 million literates in the Hindi areas in the whole Country, they are very lucky to be able to get 3 or 5 per cent. (Interruptions). That is all.

What to do? You have barely 3 million literates. I am giving you the figures. The position will be this. You will want to have the quota system. Then my friends will invoke democracy and they will get 40% instead of 3 or 5 per cent for the IAS; you will have 40% of the most pitiful ignoramuses from the Hindi States coming into and dominating the Central Services.

Shri Hardayal Devgun: They got less percentage in Services because they were fighting against British imperialism.

Mr. Chairman: He may conclude.

The Three-Language Formula

Shri Frank Anthony: Sir, I will conclude by referring to that part of the resolution which talks of the three-language formula. Now, with great respect, may I say to Mr. Chavan that it is a piece of palpable usurpation of authority? You know, Sir, Secondary and Higher Secondary education represent exclusively a State subject. The States will say, 'Who are you to tell us that we shall have a three-language formula?' It is a piece not only of unwarranted dictation; States like Tamil Nad will say that it is a piece of unwarranted impertinence.

Sir, my friend, Dr. Triguna Sen, is here. I like him. Unfortunately, when he performs too many somersaults, I have to be critical. When he performed one somersault he subscribed apparently in a prehensile way to the two-language formula. May I say, with great respect to him, that was one of the few sensible things—this two-language formula—of which he has been guilty so far.

Another of his somersaults has been interpreted by the U.P. Government to mean the banishing of the three-language formula. The U.P. Government has banished the three-language formula. They have not even got a two-language formula. They have got a one-language formula. They have arrogated to themselves the privilege of having a one-language formula. They went through the motions of learning a third language from the South: all that has disappeared.

Now you are going to take power in this resolution to say to them, to say to the others, when the U.P. has buried it and has a one-language formula, 'You, the Tamils, you the Bengalis....' (Interruptions).

Shri Hardayal Devgun rose.

Mr. Chairman: Please don't interrupt. Please resume your seat. I am here to look after matters.

Shri Hardayal Devgun: Can he talk in this way, Sir?

Shri Frank Anthony: I do not mind these interruptions, Sir. How will you say, when you have arrogated, when the Hindi States have arrogated to themselves, the right of having a one-language formula, how will you say to the Tamils and the Bengalis, 'You shall have the three-language formula so that Hindi may be imposed on you'?

As I said, Sir, this amending Bill is a continuing travesty of the Nehru assurance. The resolution is an even greater travesty."

(Speech Ends)

But the resolution, even in its travestied form, was not acceptable to the Hindi zealots. Every pressure, overt and covert, was used by the Hindi protagonists within the Congress Party and outside to dilute the resolution further. In the result the Government, abjectly dependent on the votes of the Hindi bloc, accepted an amendment which in effect requires the non-Hindi speaking elements to study three languages while the Hindi Herrenvolk will have the right to learn only one language, their mother-tongue Hindi.

Organised Terror Campaign

The main plank in the Hindi chauvinists' programme has been to trade in hate. A cheap, obscurantist device was to try to work up emotion among the illiterates and the semi-illiterates, which number includes not a few legislators, against English as a foreign language. In Kanpur, Lucknow, Meerut and Benares there was organised rioting in November and December, 1967. According to press reports the Hindi Sena, inspired and guided by certain political parties, even enforced a levy on behalf of the Hindi cause. Reporting on the organised violence in Kanpur, 'The Weekend Review', a Hindustan Times publication, observed that, "The scenes perpetrated by pro-Hindi fanatics in Kanpur, Lucknow, Meerut and Benares were doubly horrifying. The physical humiliation and wanton destruction suffered by the few shopkeepers who refused to bow down to the mob was pitiable." The report continued, "All these acts of vandalism were perpetrated under the paternal and indulgent eye of the police." Brij Bhardwaj, the correspondent writing this report, continued, "While this orgy of loot, destruction and arson was going on I wondered where were the police, the Government, the political leaders, the law-abiding citizens, the sages, the wizards and the moral exponents of this great country with its 'golden heritage'."

'The Weekend Review', reporting on the organised violence by the Hindi fanatics in New Delhi, pointed out that on December 5, 1967, about 500 students went round the Campus of the Delhi University shouting anti-English slogans, but since they represented only a small section of the Delhi University students, they did not succeed. It was at this stage that Hindi Sainiks from Uttar Pradesh rushed to Delhi to organise the agitation by mobilising the students in all the colleges and schools. 17 buses of the Delhi Transport Undertaking, including 4 private buses, were damaged; 6 private cars were smashed as their owners did not agree to change their number-plates. Even Parliament was not spared the latest techniques of the Hindi neo-Imperialists. As reported in the press, the Lok Sabha witnessed unprecedented scenes during the debate on the Bill to amend the Official Languages Act. A Jan Sangh member burnt a copy of the Bill in the House. "The glass-panes of the lobby doors were broken by some members; there were frequent scenes of pandemonium and persistent defiance of the Chair; unparliamentary and abusive language was used and there were even threats of the use of physical force."

Commenting on the scene in Parliament, I wrote, "The atmosphere in Parliament had to be seen to be believed. As the second seniormost member in the House I have seen the Legislative scene unfold, at the Centre, since before Independence. However bitter the occasion or the provocation, seldom was there any deliberate abdication of the well-tried and respected methods of Parliamentary debate and discussion. Today, some members, at least, show their utter bankruptcy in Parliamentary techniques by resorting to methods which would make the proverbial Fish-market blush. What saddened me beyond words was the atmosphere of sheer hate precipitated by the Hindi madmen. It was ominously reminiscent of the days in the Central Legislative Assembly immediately preceeing Partition. Legislators, who were friends till yesterday, looked at one another with blood-shot, hate-filled eyes. And the blood-shot, hate-filled eyes of the Hindi fanatics had to be seen to be believed. Quite obviously, they are prepared to divide the Country on the Hindi issue."

"For many reasons the non-Hindi elements were in a position of disadvantage. In the first place, there is no hate motivation, no exuding of fanatical madness. Outside the D.M.K. there is no organised resistance to the growing tentacles of Hindi Imperialism. Except for one notorious Hindi zealot, all members of the Congress Party were lashed by a rigorous PartyWhip. Deep and passionate feelings there were and they cut across party lines. Thus the representatives from West Bengal spoke with one voice against the menace of Hindi Imperialism. A Communist member, Shri Nair from Kerala, who did not get an opportunity to speak during the general discussion, loudly registered his protest by shouting 4 times, "Down with Hindi Imperialism" and then walked out of the House."

"The Hindi hate-campaign of violence, terror and intimidation was obviously planned. Two Ministers from the U.P. came all the way to Delhi to defy and break the law. Their conduct before and after their arrest defied description. Deliberately, Ministers had cast themselves in the role of law-breakers and common criminals. Student elements in Delhi, said to be the pawns of the Jan Sangh and S.S.P., went on a rampage. There is little consolation that they belonged to the mucker elements of the student community. The stark, shameful fact was that they were able to hold the University to ransom and by arson, loot and violence to bring the rule of law into contempt. According to press reports, in the U.P. there was open incitement to and approbation of violence by the Jan Sangh and the S.S.P. From Patna it was reported that demonstrators, led by the Minister for Local Self-Government and the President of the Bihar Hindi Sahitya Sammelan, stoned the premises of the well-known English-medium newspaper 'Searchlight' and sought to set fire to the office."

"The rule of law was paralysed in the presence of organised violence, crime and terror. We have yet to hear of commensurate punishment being meted out not only to Ministers, who deliberately cast themselves in the role of criminals, but to young brigands, mas-
ᵅ⁻⁻⁻ ˈ   udents and breaking the law with cynical impunity."

ᴉinst Hindi Spreads

violence and calculated terror in the Hindi States ːvitable reaction. Fortunately, the D.M.K. Ministry strongly condemned violence and appealed to the students to maintain discipline. Nevertheless, the anti-Hindi campaign was widespread and bitter. Trains were burnt, rail services were paralysed both on the metre and broad gauge sections of the Southern Railway.

The revulsion spread to Kerala, Mysore and Andhra Pradesh. A two-day battle completely shattered the long-held belief that Bangalore could never become violent on the language issue and also erased the misconception that Mysore would give in to Hindi domination without a murmur. There was a 30-hour reign of terror on January 22 and 23, resulting in 5 deaths, owing to police firing, and 273 persons being injured. The Chief Minister of Kerala joined hands with the Chief Minister of Madras. He pointed out that with the people of Andhra and Mysore waking up to the dangers of the Official Languages Amending Act, a strong anti-Hindi belt was slowly growing in the South and that the Congress leaders could ignore this only at their peril.

According to a news item from Hyderabad dated January 23, 1968, reports from 11 districts of Andhra showed that the anti-Hindi agitation was being intensified and spreading fast. Trains were detained and damaged at many places. Strikes were reported from many educational institutions, and in Chittoor an effigy of Morarji Desai, the Deputy Prime Minister, was burnt after the students had taken out a procession.

An ominous but sad incident was reported in The Hindu, dated January 30, 1968. Speaking at an Engineering College in Bangalore, General Cariappa referred to the fact that N.C.C. platoons had shown disrespect to the national flag at the Republic Day parade, at Mercara, at which General Cariappa was also present. The N.C.C. platoons of the Government College had refused to salute the flag because the commands were given in Hindi.

A news item, dated January 31, showed that the anti-Hindi agitation had spread to Mangalore. Students of the Government College and the Kasturba Medical College took out a procession and shouted anti-Hindi slogans. Hindi signboards at the railway station, Post and Telegraph offices and shops were disfigured and anti-Hindi slogans were written on the walls all over the city. Cinema houses exhibiting Hindi films announced their closure.

Rajaji appealed to the Prime Minister to suspend the implementation of chapter seventeen of the Constitution dealing with the official language until the political situation of the Country stabilised and the economy improved.

Protests continued to the amendment to the Official Languages Act. The Andhra Pradesh Joint Action Committee was formed by the students of Sri Venkateswara and Osmania Universities and the anti-Hindi agitation was intensified in Andhra Pradesh. B. Ramamurthy of Andhra University, a convener of the Committee, stated, "The student community in Andhra Pradesh are one with the Madras students in their total opposition to the imposition of Hindi on South India and abolition of English in the North."

In Calcutta organised anti-Hindi demonstrations were held. According to press reports dated December 26, apart from parades in the street and the shouting of anti-Hindi slogans, Hindi signboards and Hindi posters in front of shops and cinema houses were disfigured.

Even Mr. Kamaraj, the outgoing Congress President, pleaded for a change in the language policy for removing the additional burden that had been cast upon the non-Hindi entrants to the Central Services. The Chief Minister of Madras, Mr. Annadurai, according to press reports dated January 15, was of the view that without a satisfactory solution of the language issue based on the status quo ante, continuing in office would amount to abdication of responsibility on the part of the present generation to the younger generation which would be completely at a disadvantage in the all-India picture when it came of age and shouldered office twenty years afterwards.

Rajaji, once again, expressed the view that only by shelving the language issue indefinitely and restoring the status quo ante with English as the sole official language of the Centre and as the means of communication between States, could the Country be saved.

What happened to Morarji Desai's proposed visit to Madras was significant. On January 17, he was advised not to go to Madras because of his uncompromising stand on the language issue. Discretion suggested that he should divert his programme to Bangalore. But even there massive demonstrations organised by anti-Hindi agitators led to the cancellation of his scheduled inauguration of India's first cinerama theatre. Students from a number of educational institutions walked out of their classes, shouting,

"We want Kannada and English and don't want Hindi." According to press reports of January 22, the police had to fire to disperse the Bangalore students.

Kamaraj continued his protests against the amendment to the Official Languages Act and the accompanying resolution. According to press reports of January 22, he said that the recent Official Languages amendment and the resolution would place national unity in jeopardy. He expressed his regret that the people in the Hindi area do not understand the realities in the non-Hindi regions. He said that English would have to be the link language for communication between the Hindi and the non-Hindi areas because English was the only language that could be used as the link language. He said that the amendment served to sow the seeds of disintegration and pointed the way straight to separation. He wanted this to be immediately undone.

According to press reports from Trivandrum, dated January 22, the Chief Minister of Kerala, Mr. Namboodiripad, announced in the Legislature that the State Government's stand on the language question was that English would continue as the link language. Namboodiripad added that his Government's view was that people who were accustomed to the use of English should have the freedom to continue its use.

According to press reports dated January 23, the Madras State Assembly adopted a resolution appealing to the Union Government to suspend the operation of the Official Languages Amendment Act and to devise ways and means to ensure that the people in the non-Hindi regions were not subjected to any disadvantage or additional burden. The resolution, moved by the Chief Minister, recommended that Hindi commands in the N.C.C. and other units should be dropped and, if the Centre did not permit this, the N.C.C. in Madras would have to be disbanded.

The latest position would appear to be that the N.C.C., in the Madras State, if not disbanded has been put into cold storage.

Rajaji once again entered a plea for sanity. Writing in Swarajya of January 27, 1968, while protesting against the bilinguism formula, he said that it was a 'Split-India charter'. "For the Hindi regions," he wrote, "it is not bilinguism but a single language and that the mother-tongue of the people of those regions. For non-Hindi regions this bilinguism is prolonged trilinguism—English, the

regional language and Hindi." According to Rajaji, this prolonged bilinguism will be, "The cause of increasing confusion, delay,
expense, inefficiency, conspiracy and indiscipline in all Central
offices.....It will hit the young men and women of our land and bar
them from official and professional work."

The anti-Hindi resistance has continued to simmer in the South.
In Andhra Pradesh, according to reports dated January 31, 1968,
demonstrators burnt the effigy of the Prime Minister at 7 places;
several district schools and colleges were closed and lathi-charges
were made by the police. In Mangalore, Hindi signboards at the
railway station, post and telegraph offices and shops were disfigured
and anti-Hindi slogans written all over the walls.

In early February, anti-Hindi agitations continued throughout
Andhra Pradesh. The anti-Hindi agitation in Mangalore took
a serious turn. Detention of trains by students was reported. The
screening of Hindi films was suspended in Nellore and schools and
colleges in various parts of Andhra Pradesh were closed following
the renewal of the anti-Hindi agitation. Andhra University was
closed till February 18.

According to press reports dated March 6, 1968, the Madras
Government ordered discontinuance of the teaching of Hindi in
Anglo-Indian Schools and also in the State with immediate effect.

According to press reports of September 26, the Madras Law
Minister, S. Madhavan, stated that the State Government would
not allow the Central Government to start Hindi classes in Tamil
Nad, as this would be an attempt to bring in Hindi by the back-door.
It would also be an attempt to by-pass the decision of the State
Government to abolish the teaching of Hindi in schools. The
students of Coimbatore, according to press reports of October 3,
went on strike protesting against the starting of single-teacher Hindi
schools in the Madras State.

Some Hindi Imperialists, typifying their parochial and obscurantist
attitudes, persist in living in a world of illusion. Someone, because
he has to toe the Congress Party line, protests that Hindi is spreading in the non-Hindi States. Practically the next day the Mysore
Education Minister states that while Hindi might be studied in
Mysore, even if a student gets a cipher it would not affect either his
progress or his grade in educational institutions!

On our way from Madras to Bangalore, on the 20th December,

1967, our train was held up at Perambur. Fortunately, the students were not in an unduly violent mood. They satisfied themselves by defacing all the Hindi signs on the train and compartments and by making everyone, including our servants, who are Hindi-speaking, shout, 'Hindi, Down Down'.

The Hindi chauvinists have only themselves to blame for the sheer hatred for Hindi that is now building up like a blank wall over the South despite anodyne remarks from those who deny this position. The Hindi chauvinists have traded in Hate and it is axiomatic that Hate begets Hate. The 'Angrezi Hatao' movement is now coming home to roost, in an ever-widening 'Hindi Hatao' movement. After I had presided at the annual prize day of the Frank Anthony Public School, Bangalore, several South-Indian parents explained their difficulties to me. Not only Tamil and Telugu speaking parents, but parents from Mysore were distressed by this Hate psychology that had affected their children. As the boys grow older they refuse to learn Hindi, or if they are made to study Hindi, as part of the three-language formula, the psychological resistance closes their minds to its reception. Another parent from Mysore mentioned to me that before the Hindi chauvinists' Hate campaign against English there were about 40 classes run by voluntary organisations in Bangalore for teaching those who wanted to study Hindi. According to this parent those classes have been closed down because of the Hate motive propagated by the Hindi fanatics and which has now recoiled against Hindi.

Latest Developments—A National Disaster

Increasingly Triguna Sen, the newly appointed Education Minister, has proved not only a disaster but a dangerous disaster for education and unity in the Country. A novice in public affairs, that he should have been put in charge of the education portfolio at a critical juncture was a major national tragedy; wittingly or unwittingly, he has played the Hindi chauvinist game.

As a member of the Kothari Education Commission, Triguna Sen had embraced with alacrity the vital recommendations for continuing English as the link language for academic and intellectual intercommunication and in the all-India Institutes and the major universities. The Commission had worked for 21 months, took evidence on a massive scale and returned a massive report, to which Triguna

Sen was an eager co-signatory. It is not known whether Triguna Sen is an academician or only a highly qualified engineer. Be that as it may, presumably in his educational capacity he solemnly subscribed his signature to the report of the Kothari Education Commission. Then, presumably in his political capacity in a different milieu, presumably with a different inspiration, as Chairman of the Parliamentary Committee which made its report in July, 1967, blandly and cavalierly, he turned his back on every vital recommendation to which he had subscribed his signature as a member of the Kothari Education Commission. He entered no demur. In fact, he embraced with alacrity, as the Chairman of a political committee, as a novitiate politician, the dead-line of 5 years for the change-over at all levels to the regional languages as the media. As I mentioned when speaking in Parliament in November, 1967, on the Kothari Education Commission report, Triguna Sen should have been aware of the fact that this dead-line of 5 years was not only an exercise in irresponsibility but an exercise in absurdity. Triguna Sen seemed to believe that by some process of educational alchemy, all the necessary books not only at the under-graduate level but at the graduate, the post-graduate and research levels, in the various regional languages, would be forthcoming.

The U.P. Minister of Education when asked as to how he could produce the necessary books, admitted that the Central Committee on Scientific and Technological terminology had listed 940 standard works for the humanities and 395 for science and technology. He was asked how many of them his State had translated into Hindi. He said, "None". but added, "What does it matter? We have got some at the under-graduate level, but none of these minimum standard works either at the graduate or at the post-graduate level." Then he went on, "But what is the difficulty? I shall produce a committee of three, one senior teacher in Hindi, one junior teacher in Hindi and one pundit in Hindi, and in 5 years we shall have the translations we need for post-graduate and research work."

Commenting on this, in my speech in Parliament, I posed the rhetorical question whether this attitude should not make the nation weep !

When the Bihar Education Minister was asked for his reaction to this question of translation, he said that for his State it would mean having to indulge in fantastic expenditure. In Bihar they spent about Rs. 20 crores, but whether the translations would be acceptable or not was a different matter. He said that if they proceeded with this exercise of translations the bill would go up to Rs. 100 crores.

In my speech I pointed out that Triguna Sen's antics had produced disastrous results. His statements as Chairman of the Parliamentary Committee had given a handle to the Hindi States, although they did not need a handle or an excuse. They quoted him as the authority for seeking to outlaw English. Not only was Triguna Sen responsible for producing fatal fixations on regional lines, he was responsible for having killed and buried the three-language formula. One of the few sensible things that emerged from his utterances was his recommendation of a two-language formula; but under pressure, the new-found politician, promptly withdrew that recommendation. Although very new to politics he appears to have learned quickly the technique of the political acrobat and the chameleon. Having been primarily responsible for killing the three-language formula in the Hindi States, he is now making drivelling appeals to the non-Hindi States and also to the Hindi States to adopt the three-language formula.

Dr. Lakshmanaswami Mudaliar, Vice-Chancellor of Madras University, speaking at a meeting of the Central Advisory Board of Education held at New Delhi in August, 1967, revealed yet another face of Triguna Sen. He mentioned that at a meeting presided over by Mr. Chagla, the then Education Minister, Dr. Sen, as a Vice-Chancellor, would not allow the discussion to proceed till a resolution was passed that in all technical and professional institutions English must continue as the medium for as long as it was necessary!

Chagla's Resignation

On August 31, 1967, Mr. M.C. Chagla, then the Minister of External Affairs, submitted his resignation from the Cabinet addressing the following letter to the Prime Minister.

"My dear Prime Minister,

There is one tenet which I have considered to be basic to my political philosophy, such as I have, and that is the maintenance of the unity of India which should override all other considerations. I regret that, in my opinion, the educational policy of the Government is likely to threaten, if not undermine, that unity.

I am all in favour of the development of Indian languages. I also accept the position that Hindi must ultimately replace English and play the unifying role that English plays today. But I equally strongly believe that the change-over from English to regional languages must be gradual and must not impair educational standards and, in the process of the change-over, till Hindi takes the field, the teaching of English should be strengthened and not allowed to recede into obscurity. Even after English ceases to be a link language, it will have to continue as an international language which will help us to keep our contacts abroad.

The time limit proposed to be set for the change-over in the universities of five years for undergraduate studies and ten years for all stages is hopelessly unpracticable and unrealistic.

Some of the languages mentioned in the VIIIth Schedule of the Constitution are highly developed, others are not. Even the former have not got the necessary literature nor the teachers trained to lecture in these languages.

It is said that a crash programme of translation will fill up this gap. I disagree. It is not through translation but original work that a language is developed. And original works cannot be produced overnight. The Education Commission points out that careful preparation should be made for the purpose, and both the manner and the time of transition would have to be left for decision to the university system.

The motto of every university should be to work for excellence and not be a mere factory for the production of graduates. And I dread to think what will happen to excellence if teachers are asked to lecture in a language in which they are not proficient and with the help of shoddy books hastily produced to order.

What will happen to students whose mother-tongue is different from the regional language? In many cities you have different media of instruction to cater for a multi-lingual society. They will be practically shut out from universities of the State which will be teaching in the regional language. No thought has been given to this serious problem.

What will happen to teachers who are not conversant with the regional language? Most universities recruit professors on an all-India basis and make use of the best talent available. Are these professors to be turned out? And do we, after five years, make our universities purely regional with students only from the State and cease to employ teachers outside its boundaries?

I must also point out the harm that an early and unprepared switch-over to regional languages will do to the study of science and technology.

This is a scientific and technological age and the horizon of knowledge is expanding at an incredible pace. One can at least translate text-books in the humanities, but in science, apart from the text-books, the student has to keep pace with new discoveries, and this he can only do if he is familiar with the large number of scientific journals which are at present only published in English or other European languages.

Therefore, as far as science is concerned, even the translation of text-books will not solve the problem.

A large body of scientific scholars must grow up who will be publishing their researches in journals and magazines which will be available to universities. This is a long and laborious process and must take a very long time. Therefore, a sudden change-over from English to the regional languages must result in a precipitous lowering of standards, more particularly in the field of science, where, if we wish to industrialise our country and transform its economy, we need the work and co-operation of our best scientific and our best research scholars.

But I would rather deal with the threat to our unity. English, whether we like it or not, has brought about administrative, academic and judicial unity. If Hindi takes its place, no one would be more happy than I. But with the strong feelings prevailing in the south, this cannot be achieved till it has been persuaded to accept the official language indicated in the Constitution.

But, in the meantime, irreparable damage would have been done. The inter-regional linguistic bond which contributes so much towards our unity will have been snapped. Mobility of professors and students will become impossible. Administration in the Centre and Centre-State relations will all receive a severe jolt from this policy.

I have nightmarish visions of interpreters being needed in a high-powered conference to interpret what one Indian is saying to another.

This is why the Education Commission has proposed that in

major universities it will be necessary as a rule to adopt English as the medium of education because their students and teachers will be drawn on an all-India basis.

It might be said that as External Affairs Minister I have noth ing to do with education. But I believe in collective responsibility and I am as much responsible for the education policy of Government as my friend, Dr. Sen.

I do not like to remain in the Government and criticise its policy. That would be disloyalty. I want to be free to express my opinion. I, therefore, hereby tender my resignation as a member of the Government.

Parting is always sad and I am sorry to part company with you and my colleagues. I only wish I was leaving in happier circumstances.

I strongly feel that the steps we are taking are irreversible. In most matters, Government policy, if mistaken, can be corrected. In education it cannot be. It affects millions of our people and a whole generation may suffer because we are more concerned with our present difficulties and pressures and do not look sufficiently ahead into the future.

I hope you will permit me to release this letter to the press.''

(Letter Ends)

Culpable Ambivalence

The Government was culpably ambivalent on this question of regional languages as the media. In an effort to decry, if not discredit, Chagla it was implied that his resignation was premature as allegedly no decision had been taken by the Cabinet. This hardly squared with the facts or the circumstantial evidence.

I had been informed that the Cabinet was to meet and discuss this specific question of media. I met the Prime Minister, Mrs. Indira Gandhi, shortly after the Cabinet meeting on the 7th August, 1967. I was accompanied by Barrow, my colleague in Parliament. During our discussions there was no suggestion that a decision had not been taken. It became clear, during the discussions, that the Government had accepted the policy of the regional languages as the media in higher education. The only question that remained open seems to have been the length of time in which this change would be effected.

After meeting the Prime Minister, I met several members of the Cabinet who confirmed that the decision had been made, however much some of them had disagreed.

On being questioned by the press as to my reaction on Chagla's resignation, I said, "That it symbolised a tragedy for the Country as it underlined the utter helplessness of members of the Cabinet with a sense of sanity and vision in the face of Hindi chauvinism of which the Central Government was now completely a prisoner." The Deputy Prime Minister, Morarji Desai, when questioned by newspaper men during his extensive foreign tour, sneered that Chagla's resignation would not affect the Government. Admittedly Chagla did not have what is, today, rated as the most valuable asset among politicians : in the generally muddied waters of politics, today, rating depends not on the capacity or character of a person but on the strength of the group or clique that he can command. A premium is now placed on the capacity for intrigue, manoeuvering and the manipulation of groups or cliques.

Pleas For Sanity

Meanwhile, watching with increasing distress the almost cavalier manner in which the Hindi chauvinists and their prisoners in the Government were giving irrevocable hostages to disintegration, eminent Indians in various walks of life entered a plea for sanity and vision.

On September 10, 1967, the Medical Council of India adopted the following resolution.

"In order to maintain uniform standards in under-graduate and post-graduate medical education throughout the country and to utilize fully the world literature in teaching, patient care and research, the Medical Council of India is of the opinion that English should continue till such time as a link language with adequate scientific literature is fully developed to replace it."

The resolution was forwarded to the Prime Minister, all the State Governments, Universities and the Planning Commission.

On December 5, 1967, the Council of the Institute of Engineers (India) at its meeting held in Poona adopted the following resolution.

"This 451st Meeting of the Council of Institution of Engineers (India) held at Poona on 5-12-1967, having given very careful thought to the problem of technical education in the Country, and having regard to the importance of effective communication between Engineers and Technologists of the various regions of the country, and to mobility of engineers, teachers and the students between them, and with a view to keeping abreast of the progress in other countries has unanimously resolved as under:

(1) English should continue to be the medium of instruction at the graduate and post-graduate level in engineering technological Faculties.

(2) The regional language may be adopted for education up to Polytechnic level with a view to better comprehension by the students and also better and wider diffusion of technical knowledge in the masses.

(3) English should be a compulsory language when regional languages are used as media of instruction at Polytechnic level.

(4) International English terminology with numerals, signs and symbols in Roman and Arabic scripts shall be adopted in all technical education.

(5) English shall continue to be the medium for all examinations of the Institution of Engineers.

(6) At Secondary Schools the three-language formula should be adopted to include the regional language, Hindi and English so that Item Nos. 1 and 2 above can be effectively implemented."

Finally, the Bar Council of India, at about the same time, adopted the following resolution.

"The Bar Council of India, concerned as it is with securing adequate legal education, recognition of degrees in law conferred by universities in this country, ensuring high standards of professional competence and with the maintenance of an effective all-India Bar;

"Deprecates proposals to switch over to the compulsory use of regional languages in the High Courts and in Universities, and calls attention to some of the disastrous consequences of a hasty switch-over."

"This Council is of the opinion that deep study and felicity in the use of one common language are vital to the existence of an all-India Judicial cadre, the Supreme Court and a competent all-India Bar, each of which is in turn indispensable to national integration."

Madras Language Convention

On the 4th and 5th November, 1967, a historic language convention was held in Madras City. The venue was the magnificent new auditorium of the Madras University. About 3000 delegates from every part of the Country and from practically every State had taken the trouble to attend. The auditorium of the Madras University has accommodation for 5000 persons and was packed to capacity. This was in spite of the fact that the organisers only permitted a 1000 passes for students.

Mr. K Subba Rao, retired Chief Justice of India, inaugurated the Convention and Dr. A. Ramaswami Mudaliar presided. I was invited to attend and was among the principal speakers.

Inaugurating the Convention, Subba Rao said that the language problem should be left to be solved by the coming generation and that the status quo should be maintained until a consensus solution was found. Subba Rao warned that any attempt "To force Hindi down the throats of unwilling people will certainly lead to the disintegration of the Country." "The best course", he said, "is to have the status quo and to continue English as the official language and also as the medium of instruction in colleges."

If Hindi was accepted as the official language, he felt the Official Languages Act ought to be amended to ensure that English was continued till all the States agreed to the change-over.

Subba Rao underlined that English must continue to be the sole language of the Supreme Court and the High Courts and that it should be the medium of instruction in professional colleges, research courses and post-graduate studies.

Continuing he said, "Replacing English by regional languages as a medium of instruction at the university level is a delicate and difficult task and its phasing and steps should be left entirely to expert educationists."

Subba Rao felt that the States should make sincere attempts to encourage scholars to conduct journals and write books on various subjects in the regional languages. It was not enough, he said, to have an idea; it must be pursued with vigour.

Opposing the three-language formula, Subba Rao said that "It worked unevenly on the people of different States, besides burdening the child with unnecessary languages at the expense of knowledge. The illogicality of the three-language formula imposition will be apparent if a person in a Hindi region is compelled to take one of the languages other than Hindi and English."

He stated, that "A boy with a flair for languages may learn many, but that is an unnecessary burden both to an average and also to a bright one who had no aptitude for languages."

At the University level, Subba Rao said, there must be bilinguism— English and the regional language, the first for professional colleges and for science subjects and the latter for the humanities. He continued that in the demand for the replacement of English by Hindi as the official language and for all other purposes he saw the only reason for the whipped-up agitation for a quick change-over was a sense of false prestige and an inferiority complex.

"This propaganda", he said, "may have had a sentimental appeal during our freedom struggle, but after Independence it has none. We must behave like a mature nation and enlightened self-interest, here or elsewhere, should be our guide." He added, "We must eschew the bad and retain the good, irrespective of its source, foreign or indigenous. English is one of such good things."

Pandit Hirdaynath Kunzru said that to a certain extent it might be true that education was best imparted through the mother-tongue, but education only had value if it brought the students in touch with the people and the world for which English was necessary. Even subjects like economics, politics and sociology could not be properly discussed in isolation from the rest of the world. Hirday-nath Kunzru said that the Union Education Minister, before he left for Moscow, stated that he was not against the retention of English at the University level. If Dr. Sen had mentioned this from the very beginning, they would have been spared the trouble of having this Convention. Dr. Kunzru said that the Convention should arouse the intelligentsia of the Country to the dangers of isolation from the world. They should stand up and prevent the Country

from reverting to a situation from which Raja Rammohan Roy had
rescued it 150 years ago. He reminded the Convention how Raja
Rammohan Roy had fought against the then existing system of education (1816) and demanded a liberal education in English.

I do not propose to reproduce my speech as I addressed the Convention for some considerable time. Among the main points made
by me was that, because of the political overtones and the increasing political pressure by the dominant Hindi bloc in Parliament, an
objective approach to educational problems and, indeed, to the
larger interests of the Country had become more and more difficult.
I said that the mother-tongue theory necessarily had an emotional
appeal, but in the context of a polyglot country it cannot have uniform significance or validity. Where over 350 million people cannot read or write a single language and where, according to a conservative estimate, there are 179 languages and 544 dialects, it is
unreal to talk of acquiring knowledge through the mother-tongue
which may be little more than a dialect and with not even the most
elementary primers or books in any discipline. I said that even
after the linguistic re-distribution of the States, the different regions
were anything but unilingual : the imposition of the regional languages as media would, therefore, mean denial of the mother-tongue
to millions of people.

I stated that for several millions of Indians, English is the language spoken in the home. At any one time there are between 4 and
5 million students studying through the medium of English from the
primary up to the university stage. This represented a very high
percentage of those who have the opportunity for education.

I underlined that there could be no rigidity about the mother-
tongue as the medium. This position was underlined by conditions
in States like Assam, Nagaland and the Hill-tribe areas where, in
order to make education meaningful, English had been adopted as
the medium of instruction not only for higher education but at the
school stage.

I said that English-medium schools represented the only all-
India system of secondary education in the Country. It is to these
institutions alone that the children of members of the armed forces
and government servants, who are liable to transfer, can look for
the continuity of their education.

I said that from the legal and constitutional position any Indian would have as much right to start an English-medium school as to start a Hindi-medium school. In fact, for several reasons, the right is stronger. Unlike Hindi, English gives access to the widest horizons of knowledge : unlike Hindi, English gives access to the highest reaches of professional and technical attainment : and, unlike Hindi, English is an all-India language with adequately trained teachers available everywhere to teach the different subjects through the medium of English.

I pointed out that, as held by the Supreme Court, English is as much an Indian language as any other language of the Country because it is the language of a recognised Indian minority, the Anglo-Indians. Recently, Nagaland affirmed its adoption of English as its official language, thus giving English parity with other regional languages. In a sense, English has a superior status in law to the regional languages in the VIIIth Schedule, because it is not only the associate official language but also the language of the Constitution, of the Supreme Court and High Courts and of authoritative legislation.

I mentioned that in any democracy, especially in India with its bewildering polyglot structure, liberty of thought and expression was the most precious of the fundamental rights. The parent has the fundamental right to determine the kind of education he wants for his child. It has been held by the Supreme Court that the child is not the creature of the State and that those who nurture him and direct his destiny have the right, coupled with the duty, to prepare him for his obligations in life. To preserve the secular concept, there are several provisions in the Constitution underlining the right of a child belonging to any language group to go to any institution either run or aided by the State, whatever the medium may be. One of the fundamental freedoms of our Constitution is that of speech and expression : freedom of expression would include the freedom to imbibe thought and culture through any medium. Any attempt by the Hindi chauvinists to discriminate against English would also offend Articles 14 and 16 of the Constitution which guarantee equality of treatment and opportunity.

I said that de facto English is the link language, today, in higher education. Hindi has, in fact, no place and can never have any place because of its complete lack of an elementary corpus of books and of knowledge. Given the option, even in the Hindi States the overwhelming number of students have opted for English at the University stage. English is, in fact, today the only all-India language, at any rate in higher education. Apart from being the only cement, administrative and judicial, it is par excellence the only bond of educational and, indeed, emotional integration.

On the second day of the Convention, Dr. C.D. Deshmukh, then Vice-Chancellor of the Delhi University and a former Chairman of the University Grants Commission, proposed the adoption of "Bhasha Bharati" written in the Roman script, suitably provided with additional diacritical marks and written in one tier instead of three to avoid wastage. Dr. Deshmukh said that the nation's interests demanded that they did not weaken the grasp of English which would be the only international language to help them achieve the delayed objective of developing their regional languages. Deshmukh said that English was the only adequate medium of communication at the intellectual level. Hindi could not be thought of in this context, being no better developed than the other regional languages, perhaps worse. In his view Hindi had not yet developed as an all-India language and the Country's interests required that English be continued as an associate language for an indefinite period both at the Central and the State levels.

Deshmukh felt that there was some truth in the almost universal proposition that the Indian languages had not yet developed a "literature of knowledge". It was surprising that despite significant works by scholars over the last 100 years, Indian languages had not produced a "literature of knowledge". India could not depend upon translations forever.

Rajaji, still going strong at 89, addressed the Convention at 4 p.m. on the second day. Rajaji cautioned that the battle against Hindi imposition would be a long one. He said that the battle would not be easy because the Central Government had secured a strong army behind it for its wrong policy. From his knowledge of people in the North, they would fight hard for Hindi.

Rajaji said that the fight should not be through direct action, but by exposition of the truth in the best manner. They could not fight the battle with hesitating steps. Rajaji wanted everyone to pledge to fight to keep English in its present position.

Rajaji said that those who had Hindi as their mother-tongue did not understand the full implications of what they were trying to do.

They thought that just as they learnt English, the Tamils could and would one day learn Hindi. But Hindi was a totally foreign language to the Tamils.

Rajaji reiterated that higher education in technology and the sciences should continue to be in English not only because English had attained international status, but because the whole country wanted it. He said to those who wanted the regional languages to be introduced, "By all means use them as far as you can. But do not object to English being the medium of instruction for higher studies and for the library."

Rajaji warned that making the regional languages the media of higher education would ruin the Country. India would cease to be one Country: it would become an archipelago of isolated islands in a turbulent ocean. He asked the politicians not to interfere with students, even as the latter should not interfere with politics.

Government Exercise In Illusion

On the 17th of July, 1968, the Cabinet was reported to have approved of a national policy statement on education. Much of the old wishful thinking, the pious and, indeed, dangerous illusions are to be found in this statement. Thus there is the illusory hope of a vigorous implementation of the three-language formula at the secondary stage. As I have mentioned earlier, one of the somersaults of Triguna Sen encouraged the Hindi States to adopt a one-language formula. In reply Tamil Nadu banished Hindi. In most of the States the three-language formula is largely a hypocritical, lip-service offering. In States like Mysore, a student may get a blob in Hindi as the second or the third language : it does not interfere in the least with the promotion or, indeed, the class secured. The Anglo-Indian schools are among the very few that honestly implement the three language formula. Not only the promotion but the grading, in the Anglo-Indian schools, depends on the marks secured in Hindi, if it is the second language.

The so-called national policy statement also contains the illusion of developing Hindi as the link language. There is the continuing failure to distinguish between Hindi as the official language and as the link language in higher education and in the higher judicial echelons. In spite of all the dangerous self-deception that dogs a Hindi-ridden Central Government, there is not the remotest possibility, in any foreseeable future, of Hindi ever being adopted by the non-Hindi States as the medium in higher education. The adoption of Hindi as the language of the High Courts is an equally wild illusion. The only glimmering of commonsense that appears through this statement is that, at least, the exercise in absurdity of prescribing a time-limit of 5 to 10 years, for the change-over to the regional languages as the media at the University stage, has been abandoned. There is the usual tongue-in-the-cheek offering to the need for continuing emphasis on the study of English. But no one in the Government seems to have either the courage, the vision or, indeed, the commonsense to state frankly that without the continuance of English as the medium in the higher reaches of education, especially in science, technology and research, India will leap back into the bullock-cart age, apart from disintegrating educationally, politically and emotionally.

Increasing Breach Of Faith

As I had anticipated, when characterising the amendment to the Official Languages Act and the accompanying resolution as a continuing travesty of the Nehru assurance, the Hindi fanatics in the Central Government and in the offices of the Central Ministries are going ahead with the progressive imposition of Hindi. I had pointed out in my speech in Parliament that the Act, despite the amendment, and more especially the resolution, contained all the instruments for the rapid and, indeed, blanket imposition of Hindi. That is now happening. According to a press report of the 7th October, 1968, the Government has issued to the various Ministries and Central organisations directives which ensure the progressive imposition of Hindi. Even the anaemic provision for a translation in English will not be operative where the staff concerned, both in the originating and the receiving Ministries, have acquired a working knowledge of Hindi. With typical tortuousness, a working knowledge of Hindi has been equated to a pass in Hindi at the matriculation examination or its Pragya equivalent in the Hindi teaching scheme, or in a departmental test.

Some of the peons in my office have done not only their Matriculation but Intermediate through Hindi. This ignorant, semi-illiterate type will now set the standards for drafting in the Central Administration.

With the fetish for fabricating statistics to show the alleged spread of Hindi, we can also expect a wholesale passing in the departmental tests of those who have not even reached the semi-illiterate standards of the Hindi Matriculate.

According to this latest exercise in Hindi imposition madness, the noter will not be asked to provide a translation. The difficulty will be for the really educated government servants to supply translations to the productions of these semi-illiterate neo-Hindi Matriculates and pseudo-Matriculates.

If this madness persists, it will not be long before the Central Administration, already snarled by almost chronic inefficiency, delay and red-tapism, sinks to the cesspool level of the average Corporation run through the medium of Hindi.

Apart from anything else, this race for Hindi imposition is a deliberate dishonouring of the repeated assurances of permanent bilingualism given to the deluded inferior citizens of Hindi India—the non-Hindi speaking majority, the new class of Untouchables.

Latest Bitter Fruit

On the 8th September, 1968, I addressed a meeting of the Heads of 30 Anglo-Indian Schools in the U.P. The Heads had met because they were perturbed over the recent prospectus issued by the Lucknow University.

This prospectus prescribes Hindi as the exclusive medium for the examination of 1971 onwards for the B.A. and B. Sc. (general classes) and from 1970 for the Faculty of Commerce.

Apparently a similar prospectus has been adopted by the other Universities in the U.P. For the linguistic minorities this step is the latest bitter fruit of Hindi Imperialism. It is a brazen, contemptuous violation of the Supreme Court decision of 1962 in the Gujarat University case to which I have already referred. The principal ratio handed down by the Supreme Court was that neither a State Legislature nor a University had the power to prescribe either Hindi or Gujarati as the exclusive medium and, therefore, a fortiori had no power to outlaw English. This decision of the U.P. also deliberately ignores the recommendations of the Sampurnanand Emotional Integration Committee and the Kothari Education Commission. A reference has already been made to these recommendations. The Sampurnanand Emotional Integration Committee had, among other things, recommended that English would have to be at least the additional medium to prevent academic fragmentation and to maintain intellectual and, indeed, emotional integration.

The Kothari Education Commission has, among other things, recommended that in the All-India Institutes, major universities and colleges in the metropolitan areas English will have to continue as the medium to ensure the mobility of students and teachers and the maintenance of standards.

In the U.P. where approximately 70,000 students are in the English-medium schools, nearly 2000 pass out of these schools each year and the majority seek entry into the U.P. Universities. There are also several colleges which have English as the medium of education.

Apart from being flagrantly illegal and unconstitutional, this latest expression of Hindi chauvinism strikes a vicious blow at the linguistic minorities whose mother-tongue is other than Hindi. It will make it impossible for parents from other States residing in the U.P. to educate their children in the State. Apart from anything else, this policy is a deliberate dishonouring of the Nehru formula of bilingualism.

The Hindi States are already the most backward in the Country, having the highest incidence of illiteracy and the lowest incidence of performance in any field. This latest exercise in obscurantism will ensure that the Hindi States will fall further into the rear. The students, already backward, will be cut off from institutions that give access to the highest reaches of attainment in science, technology and research. In fact students from the U.P. will now be confined to a frog-in-the-well existence in their own State. Few, if any, of them will be employable in trade or industry outside the U.P.

Fallacies Of Hindi Imperialism

The Hindi Imperialists have perpetrated many fallacies in their attempts to justify the blanket imposition of Hindi. The most familiar argument is that it is repugnant to the self-respect of the Country to have a foreign language as the national language. In the first place, the Hindi chauvinists have increasingly perverted the position that was given to Hindi in the Constitution. Although the language issue was not a live issue during the framing of the Constitution, there was considerable opposition to Hindi being accorded the place even of the official language.   This opposition was especially marked in the Congress Party itself where the decision to make Hindi the Official language just scraped through.

In any event, the framers of the Constitution deliberately scouted the idea of Hindi being the national language.   It was realised that in the bewildering multilingual Indian context, there could not be a single national language   especially as many of the other Indian languages, such as Tamil and Bengali, were much older, much richer and infinitely better developed than Hindi.   All that was intended under the Constitution was to have an official language which would be used for official purposes of the Union and for certain limited purposes, such as Inter-State communication.

But having got Hindi into the Constitution as the official language, the appetite of the Hindi chauvinists has grown with feeding.   Immediately they set up the cry of the Rashtriya Bhasha, that is, the national language, which was never contemplated by the Constitution.   In their efforts to mollify the other principal regional languages, the device of referring to the languages in the VIIIth Schedule as national languages was adopted.   It was conveniently forgotten that once the designation of national was adopted in respect of languages, it would necessarily postulate that the regions in which these are current represent a congeries of national entities.   Once Hindi could be described as the national language, it would immediately give a handle to the Hindi chauvinists, at the Centre and the Hindi States, to seek to impose Hindi on the Country in all the connotations of the word national.

There is a vast difference between an official and a national language.   Several countries while having their respective national languages have, for many reasons, accepted English as their official language.   Thus, Ghana has both a national language and English as the official language.   The fiercely proud Irish, despite their bitter and bloody struggle with the British, made English their official language and Gaelic the national language.

There is not the remotest whisper of a suggestion in the Constitution that Hindi should be the link language in higher education.   It is not the link language in higher education even in the Hindi States.   Deliberately, the Constitution had excluded Hindi as the link language in the judicial sphere.   Thus, Article 348 draws a clear distinction between Hindi as the official language and the language to be used in the judgments of the Supreme Court and the High Courts, in their proceedings, and as the authoritative texts of bills, acts, and of all orders, rules, regulations and bye-laws. There is no prescription of time, as regards the use of English and there is no hint of Hindi being the language of the Supreme Court and the High Courts or supplying the authoritative texts in respect of legislation at the Centre and in the States. Article 348 (3) goes even further : it provides that even where the Legislature of a State has prescribed any language other than the English language for use in Bills introduced in or Acts passed by the Legislature of the State or in Ordinances promulgated by the Governor or in any order, rule, regulation or bye-law issued under the Constitution by the Legislature, a translation in the English language of the same shall be deemed to be the authoritative text thereof. This was an inevitable corollary to the position recognised by the framers of the Constitution, that an amorphous, undeveloped language, like Hindi, without any scientific or legal vocabulary just could not be drawn upon to supply the authoritative text for legislation.

The position with regard to institutions of higher education and research and the scientific and technical institutions has also been settled by the Supreme Court in the Gujarat University case already referred to. The co-ordination and determination of standards in these institutions is vested exclusively in Parliament, under entry 66 of List 1, that is, the Union List. The sole instrument of co-ordination is the English language. The Supreme Court recognised this in the Gujarat University case and struck down the attempt by the Legislature and the University of Gujarat to introduce either Hindi or Gujarati as the exclusive medium. In the Supreme Court decision there is the explicit recognition of the fact that the maintenance and co-ordination of standards in higher education can be achieved only through the English language.

Hindi More Foreign Than English

While trying to stigmatise English as a foreign language, the Hindi fanatics have forgotten that in the non-Hindi speaking regions, especially in States like Tamil Nadu, Hindi is infinitely more foreign than English. As a result of 200 years of acclimatization English has permeated evenly not only the educated but the uneducated pattern. The Hindi obscurantists have yet to learn the elementary fact that a language has no nationality : it belongs to the people who use it and have made it their own. English has become part of the warp and woof of the texture of Indian thought, education and, indeed, culture. The Supreme Court has now placed its imprimatur on the position that English is as much an Indian language as any other of the languages of India, as it is the language of a recognised minority, the Anglo-Indians. In fact, English has a position superior to any of the languages mentioned in the VIIIth Schedule because, as I have already mentioned, it is the language of the Constitution, the language of the Supreme Court and the High Courts, and the language of authoritative legislation.

Since English was adopted by Nagaland, in September, 1967, as its official language, English has also become a regional language, a position not occupied by several of the languages included in the VIIIth Schedule.

At any one time there are between 4 and 5 million students pursuing their education through the medium of English from the primary to the university stage. As I mentioned in one of my speeches in Parliament, the total number of literates in Hindi, throughout the Hindi area, is barely 3 million. In spite of the fact that the linguistic census is usually doctored in order to project an exaggerated image in favour of Hindi, the 1961 Census shows that English is the most largely known second language. More than 11 million have shown English as their second language, whereas barely 9 million were listed with Hindi as their subsidiary language : this was in spite of the fact that Hindi was enforced as a compulsory second language in many of the non-Hindi States.

English is not only an Indian language but a world language which, unlike Hindi, gives access to the world horizons of knowledge, progress and achievement. It was through English that Indians became aware of their history. It was, in fact, through English that India achieved both an intellectual and educational renaissance. It was contact with the English language that imparted to Indian leaders and thinkers the spirit of freedom and liberty that informs British history and literature. It was the English language that enabled the leaders of Indian thought and action to meet together and forge policies and programmes for unity of action and for achieving freedom. It was through the English language that Indian writers were able to interpret not only the ethos of India's freedom movement but the Indian ethos to the outside world. It was through English that India jumped from mediaevalism into the modern age.

As observed by Prof. Pandit, Head of the Department of Linguistics of the Delhi University, "This notion of language rivalry—unless the richer language disappears, the poorer one will not 'get a chance'—has clouded much of our thinking on language. Our goal in the education system should be not to remove English from the system but to ensure that once a discourse in Indian languages begins, it will gain momentum only by interaction with English. Knowledge of English and not its absence is a precondition for the development of Indian languages." Prof. Pandit further observes, "Our languages, which had only a belles-lettres tradition and which did not have any traditions of scientific and serious prose, have acquired newer expressions and traditions under the constant influence of bilingualism with English. This is a major factor in the 'development' of Indian languages. This could happen because we have had genuine bilingual authors and speakers like Mahatma Gandhi, Tagore, Rajaji and almost all the late 19th century members of our intelligentsia, who believed in sharing their experience with the people by way of an autobiography or diary if nothing else."

Greatest Canard

Not only one of the greatest fallacies, but one of the greatest canards perpetrated in Republican India is that 42 per cent of the people are Hindi-speaking. This is a deliberate fabrication. The 1951 census was obviously inflated to give a deliberately false picture. That census shamelessly included the figures for no less than 77 languages and dialects which had nothing to do with Hindi. Thus the figure for Urdu, Punjabi, Rajasthani and a host of other languages and dialects had been falsely included in the Hindi census. Equally, the 1951 census had been doctored to deflate the number of the English-speaking persons : only those were included whose mother-tongue was English so that there was the egregious figure of 171,000 shown as English-speaking. This did not even represent the number of Anglo-Indians whose mother-tongue is English. At any one time there are about 4 to 5 million students studying through the medium of English. Yet deliberately the

1951 census was fabricated to exclude all these people even as English-knowing.

No Tradition

Even in the Hindi States barely half per cent of the population understand the new Hindi with its artificial monstrosities and re-surrections from a dust-bin of dead words created by self-styled literati and self-appointed lexicographers in their frenetic attempts to enlarge the poverty-stricken Hindi vocabulary. As pointed out by Dr. Suniti Kumar Chatterjee, the famous Indologist, the Hindi sought to be evolved today is 'Khari Boli Hindi' which had no existence prior to 1850. As pointed out by another distinguished Indian, Hindi has no political or administrative tradition. Through out Indian history it has never been the language of a State because there has never been a Hindi State. Today, the Hindi chauvinists are seeking, artificially, to create a Hindi language and a also Hindi Empire of their dreams. It is a delirious illusion of the Hindi Im-perialists that the non-Hindi speaking people, especially the Tamils and Bengalis with their ancient, rich literary traditions and with their highly developed, dynamic languages, will ever enthuse over a new, undeveloped foreign language sought to be imposed on them.

Instrument Of Isolation

Another fallacy of Hindi Imperialism is that Hindi is an instru-ment of mass contact. The official language of a multilingual Country and especially of the Central Government can never be an instrument of mass contact with the people throughout the Country. The regional languages alone can, in their respective areas, be such instruments. Even in the Hindi-speaking States the new Hindi is unintelligible to the masses. In any case it is pretentious nonsense to talk of Hindi as a mass medium where over 350 million people cannot read or write a single language in a country which accord-ing to a conservative estimate has 179 languages and 544 dialects and patois. The new artificial Hindi is a supreme instrument of isolation.

Hindi is, in fact, an undeveloped regional language. The Hindi region is, in fact, a fraction of the Country and tucked away in one part. Hindi Imperialism means not only the imposition of the language of a small minority but also the imposition of an undeve-loped regional language.

Hindi Imperialism's Many Undesirable Symbols

Hindi Imperialism is a symbol of many undesirable features. In Northern India Hindi is unashamedly identified with religion. Thus the revivalists in the North are not interested only in the language but also in the imposition of their script. In the final analysis the genius and the spirit of a language have very little to do with the script. Yet the recommendation of the University Grants Commission and of the Sampurnanand Emotional Integration Committee that the non-Hindi speaking people should be encouraged to learn Hindi through the Roman script is bitterly opposed. The motive is entirely religious. According to the North Indian revivalists the Devanagari script is identified with the religion of a particular section of the people, with their Shastras.

For the linguistic minorities, Hindi Imperialism is a supreme symbol of oppression. The unashamed battle-cry of a well-known Hindi Imperialist movement is, "Hindi, Hindu, Hindustan, nahi rahege Sikh, Esai na Mussalman", meaning "Hindi, Hindu, Hindustan, nor shall there be Sikhs, Christians or Mussalmans."

Discrimination

Hindi Imperialism is the symbol, par excellence, of discrimination. It is a symbol of the denial of equality of opportunity. It is significant that the Hindi-speaking States are the most backward in every respect. They have the highest incidence of illiteracy: 90 per cent of the women and 80 per cent of the men are illiterate. As I have already mentioned, there are barely 3 million literates in the whole Hindi area. In the superior service competitions, candidates from the Hindi-speaking States make a pathetic showing. Because of the lack of a corpus of books and of knowledge in Hindi, graduates in Hindi emerge as pitiful ignoramuses.

One of the principal objectives of Hindi Imperialism is to open the service floodgates to the educationally backward elements in the Hindi-speaking States. The Hindi bloc is putting unremitting pressure on the Government to have Hindi as the alternative medium for entry into the different services. A device suggested by the Hindi zealots to mislead the non-Hindi speaking section is the quota system for recruitment. If this ever materialises, it will mean for the Hindi States the largest intake in the services. They have the largest number of illiterates. As mentioned in one of my speeches, whereas at present barely 2 to 3 per cent of the Hindi elements qualify in open competition for the Central services, on a quota system based on the counting of illiterate heads, they will insist on getting at least 40 per cent.

In another sense also Hindi is a symbol of discrimination. Today, the Central Government is committed to rapidly increasing expenditure of crores of rupees for the so-called advancement of Hindi. It is difficult to understand why the money of the non-Hindi speaking taxpayers should be wasted in trying to develop, by a process of artificial respiration, an undeveloped language. If the Hindi zealots are so desperately anxious to advance their language at least they should be prepared to meet the bill themselves.

Destruction Of Pillars Of Integration

Hindi Imperialism, today, is the symbol of the destruction of national integration. The stark, if unpleasant, fact is that before the British regime the history of India was a history of tribalisms. As an eminent Indian has written, while there was a sense of Indianness there was never really a sense of Indian nationality. It was for the first time during the British regime that India achieved political, administrative and, indeed, emotional integration. There were three main pillars of national integration. The instrument of integration in higher education was the English language. Administrative integration was achieved through the All-India services trained through the English language and taught to regard India as a single integrated entity. One of the most important pillars was an integrated judiciary, especially in the higher echelons, the instrument of integration being, again, the English language.

Under the impact of policies precipitated by Hindi Imperialism, all these pillars today are steadily crumbling. If under pressure from the dominant Hindi bloc the Central Government accepts the the suicidal formula of having a multiplicity of media for recruitment to the Central services, overnight any pretence of an integrated administration will disappear. There can never be a semblance of standardisation in marking and in the moderation of answer papers as between languages completely disparate in their content and development. The introduction of such a formula must lead inevitably to the regionalisation of the so-called All-India services and the destruction of whatever capacity they have at present to maintain an integrated administration, conditioned by an all-India outlook. In the glib proposals, the snap decisions that emerge as policy a crucial; issue is usually forgotten. What will be the medium in the training institutions? The oblique motive of the Hindi Imperialists would appear to be that once they are able to fragment recruitment on the basis of regional languages, they will be able to insist that training institutions should be conducted through the medium of Hindi. This again is the wildest of self-deception: the Tamils, the Bengalis and others will not accept being trained through the medium of Hindi. Recognising this vital fact the Parliamentary Languages Committee underlined that in the training institutions the medium of entry may be a regional language but English would have to continue as the medium in the training for the Armed Forces and the Central services. If the Hindi bloc is able to browbeat the Central Government into having two streams of training, one in English the other in Hindi, the results will not only be absurd but disastrous. There will be two streams of trainees for the All-India services: the basis will be laid at least for dividing India into two increasingly watertight and hostile service compartments.

One of the illusory recommendations of the Parliamentary Language Committee was that, ultimately, Hindi should be the language not only of the Supreme Court but of the High Courts. Here again, it was a case of the Imperialist wishful thinking having gone mad. It is the most delirious form of self-deception to imagine that if English is displaced Hindi will ever be accepted as the language of the non-Hindi speaking High Courts. It is an even more delirious form of self-deception to hope that Hindi can ever, at any time, become the language of the Supreme Court. Legal interpretation and precedent have hardened over a period of many generations around not only the shades of meaning of a single word, such as, 'may' or 'shall', but around nuances of shades of meaning. It is anyone's guess as how many aeons of time it would take for such legal interpretation and precedent to harden around the new, amorphous, undeveloped Hindi. The present world horizons of law and jurisprudence accessible to Indian lawyers and judges through English would be constricted to the horizons of the judgments of the former High Court of Madhya Bharat. Overnight one of the greatest pillars of national integration, the whole unified legal and judicial fabric, would be perverted and destroyed.

Already, although Hindi cannot be the language for judgments and orders in the High Courts, in the Hindi States some of the High Courts have the records printed largely in Hindi. The result for the litigants from these States has been disastrous. The average cost of translating a single page of a Hindi record into English for the purpose of the Supreme Court record is from Rs. 6 to 7. With the smallest record running into anything between 200 and 500 pages the cost of translation from Hindi to English runs into several thousands of rupees. This is apart from the usual cost of printing or cyclostyling the record, which is also appreciable, but nothing compared to the cost of translation. As a practising lawyer in the Supreme Court, I am aware that because of this new prohibitive burden of translation from Hindi to English many litigants, who would like to make a last attempt to secure their freedom through the Supreme Court, have found it impossible to do so. Because of this mad rush to impose Hindi, the poor average person seeking justice is now virtually prohibited from approaching the highest Court in the land. Up till now if a record had to be translated it was done at the district court level when the case was processed to the High Court. At that stage the translation costs are very much less than in the Supreme Court.

Symbol Of Retrogression

The Hindi chauvinists should deserve before they desire. Even the Hindi-speaking States have been unable to make any real progress in the use of Hindi. Thus the U.P. Government, after spending about 30 lakhs of rupees in the preparation of Hindi textbooks for certain purposes, had to scrap them. Even the Hindi alphabet has not yet been finalised : that used in Bombay is different from the alphabet used in the U.P. Giving evidence before the Language Commission, politicians from Eastern U.P. complained that they were unable to understand the Hindi of Western U.P. Persons associated with education are up against the supreme difficulty of determining what is the content of Hindi which varies from one Hindi State to another.

As I have already said, 90 per cent of the women and 80 per cent of the men in the Hindi States are illiterate. There are barely 3 million literates in the whole Hindi area. It has become a familiar device for the Hindi zealots to rant against English as the reason for the falling standards in education. And yet it is common knowledge that even the poorest parents shy away from the schools run through the medium of Hindi because most of them are regarded as cesspools of inefficiency and indiscipline and often of incorrigible corruption. The same sad story is to be found in most of the Universities in the Hindi States.

The University Inquiry Commission in its report submitted to the Government of Bihar, stated that things were, "Really unspeakably bad in Bihar University." The report continued, "The rot has run deep, very deep. There are casteism and factionalism, excessive litigation and violence in words and thought and deed and every kind of imaginable mudslinging. It is no longer a university."

The report further stated, "There is no peace in its cloisters, no spiritual and intellectual tranquility, no gleam of ideals, no striving after learning, no desire to follow knowledge. It is a maelstrom of violent destructive forces, a place of unrelieved darkness." A similar deep malaise was uncovered in Benares and Lucknow. In respect of the Benares University a Commission reported that there was widespread corruption and even moral turpitude in that campus. It is significant that this condition of increasing degeneration is to be found especially in Universities in the North where the medium is largely Hindi. Fortunately, this all-round degeneration is relatively absent from the Universities in the South, especially in Tamil Nadu, where the medium still remains largely English. In fact, it is the English-medium institutions, both the schools and the colleges, which stand out as beacons of hope in the widening morass of educational degeneration, indiscipline and even corruption that represent the conditions in many of the Hindi-medium institutions.

In an expansive mood, Jawaharlal Nehru felt constrained to observe that the general backwardness of the Hindi States was a reflection of the backwardness of the language.

Today Hindi is the supreme symbol of retrogression in the Country. At least several centuries behind the other major Indian langages both in content and development, Hindi imposition will mean putting the Country back not into the 18th century, as observed by Triguna Sen in one of his lucid moments, but back to the bullock-cart-cum-cowdung age.

Symbol Of Neo-Imperialism

Like all neo-Imperialisms the appetite of Hindi Imperialism has grown with feeding. The Hindi Imperialists are impervious to facts, logic and all considerations of the Country's unity and progress. Enjoying unchallenged political dominance at the Centre they are in full-throated, fanatical cry. No one is free from their insults and their antics. Whether it is the President of India, the Governor of a State, if they are not Hindi-speaking they are subjected to every expression of obscurantism, arrogance and downright uncouthness.

The Constitution contemplated Hindi as nothing more than an official language. There was never the remotest suggestion of Hindi being the national language or the link language in education. From the official language the Hindi zealots have sought to upgrade Hindi to the Rashtriya Bhasha, that is, the national language—a status which was never conferred by the Constitution.

The latest attempt of the Hindi chauvinists is to make Hindi into the Raj Bhasha, that is, the Ruling language. Without intending it, they have uncovered their motive of seeking to make not only Hindi the Ruling Language but the Hindi-speaking people the new Ruling Race—the Hindi Herrenvolk.

Unity Of India In The Balance

I am gravely perturbed by the helplessness of the Central Government to prevent the Country being precipitated into disintegration. Practically alone in Parliament, I stood out against the tragic, historic blunder of the linguistic redistribution of the States. On that issue no one could accuse me of any personal motive. I was merely fearful of the tragic consequences for the Country of linguistic reorganisation. What I had foretold in Parliament and outside has proved tragically prophetic. On the language issue, inevitably, because English is my mother-tongue and the mother-tongue of my Community, I am emotionally involved. Yet while in my humble way I have done my utmost to resist the Juggernaut of Hindi neo-Imperialism, I have tried to preserve a minimum sense of objectivity. In my capacity as Chairman of the Council for the Indian School Certificate Examination and Chairman of the Inter-State Board for Anglo-Indian Education, I have insisted that wherever possible Hindi should be the second language in Anglo-Indian schools. I have insisted on a steady upgrading of the standards of

Hindi instruction in the English-medium schools. I have expressed my deep distress at the fact that Hindi has been banished from Tamil Nadu and the Anglo-Indian schools prohibited from teaching it as a second language. What is required today is not only statesmanship but, above all, courage. Tragically, politics is the dominant, often the sole, consideration. Those who command the largest number of votes and have the largest political influence are able to stampede the Government into policies that are obviously not only retrogressive but irrevocably disastrous for the Country. The obvious motive of the Hindi Imperialists is to destroy English, to extirpate it from the language pattern of the Country. Everything they say and do is directed to this purpose. Playing politics first, even the front-rank leaders succumb to dictation by the Hindi bloc, to acceptance of policies that must spell dissolution of what remains of national integration.

It should be obvious to the meanest intelligence that if English is effaced, inevitably, because Hindi can never and will never take its place in higher education, in the training of the administrative services, in the higher reaches of the judiciary, there will be a vacuum, which can be filled only by chaos in education and certain national disintegration. Linguistic redistribution of the States was the first major nail in the coffin of India's integration. If the Central Government, from motives of political opportunism or sheer moral cowardice, succumbs to the obvious pressures of the Hindi Imperialists, the final nail in the coffin of India's integration will have been struck. No one will then be able to prevent educational, linguistic, emotional and political balkanization. Honesty, if not courage, should make the leaders realise that English is the last remaining bond of what is left of educational, administrative and judicial integration. Destroy it, as the Hindi Imperialists wish, and India will become merely a geographical name, not even a united nations. The unity of India today hangs precariously in the balance. Given the premise of continuing democratic viability, India's unity hangs by the bond of English.

CHAPTER XII

THE SOCIAL AND THE PSYCHOLOGICAL PATTERN

Life-Line Of The Community

FROM Beverley Nichols to Nirad Chaudhuri much ignorantly presumptuous, even malicious, nonsense has been written about the Anglo-Indian Community, especially about its alleged psychological inhibitions. No one who is not close to the Community, who is not aware of its social stratification, the educational and social matrix from which it has emerged can pretend to pontificate about its attitudes whatever unctions he may apply to his shallow, meretricious writing.

Broadly, the Community falls into three classes, namely, an upper-middle class, a lower-middle class and what may be described as the lowest stratum, but not in a derogatory sense. This stratification depends also on the period of which a person may be writing.

The pattern of work and service in the Community has changed at certain periods of its history. In the upper-middle class I would place those in business, the professions, officers in the defence and civil services and some of the Anglo-Indian planters and gentlemen farmers. The lower-middle class is largely made up of subordinates in the Railways, Telegraphs and Customs. With the decrease in the number of Anglo-Indians entering these services the lower-middle class consists, today, mostly of members working in business firms in a subordinate capacity, teachers in the lower categories, members working in Embassies in a subordinate capacity. The lowest class in the Community consists not only of the unemployed but also the under-employed. The class structure of the Community however, is not a hide-bound caste structure. There is vertical mobility. Sons of subordinate Government servants, having been given the necessary opportunities by their parents, enter the superior services, the officer-cadres of the Armed Forces, and thus move into the upper-middle stratum of the Community.

Girls from the lower-middle class of the Community have often married the best placed Anglo-Indians and, indeed, often the best placed European officials and businessmen. The girls of the Community, in fact, have shown, to whatever stratum they belong, a tendency to greater refinement and greater response to opportunities than their brothers. Perhaps this is true of any community. In my close association with schools such as the Frank Anthony Public School, New Delhi, which is a co-educational institution and has a large number of Hindu children from the best families, I have noticed that the sisters are usually more refined and better behaved than their brash brothers who often make a fetish of even crude behaviour.

Inevitably, perhaps, the Anglo-Indian social pattern has been conditioned by the larger pattern surrounding it. Thus in what may be described as the pre-Mutiny period there was the freest of social intercourse between Anglo-Indians and members of other communities. That was also largely true of the British. Before the Mutiny the social pattern was less subject to definition or, indeed, regulation than in later years. During the 18th century no artificial or warped imperial code had been imposed on British social life. Before the opening of the Suez Canal, British officers, civilian and military, almost invariably looked for their brides among the Anglo-Indian Community. There was also intermarriage between British and Indian families at the highest level. After the opening of the Suez Canal and more especially after the Mutiny, the pattern changed radically. The influx of British women made a profound impact. For practically all these women India was an avowed marriage market. Arriving in India they found serious competition from the Anglo-Indians. By and large, Anglo-Indian women were more attractive than their British competitors. The Anglo-Indian women had the small bone structure and the general petite physical make-up of the East, to which their colouring imparted a vitality and distinctiveness which recalled the beauty of Greece and Syria. Apart from the blonde Nordic types, auburn, light brown or dark hair accentuating liquid brown or flashing green eyes set in clear, soft features of burnished wheat or gold made an ensemble which has inspired not a little lyricised writing even among European commentators.

Coming to a society in which British men freely married Anglo-Indian girls, the British women evolved an insidious, almost viciously malicious, social code directed to the elimination of this competition. It was a tribute to the astuteness of the British women's instinct and their capacity for self-preservation in the marriage market, that a wall of social exclusiveness was drawn increasingly around British society. The British clubs grew in numbers and a rigid social code was enforced. Members of other communities including Anglo-Indians were squeezed out. After that in the British clubs, military or civilian, entry was virtually impossible. There were stray exceptions of Maharajas or highly placed Hindu or Anglo-Indian officials entering these clubs, but these were consigned to the position of the proverbial social fish-out-of-water.

The social barriers continued to grow higher. All manner of nuances were evolved even among the British. Among those admitted to meet a British official and his wife in their home there were careful gradations. The least acceptable socially were invited to tea : the next in the social hierarchy among the non-British communities would be invited to cocktails : dinner was usually the preserve of the British officials inter se. The extent to which this social pattern permeated British society was demonstrated by the fact that even the British clergy were hide-bound by it. The average Garrison Chaplain attached to a British cantonment was as much a creature of social prejudice as the most dyed-in-the-wool British official.

In the mofussil areas where clubs existed the social barriers were less rigid. Because of the smallness of the British population officers from all communities were usually admitted to the local 'burra' club. But once the British officers migrated to cities or metropolitan centres they fell into the more rigid British pattern. Indian officers who had access to the 'burra' club in the mofussil were rigorously excluded from the British 'burra' clubs in the larger towns and cities.

Two marked consequences flowed from this pattern which crystallized after the Mutiny. The average British officer, although often dedicated to his work, was essentially not only a sojourner but a stranger in India. Those who worked in the districts, inevitably came into official contact with the different sections of the people : but there was no social contact with the middle or the lower-middle classes. The British official knew nothing really of their home life, their habits and their attitudes.

The British women were even in a more insular position. Their contact with India was, usually, confined to the servant class. Their knowledge of India and things Indian was drawn largely from their observation of the servant class. The average British woman gloried in this artificial exclusiveness.

Second-class Britons, such as counter-jumpers in firms in Calcutta and the so-called Domiciled Europeans, were as rigidly excluded from the 'burra' clubs as members of any other community. The British members of subordinate rank in the gun-carriage factories—even the officers—and warrant officers in the Army were banned. These usually had their own clubs or institutes. The Anglo-Indians, except for a few officials, were subject to the same ban.

In Calcutta, the large commercial community practised social exclusiveness in an even more twisted way than the British officials. The 'burra' sahibs of Clive Street had their own social code. British commercial life was rigorously graded. Only those who were above the shop-assistant class could enter the clubs. Highly placed Britons, especially Scotsmen in the jute trade who married beautiful and cultured Anglo-Indian girls, were often compelled to resign their posts.

Some Anglo-Indians slipped into the 'burra' clubs but, usually, they did so only by masquerading as Europeans. They lived in constant fear of the discovery of their real position. I remember meeting a school contemporary of mine at a lunch with the then British Governor of Bengal—that was in pre-Independence days. The Anglo-Indian was a member of the Governor's European cricket eleven. When I casually referred to our school days he suddenly suffered from an attack of amnesia. I felt sorry for him: he was a fair Anglo-Indian but yet very much an Anglo-Indian. As long as the masquerade succeeded these Anglo-Indians enjoyed the premium placed on membership of the 'burra' club.

Some Anglo-Indians, however, despite their Anglo-Indian pigmentation, became members of the 'burra' clubs because of their official position, but they were never really at home. The men perhaps got on well enough, but the women were in an invidious position. The British women pursued their social snobbery with a certain feline deadliness. Thus not only Anglo-Indian women but

British women married to Anglo-Indians who happened to be members of the 'burra' club were usually the pointed targets not only of snobbery but of every refinement of feminine vengefulness. Some of them put a brave face on it, such as the Anglo-Indian manager of a well-known bank, whom I knew. An Oxonian who had won his tennis Blue, he had married a very charming British woman. Both his wife and Anglo-Indian mother were obviously unhappy in the club.

I recall the case of a very handsome British member of the I.C.S. who married a lovely Anglo-Indian girl. She was what in those days was referred to as a Domiciled European. With blonde hair, blue eyes and a soft complexion, she was easily the most beautiful woman in the club in question. The young Britisher was first asked to break his engagement; when he refused and married he was transferred, sent in fact into official Coventry.

I also remember the case of a British Colonel of the I.M.S. who had married a very charming, cultured Anglo-Indian woman. Their daughter, who had been educated in England, was the target of much venom among the British wives. When she married a British Artillery officer the malicious gossip was that an impecunious Artillery officer had married 'half an Indian'. Among those who purported to sit in judgment were at least a couple of British women whom I knew to have been servants in the U.K. Their marriages had been of the shot-gun variety. The husbands had been compelled by irate parents of the women in question to marry because of pre-marital complications.

Two incidents which happened in one of the 'burra' clubs in Calcutta highlighted the racist and colour antics that had been institutionalised as part of the twisted British social system.

A well-placed British businessman had married a really beautiful, talented Anglo-Indian girl. Although of the blonde variety she never tried to hide the fact that she was an Anglo-Indian. After the marriage her husband persuaded her to apply for membership of the 'burra' club. The blimps on the committee, many of whom were very much of the lower-middle class, even declasse variety in the U.K. but had constituted themselves into a self-appointed aristocracy in Calcutta, had apparently heard that the wife was an Anglo-Indian. She was asked to interview the committee. Her husband told her that the interview was merely a matter of routine, as the committee wanted to make certain that she looked like a European.

The wife kept her counsel. When she arrived the members of the committee were rather dumbfounded by her good looks. Indeed, some of them fell over one another to tell her that they would not have bothered her but the rules required an interview and that she was very welcome as a member. The young wife, however, coldly declined the honour, adding as a parting shot that, apart from her face which was obviously as white as any of theirs, she could assure them that her 'behind' was infinitely whiter. There was another incident of a British military officer married to an Anglo-Indian. After having met the committee, the wife had it conveyed, through her husband, that after she had inspected the committee she had no desire to join the club.

This kind of snobbery projected itself in varying degrees into the Anglo-Indian social milieu. Usually the better-placed Anglo-Indians, who happened to belong to a 'burra' club, would not join the clubs which were patronised even by well-placed members of the Community. Some of the Anglo-Indian wives were as "uppish" as the most upstart of British women. Even the wives of the members of the Indian Medical Department (British Cadre) considered it "infra dig" to go to social functions at the Railway Institute. Because the husbands could rise in the Department, which was reserved for Anglo-Indians, to the rank of Major, the wives felt that they were in the upper social swim.

There were several clubs in the larger towns and cities patronised by better-placed Anglo-Indians, civilian or professional men. To these clubs also went the so-called second-class British officers, those in the gun-carriage factories, warrant officers of the I.U.L. (Indian Unattached List) such as the Ordnance and the Signals and also many British officers who had risen from the ranks. In these clubs there was complete fraternization and no suggestion of any race or colour prejudice.

The Railway Institute

Anglo-Indian Railway Institutes occupy a special niche in the Anglo-Indian social scheme. The Senior Institute, the 'Inster' as it was called, was usually the preserve of the Community especially where they were employed in large numbers. These Institutes were to be found right down the line on every railway. The Institutes were usually well-off financially and provided plenty of social amenities including tennis, billiards and, of course, regular dances. For the upper subordinates including the Class II and some Class I officers who had risen from subordinate positions, and the Class III staff from station masters and loco foremen down to guards and firemen—these Institutes were the centres of their social life.

Many of these Institutes were household names in the Community, such as the Burt Institute, Lahore, the Ajmer Institute, the Kharagpur Institute and a score of others. They usually had a very fine boarded dance floor, an excellent bar and at least one super-band. The amenities, including tennis, billiards and swimming were as good as those in some of the 'burra' clubs.

Much ignorant nonsense has been written about social life at the Railway Institutes. As in any club patronised by people who have what may be described as an Anglicised way of life, there was drinking and a sense of fun.

Anglo-Indian railwaymen were in the front rank of sport in the Country. Because of the opportunities at the Institutes they produced some of the finest tennis and billiard players in the Country.

The social functions at an Institute, especially the dances, were marked by a warmth and sense of fun that characterise the Community. The smallest Railway Institute could produce a string band as good as some of the finest professional bands. Dances were punctuated by solos or duets or quartets. The smallest Institute produced not one but several girls with really attractive voices: the men also could produce their share of good singing. And, of course, the Railway Institute dance continued till the small and, not seldom, till the large hours of the morning.

It is not surprising that with so much musical talent we find, today, Anglo-Indians among the top pop singers in the world. To mention a few—Cliff Richards (formerly Harry Webb) of Lucknow, Tony Brent (formerly Reginald Bretagne) of Deolali, Engelbert Humperdinck (formerly Gerald Dorsey) of Madras, Eden Kane the son of Bert Sarstedt who was a senior Anglo-Indian official on the railway.

John Mayer, whose elder brother is working as the Headmaster of the Frank Anthony Public School, New Delhi, has achieved not a little fame in his ambition to build a bridge between the two art forms he loves—Indian and European music. Mayer won a scholarship to Britain's Royal Academy of Music.

At the age of eight he began to study the violin under Phillipe

Sandre. He wrote his first composition for strings when he was eleven. At fourteen he was a professional musician : at the same time he pursued an intense study of Indian music.

After going to Britain, Mayer studied at the Royal Academy. He was first, a violinist with the London Philharmonic Orchestra, then with the Royal Philharmonic Orchestra and, finally, with the B.B.C. Symphony Orchestra. He has played under most of the great European conductors. In his spare time while living in South London, Mayer has created 40 odd compositions that have won him a steadily growing reputation. He is described as being formidably erudite and utterly the dedicated artist.

In the July 1929 issue of our journal there is a reference to Madame Adelina Deefolts, the wife of C.J. Deefolts, an Anglo-Indian official in the Telegraph Department. She had a distinguished musical career and was known as the 'Nightingale of the East'. She had a twelve-month course under Hugh Marleyn, London's famous voice specialist, of the Royal Opera, Covent Garden, Ballad and Oratorio fame. She understudied the great soprano Elia Stralia, who took the leading part in the production of 'Elijah' at Queen's Hall. While in London, she gained two certificates of merit, sang before some of the greatest London critics and earned flattering encomia from all who heard her. Madame Alice Gomes was referred to as the 'Eurasian Patti'.

The Anglo-Indians love their little flutter, especially games like 'Housie'. They also like their whist drives, especially the older people.

Anglo-Indians have a very marked love of social life. There has been criticism even from some Anglo-Indian local leaders that without a dance or at least a whist drive the Anglo-Indians cannot be attracted to a meeting of the Association. This is not entirely correct. At the Annual General Meetings of the All-India Anglo-Indian Association an item such as the President-in-Chief's address usually attracts the largest of crowds. It is correct, however, that for an ordinary branch meeting, where no well-known leader is present, the function is inevitably joined with a dance or whist drive in order to attract the members.

There is undoubtedly a tendency in the Community to social division. This is not peculiar to the Anglo-Indians. In any community that is stratified socially, there is the inevitable tendency for the better placed to have their own centres of social life. In the larger cities and towns, in clubs which are controlled by the Community, functions on certain special occasions draw members from the different social strata. Thus, at a Christmas or New Year dance at the Gidney Club, New Delhi, will be found a number of well-placed Anglo-Indians and their families enjoying the function with those who are humbly placed. Today, the better-placed Anglo-Indians go to the general clubs patronised by senior officers and prosperous businessmen. Those in the Armed Forces have their own clubs and in the bigger cities there is also the general club.

The Calcutta Rangers Club

The Calcutta Rangers Club, one of the premier Anglo-Indian clubs in the Country, deserves a special niche in the Anglo-Indian hall of fame. The Club was founded in 1896. Apart from providing social activities for the Anglo-Indian Community in Calcutta, it has built a special place for itself in the field of sport. Some of the finest Anglo-Indian hockey and football teams have been nursed by the Calcutta Rangers Club.

The Calcutta Rangers Sweep was for many years the most popular sweep in the Country because it was also perhaps the best run. This Sweep enabled the Club to donate lavishly to charities irrespective of caste or community.

During the years 1954 to 1967, the Club donated over 240 lakhs of rupees to various charities. Thus between 1954 and 1956 a sum of over 3 lakhs was donated for the erection and establishment of the Kumud Sankar Ray Tuberculosis Hospital at Jadavpur. During the same period a sum of about 3 lakhs was donated to the Deshbandhu Memorial Society (Chest Clinic), Darjeeling. In 1953, Rs. 1,20,000 were donated towards the establishment of the Mayor of Calcutta's T.B. Clinic. Further, a sum of Rs. 1 lakh was donated to the H.C. Mookerjee Memorial T.B. After-Care Colony Society.

The Club has rendered yeoman service to Anglo-Indian education. Two trusts have been established, namely, the Calcutta Rangers Educational Fund and the West Bengal Charitable Fund. From the former, stipends are granted to a large number of Anglo-Indian students. The latter fund provides for the relief and medical expenses including hospitalisation of Anglo-Indians in straitened circumstances. Particular attention is given to Anglo-Indian T.B.

patients and in appropriate cases the cost of the entire treatment is borne by the fund.

Home Life

Family ties have always been strong in the Community. Inevitably, as in other communities, there are cases of unfilial ingratitude, but these are the exceptions that prove the rule. Perhaps the women have this filial sense in a more marked degree than the men. It is very rare, indeed, to find a daughter who does not help her parents when they are in need. Very often the old parents live with the daughter even after she is married. There are not a few cases of sons who have abandoned the idea of getting married because of their continuing support to old parents.

Before Independence and especially before the present inflationary conditions the standard of living in the Community, especially in the upper-middle class, was one of considerable graciousness. In the smaller towns, in the mofussil areas practically every Anglo-Indian family owned a house or bungalow : some of them owned several. In my home town, Jubbulpore, in which there was one of the largest concentrations of the Community comparable with Bangalore, whole lines of bungalows in the Civil Station were owned by members of the Community. In fact, there was what would now be considered an offensive anomaly—a large area known as Napier Town was reserved for Europeans and Anglo-Indians. The Europeans were those who had married into the Community. The bungalows, with their separate well-kept gardens and ranging from 8 to 15 rooms, could be owned or occupied only by Anglo-Indians and Europeans. Bangalore, Dehra Dun and several other places presented a similar pattern of Anglo-Indians owning whole lines of the very finest types of bungalows.

The homes of the better-placed Anglo-Indians were not only comfortable but, in many ways, gracious. The expensive furnishings, the cut-glass and silver-ware, the battalion of servants were part of the pattern in the better homes. The carpets, the silver-ware, the cut-glass decanters and whisky, wine and brandy glasses would be almost priceless today. The menu was typically Anglo-Indian. Breakfast was essentially an English breakfast—porridge, eggs and fruit. Lunch was Indian or what in fact was typically Anglo-Indian. In some homes after the soup there was the usual curry and rice, vegetable and other fruit or a sweet afterwards. Dinner was somewhat along the English pattern: roast, stews and pudding. The availability of good milk, pure ghee, plenty of fruit and sweets, at prices which would be considered absurdly low today, is perhaps one of the reasons why the Community was by and large physically robust. Before the motor car the better-placed Anglo-Indian families owned a buggy or horse-and-trap. With the advent of the motor car the better-placed families had their own car, some had two or even three, while the sons went to college on their motorcycles, some even sporting cars. Even the Anglo-Indian loco foreman, mail driver and, most certainly, the station master had his car.

Entertainment was usually generous. The older among the better-placed Anglo-Indians in the mofussil areas did not indulge much in club life. The social entertainment was in the home. Friends and relatives would regularly visit one another especially in the evenings. There was much musical talent in the Community. Even the averagely-placed Anglo-Indian usually had a piano in his home: the daughters and often the sons had been taught to play. Formerly, the violin was popular with the sons. The display of eats would be generous ranging from salt to sweet and, in-between, usually the well-known curry puff. Among the better-placed, whisky was the usual drink of the evening, while some preferred beer or even rum. Some of the older women had a chota or two. Actually, however, they preferred the Anglo-Indian milk-punch, ginger wine or, especially in the early days, port and lemon. Visiting friends after Church on Sunday morning was also a regular feature. There would be plenty of eats available, coffee or tea, and for the men usually beer.

Practically every Anglo-Indian home, even those of the lower-middle class stratum, was marked by food specialities. K.C. Neogy, a distinguished member of Parliament and member of the Cabinet after Independence, told me that the best curries in the Country were those made by Anglo-Indians. In the North, Anglo-Indians preferred their chapatis and parathas to rice. Dal was also prepared differently according to the region: in the North and Central India, usually it was of the solid variety: in the South much more watery. In the South the Anglo-Indian menu was famous for its mulligatawny soup which is usually mixed with rice and meat.

Easter and Christmas were marked by the preparation, over several weeks, of all kinds of delicacies in the home. Anglo-Indian wives and daughters competed in the excellence of their recipes, some of which were handed down from generation to generation. Apart from a variety of the most delicious cakes, there were a host of other specialities much to the delight of the youngsters who had been away at boarding schools for 8 to 9 months. Kulkuls, rosy cocades, guava cheese and jelly were a few among the specialities made practically in every Anglo-Indian home. The Kulkul is a dough-like mixture made of flour and rolled on a fork : it is frosted in sugar. The rosy cocade is made on a rose-mould and dipped in a sizzling mixture of sweet. The rosy cocade in the end result is a beautiful light, crisp flour sweet. There were various meat specialities—ox-tongue, salt meat, tongue and brawn-made as a delicacy from the brain of a pig—to be found in the well-stocked larder of practically every Anglo-Indian home.

Christmas and Easter were, usually, occasions for family get-togethers, especially for the Christmas or Easter lunch. Members of the family made it a point to get together from different parts of the Country. Church and especially Communion in the morning were a must. After that there was the round of visits by friends and relatives. Much cake and not a little wine, especially milk punch, and also whisky were offered. In the evenings there was, usually, much community singing, around the piano, an adjunct of practically every Anglo-Indian home. The old community songs from John Brown's Body to Polly Woily Doodle are still popular. The capacity for improvisation is also commendable : some of the improvised verses are of a near-risque character. Irish songs have always been particularly popular in the Community.

Anglo-Indians also have their own special brand of liquor. Milk punch, with a rum, sugar and milk base, is one of the finest wines to be found in the Country. It has the body of a light sherry and a taste better than the most refined light, dry sherry. My old Mother, until she died in 1951, used to send me a dozen bottles of milk punch and an equal number of Christmas cakes in December of each year when I remained in Delhi. My European friends used to go into ecstasies over the milk punch, and my Hindu friends over the cake!

Dress in the Community followed generally the European pattern of the period. As youngsters, going to church we wore shorts, coats.

stiff collars overlapping the coat with a bow-tie and boots or shoes. As we grew up we took to trousers : there were the drain-pipes, coats with short, narrow lapels and stiff collars; boaters were also worn. The frocks worn by the ladies varied according to the period. Later the men's dress changed : there was the period of the Oxford bags and coats with wide lapels. The women's frocks changed during the Charlston period.

There was much emphasis in the home on physical exercise. Sons were encouraged to take part in all games, boxing being particularly popular with the Community. Apart from the games there was considerable emphasis on body-building exercises—dumb-bells, terry-expanders and chest-expanders being the most popular. Some youngsters, especially those who went to college, took to the dand-baithak.

Religion

Apart from the loyalty to the home, Anglo-Indians, by and large, are also loyal to their church. While technically and legally an Anglo-Indian need not be a Christian, in fact the Community to-day is entirely Christian. And the Community is Christian by origin and not conversion. I should imagine that today about 60 per cent of the Community are Roman Catholics. Originally this was not the position. The children of British soldiers and officers who married women of Portuguese or French extraction were usually baptised into the Roman Catholic Church. Even at a later period when Anglo-Indians married girls from the Community, if one of the spouses was a Roman Catholic, because, apparently of the stringent code imposed by the Roman Catholic Church on its devotees, the children were almost invariably baptised into the Roman Catholic Church.

The Community, however, has been free from the denominational taint in its social and public life. It is significant that my predecessor-in-office was a Methodist : I am an Anglican. And yet the members who are largely Roman Catholic give their loyalty to the Association and its leader, uninfluenced by denominational considerations. There have been sporadic attempts by would-be leaders to exploit denominationalism in the Community : I, at any rate, have struck down any exhibition of denominationalism in the Community. Regrettably there have been attempts, at intervals, by narrow Roman Catholic journals to introduce denominationalism in the Community. All these attempts have fortunately failed because they have been scorned by the Community.

Office-bearers of the Association are elected without any considerations of denomination. While Anglo-Indian schools that are owned by the churches are largely denominational especially in the appointment of teachers, the Frank Anthony Schools underline the salutary convention of complete freedom from any denominationalism. In the Frank Anthony Schools the application forms of teachers have no place for caste or denomination.

Marriage

The marriage pattern in the Community has changed with changing circumstances. From 1639 to the end of the 17th century Anglo-Indians and Europeans married the women of the Country, Muslims or Hindus. With the growth of the Community especially after the Mutiny, this intermarriage ceased. In fact, the Community became rigorously endogamous. Marriage outside the Community was frowned upon. Yet there was no in-breeding, as this also was frowned upon. For first cousins to think of marriage was regarded as near sacrilege. In a sense, the conditions governing marriage in the Community have followed almost the pattern of British society. Thus, in the Community marriage has never been arranged. Eligible bachelors would be invited to the home but seldom, if ever, up to the 1920s, was a girl allowed to go out unchaperoned, until at least the young man had made his honourable intentions known. After World War II the pattern changed. Young men and women went out unchaperoned. It is, however, seldom that a young man lets down the girl with whom he has become friendly and intends to go steady. Broken engagements are rare. There is a strict social code in the Community that frowns upon broken engagements : the young man who reneges finds it difficult to be approved of by other parents.

Although I have visited the States, I did not spend sufficient time there to pass judgment on the morality, or lack of it, in American society. I must say, however, that during World War II the G.Is. who were posted in India, both officers and men, generally exhibited the morals of the farmyard. Some really good girls, because they were naive and not worldly-wise, fell victims to their wolf techniques. While several girls married good types of Americans, others were let down. Fortunately, the number of girls who were let down was not large and did not create a problem for the Community, as such girls usually left the Country rather than face shame and disgrace in the Community.

Some writers, even Anglo-Indians, have tended to lampoon the Community for its alleged tendency to 'improve the breed'. Undoubtedly, especially before Independence, many mothers liked their daughters to marry fair Anglo-Indians or Europeans. Marriage to Europeans, if they were of a lower class, sometimes had tragic results. Anglo-Indian girls from the very best of homes, cultured and refined, some of them having completed their education abroad, sometimes married British sergeants or warrant officers, who were much below them in education and culture. Sometimes the marriage turned out well, especially if the soldier settled in the Country and was assimilated to the social and cultural refinements of the girl's family: sometimes, also, the marriage failed because of the girl finding the habits of the husband crude and intolerable.

So far as intra-community marriage was concerned, the position of the man, irrespective of his colour, was often the determinant. Even the darkest men of the Community in good positions were accepted, perhaps with some mental reservations, as sons-in-law. This inclination to improve the breed is not confined to the Community. It is a reflection of the Hindu attitude towards caste or varna, which in its derivative form means colour. This attitude is expressed even, today, in leading dailies through advertisements that insist on the Hindu bride being fair, apart from possessing other intacta.

Many Anglo-Indian families, however, refused to allow their daughters to meet, much less marry, British soldiers. The Tommy, as he was generally referred to, however decent, tended to be stigmatised by the better placed families as a coarse and vulgar type.

During World War II, a number of Anglo-Indian girls married British or American soldiers, including some of the most highly placed officers, and migrated with their husbands after the war. Some of these soldiers and officers, however, settled in the Country and have found a place in the Community and the Country of their adoption.

The typical marriage pattern in the Community, up to the time of Independence, can be exemplified by a practical example known best to me, namely, that of my family in my father's generation. The eldest son, who entered the Provincial Forest Service, died young while still a bachelor. The second son, William Anthony, who also joined the Forest Service and retired as a senior Imperial Forest Officer, married Alice Hill, a first generation Anglo-Indian. Here I use the expression first generation to mean the offspring of a European married to an Anglo-Indian girl. During the earliest period in its history a first generation Anglo-Indian was one who was the offspring of a Briton married to a Hindu or a Muslim woman. The third son, Joe Anthony, perhaps the least educated of the brothers although he did his High School and had a Health Diploma, became a legendary figure as the Health Officer in the Jubbulpore Corporation. Mounted on horseback he was to be seen in every part of the City. He was responsible for making Jubbulpore into one of the garden cities of India. At one time a middleweight boxing champion, his name was a household word among all communities. During the epidemics, especially of plague, that used to decimate the city, he was known to go single-handed into houses, when all the Corporation staff had deserted, and carry out dead bodies himself to ensure their proper cremation. He married Cecilia Baker, a first generation Anglo-Indian : her father, an ex-soldier from the British army, had settled in the Country and married an Anglo-Indian girl. The youngest son, my father, Richard John Anthony, married Marion Knight, also a first generation Anglo-Indian : my Mother's father, William Isaac Knight, who started life as an apothecary in the Royal Artillery, settled in the Country and married an Anglo-Indian girl.

Of the sisters, two married first generation Anglo-Indians, Webb and Cole, who were Provincial Forest Officers; the third married a British ex-soldier, Bill Loveday, a covenanted hand in the railway, and the fourth married an Irishman, Joe Sullivan, who was also a covenanted employee in the railway. Thus all the brothers married first generation Anglo-Indians and all the sisters married either Europeans or Anglo-Indians.

As I have already said, after the Mutiny the Community became rigorously endogamous. Marriages outside the Community were frowned upon, except to Europeans. Some people have sought to criticise the Community for its insularity, but, once again, it was a reflection of the caste system. Parents would not give their consent not only to the daughters but even to the sons marrying into other Indian communities. Thus, I recall the case of one of my cousins, the daughter of William Anthony, who because of her father's position and membership of the 'burra' club used to meet well-placed members of other communities. A highly educated girl she grew friendly with a highly cultured Brahmin, a member of the I.C.S., who was the local district magistrate. My uncle, always the perfect gentleman, perhaps had his mental reservations. Such reservations are to be found in every community and more especially in India with its rigid caste inhibitions. Even in the most progressive communities there are reservations, in respect of marriage, flowing from differing religions and differing ways of life. But my aunt, a rather typical Anglo-Indian woman, had rather explicit reservations. In no uncertain terms she told both the Brahmin member of the I.C.S., when he asked for my cousin's hand in marriage, and the daughter that she could not prevent them from marrying but she would certainly ensure that they and their children would never darken her doors. That put an end to the friendship. The 'Maha-Brahmin' was out-Brahmined. I met this gentleman later when I was a member of the Central Legislature : he was then the Secretary of one of the most important Departments of the Central Government before Independence. I sometimes wondered whether he resented the Community because of his early experience and his first attempt at marriage. This cousin of mine married an Anglo-Indian clergyman. Today, they are in the U.K., where the husband has a comfortable living.

'Genuine' Anglo-Indians

In my chapter on Gidney I have referred to the complex in the Community in respect of 'genuine' Anglo-Indians. Cedric Dover, the internationally famous Anglo-Indian author and biologist, has satirised this tendency as 'The urge for purity among the impure'. To an outsider it would seem not a little ridiculous for a community of mixed blood to talk of 'genuineness' implying, as it were, an insistence on being 'genuine' half-castes. Yet this complex is there, a reflection of the herd consciousness that characterises so much of Indian society. It also underlines an essential pride of Community, a sense of Community self-respect.

Inevitably, in a community of mixed origins there has been assimilation over the centuries. Because of this assimilation, despite diverse origins, British, French, Dutch, German, Portuguese and even American, the process has led to what I have referred to as homozygosity, that is, certain common physical characteristics—a single language, English, and a common identifiable way of life.

We see the same process, of course on a much wider scale and along a more diverse colour and racial spectrum, in a country like America. American society represents the most miscellaneous of ethnic cocktails. Apart from the white and off-white intermixtures, as I have mentioned in the Introduction, at least 1,00,000 Negroes after going through the stages of quadroon and octoroon are assimilated each year to the white American nation. According to leading scientists, in another 500 years there will not be a single so-called white American without an admixture of Negroid blood.

The claims to ethnic purity and superiority by the British have exercised the wit of literati for centuries. Huxley says that the British are among the most hybridised of races in the world and he is proud of it. Huxley also tells us that the Britisher is not only a mongrel, but it is his mission to be a good and effective mongrel. In a mood of confession Daniel Defoe wrote his 'True-Born Englishman'. At least the following passage is perhaps worth salvaging from obscurity.

> "Thus from a mixture of all kinds began
> That heterogeneous thing, an Englishman :
> In eager rapes and furious lust begot
> Between a painted Briton and a Scot;
> Whose gendering offspring quickly learnt to bow
> And yoke their heifers to the Roman plough;
> From whence a mongrel half-breed race there came,
> With neither name nor nation, speech or fame;
> In whose hot veins new mixtures quickly ran,
> Infused between a Saxon and a Dane;
> While their rank daughters, to their parents just,
> Received all nations with promiscuous lust,

> This nauseous brood directly did contain
> The well-extracted blood of Englishmen.''

Because of an almost bewildering succession of invasions, India can at least hold its own in the diversity of its multi-ethnic society. It was partly because of the spurious assumption of British racial purity and superiority as a part of their artificial Imperial Code that the Anglo-Indians, especially of the fairer variety, tried to escape by claiming to be European. They failed to realise that there is no such thing as national or race purity. There has not been a pure race or nation for ten thousand years. Race mixture, in fact miscegenation, represents the biological history of mankind. I have referred to Cedric Dover's dictum, which is scientifically true, that "There are no half-castes because there are no full-castes." The history not only of Europe but of every conquering nation is the history of energetic mongrels.

In every department of life it is the good hybrid that is the most enduring, the most fertile and of the finest quality. The most sought after and the best milk producers in the Country are the hybrid cows, which might be called Anglo-Indian. Today, as part of India's programme to meet the food deficiency resort is being had increasingly to the hybrid varieties of wheat and other cereals. Facile prejudice against the so-called hybrid stems from ignorance of the historical and biological processes. Agriculturist scientists, cattle-breeders and experimenting geneticists are constantly proving the superiority of the hybrid variety. This simple, scientific truth has yet to dawn on race-conscious historians and pretentious biologists.

I have referred in the Introduction to the dictum of Lord Olivier, the famous scientist, that persons of mixed blood are potentially the most competent vehicles of humanity. It depends on what level and at what stage of civilization the mixture takes place. If the off-spring is the product of a low-class British Tommy and a servant woman the result is not likely to be a competent vehicle of humanity. But where intermarriage has been at middle-class or at upper-middle class level, the offspring have more than held their own with the finest types of the so-called unmixed races, white or brown. This quality has been exemplified in the history of the Anglo-Indian Community. It is also significant that Hindus from the middle or the upper-middle class who have married Europeans have produced some of the most outstanding Indians. Among these have been judges of the Supreme Court, High Courts and leading figures in public life especially in Bengal.

The greatest exponents of spurious doctrines of race superiority from Kipling to Hitler were obviously polygenetics. I have always been intrigued by photographs of both Hitler and Kipling: the former was the antithesis of the so-called Nordic type: Hitler's pogroms were probably motivated by a subconscious guilt complex of possessing an admixture of Jewish blood. Both in features and pigmentation, Kipling suggested ethnic admixtures with a tan not accounted for merely by the Indian sun.

As with the Americans especially, there has been a tendency among the Anglo-Indians to look with favour upon what are regarded as typically British or Irish names. Like the Americans there has been a tendency in the Community to adopt names with an Anglo-Saxon appearance. Persons with what are generally referred to as Goan names often either changed completely to a British variety or there was resort to ingenious variations which gave an Anglo-Saxon flavour: thus D'Silva was changed to Silver, Da Costa to Coster, Perreira to Perrier, Rodrigues to Rodericks, Fernandez to Ferns and so forth.

Not that British names were any guarantee against criticism because not a few Indian Christians have the most high-sounding of English, Irish and Scottish names, some being even double-barrelled. A last fling of criticism would be that in spite of the high-sounding name the person was descended from manumitted slaves, especially in Bengal where slaves often adopted the high-sounding names of their European and Anglo-Indian masters.

The term Goan is also a misnomer. Many members of the Community have what is loosely referred to as Goan names. These persons or their ancestors have never had anything to do with Goa. These names are common in the South and also in West Bengal, especially Calcutta. Of course, such names are common in Bombay but the contact with Goa would be more than likely. The names are indicative of Portuguese descent or influence and also, perhaps, of the baptising fervour of a certain type of Roman Catholic priests.

Usually the persons who talk most about 'genuine' Anglo-Indians are of the darkest variety: their protestations usually are a brash defensive front for their lineage, or lack of it, shrouded in irredeemable mystery. Once again, it is a reflection of the poor-white psychology of the so-called white nations with so little to fortify themselves psychologically that they cling pathetically to all manner of spurious attitudes.

As I have said in another chapter, the Community, because it has been endogamous for generations, emerged with certain common identifiable characteristics described as homozygosity. Yet there is a tendency even in the Community to distinguish between aquiline features, which are supposed to be of Aryan origin, and the more squat, broad-nosed features said to be possessed by Goans and ethnic groups in the South. This assumption is not generally valid because many Goans and South Indians have the most delicately chiselled features.

Apart from a number of persons having so-called Goan names, among the Community can also be found families with what are commonly known as Armenian and Jewish names. The Armenians were treated by the East India Company as Europeans. A number of them intermarried with the Community and were assimilated to it. Thus there are Anglo-Indians with such names as Chater and Seth. Jewish names are also not uncommon in the Community, especially such as Jacob, Sampson and Solomon. This is not a new phenomenon. A look at the telephone directory in London will show whole lists of persons with similar names who have been assimilated to the British nation. Among those who claim to be completely British even such names as Bose and Dutt are to be found. It is a usual pattern of assimilation in any multi-racial, multi-ethnic society. Throughout British Indian history Anglo-Indians at all levels were assimilated to the British nation.

What Gidney referred to as adulteration was a natural biological-cum-racial process. The persons who accreted were assimilated to the Community. The accretions become undesirable at the lowest level because there the assimilation is usually either not possible or even not desirable.

My objection to accretion is when it takes place at the lowest level: this class becomes a drag on the Community for, in that stratum, the accreting element is not assimilated to the way of life and the attributes of the Community; there is a tendency to parasitism, and an absence of self-reliance, independence and capacity for self-help of the average member of the Community.

Implicit in the reference to 'genuine' Anglo-Indians is the absence of qualities which the Community feels the average Anglo-Indian possesses or should possess. If an Anglo-Indian shows fright, is not prepared to accept the rigours of duty in any part of the Country, or intrigues, it is said he is not a 'genuine' Anglo-Indian.

Related to this talk of 'genuine' Anglo-Indians are certain often facile, and invalid, assumptions. Thus, there is—at least there was for decades—the assumption that the Anglo-Indians in the South were of the very dark variety. Undoubtedly, one meets an element which is sometimes almost Nubian in complexion: that is understandable in the context of an inevitable Dravidian ethnic conditioning.

As I have mentioned elsewhere, I led a delegation of Anglo-Indian Principals and Educationists to meet Jawaharlal Nehru in 1960. I do not think even Jawaharlal was prepared for the wide colour spectrum from the blond, Nordic type to the sable-hued. As it happened two completely contrasting types were standing alongside of each other when I introduced them to Nehru: one was blond, indistinguishable from any Briton, the other possessed a Nubian darkness. I saw Nehru jerk his head in a moment of uncontrolled surprise, and yet the grandfather of the Nubian-complexioned Anglo-Indian was a Briton.

In fact, some of the fairest members of the Community are from the South. As a matter of fact, Bangalore was famous for its lovely Anglo-Indian girls. Not long ago Hanumanthiah, a colleague of mine in Parliament, at one time Chief Minister of the Mysore State, referred to the sheer beauty of the Anglo-Indian girls in Bangalore. He said that as students in College they usually went to the cinema just to stare at the good-looking Anglo-Indian girls. I should mention that Bangalore was a popular settlement with the Community. Families from every part of the Country settled there, especially after the retirement of the father.

Accent And Some Differences

As in Britain or, indeed, in any English-speaking society, there are differences of accent in the Community. Writing in an ignorantly pretentious way, British authors have talked of the chee-chee accent of the Community. This is an ignorant generalisation. It is like saying that the British Nation has a Cockney accent. Accent in the Community varies from stratum to stratum and also from North to South. There is often a noticeable difference between the accents of the Anglo-Indians from the North and the South. In the South there is a tendency for the accent to be conditioned by the intonation and the inflexions of the local language. The Anglo-Indians in the North are inclined to refer to the accent of the Anglo-Indians in the South as a Madrasi accent. This again is an untenable generalisation. Among the lesser-educated members of the Community in the South there is a noticeable difference in the accent. Then again, in the Kolar Gold Fields, where there is an appreciable number of Anglo-Indians, the accent is rather different: 'there the dropping of the 'h' and the 'g' is suggestive of the accent in the old British regiments.

When I was a student in Britain, I spent one of my holidays in Wales. Apart from finding the Welsh people generally delightful and friendly, I felt that I was among Anglo-Indians. I was invited to a private dance where there were over 500 people present. I have seldom enjoyed myself more. Apart from the fact that several of the Welshmen were sporting my surname, so many of them looked like Anglo-Indians. I asked some of them whether they were from India. But to them India was merely a name. I thought they were Anglo-Indians: they thought that I was Welsh. I do not know whether their accent was like mine or mine like theirs. The accent of the Anglo-Indians has an intonation very much like that of the Welsh. I thought that our colloquialism in school, "I say, mon," was an original Anglo-Indianism. After my visit to Wales I realised that it had probably come via the Welsh.

As the leader of the Community, I have noticed certain differences between the Anglo-Indians in the South and the rest of the Country. My wife has noticed this especially, and commented upon it often. The Anglo-Indians in the South are extremely warm-hearted. When we tour, we are treated with hospitality wherever we go, but in the South the hospitality is overwhelming. Whatever part of the day or night our train halts at a station, we are plied with well-stocked tiffin-baskets, coffee flasks and so on. Although we may have just had breakfast from the dining car, at the next station we are presented with a lavish breakfast. And we dare not refuse to do justice to this second breakfast, as our people are inclined to be extremely sensitive.

There is also a certain basic refinement in the Anglo-Indians from the South, whether poor or rich. I attribute this to the fact that, by and large, Indians in the South are more refined than those in the North. South Indians claim, perhaps with good reason, that theirs has been a longer civilization, with a richer and deeper culture than that of the successively invaded North. This background of refinement and hospitality seems to have communicated itself to the Community in the South.

Alleged Social Exclusiveness

In his Autobiography Jawaharlal Nehru referred to the arrogant attitude of some members of the Community towards their fellow-Indians. I do not wish unduly to play down this attitude. It was there. I attribute it to the anti-Indian complex which permeated some of the schools, that were usually controlled by Europeans. This arrogance was also a sort of defence mechanism similar to that found among poor-whites in countries such as America and Britain where their only claim to a spurious superiority is the colour of their skin. This arrogance was to be found especially among the lesser-educated Anglo-Indians who referred disparagingly to 'Indians' apparently as the last psychological booster to which they clung in a morass of ignorance and often of poverty. With the change in the psychological pattern of Anglo-Indian education this unhappy feature will not even be a bad memory among the present youngsters growing up with youngsters of other communities in an atmosphere of mutual respect and close friendship.

Some peripatetic, muck-raking writers have exaggerated this arrogance in the Community. What they have not emphasised is that in common with the other Indian communities the Anglo-Indians often resented the British. Against acts of British discrimination the resentment was expressed in the lurid epithet, "The White Bastards!" Socially, the younger Anglo-Indians, especially, resented the British soldier. With the Community producing some of the finest boxers in the Country, the average Anglo-Indian could more than hold his own against the British soldier.

On one occasion, when I was President of the Jubbulpore branch of the Association, the branch was running a function at the local Railway Institute. I was asked to intervene in a row between some young Anglo-Indian firemen and British soldiers who had gate-crashed into the Institute bar. When I arrived in the bar the scene was in some respects amusing. Standing against the wall was a well-known Anglo-Indian driver, a light heavyweight champion who was then in his forties and known for his quiet and self-effacing manner. Four British soldiers, who were using foul language in varying degress of obscenity, were told by this driver that if they persisted in their bad behaviour they would be atomised by the young Anglo-Indian firemen. To prevent that happening he offered to take them on, one at a time. The Tommies, characterised more by brashness than a sense of discretion, agreed, conjuring up visions of perhaps wiping the floor with this middle-aged driver. A ring of spectators was formed, outside the bar, and then, believe it or not, this driver within the space of a few minutes knocked out all of them, one at a time.

This kind of tension between the young Anglo-Indians and the British soldiers was not infrequent. On the eve of Independence I was addressing a crowded meeting of Anglo-Indians at Vizagapatnam. The British soldiers of the local battalion sought to gate-crash during the dance. Immediately the Anglo-Indians of the Coastal Battery, which had been embodied during World War II, asked my permission to clear out the 'Limeys'. I advised them not to precipitate an unnecessary row. Unfortunately, after the function the Tommies and the Anglo-Indians clashed and the Tommies took a sound thrashing. I received a long complaint from the local British Commandant.

Towards the end of 1946 I referred in the Central Legislature to the raid by British soldiers on the Jhansi Railway Institute. It was decided by the Anglo-Indians of Jhansi not to admit any British soldiers to their Xmas function. In spite of this some soldiers gate-crashed and were thrown out by the Anglo-Indians. The soldiers went back and organised an attack on the Institute. Armed with bayonets and knuckle-dusters they attacked the Institute and assaulted some of the women and girls, injuring several Anglo-Indian men who resisted them with bare fists. The wanton destruction to property was calculated at over fifteen thousand rupees. My questions in the Legislature caused a furore in the press and resulted in compensation being paid to the Institute.

Much ignorant nonsense has also been written about the Community's lack of social contact with other communities. Admittedly, there is a certain social brittleness in the Community in the sense that many of its social functions are confined to members of the Community. This again is a reflection largely of the social pattern in the Country, where persons belonging to a particular community or a particular social stratum tend to keep to themselves.

In fact, Anglo-Indians are perhaps the most sociable of all the Indian communities. Even in clubs run by the Community there is a heavy demand for admission by members of other communities. Thus the Gidney Club, New Delhi, which is an activity of the Delhi Branch of the All-India Anglo-Indian Association, has a number of members of other communities, especially Hindus and Sikhs. Because it is an Anglo-Indian club, under its constitution only Anglo-Indians are admitted as full members: non-Anglo-Indians can be either honorary or associate members. Sometimes, there has been a sense of resentment shown by non-Anglo-Indians at this differentiation in membership: but that is because of the constitution of the Club. Otherwise there is an atmosphere of complete camaraderie in the Club.

Admittedly, at functions held by the Association, only members of the Community are permitted to attend, but for general functions—socials and dances—there is no restriction. The Anglo-Indian members feel that non-Anglo-Indians who wish to join the social functions should bring their wives and daughters with them: those who do, join in the gaiety as much as the Anglo-Indians.

I remember meeting a body of African students in Delhi. They mentioned that the only Indians who treated them with real friendliness were the Anglo-Indians, even those who could pass for Europeans: the other communities, especially the Hindus, treated them with ill-concealed colour prejudice.

To say that the Community does not mix socially with other communities is not only a baseless but an ignorant generalisation. Here again, it is a question of social stratification. Well-placed Anglo-Indians have friends, indeed close friends, among all communities. As a boy I recall the close friendship of my family with Hindus, Muslims and Europeans. In a way that may have been a special case because of my father's professional eminence and the fact that his patients included members of all communities.

When we were in college, all the Anglo-Indians—and there were several of us—were on the friendliest of terms with students of every other community. We were college pals, often spending our holidays in one another's homes. There was, indeed, great respect for the Anglo-Indian student. I had the privilege of being the President of the College Literary and Debating Society. I had the privilege to represent my College—Robertson College—at the Inter-College University debates, three years in succession. I was also fortunate to win the University championship for my College in all three years. When I was awarded the coveted Viceroy's Gold Medal for the best English essay in the All-India Inter-University contest, I was lionized by my colleagues—perhaps more than any Hindu student would have been. Today, with the Anglo-Indian schools, unlike the position in our time, having a majority of non-Anglo-Indian pupils, the Anglo-Indians are growing up without any of the inhibitions of their parents.

Vis-A-Vis Some Other Communities

It is a little strange perhaps, but there has not been much love lost between the Anglo-Indians and the Indian Christians. I feel this tendency in the Community, of looking with a certain disdain at the Indian Christians, is due to the fact that Anglo-Indians, who are Christians by origin, do not think much of those who are Christians by conversion.

Yet this cannot be stated as a general proposition. The better-placed Anglo-Indians are not given to the prejudices of the less-educated members who, like the British women, judged other communities by the servants they employed. A number of Anglo-Indians do considerable work for their respective churches. In this field they have close and cordial relations with leading members of the Indian Christian Community. I sometimes cannot help feeling that there is a certain resentment on the part of certain members of the Indian Christian Community, including Bishops, because of the attitude of superciliousness by some of the lesser-educated Anglo-Indians towards the Indian Christians. The relations of the Community with certain sections of Indian Christians have always been friendly, especially with those referred to as Goans and the tribal Christians in North-East India.

The sense of self-respect in the Community was outraged by the claims of the Feringis of Kerala who, while suddenly claiming to

be Anglo-Indians, also insisted on the Anglo-Indians being classified as a backward class. The Community has always had its
poor, but even the poorest among them were outraged   at the
thought that the Anglo-Indians should be classified as a backward
class merely to get a few amenities or concessions. The Anglo-
Indians are conscious of their contributions to India and they are
also conscious that, throughout their history, the Community has
been in the front rank of achievement and leadership.

For 300 years the Feringis were never accepted either by the
Government or the Community as Anglo-Indians. Unfortunately
some ambitious Feringi leaders, attracted by the Anglo-Indian
safeguards, especially representation in the Legislatures, began
to make increasingly absurd claims about the number of Anglo-
Indians in Kerala. These claims became strident in about 1955.
Actually, the Community did not know who or what the Feringis
were. An investigation was made and then it was found that
while a handful of these may, as they claim, be of dimly distant
Portuguese descent, the overwhelming majority would appear
to be converts from among the lowest and the poorest class of
fishermen, rope-makers, landless labourers and others. It was
not surprising, therefore, that they continued to be a part of the
lowest stratum of the Indian Christians and were classified as a
backward class.

The investigation also showed that, according to the 1931 Census
for Cochin, there had been a fall in the number of Anglo-Indians
from 2182 to 1717. Even then, the Census Commissioner observed,
referring to the Feringis, that, "Many of them wrongly return
themselves as Anglo-Indians, while considerable numbers return
Feringi or Indian Christian as their race. The Feringis are not
shown separately in the tables but are included in the Indian
Christians. The statistics of Anglo-Indians are therefore inaccurate and misleading."

In the 1941 Census report for Cochin, the Commissioner, commenting on the phenomenal increase from 1717, in 1931, to 9858,
in 1941, observed, "The abnormal increase in the population of
Anglo-Indians seen in part B of the Table is due to a large number
of Latin Catholic Christians locally known   as Feringis returning
themselves as Anglo-Indians during this census."

The Backward Classes Commission in its report of 1955 made

the position even more clear: it pointed out that these persons of Travancore-Cochin had been, "Mistakenly classed as Anglo-Indians." The Report also pointed out that Malayalam was the language of the Feringis and that, "They could not secure special privileges during the British rule as the Anglo-Indians did."

Gidney also faced a similar problem. There was also an element known as Feringis in Chittagong and along the East Bengal coastal area. Those Feringis tried to be included in the 1931 Anglo-Indian Census but Gidney indignantly repudiated their new-found claim: as a result the Feringis of East Bengal were not included as Anglo-Indians in the 1931 Census.

As I have said in another chapter, because of the false claims of the Feringis of Kerala the All-India Anglo-Indian Association decided not to make an issue of the Government decision to eliminate the community designation from the 1961 Census. The Community is still identified by its mother-tongue, English. The 1961 Census has thus put the position in Kerala in proper perspective. According to this Census there are about 7000 persons in Kerala who have English as their mother-tongue. This would give an adult population of Anglo-Indians in Kerala as 1000 to 1500, which represents the correct figure. As in the rest of India, persons of Portuguese descent have intermarried with the Community: this is what has happened in the case of the small number of Anglo-Indians in Kerala.

An outsider may think that the attitude of the Community towards the Feringis was prompted by communalism. Yet it would be correct to say that, perhaps, we are the least communal body of persons in India. We are certainly the least caste-conscious Community in the Country where caste unfortunately still plays a dominant role. Our attitude has nothing to do with communalism. It is a matter not only of ordinary self-respect but, for a microscopic minority, one of survival. Every community has the right to be proud of itself, while every Indian has the right to be proud of being an Indian.

Perhaps what the Anglo-Indians feel can be best illustrated by the conversation which I had, shortly after my speech in the Lok Sabha condemning the fraudulent claim of the Feringis, with a Brahmin friend. He asked me why, when the Country had set itself the goal of a casteless, classless society, I should strike an attitude that seemed to be discordant, by repudiating the Feringis.   I told him that it is difficult for a person who is not an Anglo-Indian to appreciate the position, because it involves the history of the Community, its inner thinking and feeling.   It had been argued by one or two members in Parliament that the Feringis claimed to be of Portuguese descent and since the definition of the term Anglo-Indian was posited on European descent, therefore, the Feringis were Anglo-Indians. I told my Brahmin friend that if I emulated this kind of tortuous semantics, I could argue that the Brahmins are Indians and are also Hindus, and that the Bhangis are equally good Indians and Hindus that, therefore, a Brahmin is a Bhangi.   He said nothing, but looked at me with pained surprise.   I apologised and said that was precisely what was being offered to the Community, a wanton, deliberate affront.   People who never had anything to do with us throughout our history while suddenly claiming to be Anglo-Indians also sought, in the view of the Community, to degrade it into a backward class of Indian Christians.

The Linguistic census, however, has given the quietus to the false claims by the Feringis.   By all means let these good people continue to get the benefits of a backward class of Indian Christians.   But, also, let them pursue their own way of life, which they have done apparently for centuries, during which they had nothing in common either with the history of the Community, its way of life or its contribution to India.

Leadership

In many ways the Anglo-Indians are highly respected and accepted, even before members of other communities, for positions of leadership, especially as officers in the Armed Forces.   This has been true throughout its history.   In the professions, especially in the time of my father and grandfather, Anglo-Indians were often in a dominant position.   For many years the Jubbulpore bar, one of the most prosperous bars in the Country, was dominated by Anglo-Indian lawyers.   Dr. Mendes was, in fact, the first lawyer from India to take his LL.D. from Cambridge.   After his time, Anglo-Indian lawyers, especially my grandfather John Francis Anthony and Wrixon were leaders of the bar.   Later there was William Pasley, a blond, blue-eyed Anglo-Indian over six feet in height. Pasley started life as a sergeant of Police : he then got into the provincial police service. At the age of fifty he was called to the bar in England and was for about fifteen years the dominant figure on the criminal law side. Pasley had a princely income. A master of Hindustani, he was a deadly cross-examiner. As an advocate he was not outstanding. He represented the Community in the Provincial Legislature, but made no mark there as he was not a good speaker. When I joined the bar I was shown a cupboard in which the leading Anglo-Indian lawyers used to keep the choicest of white wines which they took at lunch.

On the medical side it was customary to find Anglo-Indians as doctors and dentists. As I have said in another chapter, my father was the leading medical practitioner for many years in a field occupied not only by highly qualified Indian doctors but also Europeans.

Today, Anglo-Indians are to be found to a lesser extent in the professions. Formerly, the doctors were usually members of the Indian Medical Department (British Cadre) who had either retired from the service or had prematurely retired. Under the impetus of the Frank Anthony Scholarship Schemes, once again Anglo-Indians are taking to medicine in appreciable numbers. Many Anglo-Indians, today, both young men and women, are doing their medical degrees.

I remember at a meeting of some leading members of Parliament on the Naga question, Jawaharlal Nehru mentioned that, "Fortunately or unfortunately" the Nagas only trusted the Anglo-Indian officials. I took Nehru up on the use of the word 'unfortunately'. He replied that what he meant by the word 'unfortunately' was that it was unfortunate that the Nagas did not usually trust officers from other communities.

Exodus

There has been an appreciable exodus of Anglo-Indians from the Country. Immediately after Independence, with the holocaust of Partition and because of the sense of anxiety for the safety of their womenfolk, several thousands of members of the Community migrated mostly to the U.K. As the conditions in the Country settled down and it was realised that there was no animus against the Community and that the unfortunate happenings vis-a-vis the Muslims were not likely to affect the Community, this anxiety largely abated and so also the exodus.

After the death of Jawaharlal Nehru and the 1967 general elections there was a fresh spate of exodus. The organised anti-English riots in the Hindi States, when Anglo-Indians especially in the smaller places were exposed to insult, reactivated the anxiety in the members especially in respect of the safety of their womenfolk. The constant tirades against English and the repeated attempts, overt or covert, to drive it out of the Country, inevitably had a reaction on the Community whose mother-tongue is English. The Anglo-Indians feel, quite rightly, that if English is driven out, they can have no place or future in the Country.

The political instability that has come in the wake of the 1967 elections, with the landslide defeats for the Congress in certain areas, has added to the anxiety. In many of the States, opportunistic, motley political alliances, the new phenomenon of crossing and re-crossing of floors from the cheapest and, indeed, the most sordid of motives have accentuated considerably this sense of anxiety. In certain of the States there has been virtually no administration for years. Even at the Centre the increasing symptoms of in-fighting and political throat-cutting have not helped to induce confidence in the minorities. With all its shortcomings, the Congress Party, with the conditioning given to it by Jawaharlal Nehru, had done not a little to inspire confidence among Anglo-Indians. The treatment that I was able to secure for the Community, especially the safeguards in the Constitution, and, by and large, an attitude of understanding by Governments administered by the Congress, gave a feeling of assurance. With coalition governments in the States, often dominated by avowedly revivalist groups and parties, this assurance has receded. Essentially because of this revived anxiety, there was a fresh spate of exodus in the last two years.

Not a little anxiety has been caused by the attitude and utterances of Hindu revivalist leaders. These revivalists talk of a 'Hindu Rashtra' and a pan-Hindu culture. Even at the highest official level, there is often loose talk of integration in the sense of assimilation. In a polity which is made up of a bewilderingly diverse, multi-linguistic, multi-religious and multi-ethnic mosaic to talk of integration in the sense of assimilation is dangerous nonsense. Even the Sikhs, who can be said to be a limb of the larger Hindu pattern, would never accept assimilation in the sense of submergence. In the same way the Anglo-Indians would not accept assimilation which means submergence. Indeed, no community should be asked to accept submergence or a merging of its identity as a cultural, religious or linguistic group. If secular democracy is to have any meaning or content in India, the majority community must come to terms with this diversity. In spite of the arrogations by the revivalist leaders, Indian-ness, patriotism are not identified with any particular group, language, dress, religion or habits.

With the introduction of the British Immigration Act, which placed considerable restrictions on persons seeking to enter the U.K., emigrating Anglo-Indians looked increasingly to Australia which appeared to welcome them. Several thousands of Anglo-Indians have migrated there in the past two years.

For me this exodus has been a saddening experience because the loss has been not only that of the Community. Some of the finest elements in the Community have left the Country. Some of these were members of the Armed Forces who rendered yeoman service during the Indo-Pakistan conflict. Undoubtedly, the exodus has weakened the Community not only numerically but also in respect of its social and economic texture. At the same time, the exodus has in a way helped the Community. Many of those who have migrated were from the lowest and the darkest stratum of the Community, the boys and girls having comparatively little education. With the quotas in the the Services, especially the Railways, having wasted out, it would have been virtually impossible for these youngsters to secure gainful employment in India. They would have been a burden on the Community and also on the Country. To that extent the exodus has helped the All-India Anglo-Indian Association, which is the sole agency that is capable of doing anything effective to assist not only in educating but securing employment for members of the Community.

My own estimate is that about 50,000 Anglo-Indians, if the children are included, have migrated since Independence. I should imagine that about 25,000 have gone to the U.K., the best part of 5,000 to 10,000 to Australia, and another 5,000 to 10,000 are scattered in countries such as New Zealand, Canada and the U.S.A.

Split Psychology

Here again, much ignorant, pretentious nonsense has been written about the dichotomy in the Community. Usually the meretricious thesis is that because the Community is of mixed descent, it has no roots. I concede, straightaway, that there is a certain split psychology in the Community. That has been due not to the fact that it is of mixed descent but much more to the educational matrix from which it has emerged. As I have said in a previous chapter, until Independence and until I was elected Chairman of the Inter-State Board for Anglo-Indian Education, Anglo-Indian Schools, which were mostly controlled by Europeans, taught the pupils to look away from India and things Indian, to look up to everything British and to look down upon most things Indian. As I have said in the Introduction, the British Imperial system placed a premium on renegadism. By denying their Community, many Anglo-Indians became members of the Viceroy's Executive Council, Governors of Provinces, senior Generals in the British Army.

Because of these factors, in the present adult generation of Anglo-Indians we find this split psychology. As I have said earlier, even Gidney never referred to the Community as Indians but as citizens of India or statutory natives of India. It is the rule rather than the exception to find Anglo-Indians refer to other communities as Indians. Over and over, even at meetings of well-placed and educated Anglo-Indians, I have to draw attention to this fact: that if a distinction has to be drawn it should be drawn as between communities—Anglo-Indians, Parsees, Sikhs. Over and over again, I have stressed the fact that it is not only a solecism but a vulgarism to refer to Anglo-Indians on the one hand and Indians on the other. Unfortunately, even members of other communities including leading Hindu educationists do this. At educational meetings, over which I have presided and at which Vice-Chancellors and others have been present, I have had to correct this solecism.

Loyalty

In spite of this psychology, it is untrue to say that the Community lacks either loyalty or patriotism. The dominant tradition of the Community has been loyalty—loyalty not only to its work but loyalty to the Country.

Independence was greeted by Anglo-Indians with emotion and indeed fervour. Basil Norton's 'Song of Independence' expressed these feelings in verse.

Maha Bharat—Great India
Song Of Independence

1. Land of greatness, Land of glory,
   Motherland of ancient lore,
   Land of mountains, land of rivers
   Land of Wealth's perpetual store,
   Home of millions of earth's peoples
   Sheltered in thy vast expanse,
   Peoples born of thee O' Mother,
   Heritage of circumstance.

Refrain

March in freedom, March in progress,
Indians never will be slaves,
Conquerors come and pass forever,
With their burden to their graves.
God Almighty bless our India,
Save her children from all woe,
Make them strong and give them wisdom
Be our guide for evermore.

2. From the snow-clad Nanda Devi,
   To the point at Comerin's Cape,
   And across the East & West seas,
   Marking out the Country's shape,
   Peoples of all climes & speeches,
   Worshipping at divers shrines,
   Children, all of Mother India,
   Stamped with Mother India's lines.

3. Give us leaders brave and loyal,
   Men of brawn, and men of fire,
   Men who build, and men who labour,
   Not for selfish gain or hire.
   Let no creed or party slogan
   Lead us in disruptive strife,
   Let the flag of India's Union
   Unify our peoples' life.

4. Through the dim historic ages,

Through the darkness of the past
When the gods had fought their battles,
And the priests created caste,
When the Vedas formed the gospel,
And the minstrels sang their song,
When the Koran & the Bible,
Built the creed of right & wrong.

5. Years of patient toil and suffering
Neath the alien's iron heel
Wore out millions of our people
In the hoop of Empire's wheel;
Gone, the days of slavish serfdom,
Days of blindness, want and woe,
Let us grasp the hand of Freedom,
India free for evermore!

6. Sons of India! rise from slumber!
Till the fields and rake the soil,
Work your factories, make your engines,
Learn to labour and to toil.
Make your ships to sail the waters,
Make your planes fly far and wide,
Learn to govern wise and justly,
That peace forever may abide.

7. Let us sing the song of nations,
We are one, and we are free,
We have won our Independence
Over all our land and sea.
Let us pray for strength & guidance,
Courage, wisdom, knowledge, might,
May Almighty God above us
Lead us & defend our right.

BASIL NORTON

Mrs. Rose, a member of the Governing Body of the All-India
Anglo-Indian Association, greeted the National flag.

Flag Of Our Motherland

Flag of our Motherland, flag of the free
Our loyalty here we pledge to thee
Saffron and white and green unfurled,
Bear it aloft O winds of the world.
Father of all, we lift our eyes
As a new year dawns in the Eastern skies
Grant us O Lord the strength we pray
To lead mankind to a better day
When wars throughout the earth shall cease,
And men shall live in eternal peace.

H. ROSE

The Community is not given to parading its loyalty or patriotism, but, in crisis after crisis, including those that have overtaken the Country since Independence, our loyalty and patriotism, tested in the crucible of war, have been at least equal to that of any other community. While there have been cases of espionage and cowardice in other communities there has never been one such case brought against an Anglo-Indian.

Especially during the Indo-Pakistan conflict the upsurge of patriotic fervour in the Community was heart-warming. Anglo-Indians were as emotionally involved as any other community and as anxious to help in every way possible. Love of the 'Old Country' is marked among Anglo-Indians who have emigrated. Thus when my wife and I were in the U.K. in 1964 and the Anglo-Indians in London came to know that we were there, we were inundated with requests to attend functions organised by members of the Community. Because of the short time at my disposal, I had to decline these requests. I attended only one meeting which was organised by members of the Community at the International Tea Centre in Oxford Street. The love and the nostalgia for India are still very much there especially among the older members of the Community. Inevitably, the youngsters will grow up in a different milieu and be assimilated to a different psychology. Another noticeable feature is the sense of identity among members of the Community who have emigrated.

Some members of the Community have made exiles of themselves for several reasons. Thus, my elder brother migrated to the U.K. with a heavy heart : he did so because of the foreign exchange position which prevented him from sending his sons for further studies overseas. By emigrating he was able to give his sons the best of educational opportunities which have ensured their securing gainful employment. Psychologically he has never been happy. After the sons had completed their education and made their own life, he and his wife returned to India. But then he was confronted with the almost typical, 'Babu' attitude that marks so much of Government functioning. He was told that he could not get his pension in India unless he repatriated all the money he had taken out of the Country. To say the least, it was an extraordinary proposition, as this policy was based on the assumption that he had lived in the U.K. for 5 years on air and that all the money he had taken out of the Country was intact. Because he was refused his pension in India, he was compelled to return to the U.K. where he gets his pension not in rupees, but in sterling !

Except for the Anglo-Indians who continue to delude themselves, the large majority know that they cannot reach top positions in the U.K., Australia or indeed in any white country except for a few who might pass for Europeans. The children certainly secure gainful employment. In terms of money they earn more than they would do in India. But they realise that the top jobs are reserved for the indigenees and that the colour and race barriers will be drawn rigidly at certain levels. I constantly receive letters from Anglo-Indians in the U.K. who complain of the upsurge of race and colour discrimination there.

Finest Opportunities

What I have said to the Community from the very beginning of my leadership has materialised. I always believed, and said so repeatedly, that the Anglo-Indians, as Anglo-Indians, would get their finest opportunities in Independent India. In pre-Independence days like members of other communities and, in fact, more so, the walls of discrimination were drawn firmly around the Community. Few, if any, Anglo-Indians were ever allowed to become heads of departments, whatever their capacity and qualifications. I remember after my scathing indictment of Beverley Nichols' exercise in scatology and malice in his 'Verdict on India', my speech was applauded in Parliament. Hussan Suhrawardy, brother of Shaheed Suhrawardy, former Chief Minister of Bengal, rushed up to me and said that while I had said a good deal, he could tell me of yet another instance of deliberate British discrimination. Suhrawardy had been a senior official on the then East Indian Railway. He mentioned how a highly qualified Anglo-Indian, with some of the finest overseas degrees, had been recommended as Chief Medical Officer. The British General Manager was, however, not prepared to accept him because he was an Anglo-Indian. Yet after Independence more than one Anglo-Indian has become a Chief Medical Officer. Thus, Colin Roberston was first Chief Medical Officer of the G.I.P. Railway and then came to Delhi as the Chief Medical Officer of the Northern Railway.

Immediately after Independence the Community got very special opportunities. Replying to a question by me in the Legislature the then Defence Minister, Sardar Baldev Singh, stated that from August of 1947 to February, 1948, the number of Anglo-Indians recruited in the officer cadres for the R.I.N. was 50 per cent for the R.I.A.F. 28 per cent and for the Army 26 per cent. Addressing the Community after Independence, I mentioned that within 2 years of Independence, Anglo-Indians had been given, increasingly, positions which they had never held in 200 years of British rule. Apart from the numbers in the officer cadres of the Armed Forces, over 20 Anglo-Indians were selected for the superior administrative service which had taken the place of the Indian Civil Service. Shortly after Independence, Piggott was selected to represent the Indian Air Force in the U.K. and was awarded the coveted trophy as the best Air Force cadet in the Commonwealth.

Many Anglo-Indians after Independence have found their metier especially in the Armed Forces. In pre-Independence days the most an Anglo-Indian could become was a Major in the I.M.D. (B.C.) Since Independence Anglo-Indians have found positions of trust, in every sphere, commensurate with their ability and character.

The first Anglo-Indian to be promoted to the rank of Lt. General, after Independence, was Henderson Brooks. A talk between Krishna Menon, the then Defence Minister, and myself, however, indicated a certain quirk in official thinking. Meeting me in the lobby of Parliament, Krishna Menon mentioned that I would be glad to hear that Henderson Brooks was being promoted to the rank of Lt. General : and then he added, "But the fellow has not one but two European names." I was not amused by the tail-piece and asked him whether he expected him to have two Hindu names!

Incidentally, in his younger days, Henderson Brooks was one of the top tennis players in the Country. Readers will recall the enquiry into the reasons which led to the NEFA debacle in 1962. Henderson Brooks was awarded the Vishishth Seva Medal Class I for his work on that particular enquiry. The citation reads, "Lt. Gen. J.B. Henderson Brooks was given the difficult task of investigating the reasons for our failure in the campaign against the Chinese in 1962. Due to his tact, eye for detail and devotion to duty, the General Officer was responsible for producing a most commendable and excellent report which has been of the greatest assistance to the Indian Army. For his sterling services to the country in this very delicate matter, he has been awarded the VSM Class I."

There was a general feeling, especially in Parliament, that the report was forthright and revealing, so revealing, indeed, that the Government has not dared to allow its publication. This is part of the unfortunate tendency in the Government not to take even Parliament into confidence in military matters and to sweep under the carpet our mistakes, especially in defence matters.

Lt. Gen. Pat Dunn, the Corps Commander in the Sialkot area during the 1965 Indo-Pak war, is one of the finest fighting Generals that India has produced. It is significant that during the critical Indo-Pakistan conflict about 20 per cent of the Group Captains, about 30 per cent of the Wing Commanders and about 30 per cent of the Squadron Leaders in the Air Force were Anglo-Indians. In the Army Anglo-Indians held and continue to hold many key positions.

But for the exodus of some of our most senior people, including officers in the Navy, Air Force and Army, many of the top posts in the Country, today, would be held by Anglo-Indians. Even then in the Army we have, today, four Major-Generals : Robert Williams, Director General of Inspection; Regie Noronha, M.C., Vishishth Seva Medal Class I, with the reputation of being one of India's finest fighting generals; Edgar Pettengell of the Signals; and Frank Larkins, Director of Weapons. The number of Anglo-Indian officers in the Air Force is still appreciable. Maurice Barker is an Air Vice-Marshal. Recently, Commodore Cameron of the Navy, the Managing Director of Hindustan Shipyard Ltd., was promoted to Rear Admiral.

Leslie Johnson of the I.C.S. is the Chairman of the important Oil and Natural Gas Commission. Several Anglo-Indians are today in senior positions as members of the I.A.S. A. K. Barren, who was awarded the M.C. during the Burma fighting, was one of the several members of the Community selected for the I.A.S. after Independence. Barren, today, is Chief Secretary to the Orissa Government. K.A.P. Stevenson is Joint Secretary in the Planning Commission; Barker is Secretary to a department of the U.P. Government.

Eustace Wilson, settled in Bangalore, retired a few years ago as Surveyor-General of India. He was the first Anglo-Indian to hold this post and the second Indian to do so after Independence. He was the first civilian to be appointed Surveyor-General of India after 195 years of the existence of the Survey of India Department: before that the post was always held by a Military officer.

Melville de Mellow has been described as an institution in himself. He is, today, the Chief Feature Producer of All-India Radio and is known not only to millions of Indian listeners but has achieved not a little international fame. He won a scholarship to the B.B.C. in 1948. In 1960 he was awarded the Czechoslovak International Radio Documentary Peace Prize for the feature 'Garden of Peace'. In 1963, he was decorated with the Padma Shri for distinguished service in the field of broadcasting. In 1964 he was awarded the blue riband of world broadcasting, the Italia Prize, for the feature 'Lali and the Lions of Gir'.

de Mellow joined All-India Radio after having been an officer in the Indian Army. He has an inimitable elan, an inspirational style which at once fascinates and arrests the interest of his listeners. For their strong national fervour and stirring emotional appeal his broadcasts during the Indo-Pakistan conflict were worth several divisions in the maintenance of civilian morale. Since de Mellow came by way of the army, I should imagine that he did not have too much formal education. Yet when I listen to him on All-India Radio, I get the impression of a perfectionist, of one who is constantly seeking to achieve the attributes of artistry in his profession.

Cyril Stracey held a permanent commission in the Indian Army from 1937 to 1946: he cast his lot in with the I.N.A. in Malaya.

On release from imprisonment, he served as the Secretary of the Central Organisation of the I.N.A. at Delhi for two years. He was for a year Consul-General for India at San Francisco and thereafter served as first Secretary of the Indian Embassy at Washington. His next posting was to Paris where he was promoted Counsellor and acted for the Ambassador for a considerable spell when the latter fell ill. In April, 1965, he was appointed the first Indian Ambassador to the new-born Republic of Madagascar. His latest posting is as Ambassador to Finland. The Stracey brothers have a remarkable record of success. Pat Stracey, whose book 'Reade, Elephant Hunter' I have referred to earlier, is the eldest. Having qualified for the Imperial Forest Service, he took the place of the father, who had died when the brothers were young. Pat retired fairly recently as a Chief Conservator of Forests. He is now writing books. 'Elephant Gold' and 'Tigers' were published before his latest book on Reade. Ralph, the second brother, qualified for the I.C.S. Cyril Stracey is the third; the fourth brother, Eric, qualified for the Imperial Police and today is Inspector-General of Prisons in the Madras State. As mentioned in another chapter more Anglo-Indians are qualifying for the professions and doing courses of higher studies than ever before.

It is also heartening to see a number of Anglo-Indians going into business.

Denzil D'Monte of Madras is one of the leading businessmen of the Community. Starting from the humblest of beginnings, he gave up service in 1949 to establish the Indian Engineering & Trading Company, with a capital of Rs. 600. The Company has grown from a small trading unit and now occupies its own building in an important business locality of Madras. The Indian Engineering & Trading Company is one of the largest wholesale suppliers of certain specialised components of Auto and Diesel parts. The Company has branches in Bangalore, Hyderabad and Calcutta. There is a modern fully-equipped factory in Madras and the products under the 'DVD' brand have found acceptance in several foreign markets.

Apart from being Vice-President of the Madras branch of the All-India Anglo-Indian Association, Denzil D'Monte has multifarious activities. He is a Director of Messrs. Automac (Madras) Private Ltd., Madras and Bangalore, of Messrs. Automat Rubbers Private

Ltd., of Messrs. Automat Plastics Private Ltd., Bangalore, and Managing Director of Messrs. Pilot Engines Private Ltd., a newly established firm set up to manufacture Auto and Agricultural engines; he is also a partner of Messrs. Pressure Die Cast Products of India, Madras. Last but not least Denzil D'Monte is the owner and publisher of "Thondan", a Tamil weekly of Madras.

An index of the trust reposed in the Community was the request made to me by the Prime Minister, Mrs. Indira Gandhi, in June, 1967, to accept the Governorship of the Punjab. Mrs. Gandhi mentioned that the Punjab is a border, highly strategic State, where the political conditions are not easy, and Government wanted some one on whose judgment they could rely and who would also have the trust of the political groups and parties in the State. While thanking Mrs. Gandhi for this gesture of trust, I regretted my inability to accept the offer. I pointed out to the Prime Minister that I still have a great deal of work to do on behalf of the Community. If I accepted any kind of Government preferment, the Community would feel that I had betrayed the trust that they have so implicitly reposed in me.

Life-Line Of The Community

The All-India Anglo-Indian Association is the life-line of the Community. The well-being, indeed the very existence of the Community is synonymous with the work and achievements of the Association.

The Association has never rested either on its oars or its laurels. It is a matter of some interest that it is the oldest Anglo-Indian Association in the Country and the only All-India Anglo-Indian Association. The original Association, the Eurasian & Anglo-Indian Association of which the present All-India Anglo-Indian Association is the successor, was inaugurated on Saturday the 16th December, 1876, by the Hon'ble Sir Richard Temple, K.C.S.I., Lieutenant-Governor of Bengal, who presided at the Town Hall Calcutta, over a larger assemblage of the Eurasian Community, as it was then known, and Europeans. The Anglo-Indian Empire League, which had branches all over India, was the successor of the Eurasian & Anglo-Indian Association.

At a conference held at Allahabad from the 30th December, 1918, to the 2nd January, 1919, it was decided that the delegates of the Anglo-Indian Empire League and the Anglo-Indian Association combine to have a united body to be called, under the new provision, the Anglo-Indian & Domiciled European Association. The Calcutta Association and the Bengal Provincial Branch of the League amalgamated to form the Anglo-Indian & Domiciled European Association of Bengal. Gidney was then the President-in-Chief of the Anglo-Indian Empire League.

In 1926, the Bengal Association changed its constitution and amalgamated with the Anglo-Indian & Domiciled European Association of India, the successor of the Empire League and of which Gidney was the head. When Burma was part of India the Association took on the name of the Anglo-Indian & Domiciled European Association, India & Burma. After Burma was separated the Association was known as the All-India Anglo-Indian & Domiciled European Association. At my instance the words 'Domiciled European' were dropped in July, 1946.

When I was elected to succeed Gidney in 1942, in spite of Gidney's greatness the Association was in extremely low water financially. Although on paper it had about 90 branches, which included those in what is now Pakistan, the total funds of the Association did not run even into three figures. Fortunately, I was a bachelor and had my own resources. Not only steadily but rapidly I built up the Association infusing new life into the branches and making the Association financially viable. A noticeable feature in Gidney's time was that, by and large, the better-placed members of the Community kept out of the Association. This was perhaps due to the feeling that they did not require the assistance of the Association and the complex that socially and officially they were above those who joined, especially the railwaymen. Within a few years, I was able to change this complex. Today, it would be correct to say that very few of the better-placed Anglo-Indians are outside the Association.

Another significant feature is that, in spite of the exodus of many thousands of Anglo-Indians, the Association today is stronger in membership and resources than it has ever been throughout its long history. At a conservative estimate, more than half the Community, if the families are included, are within the fold of the Association. That by any standards makes the Association uniquely representative. Those who are not members are either the unemployed or under-employed, those who cannot afford to be members, or members of the Armed Forces who are not allowed to join even an organisation like the Association.

Some not very literate Members of Parliament, unable to answer, rationally, argument with argument, occasionally indulge in the cheap gibe that I am a nominated Member. My usual reply is that the interrupters, even if they traverse several incarnations, would never represent their constituencies as I do. I point out that, in fact, I am the only member of Parliament with an All-India constituency. Territorially, the extent of my constituency is conterminous with the Country. The All-India Anglo-Indian Association has a network of over 70 branches spreading from Delhi to Quilon and again from Bombay to Shillong.

The Association does give guidance to its members during the general elections. For the nominations of Anglo-Indians to the Legislatures, under Articles 331 and 333 of the Constitution, the Association elects or selects its nominees. There is a careful, elaborate procedure. The nominees for Parliament are elected. For the State Legislatures the nominees are selected by the Governing Body of the Association which ensures both the capacity and the representative character of the candidates.

And, yet, the Association is not a political organisation. This has been recognised by the Government since the inception of the Association and civilian Government servants are permitted to be members. It is recognised that the Association is a source of stability in times of crisis, especially during strikes. Over and over again at the call of the Association, Anglo-Indian government servants, whether in the Railways or the Telegraphs, have come to the rescue of the Administration. Essentially, the functions of the Association are to look after the educational and the cultural and civic interests of the Community.

Before me Gidney had put the Community on the map of India and secured its special recognition and special statutory safeguards under the Government of India Act of 1935.

In other chapters I have mentioned how after a long, grim struggle I was able to win for the Community special recognition in the Constitution of Independent India, with safeguards accorded to no other minority. Over and over again, the Association has entered the legal lists when the Community's educational interests have been threatened.   In other chapters I have described the numerous legal battles which, as the President-in-Chief of the Association, I have had to fight to save the Anglo-Indian schools from extinction.   These battles I fought not only as President-in-Chief of the Association but in my professional capacity as a practising lawyer.

The Association is the only organisation to which the Anglo-Indians can and, indeed, do look not only for the protection of their corporate interests but also for the redress of individual grievances. As Head of the Association I deal literally with scores of individual cases of members in the services who are seeking remedies against unjust punishment, wrongful supersessions, denial of correct emoluments and so on.

My work as President-in-Chief alone entails several hours of office routine each day.   Scores of members of the Community write to me for educational or monetary assistance, redress of their individual grievances, for scholarships for their children and also seek my legal advice.   I give them legal advice without any professional charge, if they are members of the Association.

Apart from dealing with the daily correspondence from the office-bearers of the Association throughout the Country, I make it a point to reply to every letter from members of the Community, especially from those in the humblest positions or in financial difficulties.

Apart from being the President-in-Chief of the Association and the acknowledged leader of the Community, I also edit the monthly journal of the Association : this takes up much of my time.   This journal, known, today, as 'The Review', has a circulation of almost 6,000 copies.   Apart from dealing with matters which are of interest to the Community, 'The Review' carries articles and contributions, mostly by me, on matters of general, political, legal or international interest.   A criticism is sometimes made that 'The Review' is full of Anthony's articles and speeches. This is not of my choosing.   Anglo-Indians can be extremely articlulate in debate and verbal encounter, but most of them are allergic to getting down to write an article.   To get a single article in a year even from my colleague in Parliament and the Anglo-Indian M.L.As. is like trying to extract blood from a stone.   'The Review' circulates not only to the Community but among members of the Central Government, Members of Parliament, the Judges of the Supreme Court and the Delhi High Court, the Chief Ministers and Governors of the States,

Vice-Chancellors of Universities and leading personalities. 'The Review' also circulates among members of the Community in the U.K., Australia, Canada and the U.S.A. Many of them almost cherish 'The Review' as their continuing link with India.

Among my several commitments is my membership of Parliament. I sit on the front bench of the Opposition. I am also required to give advice and leadership to the Independent Parliamentary Group which has 15 members.

In addition, as Chairman of our Education Society, which is the trust I established in 1958, I preside over the functioning of the Frank Anthony Public Schools. Apart from being the Chairman of the Board of Governors of each school, I am also the Executive Governor of the Frank Anthony Public School, New Delhi, which has over 2000 pupils. I watch the progress of the Schools from day to day. I keep a meticulous check on the teaching standards by calling for the log-books of the Heads of each School and the Record-of-Work books of the teachers. In order to conserve our resources all financial sanctions have to be first secured from me. As our Schools grow the accounts are checked not merely every quarter or half year by Chartered Accountants: there is a daily check.

Last, but not least, I am a busy practising lawyer. As a matter of fact, I happen to be the only Anglo-Indian and, indeed, the only Christian lawyer who practises regularly in the Supreme Court and the Delhi High Court.

Because of these five virtually full-time jobs, it is inevitable that my schedule is not only exacting but, indeed, gruelling. My day starts at 5 a.m. Seldom do I leave my office before 9 or 10 p.m. Not only am I but the Community is fortunate that I have a wife who is not only understanding but appreciative of my work and who is also dedicated to service for the Community. Thus, she was primarily responsible for building up the Frank Anthony Junior School, New Delhi, which was the gallant pioneer of our Schools' Scheme. Working in an honorary capacity she conserves the resources of the School by refusing the assistance of even a clerk or an accountant. And yet the Chartered Accountant's report of the School accounts testifies to her capacity which would do credit to a professional accountant. This is in addition to her administering the School, watching the work of the teachers and the progress of the children. She has an amazing memory and remembers the name of every child in addition to that of every parent.

I may refer here to a certain fairly widespread misconception. Not only the rising generation among other communities but many of the leaders seem to have forgotten the pigmentary texture of the Community. Not long ago one of the front-rank leaders,with whom I am quite friendly but who had never met my wife, after being introduced to her enquired as to what part of Europe she came from. My wife assured him that she was very much "Made in India": although her father was Irish, an O'Neil, he had married an Anglo-Indian and settled in the Country. But the incredulity seemed to persist. My wife told him that there were perhaps thousands of Anglo-Indians with her colouring. This fact seems almost to have been largely forgotten.

Up to Independence, at least one third of the Community were indistinguishable from the Europeans. In certain areas this proportion of the blond type was very high. Thus in the railway centres along the old B.B. & C.I. Railway 70 to 80 per cent of the Community had blond hair and blue eyes, red hair and grey or green eyes. With the exodus of a number of the lighter-complexioned members of the Community, this proportion has gone down. But the Nordic types have not disappeared.

The basic colour consciousness of Indian society can also be exemplified here. When the parents, even the better educated and especially the women, meet my wife, they ask the same question, as to which part of Britain she comes from. When she tells them that she is as good an Indian as any of them, they seem happy about the assurance but are diffident to accept it. They rationalise their doubts with the remark, "Then, you must be a Brahmin Anglo-Indian." Then my wife has to explain, rather laboriously, that in the Community there are no caste distinctions, there are no Brahmins and non-Brahmins.

The reaction of the children also is a reflection of the basic colour consciousness of Hindu society. Like children everywhere, when their brothers and sisters from other schools come to the Frank Anthony Junior School, often they get into an argument as to which is the better institution. They make assertions and counter-assertions about the uniforms, the teachers and, finally, the argument, especially among the youngest of the children, is, "But we have a white Headmistress : you haven't." Even at that very young age colour appears to be the ultimate argument !

The Association is not only the sheet-anchor of the Community's corporate life, it is also the centre of the Community's social life. It is at socials and dances held by the branches that the members have the opportunity to enjoy themselves. My wife often accompanies me on my tours. These visits represent a red-letter day in the life of the local branch and the local community. No king, crowned or uncrowned, could ask for greater loyalty and, indeed, affecttion. As we arrive the office-bearers are at the station to meet us, usually with a beautiful bouquet for my wife : if there is a railway school nearby usually the children, boy scouts and girl guides, make a guard of honour. We either stay at the local hotel or at the home of a senior member of the Community. After a quick bath and breakfast I give interviews to members who have grievances in respect of their conditions of work or service. Where there are Anglo-Indian schools I visit them to address the staff and pupils. If there is a railway workshop or public sector undertaking I usually visit it. The evening function is the piece de resistance of the schedule. Usually it starts at about 6 p.m. It is accompanied by a social and dance. In between I address the Community. Usually these functions last till the small hours of the morning. Because it is not possible for me to visit the branches as often as I would like to, my address to a branch usually lasts at least an hour. My Presidential address at an Annual General Meeting of the Association is longer. Today, I try to keep to one and a half hours but very often my Presidential addresses have lasted from two to two and a half hours. These meetings are usually packed to capacity. One of our office-bearers, who is rather a wit, commenting on my Annual General Meeting address said that when I get up to speak the passage of time should be marked not by a clock but by a calendar ! A constant theme in my addresses is, "India alone means home, in all its connotations, for the Community. India is the only Country where the Community is recognised and respected. It is the only Country where Anglo-Indians, as Anglo-Indians, can achieve the highest of positions commensurate with their character and ability."

Last, but by no means least, the Association does considerable work on behalf of the less fortunate members of the Community.

Every branch has its own poor fund and also its education fund, al-though, today, educational assistance on an increasingly massive scale is given by our Education Society. I tremble to think what would happen to the less fortunate members but for the Association. There is no other organisation or agency to which they can look for assistance.

The largest concentration of the Community is in Calcutta. Typical of the social work being done by the Association is the fact that the Calcutta branch of the Association feeds on an average about 300 needy Anglo-Indians each day. In regard to this charitable work I would pay a tribute to the East India Charitable Trust run mostly by Britons, for the considerable assistance they have continued to give to the Calcutta branch in feeding the less fortunate members of the Community. Homes for the poor and the aged, of which there are quite a number in the Country, are either assisted or run by members of the Association.

The Annual General Meetings of the Association, which are held in different parts of the Country, represent the heart-beat of the Community. The Association annual meetings are a kind of Mecca. To these annual meetings members and office-bearers of the Association from every part of the Country come as on a pilgrimage. At these General Meetings, which last at least three days, problems of the Community are discussed. Usually, the issues discussed are educational, social and civic. There is complete freedom of discussion at the Annual General Meetings. Hard blows are given and taken. And yet there is an atmosphere of camaraderie and brotherhood. Delegates go away refurbished in spirit and with a renewed sense of dedication. I am aware of the criticism, sometimes made that, 'Anthony is a dictator'. And yet those who attend our General Meetings often express their surprise at the complete latitude given by me, as Chairman, to members to question and criticise 'ad libitum'. It is only when I am convinced of the mala fides of a member or an office-bearer, that the basic motive is to disrupt or undermine the necessary discipline of the organisation, that action is taken under the rules. The comparatively few occasions on which the Governing Body has expelled members testify to the restraint we exercise in disciplinary matters.

The office-bearers of the Association are, indeed, the unsung heroes and heroines of the Association saga. I take this opportunity to salute them on behalf of the Community. Without their selfless work and abiding loyalty I might not have had the faith or the courage to persevere in the face of often seemingly impossible odds. The Association continues, more than ever, to be the lifeline of the Community.

All-Indians

. The Anglo-Indians are among the few real All-Indians in the Country, in the sense that they are free not only from communal but regional, caste and linguistic inhibitions. The Anglo-Indians are perhaps the only. Community that is at home in any part of the Country. This is exemplified by the fact that the Anglo-Indians, to whichever part they belong, settle happily in areas such as Bangalore, Jubbulpore and Dehra Dun.

CHAPTER XIII

IN THE EDUCATIONAL VANGUARD

The Frank Anthony Schools' Scheme

A NGLO-INDIAN education and Anglo-Indian schools have had a chequered career. Indeed, Anglo-Indian schools have traversed many vicissitudes, political and financial. The East India Company seldom, if ever, undertook any responsibility towards Anglo-Indian children. Between 1640 and 1660, when the children grew up literally within the sound of shot and shell, it was not necessary for them to have more than a smattering of the 3 Rs. All manner of people were employed as tutors—disabled soldiers, old pensioners, bankrupt merchants or dismissed factors. The first school to be opened was at Fort St. George (Madras), between 1645 and 1650 : that was the result of missionary effort.

Early History

The next fifty years saw a considerable increase in the number of Anglo-Indian children. Because of the growing need, Lady Campbell, the wife of the Governor of Fort St. George, sent out an appeal for funds to start an orphanage for girls. By 1787, the Female Orphan Asylum was established. After this attention was paid to the male children and the Male Orphan Asylum was opened on the pattern of the Calcutta Orphan Asylum, which had been opened there in 1783. There was a generous response to the appeal for funds. All ranks below Field Officers contributed two days' pay and the Generals and Field Officers gave more. At the close of the 18th century the school was financially quite well-off and the number of boys increased from 150 in 1790 to 200 in 1792.

A number were the orphans of non-commissioned officers and private soldiers and were given free education : the rest, the children of officers, paid 3 pagodas for the education and maintenance of each child. A pagoda was the equivalent of about 8 or 9 shillings, that is, equal to about five rupees. All the children were Anglo-Indians. The boys were admitted at the age of 4 and at 14 they were apprenticed as artificers, surveyors and sailors. The Female Orphan Asylum confined itself to Anglo-Indian children born of regular marriages. There was no provision for children born out of wedlock. The Madras Male and Female Asylums continued into the 20th century when they were merged into the Lawrence Asylum at Ootacamund and the Civil Orphan Asylum at Madras.

The Vestry School at Trichinopoly is one of the oldest institutions having been established in 1772 for Anglo-Indian and European boys.

During the 18th century three types of schools—charity, military and private—were established around Calcutta, after the Madras pattern. In 1731 with the aid of S.P.C.K. the Charity School was opened in Calcutta. The school continued to prosper and by 1787 its funds had increased appreciably, when it was decided to extend education also to girls. For several years these institutions continued to be separately maintained. In about 1800 they were amalgamated and called the Calcutta Free School. At that time there were about 150 children, boys and girls, in the school.

In order to meet the needs of the children of officers and soldiers dying in indigent circumstances, the Military Orphan Society was formed in 1783. Two schools were established at Howrah. The Upper Orphan Asylum catered for the children of officers and the Lower Orphan Asylum for the children of other ranks. By 1795 these schools were in a prosperous condition. According to Carey, these schools were, "A harbour of refuge for bachelors in want of wives. Balls were given expressly for the purpose of securing proposals of marriage for the young ladies. Persons in want of wives frequently made their selection of an evening. Officers in the upper provinces sometimes travelled a distance of 500 miles to obtain a wife in this way. The suitors had to satisfy the authorities of the school that they were men of good character and in a position to support a wife. The girls were left entirely free to accept or reject their suitors and were never forced into marriage."

For a little more than 60 years the Upper and Lower Orphan Asylums did most useful work for the Community. Gradually, they began to decline. In 1846, the Upper Orphan Asylum was given up and this was followed a few years later by the Lower Asylum.

Because of the growing demand for education by the Anglo-Indians a large number of private and, indeed, mushroom schools were started by individuals. Most of these disappeared after a few years on the death or retirement of the founder. In the majority of the private schools a number of boys from other communities were also admitted. Thus in Calcutta, Bengali lads from the best families attended these schools. Even in those days in the private schools the day-scholars paid as much as Rs. 16/- per month.

At the beginning of the 19th century the East India Company had established high schools and colleges for Hindus and Muslims, but nothing was done for Anglo-Indians. In Macaulay's famous Minute of 1835 there was no reference to education either of Anglo-Indians or Europeans. The Wood Despatch of 1854, which envisaged a comprehensive system of Indian education and has been referred to as the Magna Carta of English education, only made a passing reference to the "Requirements of an increasing European and Anglo-Indian population." It made no suggestions as to how to meet these requirements.

Self-Help

In spite of the Government's neglect, in the first two decades of the 19th century many schools were established. The majority of these schools were started by public subscription and continued to be supported by donations from Anglo-Indians and Europeans. Between 1830 and 1850 persons like General Claude Martin and Capt. John Doveton, an Anglo-Indian officer in the Nizam's Army, donated large sums of money for the education of Anglo-Indians.

Anglo-Indians also started schools with money raised by themselves. The Parental Academic Institution, Calcutta, was in a sense the first Anglo-Indian school because it was both established and administered by the Community. Funds for setting up this school were raised entirely by the Community. At a meeting at the house of John Ricketts it was decided to form a society, "To promote the education of our children by projecting an institution which shall be managed by a Committee chosen from among the body of parents, guardians and friends." The school was established at 11, Park Street, and classes were begun on the 1st May, 1823. It was a non-sectarian Protestant school. Unfortunately, because of religious differences in the Managing Committee, the Anglican members were permitted to separate and set up their own school which was called the Calcutta High School.

The Calcutta High School was taken over by the Bishop of Calcutta in 1836. At that time it was known as the Calcutta Grammar School. In 1845, Bishop Daniel Wilson, the first Metropolitan of India, took over the school and revived it under the name of St. Paul's School because of its close association with St. Paul's Cathedral, Calcutta. In 1863 it was transferred by the Metropolitan to Darjeeling.

The Parental Academy continued to serve the Community for more than thirty years. Because of the generous bequest in 1855 by Capt. John Doveton, it was raised to the status of a college. In those days it was regarded as a model among colleges. Owing to a dearth of pupils it was closed in 1916, after a very fine record of 60 years. Of the fifty thousand pounds donated by Doveton for the advancement of Anglo-Indian education twenty-three thousand were given to the Parental Academy, which Doveton had assisted even earlier. On the closing down of the Academy this endowment was used to pay for the education of Doveton foundationers in selected schools.

The Dharamtollah Academy, Calcutta, came into existence in the beginning of the 19th century. It reached its zenith with the arrival in 1813 of David Drummond. It began to decline after 1823 and with Drummond's retirement it merged into the Verulum Academy. Henry Derozio, the Anglo-Indian boy genius and poet, was a pupil of Drummond's Academy: in fact, he was Drummond's favourite scholar.

With the appointment of the first Bishop of Madras, there was a large increase in the number of schools between 1815 and 1835. Apart from the Military Orphanages for which there continued to be a great demand, it was thought necessary to establish similar schools for the children of civilians. The Civil Female and Civil Male Asylums were opened in 1815 and 1823 respectively.

The Anglo-Indians of Madras sought to emulate the efforts of the Community in Calcutta and started a Madras Parental Academy. The Community was, however, smaller in number and poorer than those in Calcutta. In 1834 it almost had to close down the school for want of funds. Bishop Corrie took it over and remodelled it on the lines of a British Grammar School. In 1836 it was renamed the Madras Grammar School. After his death the school was redesignated the Bishop Corrie Grammar School.

The Bishop Corrie Grammar School was open not only to Europeans and Anglo-Indians but to other communities who could afford the fees. According to the second report in 1838, there were 139 pupils on the rolls : 109 were Anglo-Indians including 21 boarders, and 30 members of other communities.

Bishop Corrie had underlined the need for more schools for girls. After his death the Bishop Corrie High School for girls was started.

In Bengal, the Anglican Church also began to establish a better type of school. Through the efforts of Bishop Middleton a boys' school associated with St. James' Church was opened, in 1823, with the help of the S.P.C.K. A girls' school was opened in 1830. From about 1830 and onwards the Roman Catholic Church also began to establish schools for members of their faith. Two Church schools were established, one for boys and the other for girls. In 1834 St. Francis Xavier's College, Calcutta, was opened by some Jesuits from Europe.

During the later part of the 18th and the early part of the 19th centuries, with the building of new cantonment stations and the strengthening of some of the older stations, the need for schools also became urgent. Several schools were established in garrison towns such as Bangalore, Cawnpore, Meerut, Secunderabad and Vizagapatam. St. Mark's was established in Bangalore; the Lawrence Royal Military School, in Sanawar, was founded in 1847 by Sir Henry Lawrence for the education of sons and daughters of British soldiers in India.

John Claude Martin, a French military adventurer who settled and died in India, amassed a large fortune partly in the service of the Nawab of Agra. Before his death he left a sum of Rs. 160,000/- for the education of European and Anglo-Indian children. It was ultimately decided by the Supreme Court in Calcutta that the bequest should be devoted to two schools in Lucknow and Calcutta. La Martiniere, Lucknow, was built in 1830 on the ground which had already been purchased for the purpose. Six years later La Martiniere, Calcutta, was founded.

Dr. George Edward Lynch Cotton came to Calcutta as the Metropolitan of India in succession to Bishop Wilson.   He had served as an Assistant Master at Rugby under the famous Dr. Arnold.   Fresh from the headmastership of Marlborough, he saw that the best way to help the Anglo-Indians was to give them good schools.   At the thanksgiving service in St. Paul's Cathedral, Calcutta, on the 28th July, 1860, he appealed for funds to establish institutions for Anglo-Indian (Eurasian was the word then used) and European children. He evolved a scheme to establish a chain of efficient schools for the Community throughout the Country.   In the same year he submitted a comprehensive report to the Government.

In response to the scheme put forward by Bishop Cotton, Lord Canning wrote his celebrated minute of the 29th October, 1860. This was referred to as the Magna Carta of Anglo-Indian education.

Lord Canning's Minute was approved by the Secretary of State. In about 16 years 10 good schools were founded in the main hill-stations in India from the money raised by private subscription. After Bishop Cotton's death in 1866, the money collected assumed the character of a memorial fund.

The school founded in 1867 in Simla was named after Bishop Cotton.   Two other Bishop Cotton Schools were established, one in Nagpur in 1863 and the other in Bangalore in 1865.   The Cainville House School for Girls, Mussoorie, was founded in 1864.

In the Bombay Presidency the Bishop's High School for boys was established in 1864.   The Diocesan Boys' and Girls' Schools were established in Naini Tal in 1869.   The Breek's Memorial and St. Stephen's School for Girls were established in the Nilgiris in 1876.

A Commission appointed in 1871 to enquire into the condition of these schools reported that the proposals of Lord Canning's Minute had been overlooked and that out of an estimated total of 26,649 Anglo-Indian and European children of school-going age only 15,067 were actually under instruction; the rest—between 11,000 and 12,000—were growing up without any education.

In 1876 the Anglo-Indian Association made representations to the Government underlining the vital need for education.   In 1879 Lord Lytton took up the question observing that it was incredible that in spite of Lord Canning's warning so little had been done by the Government in nearly twenty years.   In November, 1879, Lytton appointed a Committee with Archdeacon Baly, the Archdeacon of

Calcutta, as Secretary to enquire into Eurasian and European education and to report on the educational requirements of the Community.

After consulting Local Governments on Archdeacon Baly's report, Lord Lytton wrote his famous report on the 31st August, 1881. On this minute the Government of India decided to make European education a special department of Public Instruction. 'European Education' remained the official designation until 1932: after that it was changed to 'Anglo-Indian Education'. The schools were designated 'European' to distinguish them from the other schools. The term 'European' was defined as meaning, "Any person of European descent, pure or mixed, who retains European habits and modes of life": the definition included the Armenians. This was in deference to the fact that the East India Company had, in recognition of their special services, classified the Armenians as Europeans.

In 1882 the Government of India appointed an Education Commission for Indian education. As European education had already been the subject of a report by a Special Committee, it was excluded from the Commission's terms of enquiry. Lord Curzon called a conference of all Directors of Public Instruction in September, 1901, to review the whole field of education. At this conference it was observed that there were no special rules for education in the European schools. It was suggested that the Bengal Code, after suitable revision, be made the basis of a common code for the whole Country.

In 1902 a Committee consisting of all the Inspectors of European Schools in India, with the Director of Public Instruction of Burma as President, was entrusted with the revision of the Bengal Code. After approval by the Provincial Governments, it became in 1905 the All-India European Schools' Code.

The 1911 Census Report showed that every European and Anglo-Indian child in Burma was attending school. Illiteracy was rare in the United Provinces. In the large cities of Calcutta and Madras, however, there had arisen a population of destitute Anglo-Indians living in the worst of slum conditions. The children were neglected. The Census underlined that while a part of the Community had achieved a considerable advance in education and economic status, there was a recession among the poorer sections.

Before the Census, there was an unofficial conference of all the Protestant schools. This conference was called in December, 1910, by Sir Robert Laïdlaw, a successful Calcutta merchant who took a deep interest in the education of Anglo-Indians. The conference addressed itself to the finding of ways and means for concerted action to provide the necessary educational facilities to the Community to enable it to meet on equal terms the increasing competition they would encounter in their efforts to secure an honourable career in the land of their birth. The Committee estimated that a sum of £ 250,000 was necessary to meet the needs of the schools. It was decided to make the necessary appeals not only in India but in the U.K. and the Colonies. A London Committee was formed, which included the Archbishop of Canterbury. The appeal was launched in 1911 and was given a good start by Sir Robert Laidlaw himself who donated £ 50,000. The Church of England contributed £ 20,000. Altogether, a sum of £ 90,000 was collected.

In July, 1912, the Government of India summoned a conference on the education of the Community. It was presided over by Sir Harcourt Butler, the Member for Education. The Butler Commission underlined two of the most urgent needs of the Community. It recommended extension of education to all those children who did not attend school and improvement of the salary and prospects of teachers. It also recommended a more modern and practical type of education for the majority of the boys.

On the question of examinations it deplored the vicious competition that had been introduced in schools by the Code in the earlier years. It expressed the hope that education would not be sacrificed to examinations and that girls, especially, would be saved from wanton mental and physical strain.

On the question of teachers' salaries a resolution was adopted, declaring that these should be raised to give the teachers a respected professional status. The salaries should be on an incremental scale for a period of 10 years and it should be obligatory on all schools to have a provident fund scheme. The Government, however, refused to assume full responsibility for Anglo-Indian and European education because a great majority of the schools were denominational.

Very little concerted action was made during the next 20 years.

Later History

During 1918-1919, an unofficial body, with Sir Alfred Pickford a prominent Calcutta businessman, as its Secretary, undertook an enquiry into the conditions of the Community in Calcutta. The Sub-Committee on education found that there was ample provision for even the children of the poor, but the education given in the majority of the elementary schools did not equip them sufficiently to command a decent wage. It recommended more preparatory schools in mofussil stations and, for the majority of children, a more practical type of elementary education with a definite vocational bias after fourteen. The report also recommended the formation of a technical institution in Calcutta.

With the introduction of the reforms in 1921, education became a provincial transferred subject, that is, under the control of the Minister responsible to the Legislature; Anglo-Indian education was classed as a 'Provincial reserved subject', that is, under the control of a member of Council. But as the grants-in-aid were subject to the vote of the Provincial Legislature, the protection was often inadequate. Although the Governors were, under the Instruments of Instructions, authorised to restore these cuts by certification, they seldom, if ever, did so. In the Community's memorandum to the Indian Statutory Commission, commonly known as the Simon Commission, instances were given of the cuts, particularly by the Bengal Legislature, which the Governor consistently refrained from restoring.

In his memorandum to the Simon Commission, among other things, Gidney had asked that Anglo-Indian education be made a Central subject, because it would thus be easier to maintain uniformity in standards and curriculum which was necessary for an all-India community such as the Anglo-Indians, who were subject to transfer from one part of the Country to another, especially in such services as the Railways and the Telegraphs.

The interim report of the Statutory Commission, known as the Hartog report, however, felt that provincial control would be better. As a result of the Round Table Conference, the Irwin Committee was appointed to deal with Anglo-Indian education. This Committee recognised, "The special needs and circumstances of the Anglo-Indian Community and the necessity of maintaining a proper and adequate standard of education." The Committee recommended that instead of education being made a Central responsibility, its uniformity could be secured by other means, such as the formation of an Inter-Provincial Board and Provincial Boards of Anglo-Indian education.

The third session of the Round Table Conference noted the report of the Irwin Committee and, in keeping with the recommendations, a conference on Anglo-Indian and European education was held in New Delhi, on the 6th and 7th April, 1933.   The Conference, which was opened by the Viceroy, was attended by twelve members apart from observers.   Gidney was one of the members.   The Conference discussed the functions and constitution of the Inter-Provincial Board. The inaugural meeting of the Inter-Provincial Board was held in Delhi in June, 1935.   The proceedings were opened by the Hon'ble Khan Bahadur Mian Sir Fazl-I-Husain, K.C.S.I., K.C.I.E., Kt., Member of the Viceroy's Executive Council.

The second meeting of the Board was held in New Delhi on the 17th and 18th February, 1936.   This meeting was convened by Sir · George Anderson, Educational Commissioner with the Government of India, who was the Secretary of the meeting.   At that meeting the rules of procedure and constitution of the Inter-Provincial Board for European and Anglo-Indian Education were adopted.

1944 Commission

In 1944, the Inter-Provincial Board for European and Anglo-Indian Education set up a Commission.   I was asked to be a member.   But as I was due to visit the U.K. to present the case of the Community to the British Cabinet, I nominated Mr. Meredith Doutre, then Principal of Christ Church Boys' School, Jabalpur. Mr. K.G. Saiyidain, later Education Secretary to the Government of India, was one of the members.   The Chairman was Bishop Barne, Bishop of Lahore.

The Commission toured and took evidence from the 26th September to the 19th December, 1945.   In Chapter II of its report, the Commission observed, "The Community has always attached the greatest importance to the education of its children.   The fact that practically every child between the ages of 6 and 11 has been to school indicates that the Community is a hundred per cent literate." The Commission recorded its agreement with the view that the future of the Anglo-Indian Community was bound up largely with the existence of Anglo-Indian schools.

The Commission considered the position of 316 primary and secondary schools designated as 'Anglo-Indian'.   Of these 247 were located in the plains and 69 in the hills.   There were 180 boarding schools and 136 day schools. The Commission observed that there were 33 orphanages of which 10 were located in the hills and 23 in the plains and that there was room for a further increase, particularly in the larger towns like Calcutta, Bombay and Madras. Of the 69 Railway schools designated as 'Anglo-Indian', 62 were primary, 4 middle and 3 high schools.

The Commission observed that out of every 100 Anglo-Indian children in the lowest class, approximately 83 proceeded to the middle school stage, 45 to the high school stage, 5 to the Intermediate or Cambridge Higher School Certificate stage, and 2 to the University degree stage.

The Commission underlined the fact that the average income of the Anglo-Indian parent was from Rs. 150 to 200 per month, and because of the increased cost of education many parents found it difficult to continue giving their children further education. It also pointed out that a large percentage of the pupils did not like to continue with a purely literary and academic type of education which was not congenial to their aptitudes. The Commission referred to the fact that it was well known that the young people of the Community had a natural aptitude for handling tools and machines.

The Commission further pointed out that technical education was of vital importance. It recognised that technical education could not be given in Anglo-Indian schools because of its prohibitive cost. Anglo-Indian boys, therefore, have to make use of the new technical schools envisaged in the Sargent Scheme.

The Commission underlined the need for improved standards of teaching in Indian languages and recommended that the teaching of Indian languages should be compulsory from the Primary to the High School stage. It pointed out that unless the children had a reasonable mastery of one of the Indian languages, there would be a feeling of estrangement between them and the rest of the Country. One vital matter to which the Commission drew attention was that, "The creation of the right attitudes and values is more a matter of the teacher approach and outlook than of the actual content of the syllabus." The Commission recommended an All-India Central Training College for men and women. In such a college there would be a sufficient intake of pupils to ensure adequate equipment and proper staff.

The Commission noted that there had been no increase in the

Government grants and, in effect, the cost borne by the Government had decreased by 11 per cent. During a period of 19 years, the cost on education had gone up by 42 per cent, the burden of which had fallen entirely on Anglo-Indian parents. The Commission pointed out that while expenditure by Government on non-Anglo-Indian institutions since 1926-1927 had increased by 29 per cent, expenditure on Anglo-Indian schools, during the same period, had decreased. It also observed that the majority of the Provincial Governments had so interpreted the educational guarantees for the Anglo-Indian Community that what was meant to be the statutory minimum had become a statutory maximum of aid. The Commission pointed to the fact that the burden borne by the Anglo-Indian parent was considerably higher than that borne by an average non-Anglo-Indian parent in a non-Anglo-Indian school.

The Commission also referred to the progressive decrease in the number of Railway schools. From 95 they had been reduced to 69. The Commission felt that if these schools were abolished, many Anglo-Indians would be deprived of the opportunity to secure a suitable primary education for their children.

When the Commission's draft report was sent to me in 1946, I submitted my comments, which I am glad to say were accepted by the members. Some of these comments are reproduced below. They show that because Anglo-Indian education continued to be largely dominated by Europeans who were not in touch with the psychological milieu in the Country and the real needs of the pupils, most schools continued to subscribe to educational policies which were at least psychologically outmoded.

Some of my comments were as follows.

"I feel that the Commission's view, as set out in paragraph 6, concerning instruction in the Indian languages, does not go far enough. I consider that the recommendations of the Commission on this subject are completely inadequate. Even in the past, Anglo-Indians have been seriously handicapped in the employment market by the absurdly low standard of instruction in the Indian languages. With the momentous political changes and the avowed policy to introduce the regional languages, increasingly, as the media of instruction in the Universities, Anglo-Indian education, if the present standard of instruction in the Indian languages is continued, will be economically suicidal for the Community. Not only will Anglo-Indians not be able to pursue courses of higher studies but they will be disqualified for employment in the most ordinary appointments."

"I have always felt that our schools have been hide-bound by British insularity in the teaching and learning of Indian languages. I have never agreed that it is not possible for the Anglo-Indian to acquire in the Indian languages facility equal, or almost equal, to the standard of his mother-tongue, English. Whatever the inhibitions of our educationists may have been in the past, necessity must now compel our schools immediately to raise the standard of instruction in the regional languages. Further, it is not enough merely to indicate some sort of a levelling up. We should prescribe as the standard of instruction in the regional languages, for our schools, the standard obtaining in non-Anglo-Indian schools. This is not only not an extravagant demand, but under present and, inevitably, under future conditions, absolutely necessary if the Community wishes to survive economically."

Other Comments

"I feel strongly that the phraseology used in certain parts of the Commission's report is psychologically ill-conceived. I refer to the use of the phrase 'without losing their European identity', which appears on page 9 of the Report. Such a phrase in no way strengthens the claim of the Community which does insist on the preservation of its Anglo-Indian identity. My objections to such phraseology are threefold. It tends to perpetuate national apart from a community identity. It gratuitously provokes resentment in the minds of members of other communities who may well read into such phraseology the desire on the part of the Community to perpetuate some form of arrogance and snobbery. This is a very real psychological danger which the thinking Anglo-Indian is very fully aware of."

"The second objection is a legal one. Europeans will be aliens in the New India. Any claim to a European identity will provoke the reply that we should seek to preserve it in Europe and not in India. Further, no Indian Government will regard it as an obligation, either moral or legal, to make provision for the preservation of any European identity."

"My third objection is that such phraseology cuts across the position which I, as the leader of the Community, have taken up in my efforts to secure a place for the Community in the life of the Country. This place and the very recognition accorded to the Community in the Constituent Assembly have been due entirely to the policy of the All-India Anglo-Indian Association in insisting on the fact that Anglo-Indians are Indians by nationality but Anglo-Indian by Community."

"I also consider the phraseology used on pages 14 and 18 of the Report as likely to cause resentment. I refer to the clause, "To preserve the essential characteristics of these schools, the admission of Indian pupils should not exceed 40% of the total enrolment of the school" (page 14), and the expression, "That the admission of Indian pupils to Anglo-Indian schools should continue" (page 18). A gratuitous distinction has been made between Indians on the one hand and Anglo-Indians on the other. It has been an intensely difficult task for me to break down this distinction in the political sphere. But, on this breaking down has depended the continuing recognition of the Community in the new political set-up. It will be most unfortunate for Anglo-Indians themselves, in the Report, to attempt to revive outworn ideas, which have done the Community considerable harm in the past. I have already made it clear that our whole claim to a place of recognition in India is based on the fact that we are Indians by nationality and Anglo-Indians by Community."

Discrimination

Up till 1947, European and Anglo-Indian education as it was called was dominated by the Europeans. In his own way Gidney did his best to wear down the inhibitions and prejudices obtaining generally in these schools. A persistent demand by Gidney was for larger employment of qualified Anglo-Indian teachers in the higher posts and for members of the Community to be on the Governing bodies of schools. Gidney canvassed this demand strongly before the Hartog Committee, which was an auxiliary of the Simon Commission.

The most outstanding evidence, on behalf of the Community before the Hartog Committee, was by the Rev. G.C. Rogers, Headmaster of Christ Church Boys' School, Jubbulpore.

There is an observation by Gidney in the June, 1929 Review to the following effect:

"Rev. Rogers' evidence stands out conspicuously as the best

tendered by any member of the Community. He impressed the Committee in his inimitable way and I am told that he did much to eradicate any doubts that were entertained on the subject of Anglo-Indian education being entrusted to Anglo-Indian teachers."

Efforts had been made to secure at least one representative of the Community on the Governing Bodies of La Martiniere, Calcutta, and Dow Hill Girls' School, Kurseong. Through the Anglo-Indian Review Gidney carried on an unremitting campaign. Thus, there is a reference in the June 1929 Review to the blatant discrimination practised in La Martiniere, Calcutta. There were seven imported European teachers—the highest receiving a salary of Rs. 1200 and the lowest Rs. 550 per month, almost a princely scale at a time when the purchasing power of the rupee was almost ten times what it is today. But there were only two Anglo-Indian teachers. When the School was in financial difficulties, the school authorities fell back on Anglo-Indian teachers. But after a munificent bequest by Sir Paul Chater, Anglo-Indian teachers were replaced by European teachers.

Gidney referred to the fact that Christ Church Boys' School, Jubbulpore, and Philander Smith College, Naini Tal, two of the finest schools in India, were entirely staffed—from the Principal downwards—by Anglo-Indians. Gidney and Rogers, even more strongly, refuted the evidence given by Wordsworth and Holmes of La Martiniere, Calcutta, who indulged in much special pleading for continuing European hegemony in Anglo-Indian schools. Gidney referred to the fact that the La Martiniere Governing Body did not have a single member of the Community on it.

There is a reference in the August 1926 Anglo-Indian Review to the fact that one of the younger European assistant masters at La Martiniere, Calcutta, wished to marry an Anglo-Indian girl. When he sought permission from the Principal, he received a letter on behalf of the Governing Body threatening him with dismissal if he contracted the marriage. This was in an Anglo-Indian school where over 90 per cent of the pupils were Anglo-Indians !

The Rev. G.C. Rogers

The Community has produced many outstanding teachers. I remember K.C. Neogy, a distinguished member of the Cabinet after Independence, telling me that what he had learned in life he owed to some great Anglo-Indian teachers in Bengal, at whose feet he had sat. George Rogers lived and worked at a time when there was a blank wall of discrimination in the European and Anglo-Indian Schools against Anglo-Indian teachers. The most declasse European would invariably be projected over the head of the most outstanding Anglo-Indian teacher. It was regarded as sheer educational heresy for an Anglo-Indian school to have an Anglo-Indian Head. Boards of Governors, usually entirely European, ensured that no Anglo-Indian was appointed to a Headship. George Clement Rogers, an orphan boy, forged his way through seemingly impossible difficulties and was among the pioneering Anglo-Indian Heads of schools. I made it a point to go down from Delhi to preside at a condolence meeting held in my old school Christ Church, Jubbulpore. George Rogers had passed away at Bangalore towards the end of April, 1948. My address at the condolence meeting held in May recaptures a certain contemporary atmosphere.

"The news of Mr. Rogers' sudden death came as a shock to me. I have no doubt that it came equally as a shock to those who had the privilege of being his pupils or of working with him. He had a rare gift not only of commanding respect, without forcing it, but also of inspiring deep and abiding affection in his pupils."

"As one who sat at his feet from the beginning to the end of my school career, I know I shall be forgiven if I reminisce. The name of George Clement Rogers was a household word in Anglo-Indian homes throughout the Country. Personally, I regarded him as one of the very greatest of educationists the Anglo-Indian Community has produced. An orphan boy, by dint of character, tenacity and private study, he acquired the highest of educational qualifications. His life and his work were synonymous with Christ Church. I remember his telling me that he took over the School when it had less than 30 pupils. He lived to see it grow, and to guide it into one of the premier institutions of the Country. An education commission, which toured the Country in 1926, placed Christ Church School among the six best schools in India. He was perhaps the first Anglo-Indian to be a Headmaster in India or at any rate the first who commanded universal respect. He was one of the few Anglo-Indians who could meet, on absolutely equal terms, the European. He never tolerated patronage from the European, however highly placed. He was a powerful and lucid speaker and a preacher who attracted crowds. British Bishops trailed as pygmies, dwarfed by

George Rogers' massive intellect and deep scholarship. I also know that many Europeans resented his scholarship and ability. As an educationist, George Rogers had a rare gift, not given to many teachers—that of inspiring the confidence and love of his boys. He always put us on our honour, and few of us ever betrayed his trust. Often, deliberately, he would walk out of an examination hall, and thus leave us without an invigilator, knowing that we would not crib."

"As a builder of character he left an indelible impression on those who passed through the portals of the School. He had a habit of emphasising principles and morality by quotations. Three of them stand out vividly in my memory. How often we heard him say to a pupil, 'Boy, soil anything but never soil your honour'. He was fond of reciting the verse from Tennyson which runs,

> "I held it truth with him who sings
> To one clear harp in divers tones
> That men may rise on stepping stones
> Of their dead selves to higher things."

The words of the Psalmist,

> "What shall it profit a man if he gains
> the whole world, but lose his own soul?"

represented another quotation of his.

"George Rogers was a profound scholar of English. This scholarship was furbished by a deep knowledge of Latin. He spoke and wrote English with absolute confidence, in the knowledge of his mastery of the language. He was a purist both as regards phraseology and enunciation. At his feet I learned a critical appreciation of English helped by an invaluable study of Latin. He taught us not so much of dead grammar as of living syntax. No pupil could ever forget Rogie's (as we affectionately called him) insistence on correct pronunciation : when a boy asked for 'invites' instead of 'invitations' Rogie's immediate reply used to be, "Boy, I shall flog you if you use that word again; if you want invitations ask for invitations." When a boy talked of 'married' (mareed) he immediately checked him and made him pronounce it over and over again as married (marrayed). No pupil was allowed to say forty (fortee). In all such words he emphasised the last syllable. And so I can go on to give hundreds of instances where he broke pupils from all tendency to speak with what is popularly known as the 'Chee Chee' accent."

"As a sportsman, George Rogers had few equals. Even as he grew older and wider in girth, he played cricket with an impeccably straight bat, and bowled a deadly googly. Those were the halcyon days of sport in the School, when Christ Church swept everything before it in sport: when the School eleven used to whip European teams with County bats and Christ Church Old Boys' won the Aga Khan hockey trophy three years in succession. One of the things which Rogie pointed to with a certain amount of pride was a framed scoring sheet showing that the School eleven had skittled out the first eleven of the Hampshire Regiment for a blob. That he regarded as a world record."

"For twenty-eight years George Rogers served Christ Church. For me it is a bitter thought that he left the School under unhappy circumstances. It is often said that a prophet is not without honour save in his own country. Little, malicious people made it difficult for Rogie to carry on. Rather than face their petty malice, he resigned. He left largely unsung and unhonoured. I was able to undo, partly, the ingratitude served out to him by Jubbulpore. Although he had been retired for about 10 years, in 1944 I asked the Viceroy to confer the O.B.E. on him, which was done."

"George Rogers was not only an educationist. While he was here no Anglo-Indian boy, however poor, was refused education. Countless lads owe everything to him. He kept them in school free of charge. He fed and clothed them. He also rendered honorary service to the Church as Honorary Chaplain for many, many years. He was inordinately proud of his Community. For 17 years he represented the Anglo-Indian Community in the Central Provinces Legislature. Needless to say that with his scholarship and ability he represented the Community with distinction. He accompanied the late Sir Henry Gidney in order to give evidence before the Hartog Education Committee which was an auxiliary of the Simon Commission. He was also for many years a member of the Jubbulpore Corporation. He was proud of being an Indian and proud of being an Anglo-Indian."

"It is said that monuments in brick and mortar are but temporary—that the only monuments which endure are those enshrined in the hearts and the minds of men. I have no doubt that this permanent memorial will endure among his pupils wherever they may be."

Inter-State Board For Anglo-Indian Education

Immediately after my taking over the leadership of the Community, in 1942, I addressed myself to the dangerously outmoded psychology obtaining in some of the European and Anglo-Indian schools. In speech after speech, I underlined the fact that while the teaching in these schools may be good, the psychology was bad. The tendency was to glorify everything that was British and, equally, to denigrate everything that was Indian. During my tours to every part of the Country, I made it a point to address the staff and pupils of the schools. My talks not seldom provoked ill-concealed resentment from the British staff. I told them that they were, at best, birds of passage and as the accredited leader of the Community I could not stand by and allow them to perpetuate attitudes and values which would invite destruction for the Community.

A measure of this reactionary attitude was the fact that in spite of all his efforts Gidney could not even become a member of the Inter-Provincial Board for European and Anglo-Indian Education.

In November, 1947, I was unanimously elected the Chairman of the Inter-Provincial Board for European and Anglo-Indian Education. The Provincial Governments and the non-official members, which included several Europeans, joined hands to elect me as Chairman. There is the following report in the December, 1947, Anglo-Indian Review.

"We are glad to say that the official and non-official members have endorsed the President-in-Chief's election, and particularly the Provincial Governments. We have reason to believe that some maliciously inclined nondescripts endeavoured to get the Madras Government not to accept the change. We are glad, however, that the Madras Government appreciating the malicious character of this obstruction, ignored it and sent a telegram approving of Mr. Anthony's election as chairman." I should make it clear that the nondescripts referred to were not Europeans but Anglo-Indians.

My election marked a water-shed in Anglo-Indian education and the increasing control by Anglo-Indians in formulating educational policy for Anglo-Indian schools.

In my first address to the meeting of the Inter-Provincial Board held in New Delhi on the 10th January, 1948, I underlined the need for eradicating the wrong psychology in Anglo-Indian Education. I pointed out that while I recognised that the standards were good from the purely educational point of view, the psychology was wrong. I warned that unless the psychology was changed, it would destroy the schools, the education and the position of the Community in the Country.

I illustrated not only the harm but the hostility that this wrong psychology in Anglo-Indian schools had built up against the Community. I had been approached by the Board, before I assumed the position of Chairman, to get a grant from the Government to enable a survey to be made of Anglo-Indian education. I was asked to discuss the matter with a senior official in the Education Ministry. His first reaction was a blunt refusal of my request for the grant. I then suggested that we should both drop our official attitudes and speak as individuals. He said, "I am glad you have asked me to do that. I was educated at an Anglo-Indian school. I owe what I regard as my good education to my school. But all the while I was in that Anglo-Indian school I could not openly with self-respect say that I was an Indian." I told him, "I agree with you : that psychology still exists. I am glad that it does not exist today as it did before but my whole object in coming to you with this request is first to destroy that psychology. I myself realise that it exists. I realise its dangerous character and I want our education to be reformed. That is my main purpose in coming to you." He said, "If that is your object you can have your grant." That is how I got the funds for the 1944 Commission on Anglo-Indian Education.

I emphasised to the Board that I had regarded some Anglo-Indian schools, because of the wrong psychology for which the European educationists had been responsible, as hot-beds of anti-Indian complexes. The schools, because of this wrong psychology, had not only made the Indian, as he was called, work under a sense of discrimination, but had taught Anglo-Indians to look away not only from their Country but from their Community.

At this meeting on my proposal the term 'European' was dropped from the name of the Board. I explained that this change was long overdue as neither the Board nor the schools would come within the purview of the constitutional safeguards I had secured if they continued to use the designation 'European', as the safeguards were only intended for Anglo-Indian education and Anglo-Indian schools. Since the reorganisation of the States, the Board has been known as 'The Inter-State Board for Anglo-Indian Education'.

Over the years the Inter-State Board has performed functions and done work that have been decisive in maintaining uniformly high standards in Anglo-Indian schools throughout the Country. The Board laid down a formula by which glaring disparities between the salaries of the Principal and the top staff and other members of the staff were removed. It became, increasingly, a paramount instrument for co-ordinating the standards of almost 300 schools throughout the Country. Today, there are about 268 schools recognised as Anglo-Indian.

Because of the uniformity of standards introduced by the Inter-State Board, this system of education has not only survived but taken its place in the vanguard of Indian education. The schools are sought after increasingly by parents of all communities.

I have repeatedly underlined that the term 'Anglo-Indian' is not used in any communal sense. It denotes a system of education with certain attributes. The Inter-State Board filled the breach at a crucial, transitional period in the life and history of the Anglo-Indian system of education.

The Board has much work to do. It is at present in the process of formulating a uniform modern syllabus for schools and also revising the syllabus for Anglo-Indian training colleges. I am glad to say that the Central Government and the majority of the States continue to be associated with this Board, and to make subventions which enable it to continue its very valuable work.

Anglo-Indian Schools

Anglo-Indian schools, today, cater for a majority of non-Anglo-Indian children. They serve a national purpose in education. They form the largest group of what may be referred to as All-India schools.

I have insisted that the three-language formula be implemented in these schools. Although I have been one of the strongest opponents of Hindi chauvinism, I have always been acutely aware that political considerations must not be allowed to interfere with the quality of education and the educational needs of the pupils.

Today, however, the three-language formula has become little more than an empty slogan. The Anglo-Indian schools are among the few that really and honestly seek to implement this formula. More and more it is being honoured in the breach than in the observance. The Hindi States, encouraged by the almost irresponsible statements of Triguna Sen, the Education Minister, advocating the rapid introduction of the regional languages, killed the three-language formula. The Hindi Herrenvolk have arrogated to themselves the right to learn only one language, Hindi. Reacting strongly to the Hindi chauvinists' thrust, Tamil Nadu has also helped to bury the three-language formula. Hindi has now been banished from the scheme of studies even at the school stage in Tamil Nadu. This is tragically unfortunate because with English as the medium and Hindi as a permissible second language, at any rate in Anglo-Indian schools, children were able to transfer from one part of the Country to another without difficulty. There was no serious dislocation of their scheme of language studies. Tamil Nadu's dictat will be a crippling blow to non-Hindi-speaking children studying there. Thus Anglo-Indian and other non-Tamil elements, although long in the State, usually took Hindi as their second language. This was because of the liability of the parents to transfer all over the Country where instruction in Tamil is just not available. The Anglo-Indian schools still seek to continue with the three-language formula. In the Hindi States and Delhi, English is of course the medium, Hindi is the second language and, usually, Sanskrit the third language. In States like Bengal and Mysore, which permit Hindi, a large number of pupils from outside the region take Hindi as the second language, in which case the regional language is taught as the third language.

Article 337 of the Constitution which guaranteed grants for the benefit of the Anglo-Indian Community as made in the financial year ending 31st March, 1948, has now wasted out. That article contemplated a reduction every three years by 10% of the amount of the grant till, at the end of ten years, to the extent to which they were a special concession to the Community, they would cease. This guarantee ceased to operate after 1960.

Some States, however, continue to make grants, especially indigent grants, to Anglo-Indian schools. Quite frankly, some of the poorer schools would find it difficult, if not impossible, to provide education to the poor children without these indigent grants. With the wasting out of the constitutional guarantee under Article 337 in

1960, however, the legal position with regard to the grants has changed. When I argued the case on behalf of the Anglo-Indian schools in the Kerala educational reference in the Supreme Court in 1958, the basic ratio which I was able to secure from the Supreme Court was that since the grants to Anglo-Indian schools were not grants in the ordinary sense they were not ex-gratia, being under a constitutional obligation, therefore the State Governments could not treat the Anglo-Indian schools as if they were aided schools in the ordinary sense. Schools which are aided in the ordinary way are liable to considerable Government control, indeed interference with their internal administration. That was the effect of the Supreme Court opinion in the 1958 reference.

Anglo-Indian schools could not preserve their character and, indeed, their independence or the competence of their management, if they were subject to interference by State Governments. Because of this Anglo-Indian schools have increasingly given up aid although some State Governments have offered it to them even after the wasting out of the constitutional guarantee. Quite frankly, I have advised them to do without aid because aid can at any time become an instrument for garrotting these schools.

In terms of the Supreme Court's opinion in the Kerala education reference, if a school takes aid the State education authorities have the power even to appoint and remove the Manager of the School. With such power in the hands of State Governments, Anglo-Indian schools could never preserve their character. A school may well be told that their manager shall be from another community, the majority of their teachers from some other community not even Christian. Because of this very real danger, I have advised Anglo-Indian schools not to take aid if they can possibly do without it.

An unhappy and indeed grimly ironical consequence of this is that the Anglo-Indian Community is perhaps the only community in India whose children are not getting any kind of Government assistance. While under Article 45 of the Constitution the Government is enjoined to provide free and compulsory education to all children until they complete the age of 14 years, this injunction is in fact meaningless for the Anglo-Indian Community.

There are two reasons for this. Firstly, more and more Anglo-Indian schools have come out of aid because of the very real danger of an attempt to strangle them by mala fide interference. Secondly,

it is not the policy of State Governments, indeed of any State Government, to run English-medium schools. Thus the education of the
poor children of the Community represents a burden to be borne
entirely by the Community.

A significant fact not sufficiently appreciated is that with Education being a State subject, and with the increasing emphasis on regional and parochial trends in education, the only All-India schools
are the Anglo-Indian schools and a handful run by the Central
Government. The contribution of the Anglo-Indian Schools in
preserving some integration in education and educational standards
is out of all proportion to their numbers. They are a unique
and, indeed, an irreplaceable boon for children of parents who
are liable to transfer from one part of the Country to another.
Thus for members of the Armed Forces and the Central services
and for the business community, these schools represent the only
guarantee of the continuity of the education of their children. The
Anglo-Indian schools are among the few that, in fact, attempt to turn
out All-Indians, that is, boys and girls, young men and young
women, free from the inhibitions of regionalism, communalism,
linguism and casteism.

Council For The Indian School Certificate Examination

For some time I had been worried by the likelihood of certain
State Governments suddenly refusing to give us facilities for a worthwhile examination through the medium of English. By the simple
device of doing away with the English-medium examination, a State
Government hostile to the English language could pull the carpet
from under the feet of the English-medium schools. In fact, there
had been a warning that States such as the U.P. and Madhya Pradesh, after a period of a few years, would discontinue the facility for
taking a secondary or higher secondary examination through the
medium of English. I, therefore, cast around for an All-India English-medium examination on the continuance of which we could rely.

My first idea was to liaise with the Central Board examination
which had been set up, in the first place, for the English-medium
schools in what were then known as the Part C States. When I
made this suggestion, however, at a meeting of the Inter-State Board
for Anglo-Indian Education the official representatives of the State
Governments were in general disagreement. They felt that the

Central Board examination did not offer adequate standards and that it would adversely affect the standards in Anglo-Indian schools. After that I got in touch with the Cambridge Syndicate.

The Central Government was also negotiating with the Cambridge Syndicate as they were disposed to take over and run the old Senior Cambridge examination in liaison with the Cambridge Syndicate. Perhaps I moved faster than the Central Government.

The then Chairman of the Syndicate, Sir Ivor Jennings, Master of Trinity Hall, Cambridge, and a famous writer on Constitutional law, came to Delhi to discuss the position with me. Ultimately, I was able to persuade him to allow the Inter-State Board for Anglo-Indian Education to initiate the Indian School Certificate examination in India.

I pointed out that the managing body of the Council would have to be an Indian body as, otherwise, there would be psychological resistance. I also pointed out that the majority of the English-medium schools in the Country, or at least the best English-medium schools, were supervised by the Inter-State Board for Anglo-Indian Education and had a vested interest in a first-class English-medium examination. The proposed Council would, therefore, endeavour not only to maintain but develop the standards of the examination which had been evolved by the Cambridge Syndicate. Above all, I pointed out that the Council would adapt the examination to the needs of the children in the New India.

It was thus that, in 1958, the Council for the Indian School Certificate examination was established. I had the privilege of being elected its first Chairman and since then I have been re-elected Chairman. The Council is an all-Indian body. It includes representatives of the Inter-University Board, the Public Schools including the Sainik schools and Air Force schools and a large number of English-medium schools and, of course, the Anglo-Indian schools. The Anglo-Indian schools represent the largest number affiliated to the Council.

The Council has gone from strength to strength. Today, about 259 of the leading English-medium schools in the Country are affiliated to it. Indeed, more English-medium schools are affiliated to the Council than to any other English-medium examination in the Country.

All the leading Universities have recognised the Council examination as equivalent to the Higher Secondary examination or the P.U.C (the Pre-University Course). The Council examination is also recognised by the Union Public Service Commission. So far as the Defence Services are concerned, a certificate that a student has qualified in Class X, although there is no external examination, is accepted for entrance into Khadakvasla for training in the officer cadres. Such a certificate is also accepted by the Railway administration for entry into several categories.

The Council is not merely an examining body. It has several subject sub-committees which are constantly reviewing the content and syllabus and ensuring that the examination keeps abreast of the latest developments and techniques of education in the most advanced countries. It is recognised that the English Language standards are as high as, if not higher than, those obtaining in many of the Indian Universities.

In 1964 when I visited the Cambridge Syndicate, I was happy to see an analysis which showed that the standard of attainment in English language of the pupils taking the Council examination was twice as high as that in the other countries of the Commonwealth taking comparable examinations. But it is not only in English that the Council seeks to maintain high standards. Workshops and seminars have been constantly held which have enabled the Council to evolve advanced techniques for the teaching of Indian languages. In this work the Council has been helped by liaison with the special Linguistics Department of the Poona University and language experts from abroad. The Indian language papers are all set and examined in India.

The Council pays particular attention to the teaching of Science and Mathematics because we feel that in this rapidly advancing technological age India dare not fall behind. As a matter of fact, a recent UNESCO team of educational experts underlined the comparatively low standards of teaching of Science and Mathematics in India. The Council is alive to this challenge. There is a considerable debate going on even in the most advanced countries as to the correct method of teaching Science and Mathematics.

As a pre-condition to affiliating a school, the Council insists on well-equipped laboratories. A recent Science Talent Search survey conducted by the Government showed that in the top merit list of 31 candidates who had done the Council examination 11 had been selected, whereas out of 340 Higher Secondary candidates only 14 were selected. The Government survey attributed this result to the fact that in the schools affiliated to the Council the training of the pupils was better and science laboratories were better equipped. The survey also pointed out that the students who did the Council examination had a wider background of reading and were taught to think. There is still too great a tendency in most schools to make the students learn by rote. There is the general belief that the funnelling of facts and figures into the memory of the children is a substitute for knowledge and capacity to think.

It is recognised that the standards of the entrance examinations for the Indian Institutes of Technology are the most exacting. Indeed, the elite of India's educated youth compete for entry into the I.I.Ts. It is significant that over 60 per cent of the boys who qualify for these Institutes come from the schools affiliated to the Council examination, although the number of competitors from these schools is comparatively much smaller than the number from the Higher Secondary schools.

The Council has had the inestimable advantage of liaising with the Cambridge Syndicate. Over many decades the Syndicate has evolved a system of standardising the question papers, of moderating and marking answer papers, which has acquired the refinements of an art if not of a science. More and more, the Council is taking over the setting and examining of subject papers in India. I am glad to say that the Cambridge Syndicate has a plan to train examiners in India for this purpose.

I might relate an incident which is significant. I was speaking at a meeting which was presided over by the then Education Minister of the Mysore State. I mentioned that the system which had been evolved by the Cambridge Syndicate over a period of many decades required that the question papers should be set two years in advance, so that standardisation could be done with scientific precision. In reply the Minister said—I think he was part sad and part jocular—that if in India they set question papers even two months in advance, they would all leak out !

Unfortunately, however, there is growing confusion in the educational pattern. Education appears to be falling increasingly into regional even parochial patterns. The glorification of regional and parochial trends in education will mean not only the restriction of educational horizons but of opportunities for the students. The creaion of parochial enclaves will, inevitably, precipitate the corresponding creation of psychological and ultimately political enclaves. In fact, such parochial trends in education will inevitably spawn national disintegration.

Another ominous development is the tendency of politicians, savouring new-found power, to seek to regiment education. In some areas, power-hungry politicians are seeking to enlarge their empires by interfering in the internal mangement of the best Universities, the best colleges and the best schools. The disastrous results are already increasingly evident in intrigue, nepotism, indiscipline and an absence of the minimum of educational standards.

In this welter of growing confusion and widening desert of disparate and falling standards the independently-run colleges and schools stand out as an oasis of stability and progress. They are among the few beacons of hope for the survival of minimum educational standards in the Country.

Unfortunately, in some States there is a growing attitude of nihilism towards independently-run schools. Politicians, who know nothing about education generally and certainly nothing about the functioning of the best schools, seek to interfere with or destroy them mouthing all kinds of spurious slogans. In the name of socialism some politicians are seeking to equalise poverty in education. Among some politicians there is an attitude suggesting ignorant prejudice combined with ill-concealed envy. What they are unable to emulate in standards and discipline, they wish to destroy.

In an open society and, indeed, in any progressive society it is recognised that freedom in education is the life-breath of education. Government regulation is permissible in prescribing for such matters as a proper syllabus, proper text books, suitably qualified teachers, suitable buildings. By these tests the independently-run schools stand out in refreshing contrast to the average Government-run institutions. Unfortunately, there is a growing psychology in some States to make it increasingly difficult for the independent schools to run. All manner of pressures, overt and increasingly covert, are being exercised to hamstring these schools. The petty politician who has been responsible for precipitating instability and near chaos in the Country is now seeking, in some States, to impose his deadening and destroying hand on the few remaining institutions that continue to maintain educational standards, discipline and character-building.

In the event of a frontal attack inspired by mala fide political motives, fortunately an independent judiciary is still there to enforce the fundamental freedoms of the Constitution. One of these is the right of the parent to choose the kind of education he wants for his child. Another is the right under Article 30 of the Constitution, given to minorities based on language or religion, to establish and administer educational institutions of their choice.

The Secretary of the Council since its inception has been A.E.T. Barrow. Barrow, in fact, has been my colleague in Parliament since 1950, and is commonly known as the second Anglo-Indian M.P. Barrow is a self-effacing type without the flamboyance and articulateness of the average politician. He is, however, one of the best informed educationists in the Country on secondary and higher secondary education. He has served with distinction on a series of Government committees and commissions.

Today, leading educationists who have not been infected by motives of language chauvinism or political vandalism recognise that the standards set by the Council are in the vanguard of Indian education.

The Council represents one of the greatest instruments for integration in the educational pattern and the maintenance of uniform standards at least at the secondary and higher secondary stage throughout the Country. Because of these uniform standards, the Council is also able to ensure in the affiliated schools the mobility of the best teachers from one part of the Country to another. The Council schools also represent a unique boon for the many thousands of parents who move from one part of the Country to another.

The schools affiliated to the Council are rendering invaluable national service. These schools are free from the taint of regionalism, linguism and communalism.

Those who can afford it invariably choose independently-run schools and especially those that are affiliated to the Council examination. Ministers and politicians who talk most loudly and glibly against independently-run schools are the most clamorous in the queue to have their children and grandchildren admitted to Anglo-Indian and similar schools. The children and grandchildren of some of the most raucous of the Hindi zealots will be found in the schools affiliated to the Council.

The Frank Anthony Schools' Scheme

The Anglo-Indian Schools prospered because of the guarantees for Anglo-Indian education which Gidney was able to secure under Section 242 of the Government of India Act of 1935. They continued to prosper because of the Constitutional guarantees which I was able to have included in the Constitution under Article 337. But they prospered most, after Independence, because of the several battles that I fought and, fortunately, won in the Supreme Court.

In about 1954, I addressed a conference of Church proprietors of Anglo-Indian schools. Quite frankly, I was taken aback by the attitude of some of the proprietors. I came away convinced that some of them, at least, would change the character, including the medium, of their schools, when it suited them.

There was also the sorry, indeed sordid, spectacle of schools founded for the Anglo-Indian Community being diverted from their original trust purpose. Thus, the Bishop Cotton Schools were founded specifically for the benefit of the Eurasian Community, as the Anglo-Indians were then known, and yet the Bishop Cotton School, Simla, ceased some time ago even to pretend to be an Anglo-Indian institution. The same fate has perhaps overtaken the Bishop Cotton School, Nagpur. The Bishop Cotton School, Bangalore, still continues as a recognised Anglo-Indian institution, although it can hardly be said to be administered by the Anglo-Indian Community. Lovedale, Ootacamund, was founded for the benefit of European and Anglo-Indian children. As I have mentioned earlier, the Madras Male and Female Asylums founded specially for the Community were merged into the Lawrence School, Ootacamund. These were taken over later and became an Anglo-Indian trust. With the wasting out of the Europeans, the sole residuary beneficiaries were the children of the Community. The trustees, presumably all of them British and presided over by a British bishop, cynically destroyed this trust when they decided to hand it over to the Central Government. For some considerable time the Central Government went through the motions of implementing the trust purpose by giving scholarships to Anglo-Indian children. When I visited Lovedale—in about 1950—I found that the staff had been completely de-Anglo-Indianized. There was still a fair number of Anglo-Indian students on scholarships as a continuing gesture to the fact that the School was an Anglo-Indian trust. After discussion with the Principal and the staff I could not resist the conclusion that there was a policy of discrimination against the Anglo-Indian pupils. Anglo-Indian parents had already complained to me of this growing discrimination. Anglo-Indian children were made to feel that they were there on charity. Inevitably, even those Anglo-Indian parents, who were entitled to send their children to Lovedale, discontinued doing so. Thus an invaluable education trust meant for the Community was destroyed.

There are many Anglo-Indian Schools controlled by various Churches, especially Roman Catholic and Anglican Schools, to which the Community owes a great and, indeed, an irreparable debt. Many of these schools continue to render invaluable service especially to the less fortunate children of the Community. I refrain from naming some of the schools that continue to render yeoman service as I might omit to mention some of the most deserving. Yet I am bound to say that many of the Church schools have no ordinary sense of gratitude, and this applies specially to the financially better-placed schools. They do little, if anything, to help educate deserving Anglo-Indian children. They forget that they were built up almost exclusively with the money of Anglo-Indian parents when 90% of their pupils were Anglo-Indian. In addition, they received, for decades, grants in the name of the Community— building grants, development grants and so forth.

I have always subscribed to the thesis that without its schools and without its language, English, the Community would cease to exist. As I saw some of these unfortunate trends in some of the Anglo-Indian schools I formed a dream of setting up at least 20 schools that would not only be established but administered by the Community. In pursuance of this dream, humbly, precariously, I started the Frank Anthony Junior School, in New Delhi, in January, 1956. Because we had to husband whatever resources we had, I asked my wife, who is not a teacher but who completed her training overseas as a Secretary and a Beautician, to help out by being the Honorary Manager. Slowly, gradually, almost painfully, that pioneering venture grew. Unfortunately, like all communities, the Anglo-Indian Community has its own perverse, malicious element. Even this humble beginning was sought to be sabotaged by some members of the Community. In fact, I had to kick out, almost literally, from the Governing Body at least one of the members who had sought to induce the parents to withdraw their children. Nurtured by my wife, this little school grew and prospered. Today, it has its complement of children and has to refuse a large number of applicants. The School is housed in what is known as the Gidney Club, New Delhi: because of the limitation of space we cannot admit more than about 230 children. This Junior School was the gallant pioneer of my dream which has steadily grown into a reality.

In May, 1958, I established the All-India Anglo-Indian Education Society. It is a registered education trust and under its constitution the resources are devoted exclusively to education and the promotion of the educational interests of the Community.

I, then, contemplated a more ambitious venture, namely, to open a Public School in New Delhi. Members of the Committee of the Education Society were extremely dubious when I put this proposal to them in rather ambitious terms. Some of them, without expressing it, gave the impression that they regarded my plan as a wild man's dream. They did not know how it would be possible for me to raise the minimum initial funds that would be necessary. We would require a few lakhs for the scheme even in the first stages.

Fortunately, the Calcutta Rangers Club, a well-known Anglo-Indian institution to which I have referred earlier, gave me generous assistance. Even on their Managing Committee there were members who opposed my request as they felt that my whole scheme was hare-brained. The majority of the Rangers Committee members, however, decided to make a donation of Rs. 3 lakhs as a gesture of appreciation for my services to the Community. With that money and the money subscribed by the branches of the All-India Anglo-Indian Association, in response to my repeated appeals, the Frank Anthony Public School, New Delhi, opened in January, 1959. It opened in tents with about 120 children. Half the children were transferred from the Frank Anthony Junior School. For me the next few years represented a period of grim anxiety, sleepless nights and anxious days. To cut a long story short, the School prospered as a result not only of effort, time, money but, indeed, the blood that was put into it. Today, the Frank Anthony Public School, New Delhi, is a magnificent institution in more ways than one. Housed in a beautiful four-storeyed structure, it is one of the landmarks of Delhi. Mrs. Vijayalakshmi Pandit, who presided at one of our functions, commented that the School had the appearance of a picture post-card school. The School has built up an enviable reputation on the academic side. Today, it has about 2300 children on the rolls. We are now proposing to put down an additional four-storeyed structure in order to accommodate the insatiable demand for admission. At present we have a four-section pattern up to Class VII and then a three-section pattern up to Class XI. Opinions will vary about having a school which is almost the size of a small university. We have, by dint of experience, evolved our own system of carefully checking the work not only of the pupils but of the teachers, with Heads of Departments in the Junior and Senior sections. There is a most careful procedure for checking the record-of-work books of the teachers. There are regular meetings held not only of the Heads of Departments but of each Faculty.

In 1965, the Education Society set down the Frank Anthony Public School, Calcutta. Here again we were fortunate. The School was able to start because the Education Society received a donation of almost 3 lakhs from the Calcutta branch of the All-India Anglo-Indian Association which had received certain windfalls. Once again, the Rangers Club gave me a loan of 3 lakhs on my verbal assurance of repayment. The Calcutta School has grown steadily. There again, I regret to say, was an attempt by evil elements in the Community to sabotage the scheme. A campaign, encouraged unfortunately by a denominational Roman Catholic Calcutta paper, sought to denigrate the institution especially because of the locality and predicted its inevitable failure. The School, today, has over 800 pupils on the rolls. Recently, the Education Society acquired the adjoining property. Apart from the original structure, our plans include the laying down of a four-storeyed modern school building.

In 1967, the Education Society set down the Frank Anthony Public School, Bangalore. I was fortunate to locate a fine plot of land in a good locality. The first floor of the projected magnificent four-storeyed building has already been completed. The School opened in January, 1967, with 53 children on the rolls : today, it has more than 300 pupils.

Among my other commitments, I watch the progress of these schools from day to day. In Delhi I function not only as the Chairman of the Board of Governors, but as the Executive Governor of the school. The Principals of the Calcutta and Bangalore Schools report to me at least twice a week. All major items of expenditure require my previous approval. There is a vigorous internal checking of the finances. In the Delhi school the checking is done from day to day by Chartered Accountants. While no necessary expenditure is refused by me there is a ruthless checking of any attempt to work to any of Parkinson's laws or to unproductive, horizontal proliferation.

Increasing Scholarships

While the Education Society has been building, it is also giving, increasingly, scholarships to assist the deserving boys and girls, young men and women of the Community. Today, the Education Society is giving over 300 scholarships. No application for a scholarship for higher education is refused. At the School stage the scholarships were first confined to the last two years, but now the scholarships are being extended to cover the students in the last three years of their school career. As the scheme expands I hope to extend the scholarships to cover the lowest classes.

Because of the scholarships now increasingly available, more Anglo-Indians are pursuing courses of higher education, today, than they have ever done. All that they needed was the necessary financial assistance. It is heart-warming, when I visit branches, to meet parents who are unable to find words adequately to thank me for the opportunity given to their sons or daughters to qualify as doctors, engineers, teachers: fathers press my hand in a gesture of speechless gratitude: mothers, with tears in their eyes, kiss my hand. That is reward, indeed, if any reward is needed!

While there are a number of schools recognised as Anglo-Indian, I regret to say that very few, indeed, play their part in training Anglo-Indians for the teaching profession. There is no Anglo-Indian school in the Country that trains anything like the number of young men and women being trained by the Frank Anthony Schools' Scheme. We seek to turn out between 4 to 6 young trained men teachers each year. The course is for two years and the Education Society gives a stipend of about Rs. 160 per month to each trainee. This is in addition to the large number of scholarships ranging from Rs. 25 to 50 per month given to young men and women of the Community training to become teachers.

Contrary to the general impression, the Anglo-Indian Community is relatively better educated than any other community. Apart from the fact that it is a hundred per cent literate, a higher percentage of its young men and women proceed to the University than from any other community except, perhaps, the Parsees. About 10 per cent of Anglo-Indians are now pursuing courses of higher education. Apart from entering the professions and the officer cadres of the Armed Forces, Anglo-Indian lads are competing successfully for the Indian Institutes of Technology, which attract the elite of India's educated youth. For those entering the officer cadres of the Armed Forces, the Education Society has set apart ten scholarships per year to-meet the full cost of the training.

I have already underlined that the Community cannot, like certain other sections, look to Government for educational financial assistance. Apart from the fact that English-medium schools are not run by State Governments, aid is being used by some State Governments as an instrument to throttle the English-medium schools.

A tragic development was that after Morarji Desai became the Finance Minister, he was responsible for a measure which must do irreparable injury especially to the minority communities. An amendment was made to the Income-Tax Act so that from the 1st of April, 1962, under Section 13(b)(1) charitable trusts and institutions created or established for the benefit of any particular religious community or caste will be liable to the crushing incidence of personal taxation. Fortunately, the Community's trust was founded before the 1st April, 1962.

When I came to know about this proposed amendment, I took urgent action. I saw Morarji Desai, but he was his usual self-righteous, intransigent self. I then saw Jawaharlal Nehru who was more understanding. He tried to persuade Morarji to modify the proposed amendment so that it would not affect the minorities. The most Morarji was prepared to do, as a concession to me, to delete the word 'race'. He felt that with the deletion of the word 'race' the Community would not come within the purview of this amendment. Obviously, the Community is not based on caste. It can also be argued that it is not based on religion, as religion is not a necessary attribute of the Anglo-Indian. Although the Community is, in fact, Christian, if an Anglo-Indian adopts any other religion, he does not cease to be an Anglo-Indian.

Presumably, this imposition on the minorities was made in the name of secular democracy, as it is misconceived by some leaders, in order to discourage communalism.   In fact this incubus is not only a negation but a perversion of the secular concept.   While most States cannot give any help to Anglo-Indians because they have no English-medium schools, in future the Anglo-Indian Community along with other minorities will be hamstrung in any attempt to set up charitable trusts.   I am bound to say that this amendment was not only reactionary but, in effect, viciously communal.   While States cannot and some will not help the minorities, the minorities, after the 1st April, 1962, will be prevented from setting up trusts for helping themselves.   Such trusts will be mulcted in income-tax to such an extent as to make it impossible for them to grow or prosper.

Courage Is Destiny

The Frank Anthony Schools have done me the honour to adopt my personal motto, 'Courage is Destiny'.

The School Song, also entitled 'Courage is Destiny', was composed by A.E.T. Barrow and his son Trevor, who is a highly qualified teacher.

The song, set to a rather stirring tempo, is sung by the pupils with an almost perfervid gusto.

1. May all we learn here in our School,
   By thought and deed be shown;
   Let living truth within us rule
   And seeds of love be sown;
   That Men in all our deeds may see,
   Courage is Destiny !
   Courage is Destiny !

2. We pray for Grace, Serenity,
   To keep a humble mind,
   That we may learn true Charity,
   To love all humankind.
   That Men in all our deeds may see
   Courage is Destiny !
   Courage is Destiny !

3. Undaunted, though alone we stand,
   Upholding what is right,
   Proud children of our Motherland,
   With truth our stay and might.
    That Men in all our deeds may see,
    Courage is Destiny !
    Courage is Destiny !

4. All that is good may we retain
   When scattered far and wide
   May we our Destiny attain,
   With Courage as our guide.
    To show that by our constancy—
    Courage is Destiny !
    Courage is Destiny !

The School magazine is entitled 'Courage'.

Today, our Education Trust properties are more than half a crore of rupees or more than 50 lakhs. And this is only the beginning. I hope and, indeed, pray that my dream of at least 20 schools is realised in my life-time.

The Frank Anthony Schools' Scheme is the greatest hostage that the Anglo-Indian Community has given, throughout its history, to its educational advancement and future well-being. With the guiding motive of Courage, this scheme has enabled the Community to look to the future with faith and confidence.

CHAPTER XIV

SAGA OF CONTINUING SERVICE

THE Community's traditional qualities of courage and loyalty have been expressed, over and over again, in its service to Independent India. From the 16th to the 18th August, 1946, there was an orgy of fratricidal communal killing in what came to be known as the 'Great Calcutta Killings'. During this terrible period when Calcutta flowed with blood, thousands of Hindus and Muslims sought refuge in Anglo-Indian homes. The Anglo-Indian Community offered them sanctuary. Be it said to the credit of the Community that although many Anglo-Indians were threatened not only with reprisals but with death for sheltering refugees, they refused to be intimidated.

The Anglo-Indian Civic Union

The Anglo-Indian Civic Union, formed under the auspices of the Calcutta Branch of the All-India Anglo-Indian Association, rendered notable service. The area leaders of the Anglo-Indian Civic Union met the leaders of the predominant community in a particular area and by their tact and persuasion were able to get them not to interfere with the Anglo-Indians in their humanitarian work.

One of the most notable services rendered by the Anglo-Indian Civic Union at the time was the rescue of about 5,000 Hindus and an equal number of Muslims from the worst affected areas. Members of both communities, who faced almost certain death, were evacuated by the Civic Union to areas of safety.

In many cases the persuasion of the Anglo-Indian members of the Civic Union succeeded in gaining complete immunity for the minority of Hindus or Muslims in a particular area and even in securing pacts of non-aggression or of joint defence of a particular area by all classes.

To those Hindus and Muslims who preferred to remain in their homes, the Anglo-Indians brought food and water. They also took messages from them to their friends and relatives outside.

The telephone services were manned almost exclusively by Anglo-Indian girls who were escorted to and from duty by members of the Civic Union. These escorts were unarmed and did their work in the face of the gravest danger to themselves. The telephone authorities were caught entirely unprepared. There were no duties listed nor were any arrangements made so that the girls could either eat or sleep at the Exchange. Yet Anglo-Indian girls remained for days together at the Exchanges. They were virtually the only Community who reported for duty and kept to their posts.

Members of the Anglo-Indian Civic Union freely assisted the Fire Brigades when very often they were either deliberately obstructed or rendered helpless by members of the dominant community. At one big fire inexperience cost an Anglo-Indian his eye, the hose slipping from his hands.

In addition, the Civic Union supplied workers to assist at Writers' Buildings (the heart of the Administration), the Red Cross Society and at refugee centres such as those set up at St. Xavier's College. Better placed members of the Union put their cars at the disposal of all those who needed them. One of the principal tasks undertaken by the Union was to secure male and female workers for the hospitals as stretcher-bearers and nurses and particularly for the Presidency General, the Shambhu Nath Pandit, the Lake and the Medical College hospitals.

School Children Rescued

During those days of savage communal strife and bestiality I received news that about 150 children in various schools in Pakistan wanted to come to India : most of the children were Hindus studying as boarders in Anglo-Indian Schools. I immediately addressed Dr. John Mathai, Minister for Railways, and K.C. Neogy, Minister for Refugee Relief and Rehabilitation. As a result a special train was run from Delhi to Amritsar. At my request the Army authorities also provided a military escort. I sent two young Anglo-Indians, the President and Vice-President of the Anglo-Indian Youth League, to Amritsar with the train. I had already sent a message to the former President of the Moghalpura branch of the All-India Anglo-

Indian Association. He brought the children by road convoy to Amritsar. At Amritsar the arrangements were perfect. The Special sent from Delhi was waiting and so also the escorts from the Anglo-Indian Youth League. The children were brought back safely to Delhi and joined their parents in different parts of the Country.

The Kashmir Campaign

In the critical Kashmir campaign the Indian Air Force played a decisive role and in that decisive role the services of the Anglo-Indian pilots were specially decisive. More than half the awards for gallantry to fighter pilots were made to Anglo-Indians. The first pilot to volunteer for operations in Kashmir was an Anglo-Indian, Michael Blake. He led the first attack in the Skardu valley. Leslie Blunt was the first Spitfire pilot to land at Srinagar when it was surrounded by the enemy. Desmond Pushong, flying a Dakota, was the first to land at Poonch while the airstrip was being heavily shelled by the enemy. Anthony Suares was one of the band of the transport crew who carried out continuous operations in Kashmir for a long period. Barty landed his Dakota in an airstrip which was between 450 and 550 yards long and 100 feet wide, in order to take off 8 seriously wounded soldiers. Wilks, Clarke, Barrett, Suares and several others were among those who were awarded the Vir Chakra which corresponds to the British Distinguished Flying Cross. These citations for gallantry make proud reading. All the citations are equally inspiring and picking out only some would seem to be invidious. Because of the need to conserve space, however, the citations only of Blake, Blunt, Barty, Pushong and Barrett are given below.

Blake

"Flt. Lt. (now Wing/Commander) Michael Patrick Owen Blake (2630) set a high standard of flying in the Jammu and Kashmir operations as a Flight Commander. Being the first to volunteer for operations in Kashmir, he led the first attack in the Skardu area, flying over difficult and dangerous country."

"This officer rendered valuable service in the defence of Poonch. He, during the critical days in Poonch, gave close support to our besieged garrison there and was often responsible for neutralising enemy strongholds in that vicinity. In almost all of these attacks, he achieved results by pressing home the attacks on the enemy at great personal risks. By his fine example he inspired confidence in other pilots of his Squadron.

"For his outstanding leadership as a Flight Commander in the Jammu and Kashmir Operations, he has been awarded the Vir Chakra."

Blunt

"Flt. Lt. (now Wing/Commander) Leslie Richard Dickenson Blunt (1994) was one of the first Spritfire Pilots to land at Srinagar when it was surrounded by the enemy and about to fall. He operated with zeal and vigour and thus helped to throw back the enemy from the gates of Srinagar. In a very short space of time this officer carried out twenty-three operational sorties against the enemy and achieved remarkable results."

"He stood out amongst his pilots for his keen enthusiasm and dash. His bombing and gunnery helped to break up many enemy advances at crucial moments."

"For the excellent results achieved by him during the Air Operations over the outskirts of Srinagar, he has been awarded the Vir Chakra."

Barty

"On 19th June, 1948, at Poonch information was received from our column at Potha that there were twelve seriously wounded casualties to be evacuated from Potha. The Austers which were sent here by Jammu for that purpose were only able to evacuate four of them when they ran short of petrol.

"In the meantime a Dak had landed in Poonch piloted by Flying Officer D.O. Barty (3129). He had orders to unload his supplies in Poonch and proceed back to Srinagar. His Dak starboard engine was giving him trouble.

"The airstrip at Potha was only between 450 and 500 yards long and 100 feet wide and the surface was in a series of steps and very bumpy. There was only one way of approach to the airstrip as at the other end there was a hill and it seemed absolutely impossible to land a Dakota on that airstrip. Flying Officer Barty decided that he had to help those eight lives which were at stake and proceeded to carry out his mission. He said he had seen this strip during the supply drop in the day and considered that he could land a Dak there. The undertaking was a great success."

Pushong

"Flying Officer (now Sqn/Ldr) Desmond Eric Pushong (3122) has to his credit a considerable number of hours of flying in the Kashmir Operations as a Dakota Captain. His dauntless courage, determination and sense of duty were a source of inspiration to other pilots."

"In initial stages of the Kashmir Operations, when our garrisons were surrounded in the Mirpur, Kolti and Poonch areas, this officer carried out supply-dropping under intense enemy fire, and always defied the enemy with a grim determination. He was the first to land at Poonch whilst the airstrip was being heavily shelled by the enemy."

"On 21st March, 1948, when Poonch was hard pressed by the enemy, he made a night landing without any landing aids, to deliver some equipment of vital importance to our garrison and thus helped our troops to beat back the enemy. He further rescued the stranded crew of another aircraft which had been damaged earlier by enemy shelling.

"For the outstanding services rendered by him during the Kashmir Operations, he has been awarded the Vir Chakra."

Barrett

"The late Flight Lieutenant A.W. Barrett flew 80 operational hours within a short period of two months during the Jammu and Kashmir Operations. Although he was hurt on several occasions he carried on cheerfully and showed exceptional courage and a high sense of duty. Whilst attacking enemy positions near Poonch, he was injured but immediately after recovery he resumed operational flying."

"Again over Mendar Valley he was hit in the face by shrapnel from the enemy Anti-Aircraft-fire while going into attack. Although he was bleeding profusely, he pressed home the attack with determination and destroyed the enemy post. His love for operational flying was a source of inspiration to the other pilots of his Squadron.

"For the distinguished services rendered by him during the

Jammu and Kashmir operations he has been awarded the Vir Chakra."

Incomparable Railwaymen

The Indian Railways have been built literally on the blood and bones of the Anglo-Indian Community. In times of the greatest stress, whether in war or during the most convulsive strikes, the Anglo-Indians have kept the wheels of India's life and economy moving. The same traditions have been continued in Independent India. During the several strikes since Independence, the Railways have been kept working because of the loyalty and courage of the Anglo-Indian Railwaymen. It would require many chapters to give a detailed account of these services. A brief reference may, however, be made to the fairly recent strike, in July, 1960, which was especially bad in the Eastern and, to some extent, the Southern sectors.

On the eve of the strike I had sent out a circular to our branches, which include a large number of railway branches, expressing my confidence that Anglo-Indian Railwaymen would perform their duties loyally and without fear as they have always done.

I give below some of the replies received by me. They may not deserve prizes for their literary finish or even grammatical correctness but they recapture the 'rough diamond' qualities of courage and steadfastness of the Anglo-Indian Serviceman. From Adra, a key centre on the Eastern Railway, I received the following report: "I am happy to inform you that here in this town of Adra every Anglo-Indian acknowledged your press-release and took your advice not to participate in the strike. Because we deliver the coal to Tatas, Bhilai, Rourkela, Martin Burn, the minerals to Durgapur and Burnpur, the strikers struck hard here. Under threats of violence, of slashing of wives and children, stone-throwing and brick-batting the boys, not only the employed but the unemployed and retired men went to their duties and managed to keep, under awful conditions, skeleton passenger and essential freight services going with such determination that we broke their backs before the Territorial Army arrived. Steam Locos were sometimes manned by three Anglo-Indian drivers, who worked as driver, fireman and second fireman. At cabins, level-crossing gates, yard control offices and where others had to come for duty at night, with no call-boys working, the lads went and escorted their relievers to duty —their wives and mothers gallantly staying alone while the strikers knocked on the doors and tapped the windows to break their morale. One probationary officer (Srivastava) remarked, while working as a Guard, that he had never been through such an experience (40 hours duty in the collieries) and had never seen such devotion to duty of three Anglo-Indians, his DUB leader drivers even filling coal in baskets carrying it on their heads and loading it on their engine fenders when we fell short of lads. Chakradharpur sent us the Anglo-Indians to help work trains from this area to say little of working trains here and back—sometimes 40 hours on duty on the road—passing closed down stations—opening regulators and then ducking to avoid being struck down by stones and arrows."

From Kharagpur, where there is a large Anglo-Indian Community and which centre occupies a strategic position on the Eastern Railway, I received the following account: "This is to report on the conduct of the Anglo-Indians at Kharagpur. The boys rose splendidly to the emergency, easily winning the esteem of all the officers with their round-the-clock service. It was accepted as a challenge and without Police protection, hemmed in by personal threats, by hordes of strikers, and with their home-folk exposed, the lads kept the wheels moving. I met the top officers (over a threatened situation) and returned proudly having heard great comments on Anglo-Indian loyalty and gameness."

"The strike at Kharagpur was singularly successful—on bleak days the attendance fell to 3% in the Workshop, 11% in the Loco-shed, 20% in the Traffic and to about 24% in the Engineering and Electrical Departments. Most offices fell to about 3%. All these figures do not include the Anglo-Indians."

"The Police took it easy even when threats, processions and a few cases of violence punctuated those five difficult days."

"The lads served because the Administration relied on them. No personal advantage was sought—food or money for stay-in-staff was not offered, nor demanded."

From Jabalpur the report read:

"I am glad to inform you that all the members of the Community including the lady workers were at their posts, and I venture to say that this act was the main reason of frustration of the planned strike, at least in so far as the Telegraph Office at Jabalpur was concerned."

"I feel that we can be proud of the loyalty displayed by the members of the Community attached to the Telegraph Office and also the members of the Community serving on the Central Railway, Jabalpur Division.

"We have also received a letter from the Commissioner, Jabalpur, thanking us for offering our services to meet the strike situation."

From Arkonam, in the South, the report was, "Although Arkonam was not a strike area except for the Postal Department, our staff had to work into strike areas, and this was done without calling for escorts or police protection. In the Bangalore and Perambur areas, our crews faced a lot of hazards, such as stone-throwing and hooliganism, but by dint of tact and determination they overcame these difficulties and worked their trains and maintained the life-line of the nation, and turned aside the aims of the strike."

From Hubli, another key railway centre in the South, the report was summed up in the following words, "All Anglo-Indians, employed in the various branches of the Railway at Hubli, remained at their post during the whole period of strike, except for severe cases of sickness."

From Podanur, in the South, the report underlined the services of the Community in the following words, "I am extremely glad and proud to inform you that your sound advice to Anglo-Indians had been well heeded: we, in turn, realising that the Indian Railways were literally built by us the Anglo-Indians sought not only to protect, but efficiently to work this great transport system. Every Anglo-Indian had risen to the occasion and conducted himself loyally in this crisis. Every member of the Community sincerely thanks you for your expert judgment and valuable advice."

The report from Bhusawal, a key centre on the Central Railway, symbolished the services of the Community: "It was the united stand of all Anglo-Indians to help the Railway and the Country. Bhusawal being the heart of the Central Railway was firm and strong and pumped energetic blood and vigour to all its co-workers of different communities."

Many Anglo-Indians were given special civilian citations for bravery and awards of different kinds.

At Asansol alone, one of the worst-affected strategic centres, 4 Anglo-Indians were given citations for outstanding work and courage. The citation of C.C. Dragwidge was typical. It read as follows :

"Shri C.C. Dragwidge,
Yard Master, Andal.

"On the 12th and 13th July, 1960, when all other staff had been forcibly evicted by the strikers from the Andal West Cabin, Shri C.C. Dragwidge, the Yard Master, remained steadfast at his post of duty. Even when he was surrounded by a mob of 200 persons on the 13th of July, and despite their attempts to intimidate him and force him to leave the Cabin, he stuck to his post till the Police arrived and dispersed the crowd. On the afternoon of the same day when the Divisional Superintendent, Asansol, visited the Andal West Cabin, he found Shri Dragwidge still working single-handed, although other staff were afraid even to move in the vicinity of the Cabin. "

"In appreciation of the high courage and devotion to duty displayed by Shri Dragwidge, the General Manager, Eastern Railway, is pleased to sanction him a reward of Rs. 400/-."

Beyond The Call Of Duty

Hundreds of Anglo-Indian railwaymen have, since the founding of the railways, literally given their lives in the line of duty. A recent example was that of P.D. Carroll who gave his life to save the Bombay Mail of which he was the driver. He died so that his crew and the passengers he was carrying may live. Carroll was the driver of the Up Bombay Mail on the 20th March, 1959. The Mail had been given the all-clear signal. Suddenly Carroll sighted an obstruction on the track which had been caused by a Diesel Goods train ramming another stationary Goods train. Oblivious to his own safety and conscious only of his duty, towards the passengers he carried and also to his fellow staff, he jammed on his brakes and hung on while calling to his firemen, "Jump for your lives. I will save the train." As a result of Carroll's split-second action the speed of the Mail was considerably reduced. Nevertheless the momentum was such that the engine and tender left the track and spilled over the embankment. Carroll had succeeded in saving the lives of his crew and hundreds of his passengers, but in doing so had sacrificed his own. Carroll had to be dug out from under his engine where his crushed leg lay pinned beneath the steel girders. Later on, his leg was amputated. He put up a courageous fight for his life, but ultimately passed away on Sunday, the 22nd March, 1959.

Old and young of all castes, creeds and communities, including many of the passengers whose lives he had saved, called at the hospital to enquire after Carroll's condition. Thousands of persons without distinction of caste or creed attended the burial ceremony.

In recognition of Carroll's heroism and devotion to duty, his widow accepted, on his behalf, the posthumous award of the Ashoka Chakra Class II. In addition the Railway Administration made a special contribution to his Provident Fund.

Replying to my letter of congratulation and condolence, Mrs. Carroll wrote, "In 1929 he joined the railway. About three years ago he was offered a Loco Inspector's post, but he refused the same as he always said, 'I love my engine and will never give up driving.' I often told him, 'You work too hard and you will yet die on that engine'—little did I think my words would come true. May God rest his soul in peace."

A reference to two outstanding examples of Anglo-Indian courage, beyond the call of duty, would not be out of place. They were Gloria Berry and Captain Eric James Tucker.

Brave Daughter Of India

The citation mentioning the award of the Ashoka Chakra Class II posthumously to Gloria Berry read as follows:

"Soon after the explosion of the bomb which occurred on the Air India International Constellation 'Kashmir Princess' on the 11th April, 1955, while on its flight to Djakarta, the whole interior of the aircraft including its cockpit was filled with smoke. Acting immediately on orders of the Commander, Miss Gloria Berry distributed life-jackets to all passengers. By the time this was done, the ill-fated aircraft was rapidly losing height. Even then Miss Berry did not care for herself but went into the cockpit and tried to distribute life-jackets to the crew. As the crew would not listen to her while controlling the plane, she insisted and personally fixed the jackets on them. It was this cool and calculated act of Miss Berry in the face of certain disaster which in the end saved three lives though it cost her own."

Gloria's mother received the award at the investiture ceremony held at Rashtrapati Bhavan on Friday, the 11th October, 1957.

A daughter was born to Dr. Berry of the I.M.D. and Mrs. Berry at Jubbulpore on the 25th July, 1932; she was christened Eva Margaret Gloria. Gloria completed her education at the Cathedral Girls' High School, Bombay. On leaving school she joined service with Air India International. Gloria was on the inaugural flight of the 'Kashmir Princess' to Singapore. It was by a tragic coincidence that it was also to be her last flight. She was due to be married in April, but postponed the marriage in order to do this trip as she was anxious to see Indonesia. The supreme courage of this young Anglo-Indian woman was rightly acclaimed by the whole nation. Gloria Berry has added yet another shining name to the illustrious roll of honour of Anglo-Indian women who have put devotion to duty even before life. Gloria Berry was the first woman in Independent India to be decorated for supreme gallantry.

Captain Eric Tucker

The only award for gallantry made to a member of the Armed Forces at the Republic Day Parade held in January, 1959, was to the late Capt. Eric James Tucker of the Maharatta Light Infantry. According to an Anglo-Indian general, under whom he had served, Tucker had died as he had lived. He was known to his friends for his qualities of loyalty and open-hearted generosity. He never hesitated to deny himself in order to assist a friend. Tucker's citation read as follows:

"Capt. Tucker was assigned the task of opening the line of communication from Chakabama to Phek, a distance of 42 miles, and thereafter to Meluri, a further distance of 20 miles, to destroy the hostile concentrations at Meluri. This he successfully achieved on 9th October, 1956. He had, however, to abandon Meluri for want of supplies and he made a dash for Phek on 11th October, 1956. After revictualling he again left for Meluri on 13th October, 1956: his company encountered a large number of hostiles armed with automatics and rifles, but they fought their way with great courage, inflicting many casualties on the hostiles, and reached Meluri on 15th October 1956.

"Employing feats of skill in clearing the many and varied obstacles on the road, showing great leadership in effecting the crossing of the turbulent river 'Tizu' running in spate, eliminating and neutralising hostile resistance opposing the advance with courage and determination, infusing great confidence in the troops, under his command,

Captain Tucker achieved this task in the short period of 9 days."

"Subsequently, Captain Tucker carried out many arduous and hazardous tasks against great odds. Late at night on 1st April, 1957, getting information about a hostile concentration at Chipokatama, he immediately proceeded to the place, and negotiating the labyrinthine tracks, in the dark jungles, took the hostiles completely by surprise. Disdaining the withering fire from the hostiles, Captain Tucker charged the hostiles' position with a section without the least consideration for his personal safety and captured four hostiles armed with rifles, including their leader."

"On 18th July, 1957, at Vishyepu Captain Tucker with a small party successfully outmanoeuvred a large hostile body, inflicted heavy casualties and captured a large number of prisoners. He led his men into the midst of the hostile concentration through a curtain of bullets. He displayed an extremely high order of valour, courage and determination and acted with utter disregard for his own safety."

"Finally, on 2nd August, 1957, Captain Tucker was proceeding from Khuzami to Kivikhu with a platoon. At mile 69/70 hostiles who had obtained prior information of his move lay in ambush in the thick undergrowth. After allowing the leading section to pass through, the hostiles suddenly opened fire with automatics and rifles on him from close quarters. Hit on his face and legs, he stood his ground and engaged the hostiles with his sten gun firing from the hip until the magazine was empty. He then charged at the hostile position with a grenade, but a further burst of automatic fire hit him on his chest and he collapsed and died."

"Throughout his service in the Naga Hills, the late Captain Tucker displayed great devotion to duty, having undertaken tasks far beyond the call of his normal duty. He never cared for his personal safety and infused great confidence in the men under his command by his most conspicuous courage and valour. So many situations so bravely faced by this young officer have been a source of great inspiration to his comrades."

Tucker's young widow received at the parade, at which the Duke of Edinburgh was a special guest, from the President of India the posthumous award of the Ashoka Chakra Class I to her young, gallant husband. There is little doubt that if the campaign against the Naga hostiles was treated as a regular military undertaking, Tucker would have been awarded the Param Vir Chakra, the Indian equivalent of the V.C.

Writing to me, Mrs. Sybil Tucker, stepmother of Eric Tucker, gave details about the family. Among other things she wrote, "Eric was one in a thousand—a most dutiful son, loving, obedient, kind, and always out to help anyone in trouble. As a child he showed signs of leadership. He was very popular. His colleagues looked up to him for advice. He was specially fond of reading good literature, fond of music and singing, good at dramatics, and played hockey and football."

Interludes

In another chapter I have referred to Regie Noronha being decorated with the M.C. and Bar during the Burma campaign. With the rank of Brigadier, Noronha was the Commander not only of the Indian but other U.N. Forces in the Congo. For his exceptional service there he was awarded the Vishishth Seva Class I Medal. The citation reads as follows:

"During his tenure as Commander, Indian Independent Brigade Group, Brig. R.S. Noronha, MC, was appointed Commander 'B' Sector, which included units from Tunisia, Ethiopia and Ireland and smaller detachments of Arms and Services from many other countries. He was largely responsible for the efficient functioning of 'B' Sector."

"In November, 1962, when Elizsabethville was surrounded by a chain of road blocks, Brig. Noronha was largely responsible for the behaviour and conduct of troops in 'B' Sector in the midst of considerable provocation. It was due to his inspiring leadership and his ability to get on with people that a hostile public began to respect him and his command. During the operations against the mercenaries, Brig. Noronha's troops were largely responsible for clearing Elizsabethville and in addition providing the main thrust towards Jadotville and Kolwezi. He planned the crossing of the Lufira river and the seizure of Jadotville brilliantly. Throughout these operations, Brig. Noronha was always at the head of the advancing column. His bravery, cheerfulness and leadership in these difficult conditions have become a legend in the Congo. Due to his personal intervention and risk to his own life, he was able to arrange a peaceful final entry of his troops in Jadotville. His bravery became manifest again when his party was attacked by a group of mercenaries near the Dikulwe river. Under his personal direction, he organised his small party to force the attackers to withdraw."

"In recognition of his devoted and distinguished services of the most exceptional order both as Commander of 'B' Sector and the Indian Independent Brigade Group in the Congo, Brig. Noronha has been awarded the VSM Class I."

The international press referred to him as, "The gutty Indian soldier who took Elizsabethville with a swagger stick." According to the press reports, Noronha went in alone, unarmed, in his jeep, to face the trigger-happy crowds of mercenaries and Congolese soldiers : by sheer, cold courage he was able to take Elizsabethville without firing a shot.

Regie Noronha's sister is one of the most respected office-bearers in the All-India Anglo-Indian Association. A selfless worker she has been the Vice-President of the Golden Rock branch of the Association for several years.

Squadron/Leader T.G. Jones was awarded the M.C., in 1951, before he was seconded to the Air Force.

In February, 1951, Wing/Commander J.J. Bouche, Wing/Commander O.D. Dodsworth and Squadron/Leader A.N. Todd were mentioned in despatches for gallantry.

The trouble in the Naga Hills saw Anglo-Indians in the Air Force doing their duty with typical steadfastness. The citation of the award of Ashoka Chakra Class III to Squadron/Leader T.L. Anderson shows that he was assigned the task of dropping supplies in two zones which were not only small but difficult of approach since flying over that area was full of hazards owing to treacherous air currents at the dropping zones. "As the operations could not be put off, Sqn./Leader Anderson volunteered to carry out the task. He flew four sorties between the 19th and the 25th October, 1956, and dropped the necessary supplies."

The citation shows that this "Hazardous task was a trial of both courage and skill. The fact that the dropping zones had to be subsequently abandoned as being too dangerous for air-drops goes to show the extent of risk that the officer had accepted and the determination that he displayed."

Chinese Aggression

Under the powers conferred by Article 352 of the Constitution, the then President of India declared, on the 26th October, 1962, that a grave emergency existed whereby the security of India was threatened by external aggression. The Chinese had treacherously attacked India. The Annual General Meeting of the Association was in session at that time in Calcutta. On the morning of the announcement of the Emergency by the President, before commencing with the proceedings of the General Meeting, I called together the representatives of the Community who were present from every part of the Country. To my request that we should immediately make a contribution to the Prime Minister's National Defence Fund there was an enthusiastic, spontaneous response. No gathering of Indians could have been inspired with a greater sense of national pride and fervour. Immediately, the Branch representatives pledged contributions amounting to 50,000 rupees. At the general body meeting I announced this contribution amid fervid acclamation. Shortly after that the Rangers Club, a well-known Anglo-Indian institution of Calcutta, handed me a cheque for 50,000 rupees for the National Defence Fund.

To my appeals addressed to the Branches of the Association and the Anglo-Indian Schools there was an immediate and, indeed, heartwarming response. The story of St. George's Homes, Ketti, was typical and moving. This School, founded as a trust for orphan children of the Community, is a well-known Anglo-Indian institution. Pocket money is given to the orphans from the trust funds to help brighten their lives. The contributions sent by this School came largely from the pocket money of the orphans who insisted on making their contribution to the National Defence Fund.

At the Frank Anthony Public School, New Delhi, over 1600 pupils drawn up in a hollow square and facing the National Flag took the following, 'Pledge to my Country',

'I promise, on my honour, to serve my Country, which is at war, in any way that I may be called upon to do.'

'I promise, to help the war effort in every way that I possibly can until the enemy is driven out of my Motherland.'

'I promise, always so to conduct myself as to preserve the honour of my Country.'

In response to my appeal the women of the Community also came forward to help in their own way. A committee of ladies, presided over by my wife, met the then Chief of the Army Staff, General Chaudhuri, and handed over 250 parcels, costing 10,000 rupees, for wounded jawans.

Ultimately the contributions that I sent to the Prime Minister on behalf of the Community amounted to Rs. 1,68,417/41.

Speaking in Parliament on the 8th November I mentioned that it was as far back as 1950 that I had warned the House that as soon as the Chinese wolf was ready, it would unhesitatingly bury its fangs and its claws in the throat and body of India. Unfortunately, at that time, we were wallowing in the illusion of 'Hindi-Chini Bhai Bhai'. Those of us who warned about the inevitability of the Chinese attack were met with ill-concealed sneers. In August, 1962, speaking in Parliament, I sounded, once again, a note of warning which proved to be tragically prophetic. I referred to N.E.F.A. as the soft under-belly of India. I said that if the Chinese moved—and I expected them to move—they would move against this under-belly. Jawaharlal Nehru reacted strongly to my speech. In effect he accused me of being a neurotic, suffering from nerves and conjuring up bogeys of Indian heads rolling in N.E.F.A. In November I referred to my unheeded warning but said that in the face of the supreme challenge to the Country all recriminations should be forgotten.

During the Chinese attack, Jawaharlal Nehru consulted with about 8 leaders of the Opposition including myself. Speaking later in the House I mentioned that the Chinese attack was in a sense a blessing in disguise. It had made us shed our illusions and our policy of almost deliberately keeping our armed forces ill-equipped and inadequately trained.

Speaking in December, 1962, in Parliament, I said that we should make it clear to our people that the reverses in NEFA were not the reverses of our fighting men, but the reverses of inexperienced and bad generalship. I said that there was no shame in admitting this. Other democracies caught unprepared have also had to dispense with their doddering generals, their arm-chair generals, their politician-generals who had broken under the grim reality of war.

I also criticised our publicity arrangements. Neither our people nor the world had been informed of the fighting in Ladakh. We had lost posts against a certain background. We had established posts in Ladakh with 20 or 30 men : they were lucky if they fought at odds of 20 to 1. In Ladakh our soldiers had killed many times their number of Chinese. Apparently they had limited supplies of ammunition. When those limited supplies were exhausted they did not withdraw : they fought with the butt-ends of their rifles; they fought and they died. I mentioned that we were overborne by the reverses in NEFA. The story of Ladakh had not been told. It was a story in the finest tradition of Indian valour, a story of grim courage, of fierce, unyielding tenacity.

Commenting on the functioning of Parliament during this crisis, Mr. Durga Das, the doyen of the Journalists in Parliament, formerly the Editor of 'The Hindustan Times' of New Delhi and at that time the Editor-in-Chief of INFA, wrote :

"The session of the Union Parliament which ended last week made history by unanimously backing the Nehru Government in facing the national emergency caused by the Chinese aggression. Even more, it marked the emergence of the Executive Committee of the ruling party as a political force. Since Cabinet Ministers hesitated to speak out their mind to their leader the Committee virtually functioned as the pressure group whose first victory was the exit of Shri Krishna Menon."

"For the same reason one person emerged as the most effective Parliamentarian, Mr. Frank Anthony, the Anglo-Indian leader nominated to the House. Besides being an old hand he has no party affiliations to inhibit his freedom of expression. Just as the Executive Committee of the Congress Parliamentary Party became the vehicle of pressure behind the scenes, Mr. Anthony became the mouthpiece of the generality of M.Ps on the floor of the House. Thus Parliamentary democracy fulfilled itself in the hour of crisis."

The Kutch Episode

Even before Pakistan's aggression in Kutch, the then Prime Minister, the late Lal Bahadur Shastri, was obviously deeply concerned. In keeping with his habit of consulting senior members of Parliament, he called in about 8 members including myself. Apart from the Defence Minister, the Chief of Army Staff was there to brief us. The briefing suggested that Pakistan had massed about two divisions on the Kutch border and that she had ample road and rail communications right up to the border. India's position was extremely bad, if not hopeless. There were no viable roads and the nearest communications centre was about 70 to 80 miles from the border. It was hoped that India might be in a position to build a minimum number of roads after the monsoon. I sounded the warning that Pakistan may not allow us to do that and may well attack before the monsoon and before we could improve our communications or even deploy our troops anywhere near the border. That, unfortunately, was exactly what happened.

On February the 10th, 1965, the Pakistani forces occupied Kanjarkot. The Indian High Commissioner in Pakistan sent a protest note on February the 18th, proposing a meeting of survey experts for the demarcation of the boundary on the ground, withdrawal of the Pakistani forces and restoration of the status quo. While India was pursuing her efforts to get the Pakistanis to the conference table, on April the 9th two Pakistani battalions attacked the Indian troops at Sardar post. On April the 10th, the Indian Army forces reoccupied the post. In the meantime, Pakistan moved the 8th Infantry Division from Quetta in addition to the two armoured battalions and the various artillery and infantry battalions she had already deployed on the border. On the 24th April, Pakistan launched an attack in brigade strength against the Indian post west of Chad Bet on the border.

At the commencement of these operations, Maj.-Gen. Pat Dunn, who was on leave preparatory to retirement, was called out of the blue to take over operational command in Kutch. The Indian forces were hopelessly outnumbered, out-gunned and in a hopelessly inferior logistical position. A member of the Cabinet told me that at a meeting of the Cabinet grave anxiety was expressed at our seemingly hopeless position. The Chief of Army Staff informed the meeting that he could only do his best under the circumstances and that he had selected not only one of the best tactician generals the Indian Army had ever produced but one of the best generals perhaps in any army in the world.

Speaking in Parliament I mentioned that the story of Kutch had not been told to our people nor adequate tributes paid to the infinitely superior tactics of the Indian operational commander, Maj.-Gen. Pat Dunn. Our jawans fighting in almost impossible desert terrain with absolutely no cover, without any real heavy equipment, with their meagre water-supply having to be carried largely by helicopters, as there was no rail or road communication, and never in greater strength than a company, inflicted ten times the number of casualties on the Pakistanis. They knocked out ten times their number not only in men but in weapons, while the Pakistani forces were shelling them continuously from the high ground on which they were deployed.

Some of the foreign correspondents, who visited the front, commented on the almost incredible performance of the Indian troops in the face of overwhelming odds and paid tribute to the infinitely superior tactics of the Indian operational commander.

In an action in Biar Bet, more than a brigade of Pakistanis moved in, as they fondly hoped, to overrun a Company. But when they moved, as they thought for the kill, another Company of our jawans had moved up. The Pakistani Brigade, caught between the crossfire, panicked, lost at least 6 tanks and suffered 144 casualties. Pakistan had obviously intended with its overwhelming strength in numbers and American armour to achieve a blitzkrieg right up to the 24th parallel, a depth of about 20 miles. In the face of the punishment inflicted by a handful of jawans fighting a battle of attrition, the Pakistanis ultimately thought discretion the better part of valour and stayed put at Biar Bet, just inside Indian territory.

The Indo-Pakistan Conflict

From the 2nd September, 1965, and throughout the conflict, the late Shastriji held frequent meetings with about 8 senior members of Parliament including myself. At the request of the Government I recorded on the 15th September a broadcast which was relayed by All-India Radio on the 16th September. In that broadcast I said: "Pakistan has declared war on India. This was the inevitable climax to years of adventurism, treacherous, repeated aggression and a philosophy of obsessive hate for India. As a member of the India-Pakistan Conciliation Committee I was one of those who had hoped and, indeed, prayed, that somewhere, somehow, Pakistan would realise that the security of the subcontinent could best be achieved by both our countries facing outwards towards the threat posed to Asia and, indeed, the world by Chinese Communism."

"I was one of the leaders of the Opposition in the Lok Sabha who supported the Kutch agreement, although emotionally I felt strongly against it. I was of the view that it required a great deal of moral courage on the part of the Prime Minister and the Government to accept that agreement because of the Nation's revulsion against Pakistan's repeated aggression and treachery. But I also felt that this agreement should be our last hostage to peace with an aggressive, treacherous neighbour. Thus when Pakistan invaded Kashmir by sending in infiltrators, I resigned in disgust from the India-Pakistan Conciliation Committee and was also insistent in Parliament that this time India must take suitable counter-action by liquidating the bases from which the infiltrators were being sent in. I realised that the late Prime Minister, Jawaharlal Nehru, with whom I had discussed the Kashmir question more than once, was right and that I was wrong. His thesis was that Pakistan conceived in hate and bred in hate, whatever gesture we made, even if we handed over Kashmir on a platter, would continue to live in hate for India and would always seek causes for tension, excuses for aggression."

"Pakistan's philosophy of implacable hate for India has been accentuated by its obvious collusion with China. Obviously under Chinese tutelage and instruction, in the well-known Chinese-style tactics of subversion, Pakistan trained Mujahids and guerillas and sent them into Kashmir. In the exhibition in Parliament House of arms captured from Pakistani guerillas and soldiers, I was amazed to see not only the range of equipment with Pakistani Ordnance factory markings but highly sophisticated weapons such as anti-tank mortars which even Pakistan was not capable of producing and which only a major nation could have imported."

Pakistan Springs At India's Throat

"Here I would like to congratulate the people of Kashmir for their refusal to give aid and comfort to the Pakistani infiltrators. This was Pakistan's first miscalculation. Pakistan had obviously banked on a mass uprising of the people of Kashmir to assist her guerillas. Foiled by the answer of the people of Kashmir, who alerted our security forces, identified the infiltrators and helped in the mopping up of the guerillas, Pakistan threw off all attempt at camouflage. She put in a powerful military thrust supported by two regiments of American Patton tanks through the Chhamb Valley across our international border. Pakistan's obvious plan was to cut India's jugular artery, to isolate our forces in Kashmir and Ladakh and then to liquidate them at will. Faced with this grim threat across our international border, India would have been guilty of wanton national suicide if she had not acted in self-defence. We had no option but to put in a diversionary counter-attack by sending our forces in the direction of Lahore."

"It is a matter not only of regret for us but it should be a matter of eternal shame for some countries that while they did not have the ordinary honesty to condemn at least Pakistan's attack across our international border, they have had the temerity to criticise us for acting in self-defence after the enemy had sprung at our throat."

Lessons From India's Reply

"I believe that even those countries that have an incurably blind spot towards Pakistan's treachery and repeated aggression will learn several lessons from India's reply to Pakistani aggression. They will learn that India's patience has been exhausted: that the Kashmir problem is dead and buried and that India will not move from her present positions in Kashmir as they are the only guarantee against a repetition of Pakistani aggression. They will learn that India's Jawan continues to be an incomparable fighting man and that our pilots with their sheer elan and fighting skill are among the best in the world. With outstanding generals that are now leading our armies, in spite of the tremendous advantage that Pakistan has with the supply of a billion and a half dollars' worth of the latest American sophisticated military hardware, our officers, jawans and airmen have more than made up by skill and valour what they lacked in armament."

"Many of our divisions are, today, mounting watch on other frontiers against Pakistan's ally, China, who is probably looking for a pretext to go to the rescue of her junior partner. Because of this, on the western front we have had to fight with a limited number of troops against Pakistan who already had a tremendous advantage because of massive American arms and equipment. But because we have relied more on our own production, time is on our side. The longer Pakistan's aggression lasts, the more decisive will be the results in our favour. Let the Country and, above all, our politicians, have patience."

Vindication Of Secular Democracy

"For India this war that has been forced upon us is nothing to be happy about. War, however limited, is neither easy nor pretty. India has a tradition of peace and, indeed, a passionate love for peace. Until the Chinese attack we had deliberately kept our defence forces very much below strength, because we sought to concentrate on urgent economic and social problems. Our reverses in NEFA were the reverses perhaps of bad generalship, but more especially the reverses of a tragic lack of equipment and military unpreparedness. Militarily, the Chinese attack was perhaps a blessing in disguise, because after that we began to put our military house in order. Today, India's objectives in resisting Pakistan's aggression are limited. There is no desire to conquer territory. Apart from giving an adequate reply to the aggressor, to teach him that aggression does not pay, a primary objective is the vindication of our faith in secular democracy. For us, today, Kashmir is a symbol of India's faith in secular democracy. The people of Kashmir, by refusing to subscribe to Pakistan's mediaeval doctrine of theocracy and religious hatred, have helped to strengthen the base of India's secularism. For India this is not a religious war, though for Pakistan, an avowedly theocratic dictatorship, the mediaeval, hysterical battle-cry has been 'Jehad'.

India's Strength Fortified By All Communities

"Today, India's secular democracy is being further cemented by the fact that the youth of every community is fighting, and dying, to repel Pakistani aggression. If I may give an example: the Community that I have the privilege to lead—the Anglo-Indians—is, along with the Parsees, the smallest community in India. But my Community, today, is repeating the story of its heroism when Anglo-Indians helped to repel Pakistani aggression in Kashmir in 1947. On that occasion the Indian Air Force played a decisive role and in that decisive role Anglo-Indian pilots played a notable part. Today, in our Air Force Anglo-Indian lads fighting shoulder to shoulder with the lads of other communities are steadily destroying the Pakistani Air Force despite its much-vaunted superiority in American planes and equipment. Another example of how India's strength is fortified by all communities is supplied by the fact that in the main sectors of the fighting, of the three Generals leading our Jawans to victory, one is a Sikh, the other an Anglo-Indian and the third a Hindu."

"War, today, is total. The civilian, perhaps even more the politician, has to show that he is worthy of our incomparable fighting men. They can show this by discipline, a will and capacity to endure whatever difficulties, whatever suffering may be in store for us. Government must also prove worthy of our magnificent fighting men. All anti-social elements must be dealt with mercilessly. The disturber of communal peace, the hoarder, the profiteer must be struck down ruthlessly. The hoarder and profiteer are still very much at large. Government has to control the hoarder and the profiteer. The Defence of India Rules are not sufficient to deal with these incurable parasites. Draconian legislation dealing out summary and extreme punishment is a necessary minimum."

"I believe that through the present trial and whatever further trials we may have to face, India will emerge a finer and a better nation, more united, more disciplined, more dedicated than ever to our ideals of secular democracy. The survival of democracy in Asia will be assured by India's success against the latest aggression by a military dictatorship steeped in mediaeval theocracy. Jai Hind."

Address At Ramlila Grounds

During the conflict I was asked to address a mass meeting at the Ramlila Grounds, New Delhi. Among the speakers were Mrs. Indira Gandhi, who was then Minister for Information and Broadcasting, and Dr. Zakir Husain, then Vice-President of India. According to the press, there were about 5 lakhs of people present at the meeting. The English translation of my speech reads as follows :
"Friends,

"The mother-tongue of the Anglo-Indian Community, which I have the privilege to lead, is English and because of that I naturally speak better in English, but as you perhaps desire that I should address you in Hindustani, I shall speak in Hindustani."

"Today, India is answering Pakistan's aggression. India had endured Pakistan's continuing aggression for many years. India had desired from the bottom of her heart that there should be peace because India had many major problems to resolve, such as putting her economic house in order, ensuring food, clothes, housing and education for our people. India has endured Pakistan's aggression in Kashmir for many years."

"As you know, after careful preparation Pakistan had attacked in strength in Kutch supported by American Patton tanks. Our gallant Jawans and Officers led by an Anglo-Indian General had stopped the enemy in Kutch although our men were completely outnumbered, had no tanks and not even sufficient water to drink. By their valour our Jawans stopped Pakistan near Biar Bet just inside Indian territory although Pakistan's intention was to penetrate at least 20 miles. Our Jawans so mauled the Pakistanis that they stopped in their tracks."

"Even after this aggression by Pakistan, India, in pursuance of her desire for peace, extended the hand of friensdhip to Pakistan. It is a matter of shame, as the Prime Minister has told us, that even while Pakistan was putting her signature to the Kutch agreement, she was making preparations for yet another act of aggression. Thus, Pakistan invaded Kashmir after having trained and equipped Mujahids and guerillas and sent them in several thousands. Pakistan has lied continuously and shamelessly as she had done in 1947. Against Mujahids and against guerillas there was only way of fighting and that was to attack their bases as was being done in South Vietnam. Pakistan invaded Kashmir obviously in collusion with China who is Pakistan's big brother. Pakistan, today, is China's apprentice."

"Foiled in Kashmir, Pakistan brazenly attacked in the Jammu area across our international boundary. Pakistan's clear intention was to cut our artery with Kashmir. In this context India was obliged in sheer self-defence to send in her troops towards Lahore."

Why Are We Fighting

"Today, our people have to keep one clear realisation before them. Why are we fighting Pakistan? In the first place we are repelling an aggressor and we have to smash that aggression. Above that, there is even a greater objective. We are fighting because India is a secular democracy. India is not a religious State. We are fighting to show that Kashmir is an integral part of India : Kashmir is an important part of India. Because the Muslims of Kashmir refused to support the Pakistani guerillas and, on the other hand, they immediately alerted our security forces, identified the guerillas, the guerillas are being mopped up by our security forces. I congratulate the people of Kashmir."

"Why is India a secular democracy?   India's strength lies in the fact that India derives its strength from every community.   This is not a war between Hindus and Muslims : it is not a religious war. This is a war between a secular democracy on the one hand and a fanatical, religious dictatorship on the other.   Today, in defence of the Country, the young men of every community are fighting : in defence of the Country the young men of every community are playing with their lives : in defence of the Country the young men of every community are laying down their lives, not only the Hindus, but Anglo-Indians, Parsees, Sikhs and others.   If I may with respect give an example.   Today, where the fighting is going on, there are three senior generals, one is a Sikh, the other an Anglo-Indian and the third a Hindu.   May I also give another example taken from my Community?   When in 1947 the Pakistani forces had reached Srinagar, they were driven from the gates of Srinagar by our Indian Air Force in which the Anglo-Indian pilots played a notable part.   The first pilot to land at Srinagar was an Anglo-Indian : the first pilot to land at Poonch was an Anglo-Indian.   Of the awards for gallantry— the Vir Chakra—made to the fighter pilots more then half were given to Anglo-Indians.   Today, also, the Anglo-Indians are in an appreciable number in the Air Force.   Fighting shoulder to shoulder with the young men of other communities, they are destroying the Pakistani Air Force.   What they are lacking in planes and equipment, they are making up by their courage and skill."

"Today, every citizen has a clear duty.   The person who spreads rumours, who tries to incite communal disturbances, is a traitor. He undermines the strength of the nation.   If it was in my power, to such persons I would mete out the death sentence.   The person who hoards food, who profiteers, is equally a traitor.   It is also true that during war the citizens will have to endure all kinds of difficulties and I know that they will be willingly endured.   Our greatest duty, today, is to maintain unity and discipline.   I am certain that from this war India will emerge more united, with our secular democracy strengthened, with our respect among nations enhanced. Jai Hind."

Throughout the conflict Shastriji had regular consultations with 7 or 8 of us, senior members of the Opposition.   The Defence Minister and the Chief of Army Staff used to be present to brief us. During this period of crisis, Shastriji won our esteem and affection more than ever. He was unflappable, quiet and yet implacable in pursuing the war while it lasted. He had a genius for being able to evoke a consensus from among the most disparate of political elements.

He could also be unshakably firm when the occasion required it. When our Armed Forces had hammered Pakistan, as he thought sufficiently, he was prepared to accept the cease-fire. Actually I was against accepting an immediate cease-fire : my assessment was that given a few more days Dunn's I Corp would break through in the Sialkot Sector and after that there would be a complete collapse of the Pakistani salient from Sialkot to Lahore. I was of the view that this would make the results decisive and prevent any distortion of facts in future by Pakistan, such as that the Indian forces halted where they did, because they were stopped by the Pakistani forces. I felt that we should not repeat the mistake we made in Kashmir. There Thimayya's forces were ordered to halt when they were in a position to have gone right up to Lahore within another twenty-four or forty-eight hours. But Shastriji was essentially a man of peace. He was of the view that we had taught Pakistan, sufficiently, that aggression did not pay and that we should now call a halt to the bloodshed and the bitterness.

Commenting on the functioning of Parliament during this period the Special Representative of 'The Statesman' wrote :

"During the Indo-Pakistan conflict two members of Parliament have conspicuously enhanced their stature. One of them is the Anglo-Indian leader, Mr. Frank Anthony, the other the General Secretary of the Congress Parliamentary Party, Mr. K.C. Pant. At the Opposition leaders' meetings with the Prime Minister, Mr. Anthony's has been a leading and constructive role. Mr. Pant has done a great deal to galvanise the Congress Party Executive into a live link between the Government and the party rank and file. Even more impressive has been Mr. Anthony's role in hammering home to the British High Commission here what India thinks of Britain's partisan stand on Kashmir."

While Anglo-Indians were playing a role, not undistinguished—out of all proportion to their numbers—in the Armed Forces and particularly in the Air Force, the Community responded once again to my appeals for contributions to the National Defence Fund. As the cease-fire appeared to be an uneasy one, contributions continued to be sent for the National Defence Fund even after the cease-fire. On April, the 19th, 1966, I handed over to Mrs. Indira Gandhi, who had succeeded the late Lal Bahadur Shastri, Rs. 1,54,056.82 as a further contribution from the Anglo-Indian Community and the Anglo-Indian Schools.

With the assistance of the authorities I was able to secure the presence of several Anglo-Indian heroes at the Annual General Meeting of the All-India Anglo-Indian Association in November, 1965. Among those present were Lt. Gen. Pat Dunn, Padma Bhushan, Wing/Commander Goodman, Maha Vir Chakra, Squadron/Leader Trevor Keelor, Vir Chakra, Squadron/Leader Denzil Keelor, Vir Chakra, and Flt./Lt. Alfred Cooke, Vir Chakra.

In my presidential address I made the following reference to the fighting role of the Anglo-Indians.

Fighting Role Of Anglo-Indians

"There is no doubt that, as in the past, the Community has during this war by Pakistan made a contribution out of all proportion to its size. Sqn./Ldr. Trevor Keelor was the first Indian pilot to draw blood against the Pakistanis and, indeed, as I have said previously, the Keelor brothers were the first literally to explode the myth of Pakistan's allegedly invincible American Sabre Jets."

"I wrote to Mr. Keelor that his two sons had made the name of Keelor a household word. Hindu parents have told me this, many of them are giving their sons the first name of Keelor."

"Then there is Wing/Commander Goodman. He was awarded the Maha Vir Chakra and Flt./Lt. Alfred Cooke the Vir Chakra. These young Anglo-Indians with their elan together with their fellow-Indian pilots made up by sheer heroism and fighting skill what perhaps we lacked in sophisticated planes. I do not want to say too much about the kind of planes we have. But in their Indian manufactured Gnats, our lads so out-manoeuvred and so out-fought the Pakistani Air Force that, as an Anglo-Indian Group/Captain writing to me said, within a few days they so put the fright of God into the Pakistani pilots that the Pakistanis refused to give them battle: instead, they diverted their heroism to the bombing of churches, temples, mosques, hospitals, dropping napalm bombs on defenceless men, women, and children."

"In the Army our Anglo-Indians fought—from what I hear—

with their customary gallantry. There was Lt. General Pat Dunn. I do not want to embarrass him. But I know something of the Kutch story : how he was called out of the blue, given that assignment, and, as I have said, being first a good soldier and a good Indian, he accepted it unhesitatingly. He went there. But you do not know the conditions under which our men fought in Kutch. We were taken completely by surprise. I was in the inner discussions with the Prime Minister. We had no tanks. I do not think Pat Dunn, he was a Major-General then, had even adequate artillery : I do not know if his men even had drinking water apart from water for other necessary Indian purposes. In Kutch they fought and thwarted Pakistan's plan, which was obviously to drive down to the 24th Parallel, a distance of 20 miles. Pat Dunn described it rather luridly to some foreign correspondents. It won't bear repetition here but it was a question of attrition tactics. Pat Dunn and his men so mauled the Pakistanis that the Pakistanis thought better of it and stayed where they were. They did not move beyond Biar Bet, just inside Indian territory.''

Then, as you know, Pat Dunn went in as Corps Commander, as Lt. General, in the Sialkot Sector. The largest amount of territory overrun by the Indian Army was in the Sialkot Sector. He was entrusted with the hard core of India's armoured strength. But perhaps what most of you do not know is the extent to which Pakistanis had fortified this whole front from Lahore to Sialkot. The story is coming in now—almost a Maginot Line of steel and concrete. Apart from the Ichhogil Canal there were pill boxes, gun emplacements, virtually indestructible. The heaviest shells only knocked out puffs of masonry. And in spite of that, you must have gathered from the press that General Dunn's armoured pincers had almost closed in around Sialkot. I do not know whether he accepts my interpretation, but I believe that had the war not stopped, as it did, and we had gone on for a few more days, the Pakistanis would have collapsed first in Sialkot and then there would have been a general collapse of the Pakistani salient from Sialkot to Lahore.''

The Dograi Epic

"And I have heard something of the story of Dograi. There also the fighting was particularly bitter. And don't believe that we fought with three Indians to one Pakistani, because, as you know, we had practically half of our Army tied down watching Pakistan's partner in crime, China. In Dograi we fought very much man to man and there was this tremendous line of steel and concrete, pill boxes and gun emplacements. Our Officers and Jawans advanced literally foot by foot on their bellies under this tremendous hail of fire. Practically the only way in which they were able to get the Pakistanis out of this Dograi area was to drop in hand-grenades and destroy, in that way, or attempt to destroy these pill boxes. And our men did it repeatedly, although it meant almost certain death. In that gallant action, which resulted in the capture of Dograi, leading his regiment, the 3rd Jats, was Lt. Colonel Desmond Hayde. He was awarded the Maha Vir Chakra. I am sorry he could not be with us today. Actually, I was unable to contact him."

Gallantry Citations

On the 24th November, 1965, Dr. Radhakrishnan, the then President of India, decorated 63 heroes of the Indian Army and Air Force with awards for gallantry made on the battlefield. It is significant, and for the Community gratifying, that of the 63 heroes decorated 7 were members of India's smallest minority.

The citations read at the Investiture ceremony were as follows.

Lt. Gen. Dunn—Padma Bhushan

"Lt. Gen. P.O. Dunn assumed command of 1 Corps on 20 May 66 which he was to raise at short notice for possible operations in defence of our borders. Troops could only be allotted to him at a later stage and as operations became probable, some of them were only placed under his command a few days before the commencement of actual operations. In fact, to achieve speed, his Corps was launched into an operation in the SIALKOT Sector while portions of it were still moving up through the PUNJAB. In spite of these difficulties, the Corps Commander integrated his troops quickly into a fighting team. The enemy committed a substantial part of his armour in his effort to stop the advance of Gen. DUNN's Corps but within a short period of 12 days the enemy's better-equipped troops were so successfully defeated that the losses inflicted on his armour were more than three times his own losses. Enemy territory gained by his troops was held against repeated counter-attacks and the Corps continued to advance steadily until the "cease-fire" brought about a halt."

"Lt. Gen. P.O. Dunn displayed high qualities of leadership, tenacity, courage and tactical ability in the command of his troops and successfully carried out the task of crippling the PAKISTAN offensive potential. He showed particular skill in the move to, on and from the operational area and in the co-ordination of the groups under his command. For his outstanding services in the defence of his country, services in the highest tradition of the Army, he is strongly recommended the immediate award of the PADMA BHUSHAN."

Lt. Col. Hayde—Maha Vir Chakra

"No. 125-Pres-65—The President is pleased to approve the award of the MAHA VIR CHAKRA for acts of gallantry in the recent operations against PAKISTAN to :

Lieutenant Colonel DESMOND HAYDE (IC-4036), 3rd Battalion, The Jat Regiment. (Effective date of award—6th September, 1965).

On the 6th September, 1965, when the initial attack on the Ichhogil Canal in PAKISTAN was launched, Lt. Colonel HAYDE, Officer Commanding a battalion of the Jat Regiment, captured the western bank of the canal against very stiff opposition from the enemy. It was primarily due to his leadership that not only did his battalion not fall back from the positions which it had occupied, but in fact moved forward in spite of continuous and heavy shelling and frequent air and ground attacks. On the 9th September, 1965, when the enemy launched an attack with Patton and Sherman Tanks, his battalion accounted for five of the enemy tanks with recoilless guns. The performance of this battalion throughout the operations was excellent and this was largely due to the great personal courage and exceptional qualities of leadership shown by Lt. Colonel Desmond Hayde."

Group/Captain Lloyd—Vishist Seva Medal Class I

"By the time Group/Captain Vernon Alexander Lloyd was appointed Officer Commanding of an operational Wing in Punjab, trouble from the infiltrators had already erupted in the Jammu and Kashmir area. Aware of the imminence of a full-fledged war, Gr./Capt. Lloyd immediately set about making preparations for it. In the limited time available he instituted passive air defence measures and spurred his officers and men to greater efforts towards improving the serviceability of aircraft and operational preparedness of the unit. As a result his Station was ready to meet the challenge when Pakistan entered the arena openly as an aggressor."

"One of the front line wings which menaced Pakistani activity in the area of Sialkot and Lahore, Gp./Capt. Lloyd's Wing was subjected to continual night bombing raids from 6th September till the day of the cease-fire. As if night harassment by his bombers was not enough, the enemy dropped paratroopers near the airfield so that they could infiltrate into it and destroy or damage our aircraft and installations thus crippling the effectiveness of the base. However, Gp./Capt. Lloyd's efforts at improving the ground defences to make the airfield almost invulnerable yielded results, and the paratroopers had to be content with sniping at the personnel servicing the aircraft at night. Despite the night bomber raids and the enemy paratroopers' forage, work of the airfield and aircraft went on with unabated vigour. An index of the unflagging zeal of the air and ground crew and of the courage and fortitude is the steadily increasing number of sorties the station was able to mount. There were 29 sorties on the 7th September, the day following the first Pakistani night raid, 74 on the 11th and 77 on the 22nd September, 1965."

"Although Gp./Capt. Lloyd had been in Command only a few days before the declaration of hostilities, he imbued by personal example every one in his Station with courage, determination, confidence in the justness of our cause and a sense of selflessness and purpose. By his fearless leadership he has rendered service of the most exceptional order to India and is recommended for the award of the Vishist Seva Medal, Class I."

Wing/Commander Goodman—Maha Vir Chakra

"Wing/Commander William MacDonald Goodman is in command of an operational Fighter Reconnaissance Squadron in the Western Sector."

"From the very first day of hostilities Wing/Commander Goodman set the pace in the Squadron, by personally leading most missions, both Reconnaissance and Ground Attack, against enemy tank and troop concentrations in the face of heavy air and ground opposition."

"His personal example and guidance was a source of inspiration to all ranks under his command, which contributed to the high morale of the unit. This was reflected in the very high state of serviceability maintained by the unit, and a number of successful strikes against the enemy."

"Wing/Commander Goodman's inspiring leadership, determination and conspicuous gallantry are in the highest traditions of the Service."

"Wing/Commander Goodman is recommended for the immediate award of the Maha Vir Chakra."

Squadron/Leader Trevor Keelor—Vir Chakra

"On the 3rd September, 1965, at about 0700 hours, a report was received from one of our radar units that a formation of Pakistani fighters was circling over our army positions in the Chhamb Sector of Jammu and Kashmir. A formation of Gnat aircraft was ordered to intercept the intruders. On approaching the area, Squadron/Leader Trevor Keelor, who was a section leader in the Gnat formation, sighted the enemy aircraft, identified them as Pakistani F-86 Sabre Jets and immediately engaged them in air battle."

"While the air combat was in progress, the F-86 Sabre Jets were joined by a section of F-104 Star-Fighters of the Pakistani Air Force. Although the balance had now tilted in favour of the Pakistanis, the Gnat formation, under the determined leadership of Squadron/Leader Keelor, continued with the attack. Unmindful of the numerical superiority of the enemy, Squadron/Leader Keelor gave chase to a Sabre Jet and pressed home his attack until the aircraft caught fire and disintegrated in the air. He broke off his attack only when the distance between himself and the enemy aircraft was so close that debris from the latter was likely to damage his own. This was the first victory of the Indian Air Force in air battle against the Pakistani Air Force."

"Squadron/Leader Keelor, who is an earlier recipient of the Vayu Sena Medal, displayed courage, leadership and determination of a high order in this, his first engagement, against a numerically superior enemy."

"Squadron/Leader Keelor is recommended for the immediate award of the Vir Chakra."

Squadron/Leader Denzil Keelor—Vir Chakra

"Squadron/Leader Denzil Keelor displayed a high degree of courage and leadership while providing fighter escort to Mystere aircraft during a strike mission on 19th September, 1965. His section of 4 Gnat aircraft was engaged by 4 Pakistani Sabre Aircraft while at 500 feet. The battle was fought below 2000 feet with enemy anti-aircraft guns engaging them from below. Through his guidance, his sub-section leader shot down a Sabre aircraft. Sqn/Ldr. Keelor then engaged a Sabre aircraft himself and crippled it. Throughout the Indo-Pakistan conflict, Sqn/-Ldr. Keelor has been a source of inspiration to both the pilots and the ground personnel because of his shining example, enthusiasm and sense of duty."

"Squadron/Leader Denzil Keelor is recommended for the immediate award of the Vir Chakra."

Flight/Lieutenant Cooke—Vir Chakra

"On the 7th September, 1965, Flt/Lt. Alfred Tyrone Cooke was leading an 'element' of two aircraft on combat air patrol. On intimation of an air raid over Kalaikunda by 6 enemy Sabre Jet Aircraft he led his 'element' without any hesitation to intercept the enemy aircraft and despite the fact that our own anti-aircraft guns had already started to fire, he fearlessly and in total disregard of his personal safety, engaged two of the enemy aircraft. The enemy aircraft, in their frantic bid to avoid action, resorted to violent evasive and counter-offensive manoeuvres but he, with firm determination and exceptional skill, out-manoeuvred the enemy and pressed home his attack with determination and shot down one of the enemy aircraft which disintegrated in mid-air in front of him. Subsequently with outstanding flying skill he positioned himself in a favourable position behind a second aircraft but he had no ammunition left. However, he kept the enemy on the run and the surviving enemy aircraft were driven away in utter chaos and confusion. Flight/Lieutenant Cooke displayed conspicuous gallantry and courage of a high order in the presence of the enemy and an outstanding sense of duty, leadership and dedication to the service in the best traditions of the Air Force."

"Flight/Lieutenant Cooke is recommended for the immediate award of the Vir Chakra."

I mention here a fact which will probably come as a surprise to many readers. I do so in no spirit of criticism. It is merely to show that very often those who have admittedly performed deeds of outstanding heroism are overlooked in the heat of battle. The battle of Dograi has rightfully taken its place as an epic in the Indo-Pakistan conflict. Lt. Col. Desmond Hayde was awarded the Maha Vir Chakra for his heroism in capturing the area around Wagah a few days before the battle of Dograi. For his outstanding, courageous leadership when gallantly leading his gallant Jats to capture Dograi he received no decoration. Several officers who were fighting in this area expressed their surprise to me, later, that Hayde, who perhaps deserved the highest available decoration for the Dograi Epic did not even get a bar to the Maha Vir Chakra.

Because of my handling in the earlier years of my professional work of a number of Court-Martial cases, military personnel continue to seek my professional assistance. Practically every case of an officer who had been dismissed or removed for dereliction of duty during the Indo-Pak conflict went through my hands at the appeal stage. Incidentally, not one of them was an Anglo-Indian. Because of this professional work I had inside information which I could not have secured even as a member of the National Defence Council. Hayde's battalion was operating in conjunction with two other battalions. Neither of these battalions did well. Both the C.Os were removed. One of them, in fact, was the only senior Indian officer court-martialled for cowardice. The performance of the 3rd Jats, whom Hayde was leading, was thus particularly crucial. Describing this battle Dewan Berindranath in his book 'The War with Pakistan' in Chapter 6 entitled 'Date at Dograi' gives details of this epic encounter.

"Dograi is about 8 miles from Lahore : it is a corner-stone in the outer defensive system of Lahore. The whole area was heavily fortified. Had Dograi remained intact, our whole position right up to Amritsar would have been in danger. The task of capturing Dograi was entrusted to Lt. Col. Hayde." Dewan Berindranath continues, "Lt. Col. Hayde, Officer Commanding the Jats, had his own plans absolutely clear in his mind. He confided it to his officers with simple words, "I have a date at Dograi. You shall see me there dead or alive."

Continuing his comments on the Dograi battle, Dewan Berindranath writes:

"Since the enemy expected the attack, the fire from Pakistani positions was particularly heavy. As a captured officer confided:

'Later, the Pakistani firing had been planned at such a close range that not even a field mouse could have got through the bullet barrage. But these fellows of yours kept on crawling undeterred by the fire.' A speciality of war preparations in the area were heavily laid mine-fields. Our men had to run over them without trying to clear them. There was no time for that."

Giving details of the battle, Dewan Berindranath writes: "It was a furious battle," said Lt. Col. Hayde while narrating to me events of the six-hour fighting. "Our tanks moved at night. This does not happen usually. It was a surprise for the Pakistanis. We attacked like lightning. They put up stiff resistance. We advanced under a hail of fire from enemy artillery and machine-guns from the pill-boxes. Many fierce engagements took place. But the right-flanking 'hook' took the enemy by surprise. They left everything and ran. We knocked hell out of 16 Punjab. Some of the enemy troops were caught in their own mine-fields. There is no denying the fact that our own toll of life was very heavy. Roughly half of our 900 men had been either killed or injured in action. But the price the enemy had to pay was much heavier. A great contribution was made in this action by our artillery. It was so effective that the Pakistani Commander, after his capture, had asked whether we had guided anti-tank missiles. He could not believe his eyes and ears on knowing that it was ordinary gunfire which had knocked out his fortifications."

Later other Anglo-Indians received awards for gallantry during the Indo-Pakistan conflict: Group/Captain David Bouche, Wing/Commander Clarke, Wing/Commander Mousinho, Wing/Commander Wollen and Wing/Commander Anderson, to name a few. It is significant that during the conflict, in our Air Force, which covered itself with so much glory, about 20 per cent of the Group/Captains, about 30 per cent of the Wing/Commanders and about 30 per cent of the Squadron/Leaders were Anglo-Indians. It is also significant that in most of the Air Force stations facing Pakistan, the Commanders were Anglo-Indians.

During the Indo-Pakistan conflict several Anglo-Indians occupied key positions at Army Headquarters. Brigadier Robert Williams was the Director of Armaments: in that capacity, for several years, he and his men were responsible, because of their rigorous and incorruptible standards, for ensuring the production of Indian arms and equipment of the finest quality. It was this quality that enabled our forces to hammer the Pakistanis in spite of the billion and half dollars worth of sophisticated arms and equipment that had been gifted to them by the Americans. Brigadier Charles Joseph was the Director of Weapons and Equipment. Brigadier Larkins was Brigadier Q in the Quarter-Master-General's branch. Brigadier Mulleneaux was Director of Movements. Mulleneaux on the military side and two Anglo-Indian railwaymen on the civilian side were primarily responsible for the movement of our troops and equipment to the Front. This was both a gigantic and intricate job. The smoothness and precision with which this crucial undertaking went through received high praise from foreign military observers.

Among those who made the supreme sacrifice were Lt. Col. Terence Nolan, Officer Commanding 2 Mahrattas, Sqn/Ldr. Marston and Flt/Lt. Carl Roberts.

Our Women

Anglo-Indian women in the Services played their part with customary devotion to duty. Three Anglo-Indian officers of the Indian Military Nursing Service were decorated for gallantry during the Indo-Pakistan conflict. They were Lt. Col. (Miss) Marjorie Shaw, Major (Miss) Glena Fernandez and Major (Miss) Thelma Stoddard. The citation of the award to Marjorie Shaw is typical and reads as follows:

"In spite of deficiencies in Nursing Sisters in the medical unit in which she was the Matron, Lt. Col. (Miss) MKA Shaw by her hard work, personal example and untiring zeal kept up a very high standard of nursing in 150 General Hospital which was located very near the cease-fire line during the operations in September, 1965. She continued to maintain these high standards under pressure of an influx of casualties. For each and every casualty, military, paramilitary and civil, she always had a word of cheer and saw that they were immediately made comfortable and promptly attended to on admittance.   She was on her feet day and night ensuring that everything possible was being done for the patients.   By her devotion to duty she set a fine example both to the nursing officers and other nursing staff of the General Hospital.   Many patients who were ministered by her expressed their reluctance to leave the General Hospital and many of them continue to write to her to express their thanks."

"For her devotion to duty and her selfless conduct she has been awarded the Vashisht Seva Medal. Class II."

Once again, in the tradition of the Community, Anglo-Indian men and women answered the call of duty with selfless devotion and unflinching courage.   Many of them served above and beyond the call of duty.

Let The Record Speak For Itself!

BIBLIOGRAPHY

ALL-INDIA ANGLO-INDIAN ASSOCIATION. The Monthly Journal: from 1926 to 1968.

ANGLO-INDIAN EDUCATION. The Report of the Commission appointed in 1944 by the Inter-Provincial Board for Anglo-Indian Education.

BIRT, BRADLEY. Poems of Henry Louis Vivian Derozio with an introduction by Bradley Birt, 1923, Oxford University Press.

BUCKLAND, C.E. Dictionary of Indian Biography, 1906, Sonnenschein & Co., 25, High Street, Bloomsbury, London.

BURCHETT, W.G. Trek Back from Burma, Kitabistan, Allahabad.

BOWER, J.A.H. Ambition Mocked Our Useful Toil, 1939. G. Claridge & Company, Ltd., Frere Road, Bombay.

BUSTEED, H.E. Echos From Old Calcutta, Being Chiefly Reminiscences of the Days of Warren Hastings, Francis and Impey, 1908. W. Thacker & Co., 2, Creed Lane, London: Thacker, Spink & Co., Calcutta and Simla.

CHATTERTON, EYRE. History of the Church of England in India Since the Early Days of the East India Company, 1924; Society for Promoting Christian Knowledge, London, (MacMillan & Co).

CLARKE. The Fortunes of the Anglo-Indian Race Considered Retrospectively and Prospectively, 1878, Madras.

COLLIER, RICHARD. The Indian Mutiny, Fontana Books.

COMPTON, HENRY. A Particular Account of the European Military Adventurers of Hindustan, from 1784 to 1803, 1892, London.

DANIELL, H. The Development of Anglo-Indian Education and Its Problems (Thesis presented at the University of Leeds, in 1941, for the Degree of Master of Education).

DEWAN BIRENDRA NATH. The War With Pakistan, 1966, Asia Press, 19, Netaji Subhash Marg, Delhi-6.

DOVER, CEDRIC. Half Caste, 1937, Martin Secker & Warburg Ltd., 22 Essex Street, Strand, London.

DOVER, CEDRIC. Cimmerii? Eurasians and Their Future, 1929, the Modern Art Press, Calcutta.

DOVER, CEDRIC. Henry Derozio, Eurasian Poet, Preceptor and Philosopher, 1930, Calcutta.

DUNN. Anglo-Indian Romance, The Calcutta Review, January, 1919.

EDWARDS, THOMAS. Henry Derozio, The Eurasian Poet, Teacher and Journalist, 1884, Calcutta.

FRASER, BAILLIE, J. Military Memoirs of Lt. Col. James Skinner, C. B. Volumes I & II, 1851, Smith, Elder & Co., 65, Cornhill, London.

HINDLE. A Survey of the Anglo-Indian Community. Report of the National Council (Y.M.C.A.), 1924 to 1926, Association Press.

HOLMAN, DENNIS. Sikander Sahib, 1961, Heinemann, London.

KEENE, H.D. Hindustan under Free Lances, 1770 to 1820. 1907, Brown Langham & Co., Ltd., 78, New Bond Street, London.

KINCAID, DENNIS. British Social Life in India, 1608 to 1937, George Routledge & Sons, Ltd., Broadway House, Carter Lane, London, E.C.

MAHER, REGINALD. These Are The Anglo-Indians, 1962, Swallow Press, Calcutta.

MORENO, H. W. B. The Call to Arms for Anglo-Indians, 1916, the Central Press, Printers & Publishers, 12, Wellesley Street, Calcutta.

PEARSE, HUGH, COL. The Hearseys. Five Generations of an Anglo-Indian Family, 1905, William Blackwood & Sons, Edinburgh and London.

RAY CHOUDHURI, SUBIR. Henry Derozio, Eurasian Poet and Reformer, 1966, Metropolitan Book Agency, 93, Park Street, Calcutta-16.

ROBBY, C. T. The Anglo-Indian Force, 1916.

SAKSENA, RAM BABU. European and Indo-European Poets of Urdu and Persian, 1941, Newal Kishore Press, Lucknow.

STARK, H.A. Hostages to India, 1926, the Calcutta Fine Art Cottage, Calcutta.

STARK, H.A. Call of the Blood, 1932, British Burma Press, Rangoon.

STARK, H. A., MADGE, WALTER. East Indian Worthies Being Memoirs of Distinguished Indo-Europeans, Printed at the Cambridge Steam Printing Works, 3, Fairlie Place, Calcutta.

STARK, H. A. John Ricketts and His Times, 1934, Wilson & Son, 37, Elliot Road, Calcutta.

SKIPTON, H. Our Reproach in India, 1912, London.

WALLACE, KENNETH. Life of Sir Henry Gidney, 1947, A. Mukherjee & Co., Calcutta.

WALLACE, KENNETH. The Eurasian Problem Constructively Approached, 1930, Thacker Spink & Co., Calcutta and Simla.

WALLACE, KENNETH. Brave New Anglo-India, 1935, the Modern Art Press, Calcutta.

WESTON, C. N. Anglo-Indian Revolutionaries of the Methodist Episcopal Church, 1938, Scripture Literature Press, Bangalore.

WESTON, C. N. Great Britain's Hostages to India, The Anglo-Indians, Their Magna Carta, 1955, Baldwin Boys' High School, Bangalore.

WILSON. The Domiciled European and Anglo-Indian Race of India, 1926, Bombay.

INDEX

If you would like us to publish your book or

If you would like to distribute our books please e mail us at our contact address:

wallenberg.press@gmail.com

Lightning Source UK Ltd.
Milton Keynes UK
24 July 2010

157450UK00001B/14/A